73

Marwick, Arthur, 1936–
942.082 Britain in the century of total war: war, peace and social
change, 1900–1967. Boston, Little, Brown ⸤c1968⸥

511 p. 23 cm. 63/–
(SBN 370 003863 1)
Bibliography: p. ⸤462⸥–48 ⸤.

1. Gt. Brit.—Hist.—20th cent.   I. Title.

DA566.M34   942.082

(B 68–11555)

68–110065

BRITAIN IN THE CENTURY OF TOTAL WAR

Britain in the Century of Total War

WAR, PEACE AND SOCIAL CHANGE
1900–1967

ARTHUR MARWICK

An Atlantic Monthly Press Book

LITTLE, BROWN AND COMPANY   BOSTON   TORONTO

LIBRARY OF CONGRESS CATALOG CARD NO. 68-17276

FIRST AMERICAN EDITION

ATLANTIC—LITTLE, BROWN BOOKS
ARE PUBLISHED BY
LITTLE, BROWN AND COMPANY
IN ASSOCIATION WITH
THE ATLANTIC MONTHLY PRESS

For
Helen and Louise

Contents

PREFACE

The arguments at the heart of this book have been paraded before various academic colleagues of many nationalities, at various times and in many settings, ranging from formal conferences to private parties and public bar-rooms. Many of my students must be sick to death of them. Without the comment and criticism of colleagues, students and friends it would not have been possible to write this book. I owe a particular debt to Mr Arthur Bowler of the State University of New York at Buffalo who saved me from many errors of fact and style perpetrated in the original typescript.

This book is about the social effects of modern war; and about Britain (not England) in the twentieth century. I wish I had written more about Wales, especially since I have had to say so much about two Welshmen, David Lloyd George and Aneurin Bevan. The problem is simply that separate Welsh statistics are much less easy to come by than separate Scottish ones; there is, furthermore, still something of a shortage of secondary works on modern Wales. I have not attempted to deal with social developments in Northern Ireland, which is part of the United Kingdom, but not of Britain.

For permission to quote copyright material acknowledgments are due to: George Allen and Unwin Ltd for extracts from *Keeling Letters and Reminiscences*, F. H. Keeling; Chapman and Hall Ltd for an extract from *Sword of Honour*, by Evelyn Waugh; MacGibbon and Kee Ltd for an extract from *Disenchantment*, by C. E. Montague; Mr Harold Owen and Chatto and Windus Ltd for the poem 'The Parable of the Old Man and the Young', from the *Collected Poems* of Wilfred Owen; Eyre and Spottiswoode and David Higham Ass. Ltd for an extract from *The Day of the Sardine*, by S. Chaplin; Faber and Faber Ltd for extracts from two poems by W. H. Auden, an extract from *Outline: An Autobiography and Other Writings*, by Paul Nash, and, as also to Mr George Sassoon, for 'The General', from *Counterattack*, by Siegfried Sassoon; William Heinemann and Co. Ltd, as also to Rosica Colin Ltd, for an extract from *Roads to Glory*, by Richard Aldington, and, as also to Laurence Pollinger, Ltd, extracts from *It's a Battlefield*, by Graham Greene, and for extracts from *Angel Pavement, English Journey* and *Three Men in New Suits*, by J. B. Priestley; Michael Joseph Ltd for an extract from *A Picture to Hang on the Wall*, by S. Hignett; Longmans, Green and Co. Ltd for an extract from *Gentian Violet*, by Edward Hyams; Macmillan and Co. Ltd for extracts from *Reconstruction* and *The Middle Way*, by Harold Macmillan; the Oxford University Press for an extract from *Diary with Letters*, by T. Jones; Weidenfeld and Nicolson Ltd for an extract from *Political Adventure*, by Lord Kilmuir; the Controller of H.M. Stationery Office for excerpts from British government publications; the keeper of the Public Records for permission to quote from material in the Public Records Office.

CHAPTER ONE
War, Peace and Social Change

History has been defined as a dialogue between the present and the past. Hopefully it is also a dialogue between the historian and his audience. At the core of this book lies a series of generalizations about the relationship between war and social change, presented to the reader not as a group of immutable 'laws', but simply as a possible guide (and goad) through a gigantic historical and sociological problem, and, more positively, as an explanation of some of the paradoxes of Britain's recent social history. Marxists have always been firmest in stressing war as an agent of change: 'war', said Trotsky, 'is the locomotive of history.' Other historians have found it unreasonable to suppose that war, the most unpleasant and destructive of all human activities, can make any contribution to human progress: Professor J. U. Nef devoted a substantial volume to that very theme and Professor Toynbee has insisted upon the incompatibility of war and the advance of civilization;[1] sociologists have tended to concentrate on the interesting, but incomplete, notion of war as 'disaster'[2]; and a number of recent narrative histories of twentieth-century Britain have played down the First World War as little more than an interruption in the steady course of social and political development.[3] Renewed interest in that particularly horrific war, however, has led to a refocusing on the general problem: Professor Geoffrey Barraclough has told historians that they should give up seeking the causes of the war and start studying its consequences,[4] something which, for Britain, I, and for Germany, Professor Gerald Feldman, had already done.[5] In his most recent major work Mr A. J. P. Taylor has directed attention to some of the bigger issues with one or two of his most vivid sentences[6] and in October 1967 an Institute of Contemporary History conference discussed 'the Impact of the First World War'. Earlier Dr Philip Abrams had made a most impressive attempt to bring into use some of the tools of sociological analysis; though finally, in speaking of what he

called 'The Failure of Social Reform: 1918–1920' he decided that
the First World War was accompanied by little real social change
in Britain, concluding a trifle lamely that

the one group in English society to which the war brought a significant
extension of social and political prestige was middle-aged propertied
women.[7]

It will be a basic contention of this book that two wars have
played a substantial, though unequal, part in furthering social
change in twentieth-century Britain, and a primary purpose to show
why this was so. There will be no attempt to generalize about the
'consequences' of war, for to talk of a war having consequences –
save at the most direct level of 'so many killed,' 'so many houses
destroyed,' and so on – is really a wrong use of language. War is, in
its very essence, negative and destructive; it cannot of itself
create anything new. What I shall try to do is to isolate the four
aspects of war which are relevant to social change, and thereby
endeavour to demonstrate the four *modes* through which war
affects society. The consequences – so-called – of the war will be
the final identifiable products – Acts of Parliament, new wage
rates, changes in the social structure – resulting from war's fourfold
reaction with existing society, and with the agents of change already
apparent in that society. Obviously the whole exercise is valueless
without a deep knowledge of the nature of a society on the eve of
the war it is proposed to study: the methods of the sociologist
serve little purpose without the knowledge of the historian.

War, at its simplest, is a matter of loss and gain: loss of life and
limb and capital; gain of territory, indemnities, or trade concessions. War is the supreme challenge to, and test of, a country's
military institutions, and, in a war of any size, a challenge to its
social, political and economic institutions as well. War needs someone to do the fighting, and someone to furnish the weapons and
food: those who participate in the war effort have to be rewarded
(though, as we shall see, the process is much more complicated
than that of mere reward). War is one of the most intense emotional
experiences (comparable only with the great revolutions in

history) in which human beings as members of a community can be involved. In the eighteenth century the gains and losses involved in the wars were fairly easy to compute. Recent wars have tended to result in considerable material loss all round, and in the Second World War only one belligerent (the United States) showed clear gain. In another great war, the loser would doubtless be human life itself, though it is still possible to wage limited war for limited gain as India did in Goa. For Britain in the twentieth century the loss-gain aspect of war has shown itself principally in destruction of human and capital resources and of existing patterns of trade and social life: it is in this aspect that the 'disaster' studies of the sociologists have greatest relevance. War as challenge or test was neatly pinpointed by Marx when he wrote:

The redeeming feature of war is that it puts a nation to the test. As exposure to the atmosphere reduces all mummies to instant dissolution, so war passes extreme judgement on social systems that have outlived their vitality.[8]

The most obvious example of war affecting society in this way was the collapse of the Czarist régime in Russia in 1917. However, the test of war need not necessarily provoke dissolution: it can, given a determined will to victory, provoke the transformation of those institutions which in their pre-existing form have been revealed as inadequate to the new challenge – here, of course, is one key to the constructive effect a war *may* have. If the reader begins to hear a faint echo of Professor Toynbee's famous Challenge and Response theory,[9] he will not be wrong, save that I am using the idea of Test–Dissolution–Transformation in a very limited and specific context and one which must be taken in conjunction with the other three modes through which war affects society. The test of war may lead to neither total dissolution nor complete transformation, but, depending on the length of the war and the seriousness of the challenge, to some intermediate stage: so often, we shall see, this is what has happened in twentieth-century Britain.

Feudal wars were essentially waged by a small aristocratic minority which alone shared in the spoils, with the peasant masses on both sides suffering from their depredations. (However the connection between the development of the English Parliament – not of great interest to the peasants – and the crises of the Hundred Years War, has often been noted.) In modern war there is greater participation on the part of larger groups within society, who tend correspondingly, by processes which will be examined in some detail in this book, to benefit. Emancipation of the Russian serfs followed closely upon their participation in the Crimean War (that many peasants were in fact a good deal worse off after emancipation is a warning about the complexities of history, not, I believe, a warning against generalization, which is fruitful precisely in proportion as the complexities are borne in mind); the present civil rights consciousness on the part of the American Negro appears to me closely related to his participation in the Second World War, when he acquired economic status and some sense of citizenship. An extreme case is that of the members of resistance movements in the Second World War, who were the *only* effective participants in the national cause: much of the post-1945 welfare legislation in continental Europe came direct from the programmes of the resistance groups. This is all very obvious, and all rather vague: the most elaborate attempt to give the correlation between military participation and social change a precise, almost quant-itative basis, was that of the sociologist, Stanislaw Andrzejewski, who formulated what he called the Military Participation Ratio (M.P.R.),[10] a notion which was taken up briefly by Professor Richard Titmuss in a lecture on 'War and Social Policy'[11], and by Dr Abrams in the article already cited. In Dr Abrams's admirable rephrasing the theory simply states that

there is some kind of meaningful correlation between the social 'size' of a war and the process of social reform and levelling.[12]

Professor Titmuss had been more specific:

The aims and content of social policy, both in peace and in war, are ... determined – at least to a substantial extent – by how far the co-operation of the masses is essential to the successful prosecution of the war.[13]

By the parenthesis 'both in peace and in war' Titmuss suggests social significance in the threat or possibility of war, as well as in war as an actual contingency, and a similar idea lay at the root of Professor Semmel's *Imperialism and Social Reform*, which however took to absurd lengths the notion of the State consciously 'buying' support. It is not just 'social policy' – guided government action – which is affected by war, but also, irrespective of any action the government may or may not take, economic and social relationships and attitudes within and between social classes, the reference groups by which people judge their own standards of living or of liberty (one thinks of the Russian intellectuals who were profoundly influenced by contact with Westerners in the Napoleonic wars) and the moral canons by which they judge their everyday actions. In concentrating on the issues of 'social reform', Dr Abrams in his article ignored the unguided social changes which can take place during a war, which accounts for his lame conclusion about the effects of the First World War. His qualification of the M.P.R. theory is extremely sensible:

In its crude form the 'military participation ratio' theory of social reform will not do. If it is to have any value, it must also allow for the fact that different groups in society participate in a war effort in different degree, with widely varying power to influence consequential political decisions, and with a very different sense of what participation means to them.[14]

But it is not political decisions alone which matter: 'the key to history', as Marx remarked, 'lies in society, not in the State.'

The immense emotional surcharge carried by war, a matter of importance in itself, leading perhaps to bitterness, cynicism and political detachment, perhaps to a renewed interest in problems of the mind and spirit, is especially significant for the manner in which it reinforces the changes associated with the other aspects of war.

War, then, without itself creating anything, can be an instrument of social change: the more total the war, the more likely are we to see all four of the modes through which war affects society in full play; in a limited war the destructive, inegalitarian features of war are likely to predominate. But war is not the only, nor is it the most important, instrument of change. Societies which have not borne the brunt of the two twentieth-century wars have gone through processes of social development remarkably similar to Britain's. Although offering a tentative guide to the experience of all countries affected by modern war, all this book finally declares is: 'This, as it happened, is the way that it happened in Britain.' It is important, therefore, to look at the larger circumstances which, wars or no wars, were throughout the century effecting social change in Britain, as elsewhere. In all twentieth-century industrialized societies the pressure generated by the unguided activities of individuals and groups within these societies, mightily assisted by the great resources of science and technology, have been towards a greater share for the many of economic and material well-being, social status and political responsibility. Britain's twentieth-century history, in part, has, in a simple phrase, been a history of the 'rise of the working classes', a rise brought about by the growth of a sophisticated economy dependent for survival and expansion upon mass consumption by the working classes, but reinforced by the conscious entry into political and industrial action of the organized working-class movement (which, in Britain, has had a rather special flavour, apparent in that unique institution, the British Labour Party). But the organized working-class movement has not been the only participant in furthering the egalitarian process. Many persons within the classes whose selfish interests were linked to an older, more unequal structure have been impelled by some abstract concept of 'justice' or 'liberty' either to initiate, or to lend their support to, movements for change, often giving these movements a distinctly paternalist cast. Yet the old traditions and forms of an intrinsically hierarchical society have persisted, apparently setting definite limits upon the extent of equality to be achieved in Britain. At times – as, say, in the Twenties – there has been sharp conflict between the upholders of hierarchical traditions and the proponents of change (E. P. Thompson has wisely and wittily dismissed what he calls 'the phlegmatic assumption that revolutionary activity can be written off as un-English'),[15] but on the whole recent British history has exhibited the gradualness and stability for which it is famous, because, most obviously, of the renowned ability of the existing ruling class to recruit protesters from below, and, more critically, because of the willingness in the last analysis of protesting groups to accommodate themselves to the existing hierarchical framework. It is indeed because of this very tendency to gradualness that I rate so highly the importance in recent British history of the two great 'discontinuities',[16] the two total wars (as also the lesser discontinuity, the crisis of 1931). Great weight, then, will be given in this book to the two total wars; but as it is no part of my intention to distort the picture in order to suit my main thesis, a great deal of space has also been devoted to questions wherein wars and rumours of wars figure not at all. Wars are like weddings: essentially extravagant and unnecessary, but a great stimulant in a convention-bound society.

NOTES TO CHAPTER ONE

1. J. U. Nef, *War and Human Progress*, 1950. Toynbee's views stand out sharply in the extracts from the first six volumes of *A Study of History* published as *War and Civilization*, 1950.
2. e. g. Pitirim A. Sorokin, *Man and Society in Calamity*, 1942; Quincy B. Wright, *A Study of War*, 2 vols., 1942, esp. vol. I, p. 272: 'The preceding survey suggests that in the most recent stage of world-civilization war has made for instability, for disintegration, for despotism, and for unadaptability, rendering the course of civilization less predictable and continued progress towards achievement of its values less probable'. The two most valuable sociological contributions are Willard Waller, 'War and Social Institutions' in W. Waller (ed.), *War in the Twentieth Century*, 1942, pp. 478–532, and G. Sjoberg, 'Disasters and Social Change', G. W. Baker and D. W. Chapman (eds.), *Man and Society in Disaster*, New York 1962, pp. 356–84. For a fuller bibliographical review see my paper delivered to the Institute of Contemporary History, October 1967.
3. Professor Alfred Havighurst, *Twentieth Century Britain*, 1962, p. 116, writes, 'The Great War seems to us to inaugurate a new era. This is more apparent than real. If World War I changed Britain it was only in degree. The nature of the change had already been determined.' In their history of *The Social Services*, 1949, H. and M. Wickwar stress the calm continuity as between 1911 and 1920. Mr Maurice Bruce, in *The Coming of the Welfare State*, 1961, simply brings his narrative to a halt in 1914, then, with scarcely a glance over his shoulder, cheerfully starts it up again in 1918: later,

however, he does find the Second World War 'the decisive event' in the evolution of the Welfare State.

4. First of all in his presidential address to the 1966 meeting of the Historical Association.

5. A. Marwick, *The Deluge: British Society and the First World War*, 1965. G. Feldman, *Army, Industry and Labor in Germany, 1914–18*, 1966. An older work is A. Mendelssohn-Bartholdy, *The War and German Society: the Testament of a Liberal*, New Haven, 1937.

6. A. J. P. Taylor, *English History, 1914–1945*, 1966. On the First World War, p. 2: 'The history of the English state and of the English people merged for the first time.' On the Second, p. 600: 'In the Second World War the British people came of age.' See also Mr Taylor's review, *New Statesman*, 25 November 1966, of Professor Feldman's book.

7. P. Abrams, 'The Failure of Social Reform: 1918–1920' in *Past and Present*, April 1963.

8. Karl Marx, *The Eastern Question*, 1897.

9. Arnold Toynbee, *A Study of History*, 10 vols, 1934–1954, esp. vol. II, p. 260.

10. S. Andrzewski, *Military Organisation and Society*, 1954.

11. Published in *Essays on 'the Welfare State'*, 1958, pp. 75–87.

12. Abrams, *op. cit.*

13. R. Titmuss, *op. cit.*

14. Abrams, *op. cit.*

15. E. P. Thompson, *The Making of the English Working Class*, 1963.

16. For some perceptive comments on the sociological significance of 'discontinuities' see William Kornhauser, *The Politics of Mass Society*, 1959, pp. 159–72.

CHAPTER TWO

Before the Lamps Went Out

I. THE LEGACY OF HISTORY AND THE BOUNTY OF GEOGRAPHY

Britain in the twentieth century has been exposed as a country desperately short of the raw commodities upon which successful industrial enterprise is based. This is an ironic reversal of fortune: in the late eighteenth century and early nineteenth century, it had been partly through geographical advantage that Britain had achieved world economic primacy. She possessed plenteous stocks of coal and good natural communications: a relatively closely-knit country of 88,755 square miles, she was insulated from the worst upheavals of continental Europe. The varied geography of an island only 750 miles long and, at its greatest extent, 375 miles wide, is best understood if divided into three components: Lowland, Upland and Highland.[1] In the lowland regions of the South lay the original agricultural wealth of England, while it was amid the mineral wealth of the upland areas of South Wales, the Pennines and Central Scotland that the Industrial Revolution took place, creating in some parts an ugliness unsurpassed in Western Europe and in others a strange beauty of mingled industrial and natural landscape; the highland regions of Central Wales and of Scotland remained 'unspoiled', left to decay while the rest of the land prospered, unexploited (save in the interests of a few wealthy landowners), though rich in potential hydro-electric power. Only the needs of war were to halt this senseless prodigality.

An island power, Britain had the world, and the world's trade, at her feet. At the beginning of the twentieth century she was still enjoying the fruits of economic primacy, even if that was now being insistently challenged by Germany and by the United States of America. Many of the raw materials which she lacked could be drawn from the overseas empire which spread over the globe, bold patches of red on the map which delighted the eye of the school-marms and schoolchildren alike. With 35 per cent of all world trade in 1900, Britain was the world's greatest trading nation. Her more powerful and assertive inhabitants had, from the sixteenth century onwards, shown an inventiveness in developing and adapting their forms of government to accommodate the claims of new interests produced by economic change. From out of the scientific revolution of the seventeenth century and from a natural proclivity for trade they had found the means to build an industrial society, and, though not without great cost in personal suffering, they had adapted themselves to the needs of that society. In the eighteenth century and in the long struggle against Napoleon they had waged war victoriously, if not always gloriously. British power and influence, save for the loss of the American colonies, steadily spread.

Any attempt to explain these successes in terms of racial characteristics or of climatic conditions would be worthless; suffice it to say that the British population, subject in the distant past to many invasions, was drawn from widely varied stocks, but that relative isolation from Europe had enabled these stocks to be fully assimilated. Climatically the British Isles were, and are, subject to a rapid succession of invasions of a different type, invasion by varied, but distinctive air-masses: the warm damp tropical maritime from the Atlantic, often bringing fog or heavy rain; the polar maritime, frequently bearing periods of rain showers and sunny intervals; the polar continental, bringing a cold, dry biting wind, often provoking an inversion of temperature and fog; and the tropical continental, which heralds dry, stable weather and occasional heatwaves. Thus the British climate is variable, but it is also, because of the moderating influence of the sea, remarkably temperate for a country lying between 50 and 60 degrees North; the temperature seldom rises above 90 degrees Fahrenheit or falls below zero.[2] Dourness, a quality sometimes associated with the British climate, was not, as a wealth of evidence from the eighteenth century, and earlier, would testify, a special characteristic of the British people. What, from the sixteenth to the nineteenth centuries, they did undoubtedly manifest was vigour.

In the first industrial revolution of the late eighteenth and early nineteenth centuries Britons had been to the fore in scientific discovery, in invention and in the practical application of both. In the later nineteenth century there seemed to be no question of a failure in the British scientific imagination, or of British inventiveness. In electrical theory Faraday, Joule and Wheatstone were succeeded by Lord Kelvin and Clerk Maxwell, pioneer of the theory of electro-magnetic waves; J. J. Thomson in 1897 proved the existence of the electron; Joseph Swan in 1878 successfully demonstrated his incandescent electric light bulb; William Perkin in 1867 discovered how to develop aniline dyes from coal tar; Sidney Gilchrist Thomas in 1877 patented a method for a large-scale production of steel from phosphoric ore. Yet as British industry continued to thrive on old products and old methods, there was a reluctance to adopt the new ideas and the new inventions. From the start supremacy in the chemicals industry (based in part on Perkin's discovery) and in the electrical industry was assumed by the Germans and the Americans. The older organizations of science, the Royal Society, the Royal Institution and the British Association, were declining, and up to 1914 the British government showed only spasmodic awareness of the importance of sponsoring scientific research and encouraging its industrial application. But whatever the long-term implications, they were still concealed behind Britain's long lead in the production of other basic industrial commodities.

Though materially successful, the British could be taunted with being a nation of philistines. There had been no native-born musician of stature since Purcell; no architect since the Adam brothers; no painter or sculptor to compare with the great European masters; no dramatist of any significance at all between Sheridan and Shaw. Only in literature had the British excelled. Britain had no tradition of theatres and opera houses supported by local princes or dukes. In a relatively mobile society the arts tended to become a symbol of social status and among a nation of pragmatists and utilitarians had often been assessed, and constricted, by non-artistic criteria. These conditions were not created by the Victorians, but they reached their greatest intensity in the Victorian period when writers and artists seemed happy to pander to them. In turn, there was towards the end of the century a literary and artistic reaction, the Modern Movement, drawing its inspiration almost exclusively from foreign models – the Symbolists, the Post-Impressionists, Art Nouveau. Up till 1914 the practitioners or sponsors of modernism in Britain had a hard struggle to gain any kind of acceptance. But whatever the years that followed the deluge of 1914–18 were to bring in the way of political and economic decline, they also brought an astonishing reversal in the image of the British as a totally philistine nation.

It is difficult at any time to draw up a precise table of relative world power. Today most informed commentators, basing their judgement on such criteria as size, population, gross national product, *per capita* income, weapon-power, political influence, and world trading position, would place the United States of America in top position. Russia is a strong rival, ahead of the U.S.A. in some respects, far behind her in others. China is a strong potential rival. Between America and Russia (leaving China aside as a somewhat unpredictable quantity) and all the other powers there is a difference which seems qualitative rather than quantitative. It is arguable that even at the end of the nineteenth century Britain still occupied a position analogous to that of America today; with Germany perhaps in the position of Russia and America herself a little like China. But there was no real qualitative difference between these powers and the other major powers in Europe such as France and Russia. The highest peak of relative British power had been in the sixty years after the Battle of Waterloo. It is worth stressing both the shortness of this period and the way in which it arose from a fortuitous combination of British industrialization, French defeat, German disunity and American inexperience. And, it may be added, although Britain was supreme as a world power, her ability to interfere successfully in the affairs of continental Europe was practically negligible. Two points then emerge: Britain in 1900 occupied a world position which she manifestly does not occupy today; but that world position could not seriously be construed as being part of any immutable order of things.

As population increased and as the centres of economic power shifted, the circle of those who took an active interest in the community's destiny, or specific aspects of it, widened. Yet four centuries of English and British history, including a Protestant Reformation issuing in the *via media* of Queen Elizabeth, a Puritan revolution leading to a Royalist restoration, a 'Glorious Revolution' which shed no blood and little light on the basic issues it proposed to solve, a reform of Parliament which gave the middle classes votes and kept the aristocrats in power, reveal among the politically conscious at different points in time certain clear characteristics: a pragmatism never divorced from a reverence for tradition; a supreme talent for compromise; and an attachment to a somewhat nebulous concept of 'liberty'. This last can be summarily illustrated by reference to the starving coal-heavers of the 1760s who rioted for 'Wilkes and *Liberty*', or to the celebrated conversation in 1735 between Queen Caroline, lately of Hanover and Lord Hervey recorded by the latter in his *Memoirs*:

'My God!' she cried, 'What a figure would this poor island make in Europe if it were not for its government! It is its excellent free government that makes all its inhabitants industrious, as they know that what they get nobody can take from them; it is its free government, too, that makes foreigners send their money hither, because they know it is secure, and that the prince cannot touch it; and since it is its freedom to which this kingdom owes everything that makes it great, what prince, who had his senses, and knew that his own greatness depended on the greatness of the country over which he reigned, would wish to take away what made both him and them considerable? I had as lief,' added she, 'be Elector of Hanover as King of England, if the government was the same. Who the devil would take you all, or think you worth having, that had anything else, if you had not your liberties?'[3]

The economic connotation is clear: liberty, above all, means liberty to hold private property. Still, it could have another shade of meaning. The Scots (firmly associated with the English in the United Kingdom of Great Britain, after the Union of 1707) had put it defiantly as early as 1320 in the famous Declaration of Arbroath:

So long as a mere hundred of us stand, we will never surrender to the dominion of England. What we fight for is not glory nor wealth nor honour, but freedom, that no good man yields save with life.[4]

These characteristic styles of political thought and action served the British well up till the end of the nineteenth century; but thereafter, as with her former geographical advantages, they did not so well stand the test of time, particularly as they became overlaid with an element which had always been discernible among leading British political commentators on the British political scene, self-congratulation.

2. THE PROCESSES OF REFORM

We use the word democracy in two rather separate senses: to describe a form of government which, through the apparatus of a wide franchise and representative institutions, creates the opportunity for self-government; or to describe a type of society which through economic and social controls allows for the possibility of full self-development. Neither definition was applicable to Britain in the early years of the twentieth century. Indeed, there were some strongly anti-democratic (in both senses of the term) features of the British way of doing things which were to endure right into the Sixties of the present century. What Britain did have, looking at the formal aspect of the question, was representative (*not* democratic) government, with a number of very highly developed conventions. There was free speech, freedom of assembly, and a free Press – free from governmental control, that is. More than this, within the defined frame of representative government the machine was oiled by one vaunted British virtue which, in this context, was no myth: the sense of fair play. As Gladstone had put it, 'The British constitution presumes the good faith of those who work it.'[5] This, essentially, was Britain's gift to the world – not democracy (though it could be, and was shortly, adapted to democracy), but a highly sophisticated parliamentary system which worked perfectly in guaranteeing the liberties of all those whose liberties it was intended to guarantee. As a commodity for export, it was highly perishable: in place of the lubricant of good faith the engine could be run, as it had been run in eighteenth-century Britain, on jobbery and corruption – as was to be demonstrated fifty years later in at least one liberated British colony.

The five basic themes in the development of the British political system had begun to announce themselves in the eighteenth century above the ground base of jobbery. They are: the Monarchy, still in the person of Queen Victoria of real influence in the constitution, but manifestly on a steady slide of diminishing power; the elaboration of the formal position of the Cabinet and of the Prime Minister at the head of it (Walter Bagehot, editor of the influential journal, the *Economist*, commentator and prophet of mid-Victorian Britain, had given currency to the concept that British government, in essence, was Cabinet government[6] – latter-day Bagehots in the mid-twentieth century were to argue that Cabinet government was becoming Prime-Ministerial government);[7] the advance of the House of Commons as against (in the past) the Monarch and (in the present and future) the other chamber in the British Parliament, the House of Lords, partially offset by a decline in the influence of individual members of the House of Commons as against the growing power of Cabinet and Prime Minister; the notion of his Majesty's Opposition – the key element in the sophisticated game touched on above; and political parties – 'organized opinion' in Disraeli's striking phrase. The development of party took three forms: inside Parliament the grouping of members behind the respective political leadership, with party whips to ensure a certain measure of coherence; outside parliament the formation of individual local party organizations; and, finally, the linking of these local parties together in a national party organization. Fears were expressed at the turn of the century by the political scientist, Ostrogorski, that those who controlled the national party organization would be able to control the party in Parliament.[8] In fact it was already clear that if anything the opposite process was taking place – with the leadership in Parliament beginning to adumbrate control of the party organization; great freedom, however, yet remained to individual local parties.

In the development and recapitulation of these five themes, democracy played no part. In retrospect the franchise extensions of 1832, 1867 and 1884 do mark important steps towards formal democracy. Many of those who had agitated for parliamentary reforms were democrats, though none of those who conceded them

were. In 1911 only 59 per cent of the adult male population
(just under 8 million out of a total population of 40·8 million)
had the franchise, and it was clear from the complicated registration
procedure that the vote was still a privilege which a man earned
through his respectability and proven value to the community,
rather than a democratic right. As the law stood under the terms of
the 1884 Act, there were seven different types of franchise, of which
the two major ones, accounting for over 84 per cent of those
registered to vote in 1911, were the occupation and household
franchises: the former qualified the occupier, as owner or tenant, of
any land or tenement of the clear yearly value of £10; the latter the
inhabitant occupier, whether as owner or tenant, of any dwelling
house defined as a separate dwelling. Half a million among the
wealthier sections of the electorate had two or more votes; in the
election of January 1910 two especially well-qualified brothers
between them cast thirty-five votes, and then, apparently, lamented
that inadequate registration had deprived them of further votes.
The principles upon which the system was based were clearly
expressed in the rhetorical question posed in the House of
Commons in July 1912:

Is the man who is too illiterate to read his ballot paper, who is too
imprudent to support his children, to be placed on the same footing as
the man who by industry and capacity has acquired a substantial interest
in more than one constituency?[9]

Two generalizations might then be made about the state of the
franchise in early twentieth-century Britain. In the first place it
was not democratic, and it was not intended to be. In the second
place, because of the variety of franchises and the cumbersome
procedure of registration, it was even less democratic than it
purported to be. This device, the device of the inefficient machine,
is one we shall come across again.

An important aspect of traditional 'liberty' was a respect for the
rights of localities as against the central government. In England
and Wales the main lines for twentieth-century local government
were laid down in Acts of 1888 and 1894, by which sixty-one of the

larger towns were designated as county boroughs forming a single authority for the administration of local government services in their area; in the sixty-two administrative counties a two-tier system obtained, with responsibility for some services lying with the county council and others with the non-county boroughs, or urban districts or rural districts within the counties. In Scotland a similar dichotomy was created between the four major burghs – Edinburgh, Glasgow, Dundee and Aberdeen – and the counties. The local government franchises were restricted to ratepayers, but included women. Rates (local taxation) were based on property values, and not on income.

Pursuit of the question of democracy in its economic and social aspects leads into troubled waters. From medieval times British governments had been known to take action on behalf of the poorer sections of the community. In the eighteenth century there grew up a systematic economic doctrine hostile to the idea of any governmental interference of any sort in the free workings of society. The classical political economists, or *laissez-faire* school, argued against state interference on three counts: first, that on the principle of 'liberty' already noted it was philosophically wrong; second, that it was unnecessary, since Divine Providence – 'the invisible hand', as Adam Smith, greatest of the British classical economists, put it – would ensure that if each individual pursued his own economic interests, the end product would best serve the interests of the community as a whole; and, third, that it was inexpedient, since, so the classical school believed, scientific evidence could be presented showing the harmfulness of State interference and the salutary effect of economic freedom.[10] *Laissez-faire* economic doctrines were well suited to the interests of the industrial class rising to prosperity on the tide of the industrial revolution; undoubtedly they had a liberating effect on economic practices and contributed to the enormous increase in national wealth between 1780 and 1850; too rigidly observed, they also permitted the early processes of industrialization to be attended by enormous human misery and suffering. It was early apparent to politicians and reformers of various persuasions and motivations that only by government action could the worst abuses be stemmed.

At the beginning of the twentieth century a distinguished academic lawyer, A. V. Dicey, put forward the theory that up till about 1868 British legislative policy had been dominated by individualism (or *laissez-faire*), but that since then a countervalent theory of collectivism (or State interference in social and economic matters) had taken over.[11] The division now seems a rather facile one. Certainly it is true that from the 1870s we find British governments passing Housing Acts, Trade Union Acts, Public Health Acts and Education Acts on an unprecedented scale. What is more, there was a certain conscious acceptance among political leaders of what was being done – the mid-Victorians had boasted of their faith in *laissez-faire*, even if in practice they had slipped in the odd Factory Act here and there. The growth of large industrial combinations served to temper the belief that private enterprise could do no wrong; 'gas and water socialism' – the establishment in some of the bigger county boroughs of municipal water companies and gas companies, and, in the 1890s, of municipal electric tramways – suggested that there were other ways of doing right. The idealist philosophers (particularly T. H. Green and Bernard Bosanquet), teaching at the ancient universities, which was where budding politicians were usually educated, stressed the importance of the State. So it came about that Sir William Harcourt, in the last decade of the century, could make his famous remark, 'We are all socialists now.' What he really meant was, 'We are all collectivists now.'

None the less individualism and resistance to the encroachment of the State upon society remained stronger in Britain than in continental countries with their long history of *étatiste* despotisms, whether monarchical or revolutionary. In late nineteenth-century Britain there was strong emphasis on voluntary charitable work, and there was less State-sponsored social reform than in some other countries: Germany, in particular, had introduced her first national health insurance scheme in the 1880s. Social reform in Britain was confined to filling the most glaring gaps in the existing social system. The bed-rock of social provision was to be found in the Poor Law, first enacted by the Tudors in the sixteenth century, and re-enacted in 1834. Administered locally by Boards of Guardians and financed from local rates, the Poor Law provided a minimum subsistence under conditions which were deliberately designed to deter all but the utterly desperate from applying for it. Only the faintest chink was opened in the Poor Law edifice by the introduction in 1897 (by a Conservative ministry) of compulsory Workmen's Compensation, under a system whose two major defects were that litigation, which could often be expensive, was necessary on the part of the injured worker, and that success for the litigant was often represented by a lump sum payment, which was considerably less useful to him than a regular weekly pension.

Conservatives and Liberals both had social reforms to their credit: if anything the Conservative stock stood higher – their landowners and businessmen, if not their financiers, were often less solidly sold on the doctrines of *laissez-faire* than was the nineteenth-century Liberal Party. In 1900 there appeared the sickly infant which was to become a third political party: the Labour Representation Committee. Britain in the nineteenth century had her confirmed socialists, those who had a clear philosophy of how the bases of society were to be reconstructed: the Marxists centred in the Social Democratic Federation, (S.D.F.), the Gradualists in the Fabian Society, which hoped to achieve its objectives by 'permeation' of the major political parties. She also had a well-developed trade union movement, based on the 'model unions' of skilled workers established in the 1850s and the 'new unions' of unskilled workers established in the 1880s. Some of the leaders of the new unions were socialists, but in the main the concern of the unions was with immediate objectives, such as bettering wages and improving conditions. It was Keir Hardie, a miner from Lanarkshire in Scotland, who saw more clearly than most the need to bring together the socialist elements and the trade union mass. The first major effort at building a bridge was the Independent Labour Party (I.L.P.), founded in 1893. The I.L.P. was strongly socialist and largely working-class; but it failed to capture the sympathies of the unions. Yet, together with some of the more socialistically- and politically-inclined members of the new unions, it played an important part in summoning the conference which resulted in the establishment of the Labour Representation

Committee (L.R.C.). This nebulous body was essentially a loose federation of trade unions and socialist societies. Of the two men whose candidatures were endorsed by the L.R.C., and who were returned to Parliament in the General Election of 1900, one, Keir Hardie, was a socialist, the other, Richard Bell, was not. Regularly conferences of the L.R.C. resisted attempts to write a socialist objective into its constitution.

External events helped the L.R.C. along. A number of court cases, of which the most famous was that concerning the Taff Vale Railway Company, threw into jeopardy the whole principle of the right to strike by holding unions liable for all loss of profits caused by strikes. Trade unions which had held aloof from the L.R.C. now saw the advantages of an organization devoted to political activity on behalf of Labour. Somewhat fortuitously two further L.R.C. candidates crept into Parliament at by-elections. In 1903 the L.R.C. took the important step of establishing a political fund to be financed by a levy on member organizations. Seeing no threat to its own position in this new party of Labour, but concerned to minimize the cost of fighting elections, the Liberal Party, in the person of their Chief Whip, Herbert Gladstone, entered into secret negotiations with the L.R.C. designed in certain constituencies to avoid direct conflict between a Liberal and an L.R.C. candidate:[12] for the L.R.C. negotiations were conducted by the secretary, J. Ramsay MacDonald, who from unpromising origins as the illegitimate son of a Scottish servant girl had by hard work and natural talent reached a position where he was able to undertake the L.R.C. secretaryship without salary. MacDonald was a leading figure in the I.L.P.; out of an earlier liberalism he had developed a theory of socialism by slow evolution.

Assisted by the electoral agreement with the Liberals, the L.R.C. secured the return of twenty-nine candidates in the General Election of 1906. There were twenty-four 'Lib-Labs', working-class representatives returned under the auspices of the Liberal Party, one of whom at once threw in his lot with the L.R.C. – or Labour Party, as it now christened itself. But above all victory lay with the Liberals, who after twenty years of Conservative rule had secured a majority of eighty-four over all other parties. It is fashionable nowadays to stress that despite this landslide victory long-term sociological trends were unfavourable to the Liberals, in that the middle classes as a whole had by this time secured most of their major social and political objectives and therefore were turning increasingly towards the party of the *status quo*, the Conservative Party, while the growing suburban white-collar class tended to be imperialist in sentiment, and therefore also Conservative; the Liberals furthermore, being hoist with a leadership which in class composition was not markedly different from that of the Conservatives, were in no strong position to meet the aspirations of the increasingly assertive working classes. The Liberal victory, then, is often attributed more than anything else to the mistakes of the Conservatives under A. J. Balfour, a patrician of philosophical bent but no great talent for the humdrum details of politics.[13] The greatest legislative achievement of the Balfour régime, and one which aroused great hostility among nonconformists, was the Education Act of 1902. This was partly a measure of administrative rationalization in that it abolished the separately-elected School Boards (created by the Education Act of 1870 to provide non-sectarian elementary education in those areas where the religious bodies were not already providing 'adequate' education), giving their powers (together with certain new powers) to the county boroughs and county councils and (for elementary education only) to the county districts. In Scotland School Boards remained in being till 1929; in the Edwardian era many socialists argued that this was the better system as it kept education in the hands of those who were specially interested in it.[14] The major importance of the 1902 Act lay in the power which it gave to the county boroughs and the county councils to provide secondary education, subsidized from the rates, though not usually free. The controversial part of the Act was that which permitted rate aid to be given to Church schools as well as non-denominational ones of the old Board school type. Among the leaders of the nonconformist agitation against this provision was a wealthy solicitor and Liberal M.P. who had already made a mark for himself in the causes of Welsh nationalism and opposition to the Boer War, and who rejoiced in his humble Welsh origins, David Lloyd George.

In whatever fashion the election result of 1906 is to be qualified
and explained, there is no doubt that to some contemporaries it
seemed a portent of radical social change,[15] and no doubt also that
Lloyd George, President of the Board of Trade in the new government, spoke the language of radical social change. So too did
Winston Churchill, a former Conservative of distinguished lineage
who had recently crossed the floor of the House of Commons to
join the Liberal Opposition. Many influences combined to create
an atmosphere favourable to an accelerated programme of social
reform. Charles Booth, a rich shipowner had, in the massive
researches he conducted in the last two decades of the nineteenth
century, revealed the extent of privation among families in the
East End of London: one third were found to be in want.[16]
These findings were confirmed for working-class families in York by
the cocoa-manufacturer and Liberal philanthropist, Seebohm
Rowntree.[17] They were expressed forcefully by the popular
novelist Jack London, as earlier they had been by the Scottish poet,
John Davidson:

> It's a naked child against a hungry wolf;
> It's playing bowls upon a splitting wreck;
> It's walking on a string across a gulf
> With millstones fore-and-aft about your neck;
> And the thing is daily done by many and many a one;
> And we fall, face forward, fighting, on the deck.

A whole school of didactic writers, led by George Bernard Shaw,
H. G. Wells and John Galsworthy, brought discussion of social
problems to West End theatres and into the parlours and boudoirs
of the rich. Scarcely a political party in the full sense of the term, the
L.R.C. and early Labour Party could at times also add its mite as a
pressure group on behalf of society's underdogs, and it made a
special issue out of the problems of the aged poor.[18] Sensitive to
the growing interest in social problems among intellectuals and
publicists, the Conservative ministry in 1905 appointed a Royal
Commission to investigate the workings of the Poor Law. Chairman
of the Commission was a former Conservative minister, Lord
George Hamilton; but also sitting on it were Beatrice Webb, wife of

the leading Fabian intellectual, Sidney Webb and George Lansbury, an I.L.P. Socialist, whose 'bleeding heart', an Irish M.P. once acutely remarked, tended to 'run away with his bloody head'. In 1909 the Commission presented two reports, a minority report embodying the Fabian view, and a majority report which was coloured by the doctrines of the Charity Organization Society: none the less both reports condemned the existing Poor Law. In Public Health, in which governments had been long interested since epidemics affect the rich as well as the poor, special interests were at work on behalf of reform. Under the existing system the ordinary general practitioner in a poor area, often dependent for a livelihood on contract service to a trade union, was grossly underpaid, as Shaw incidentally indicated in *A Doctor's Dilemma*. Self-doctoring among the poor, too, gave rise in informed circles to concern over a growing racket in patent medicines. Some kind of extended public health provision seemed the best remedy for both evils.[19]

The Liberal government of the wealthy and well-liked Sir Henry Campbell-Bannerman, and of his successor as Prime Minister, the brilliant but somewhat passionless barrister, H. H. Asquith, sometimes prodded by Labour members, seldom opposed by Conservatives, proceeded to pass a series of social reforms which were unprecedented in scope and in number: free school meals and a free school medical service; non-contributory old-age pensions; a Children's Act; the establishment of Labour Exchanges and of Trades Boards (to raise standards in the sweated trades); a major Housing and Town Planning Act; and, after the two General Elections of 1910 had confirmed the Liberals in office, a National Insurance Scheme covering both sickness and unemployment, followed by a Shops Act and an eight-hour day for the miners. Yet to talk of this as 'laying the foundations of the Welfare State' is to sacrifice historical perspective and analysis to facile metaphor and terminological anachronism.

The concept of the 'Welfare State' as conceived three decades later implies community responsibility for five types of social need: for security in the sense of a guarantee against interruption of earnings for whatever cause; for health; for education; for housing;

and for full employment (which really is an extension of social security). In 1914 the Poor Law, despite the adverse comments on it of both majority and minority reports of the Royal Commission, remained the basis of British social security. Insurance against ill-health was confined to wage-earners earning less than £150 per annum; insurance against unemployment was confined to the five trades where seasonal unemployment was highest; claims to benefits rested upon compulsory contributions from employee and employer to what was intended to be an actuarially viable scheme; old-age pensions at five shillings a week for a single person over seventy with earnings of less than £26 per annum could not, and were not intended to, cover the full requirements of even the barest subsistence. Basic to the national health provisions of the 1911 scheme was the idea that all wage-earners within the scope of the Act (not dependants) could join the 'panel' of any doctor agreeing to join the scheme (most, after an initial show of resistance, did) and could receive free treatment from him – the doctor being recompensed out of the National Insurance funds. Administration was left in the hands of privately-run 'Approved Societies', the most efficient of which provided extra benefits such as dental treatment; others provided nothing beyond the bare minimum. Hospital treatment for the poor was to be obtained either in the charitable 'voluntary hospitals', or, more probably, in the grim infirmaries administered under the Poor Law. Only the outstandingly enlightened local authorities had begun building hospitals of their own. In 1914 the legal school-leaving age was fourteen, save that children who had secured a certificate of 'proficiency' or of regular attendance were allowed to leave at thirteen. 'Half-timers', girls and boys of twelve or over, could work for not more than thirty-three hours a week, provided they spent the other half of their time at school. Only 200,000 of the country's children got as far as secondary school, less than a quarter of those enjoying 'free places'. [20] The remainder (3 millions or so in the relevant age-group) sat out a miserable elementary education until the expiry of their allotted span, when, ignorant and uncaring, they were released upon the world. There were many Housing Acts on the statute book; all had the same weakness, illustrative of the strength of *laissez-faire* ideas and of resistance to central power; they all *permitted* the local authorities to build houses for the poor, none of them *compelled* the local authorities to do this, nor offered any financial assistance to lessen the burden on local rates. The provision of housing was the task of private enterprise, though the shortage of houses in 1913 was officially estimated as between 100,000 and 120,000; there was no shortage of evidence as to the squalor of the nation's slums. Although the introduction of Labour Exchanges was intended to reduce unemployment by increasing mobility of labour, any notion of interfering with the free working of the economy in order to stimulate employment was not only unheard of, it was unthought of – save in a somewhat unsophisticated, though not necessarily unimaginative, way by Labour M.P.s who advocated schemes of public work.

Social legislation, then, was still in 1914 of the 'filling the gaps' variety, the counterpart of an economic philosophy in which

the Government, apart from the Post Office and a few naval and military undertakings, did not concern itself with the organization of industry or the marketing of its products, did not attempt directly to influence the course of trade, and rarely intervened, except as a borrower, in the money or capital markets. . . . It was assumed that the unrestricted initiative of profit-making entrepreneurs would secure the most effective utilization of national resources, and that the consumer would be protected against exploitation by competition.[21]

In fact the immediate need was not for refinements of detailed social legislation but for a massive attack, by economic means, on the basic problem of Edwardian society: poverty. As the statistician A. L. Bowley phrased it in a social survey conducted in 1913, 'To raise the wages of the worst-paid workers is the most pressing social task with which the country is confronted today.'[22]

3. EDWARDIAN SOCIETY

Class, Edward Thompson has wisely said, is 'an historical phenomenon', 'something which in fact happens (and can be shown to have happened) in human relationships'. For the sociologist it may be

necessary to distinguish between 'class', 'status' and 'power':
these categories serve no purpose for the descriptive historian,
nor is any purpose served by the polite fiction that since the middle
classes achieved power in the nineteenth century (they didn't, of
course) there can be no upper or ruling class. If 'middle' means
anything it means 'middle' – between the upper classes and the
working classes. After all, the Victorians themselves recognized
the class distinction between the plutocracy and the middle
classes.[24] By upper class I mean that class which has power (when
it cares to assert it), power in government or over important
sectors of the economy, or power by virtue of the possession of
exceptional wealth. By working class, essentially, I mean manual
workers. The middle class is everyone else: those who are conscious
of their superiority to the workers, but who know (if they are
honest) that, the cumulative use of the organs and institutions of
representative government apart, their individual opinion on any
particular political decision is not worth a twopenny damn.
Edwardian society was marked by vast inequalities and by rigid
class distinctions, though there were forces at work steadily
modifying the more complicated and more rigid class hierarchy of
the mid-nineteenth century. An upward movement in money
incomes had compressed classes and gradations within classes.
Death duties, introduced on an inconsiderable scale in 1889 and
greatly extended in 1894 (by Sir William Harcourt) and 1909
(by Lloyd George), and income tax, graduated after 1906 so as to
treat higher incomes more harshly, and, after 1909, reinforced by
super-tax, shortened the range of disposable income available to
different classes in society. Technological advance was extending
the area reached by the basic material amenities of modern life; in
1914 this area perhaps just touched the most successful members of
the working classes: it certainly went no farther than that. The rise
of large-scale industry, with, as a corollary, the development of
insurance, banking and accountancy, involved the growth of a
suburban white-collar lower-middle class which added a new
subtlety to the class structure. C. F. G. Masterman, Liberal
politician and perceptive social commentator, drew a vivid picture
of this class in *The Condition of England*, published in 1909:

Its male population is engaged in all its working hours in small, crowded offices, under artificial light, doing immense sums, adding up other men's accounts, writing other men's letters. It is sucked into the City at daybreak, and scattered again as darkness falls. It finds itself towards evening in its own territory in the miles and miles of little red houses in little silent streets, in number defying imagination.[25]

Farther down the social scale, the expansion of trade unionism among the unskilled workers created a greater homogeneity within the working classes, though wage differentials were very jealously guarded, so that the skilled artisan of 1914 earned twice as much as the unskilled labourer.

But the major social fact was still the deep and recognized chasm which lay between the working class on the one side and respectable society on the other, a chasm which is as apparent in the plays of George Bernard Shaw as it is in the Edwardian novels of E. M. Forster. Although impressionistic studies, such as Masterman's, looked at the whole society, the scientific social surveys which are so important a part of the stimulus to change in the early twentieth century were exclusively concerned with the working classes: the middle and upper classes were subject, only the working class was object. Definitions of this separate working class are difficult to find, a clear sign of the absolute certainty as to its existence: to meet a member of it was to recognize him at once, by his appearance, by his smell, indeed, by his size, since widespread malnutrition resulting from working-class poverty meant that he was characterized also by his small stature. In 1900 the minimum height for recruits to the British Army had, with a revealing realism, been fixed at five feet. Introducing his 1913 survey of working-class conditions, Bowley did make the attempt to define his subject-matter:

The definition of the 'working class' cannot be drawn on preconceived lines. Of course, in the great majority of cases included in our Tables the principal occupant of the house was working for weekly or hourly wages, and in the great majority of houses in our samples treated as non-working class the occupier was professional, commercial or living on income from property. The necessity for less obvious discrimination arose in houses rented from 7s. 6d. to 12s. a week. If the principal occupants were clerks, travellers, teachers, shop managers or employers in a small way they were excluded from the working-class tables.[26]

Essentially this is definition by instinct, as is brought out most strongly in Bowley's inclusion of shop assistants in the working class 'if working for butchers or grocers' – but not if working for other patently non–proletarian concerns.[26]

In a total sample of 2,630 householders, 480 (or just over 20 per cent) did not instantly manifest the proletarian qualities Bowley was looking for. As a start, therefore, we might roughly think in terms of a working class which extended to 80 per cent of the total population. Altogether in 1911 there were in Great Britain 15·6 million wage-earners, men, women, boys and girls; this figure, equal to 75 per cent of the total employed population, represents the main core of the working class as understood by contemporaries.[27] To it we should, almost certainly, add the 1·2 million men and women employed as small shopkeepers, hawkers, dressmakers, etc., whose earnings were no greater than those of the average wage-earner. We might also add some of the 1·2 million salaried men and women who, because they earned less than £160 per annum, paid no income tax. According to another Edwardian commentator, Sir Leo Chiozza Money, a Liberal M.P. and enthusiastic social critic, this segment is more properly allotted to the lower-middle classes,[28] though it includes the elementary school teachers, who were almost exclusively working-class in origin and outlook.

Moving into clearly-marked middle-class territory, we have 400,000 salaried men earning over £160 per annum (it was a sign of the subordinate position of Edwardian women that the number of them who came within this category was negligible) comprising a professional group of clergymen, doctors, lawyers, engineers, writers, artists, entertainers, law clerks etc., (but not teachers, who are classified as 'salaried') totalling 330,000, and a majority of the 580,000 farmers. Finally, among the occupied classes there are 620,000 employers, who divide into a majority of small provincial businessmen, who are quite definitely middle-class, and a minority whose eminence as owners of national concerns places them in the topmost class in society. This class was an amalgam of the landed aristocracy (the more important element) and top business and professional men. The aristocracy still enjoyed the leadership of London society, a primacy in politics, whether of the Conservative or Liberal variety, and a feudal dominance over the countryside.[29] It was usual for those without aristocratic connections to work their way up by mean of the ladder of politics, as Asquith and Lloyd George did, and as Gladstone had done before them. In the relaxed atmosphere of the Edwardian era it was possible through wealth alone to scale the peaks of high society – scoffers spoke of the new 'beerage' – but less easy to attain positions of political power. The essential solidarity of the ruling class is brought out by the serious consideration given to the proposal made by Lloyd George in 1910 that the apparently bitter struggle over the rights of the House of Commons as against the obstructionist tactics of the House of Lords might be solved by the formation of a Liberal-Conservative coalition.[30] The surest sign of membership of the ruling class was education at one of the seven top 'public schools'. During the nineteenth century a desire on the part of the wealthier middle classes to give their sons a gentlemanly education had resulted in the founding of many new private fee-paying boarding schools modelled on the pattern of what were perversely called public schools – the schools attended in the eighteenth century by the sons of aristocratic families. Though by 1914 there were many institutions of secondary education which called themselves public schools, none could rival the eminence of those defined in the Public Schools Act of 1868: Eton, Harrow, Winchester, Rugby, Shrewsbury, Charterhouse and Westminster.

Though it is hard to determine *exactly* where the line between middle class and upper class should be drawn, we should probably not be far wrong to think in terms of 5 per cent upper class, 15 per cent middle class, and 80 per cent working class. The economic inequalities are apparent enough. Just under 14,000 people with incomes of over £5,000 per annum took about 8 per cent of the aggregate national income; 47,000 people had incomes of over £2,000; slightly over 1 per cent of the population took 30 per cent of the income. 2½ per cent of the population held two-thirds of the country's wealth. The average wage of the adult male industrial worker was about £75 a year; the average annual income of the salaried class was £360. Looked at broadly, about 5 million of the population (including dependants) had half the country's income to live on; the remaining 39 million had to make do on the other half. Looked at narrowly, there were 75,000 private dwelling houses with an annual value of more than £100 (£150 in London); there were 151,000 motor-cars (the luxury toys of the rich) on the roads.[31]

Two other trench lines of social cleavage are worth noting. The first is the universal prevalence of servant-keeping among the middle classes. The second is less striking at first sight, but of considerable significance none the less. Payment of income tax is not a highly sought-after social privilege, yet it is a measure of a man's respectability as a financial pillar of society and an indication of his positive stake in the community. In 1913 there were less than 1¼ million income-tax-payers, that is less than 7 per cent of the occupied population came within this pale of solid economic worth.

4. TURMOIL

From 1898 to 1914 British business basked in a long golden cycle of rising prices. But booming industry and high profits served to stress the differences between the haves and the have-nots, to accentuate the misery and squalor of the Edwardian slums. Even for the organized working class money wages failed to keep pace with rising prices, and after 1910, for the first time in half a century, real wages were actually in decline. It is not surprising that there were sharp outbreaks of industrial unrest in the years immediately preceding the outbreak of war, especially when, by a paradox of the parliamentary situation, the Labour Party found itself tied more closely than ever to the Liberal government: the two elections of 1910 whittled down the Liberal majority to a state in which it was dependent on the votes of the Irish Nationalists and of

Labour, which meant in effect that if Labour voted independently of the Government it ran the risk of opening the way to Conservative rule. The Labour Party, anyway, had been hampered by the judgement given in the Osborne case of 1909 declaring illegal the political levy upon affiliated trade unions, which, since the L.R.C. conference decision of 1903, had been the basic source of finance for the party. The position was not retrieved till the enactment of salaries for M.P.s in 1911 – itself a stage in the development of formal democracy. British trade unions, too, were influenced by the doctrines of syndicalism, which emphasized the importance of the trade union as the basic unit in the democracy of the future, and of the strike as the basic means of achieving the political supremacy of these units. In 1910 there took place a four-day railway strike in the Newcastle district, a fourteen-week lock-out of boiler-makers in the North-east shipyards, a brief stoppage in Lancashire involving 120,000 cotton workers, and a coal strike in South Wales, attended by violence and resulting in the dispatch of troops to Tonypandy. In 1911 there was a short strike of seamen and firemen, followed by dock strikes at London, Manchester and Liverpool, where troops were called in and two strikers were killed; a London carmen's strike; a number of strikes by engineering labourers; and a general railway strike, in which widespread use of troops was made: again two men were shot dead. In 1912 there were miners' strikes in Scotland and Wales, and a second London docks strike.

It was understandable that working men should break what were believed to be the conventions of British constitutional behaviour when they themselves still camped out on the very fringes of that constitution. More worthy of note was the way in which a section of the Conservative Party, feeling its interests vitally challenged by the Liberal Party in office, began to break the principles of a constitution of which they usually claimed to be resolute defenders. Not simply the party of the *status quo*, the Conservative Party was also the only resort in British politics for out-and-out reactionaries. Normally a will to power within the party had ensured that the party leadership came from the moderate wing. In the late-Edwardian period the party found itself in the nearly disastrous situation of being led from the Right.

Partly this was because of an exaggeration of the implications of the 1906 election result and an acceptance of Lloyd George's denunciations of the landed aristocracy at their face value; partly it was a consequence of the paralysis induced by a split in the party between those who continued to uphold the sanctity of Free Trade and the followers of Joseph Chamberlain, whose demand for protectionist tariffs against foreign competition was becoming ever more shrill. Under the leadership of Balfour the Conservatives launched upon a deliberate policy of using their entrenched majority in the House of Lords to destroy the more contentious Liberal measures – they were careful, however, to leave untouched Bills, such as the one which became the Trades Disputes Act of 1906, which had an obvious appeal to working-class voters. Step by step this led to the culminating folly of rejecting Lloyd George's 1909 Budget, whose Land Value duties were more shadow than substance: but then the extreme Tory peers were already terrified by the sinister shadows of socialism they imagined flickering all around them. The two elections of 1910 maintained a firm anti-Lords majority in the Commons (although the Liberals lost seats, they could rely on the support of Labour and Irish Nationalists) and events moved logically to the introduction of a Parliament Bill defining and restricting the powers of the House of Lords: money Bills were not to be touched at all by the Lords, other Bills could be held up only for two years. In both the House of Lords and the House of Commons, Conservative extremists (nicknamed the Diehards) were roused to fanatical and unedifying opposition. But the possibility that the King might be persuaded to create a sufficient number of Liberal peers to ensure the Bill's passage through the Lords (though Asquith's obvious reluctance to turn to this course brings out very clearly how close in fundamentals the leaders of his party were to those of the Conservatives) induced the wiser Conservatives to see to it that the Bill did in fact become law. Defeated and humiliated, the Conservatives noisily rid themselves of the leadership of Balfour, and, unable to settle between the two strongest contenders, Austen Chamberlain and Walter Long, chose Andrew Bonar Law, a Glasgow iron merchant who had been born in Canada.

Behind the constitutional struggle there lay a deeper question, that of Britain's relationship with Ireland. Since the seventeenth century Ireland had been governed as a colonial dependency, though the leading British settlers had had their own, very corrupt, parliament in Dublin. When Britain became industrialized, Ireland remained predominantly agricultural; and her peasantry were Catholic at a time when Protestant bigotry held that Popery was not merely anti-Christian, but likely to be unpatriotic as well. In the eighteenth century the movement against corruption and metropolitan dominance was led by the lesser members of the Anglo-Irish Protestant settler class. During the war against revolutionary France a stage of open rebellion was reached, and the British Government of William Pitt in 1800 concluded that the British position in Ireland could only be secured by a union of the Dublin Parliament with that at Westminster. The big land-lords, therefore, moved to England, leaving paid agents to squeeze their rents from the Irish peasantry; the radical Protestants left as well, so that the soul of the Irish rebellion now passed entirely to the Catholics. After 1829 the wealthier Catholics were enabled to send their representatives to Westminster, and thereafter there was always in the House of Commons an Irish party dedicated to 'Home Rule', the re-establishment of an Irish parliament in Dublin. Below the plimsoll line of parliamentary action there was, in a land subject to frequent famine and governed by a power which, repeatedly and inexcusably, showed itself unaware of the true dimensions of the economic problem and relied increasingly on repression and coercion, a steady surge of activity, which frequently broke into acts of open terrorism.

Early in the twentieth century economic conditions for the peasantry were at last beginning to improve slightly as Conservative ministries developed the practical expedient of making available long-term loans so that the peasants could set up independent proprietorships. But conditions in the slums of Dublin and Belfast were worse than ever: anti-British politics in Ireland were rein-forced by the growth of an aggressive Labour movement. Liberal governments in 1886 and 1893 had attempted to enact Irish Home Rule: the first attempt had been defeated by a split in the Liberal ranks in the House of Commons, the second by the Conservative dominance in the House of Lords. The imminent possibility of Home Rule brought to the surface the fears of the humbler Protestant settlers of Ulster in the north of Ireland, and these were deliberately stirred into violent life by British Conservative politicians who saw in the Ulster issue a means towards defeating the whole notion of Home Rule. The Liberal victory in 1906, the Liberal dependence after 1910 upon the support of the Irish Nationalists, and, finally, the feckless sacrifice by the Lords of their power permanently to thwart decisions of the Lower House, brought Home Rule back as an immediate likelihood. From 1911 Ulstermen began to arm themselves in preparation for resisting by force the sovereign authority of the British Parliament. The Nationalists, too, began to form their own Volunteer Army. While the Asquith ministry completely failed to meet the challenge to law and order and established constitutional procedure, Bonar Law not merely stepped beyond, but with both feet plunged across, the bounds of constitutional propriety when he gave public encouragement to the potential rebels in Ulster.[32]

Ever since the publication of George Dangerfield's elaborate piece of literary history, *The Strange Death of Liberal England* (1935), it has been customary to link together Labour violence, Tory intransigence, Ulster bellicosity and suffragette militance as intimations of a liberal society in collapse. To the Oxford Historian R. C. K. Ensor, 'the fabric of democracy had come into real danger.'[33] After clucking sadly over the Conservative errancy from the paths of constitutional virtue, he wagged a ponderous finger at the suffragettes and their organization, the Women's Social and Political Union (W.S.P.U.):

The vote was not sought for any practical object, but as a symbol of equality. They were obsessed by an inferiority complex. And similarly upon politics at large their militancy had more effect than their suffragism. The means mattered more than the end, and indeed conflicted with it. For while the vote presupposes the rule of free persuasion, the W.S.P.U. leaders proclaimed, by word and deed, that the way to get results was through violence. Such doctrines are always liable to become popular, when a politically inexperienced class or classes come into the public life of a nation. Often it seems plausible then to win the game by a 'try-on' at breaking the rules. But of course if others follow suit, there is no game.[34]

Whatever freedom some women may have enjoyed in eighteenth-century aristocratic circles, the rise of bourgeois industrial society was accompanied by the clear enunciation and practice of a doctrine of women's essential inferiority, socially, economically and politically. At the same time industrial society provided the conditions in which it was possible for women to organize a concerted attack upon the restrictions by which they were constrained. Amid the burst of Liberal adminstrative and legal reform at mid-century came two Married Women's Property Acts, which helped to give women an economic existence independent of their husbands. In the new passion for education of the last third of the century new educational opportunities were opened to women, though often only after hard struggles against determined resistance. Women poured into teaching (150,000 of them in the last decade of the nineteenth century), nursing, shops and offices; a few managed, against overwhelming male hostility, to struggle into the higher professions. Local government reform in the last quarter of the century gave women the opportunity to exercise political power at the local level. For women of the lower classes unremitting toil had been a fact of life for centuries. After the industrial revolution women found themselves doing the worst and the worst-paid jobs; in 1875, however, the first women's trade union was founded.

For all that was achieved, inequality between the sexes was as clearly defined in Edwardian society as inequality between classes. Instead of stressing as he did in the famous lines from *Iolanthe* (1882) that

> Every boy and every gal
> That's born into the world alive
> Is either a little Liberal
> Or else a little Conservative

W. S. Gilbert might well have stressed the politically and socially more important fact that every Liberal or Conservative was either

a boy or a gal. Education for middle- and upper-class girls was
essentially directed towards a life of gilded uselessness; working-
class women were the industrial drudges of society. In sexual morals
a double standard prevailed: behaviour that might be condoned in
a man could spell ruin for a woman. Waging in the 1880s a
successful campaign against the existence of licensed brothels in
garrison towns, Mrs Josephine Butler was striking a blow for
equality through the raising of the male standard to that of the
female. The 'new woman' of Edwardian times, reputedly, was
aiming at the enjoyment for herself (suitably encouraged by
avant-garde males) of the same standards as men. There is a good
moment in Shaw's *Man and Superman* (1901) when Jack Tanner
makes a noble speech in support of Violet's right to be pregnant
and unmarried: Violet then spurns his support and announces that
in fact she has been secretly married all the time. Richard Aldington
in the Edwardian chapters of *Death of a Hero* (1928), was clearly
irritated by the would-be advanced girl, who at the first hint of
pregnancy collapses into all the old formulas. But the use of
contraceptives was spreading. And in the last Edwardian years,
dresses began daringly to climb a few inches above the ground, and
the very shameless began to smoke in public.[35]

It was a commonplace of nineteenth-century British liberalism
that social and economic evils, if soluble at all, were to be solved by
political means. Those who demanded 'Votes for Women', therefore, were acting in the best liberal tradition; in 1867, indeed, they
had had as their spokesman in Parliament the great apostle of
liberal progress, John Stuart Mill. Purely constitutional means
were adhered to by the 'suffragists' mustered in the National
Union of Women's Suffrage Societies led by Mrs Henry Fawcett.
Given the enormous burden of inequality which persisted, and the
bitter struggles which had almost always preceded any lightening
of it, it was not surprising that in 1903 a body devoted to 'Deeds
not Words' was founded, the Women's Social and Political Union.
'Deeds' to begin with meant heckling and other disruptive tactics
at political meetings. The W.S.P.U. was very firmly directed by the
Pankhurst family, especially by Mrs Emmeline Pankhurst and her
tough (though *petite*) eldest daughter Christabel. As the W.S.P.U.

moved towards more violent courses, a splinter group, the Women's Freedom League, which went no further than the old middle-class tactic of the days of the struggle over the Great Reform Bill of 1832 ('to stop the Duke, go for gold' had been the slogan then) was founded. Within Parliament the feminists had a number of active supporters, and on several occasions there were favourable majorities for extension of the franchise to women, since the women had the support of many rank-and-file Liberals and several enlightened Conservatives. But Asquith himself was hostile, so that there was no formal government support; as Mrs Fawcett neatly put it, from the suffragists' point of view, the Liberals were an army without generals, the Conservatives generals without an army.[36] The peaceful work of the N.U.W.S.S. had achieved much; almost everything, in fact, save the final objective. It is not surprising that after 1910 militant suffragette violence intensified: a small bomb damaged the Coronation Chair in Westminster Abbey, paintings (including the Velasquez 'Rokeby Venus') were slashed, churches, railway stations and, in Scotland, three castles were damaged or destroyed by fire. The parallel with the agitation of 1830–32, when Nottingham castle was burned down, is again striking.

It was not a question of 'the fabric of democracy' being in danger. What was happening after 1910 was that an essentially undemocratic fabric, which had not been sufficiently adapted and modified in preceding years, was now subject to intense strain from forces of democracy, nationalism and economic discontent. Britain was not alone in this respect. Europe too was being swept by a wave of unrest, compounded in part of rapid technological advance leading to urbanization and disruption of older communities, in part of extreme nationalism. Everywhere there was bellicosity, signs of a will to war: poets and philosophers glorified it in advance, futurist painters elevated it to an aesthetic canon. In Britain there was ample evidence, down into the depths of society, of an extreme jingoism. Charles Booth stressed the patriotic content of the music-hall songs of the people of London,[37] the hysteria which accompanied the Boer War yielded a new synonym for patriotic jubilation, 'Mafficking', and the naval race with Germany produced the doggerel cry for more battleships. 'We want eight and we won't wait.' A wealth of popular literature visualized the nature of the coming war.[38] Among the articulate expressions of the will to war two strands of thought can be distinguished, frequently in practice intertwined. To what can be called the realists, war was a fact of life, and, in a world in which Germany was challenging British commercial and naval supremacy at every turn, practically an inevitability. A tract of 1906 advocated military conscription as essential 'if England is to be saved from the grave dangers which now threaten her'.[39] In 1909 Lord Rosebery warned the boys of Wellington College that

men will have to be more universally armed in the future than they are now. . . . There are encroaching opinions which threaten patriotism, menace our love of country, and imply the relaxation, if not the destruction, of all the bonds which hold our empire together.[40]

The strand of idealism sometimes involved little more than the conventional appeal to love of country and service of King and God, but also included the radicalism of young men anxious to cleanse British society and to purify the world. In *The Great Analysis*, published in 1911, William Archer argued that some 'great catastrophe' might be necessary before a new world order could be ushered in.

To say that the First World War developed solely out of the tensions, stresses and will to war of early twentieth-century Europe would be to give it too hard a quality of inevitability. It is possible from the point of view of British participation to define more precise economic and political causes. First, the rivalries and conflicts in the Balkans between two major powers, Austria-Hungary and Russia, and several minor nations: seemingly remote, these produced the murder at Sarajevo and the immediate cause of the war. Second, the growing awareness in Britain that her world economic position was steadily being challenged by Germany. Third, the conviction that any German aggrandizement on the continent of Europe would fatally upset the balance of power. Fourth, the manner in which the pre-war diplomacy had resolved the manifold conflicts and jealousies of nations into the rigid and highly dangerous line-up of two armed camps, Germany and Austria–Hungary on the one side, France, Russia and, at a remove, Britain on the other. For the final decisions and miscalculations which brought war as a fact, there were two circles of responsibility: on the outside the diplomatists and statesmen; at the centre the military staffs, with their conviction that in modern war speedy action and perfect interlocking of alliances were essential. Once the statesmen made their first fumbling moves to war, the military ensured that there could be no turning back.

In the month which followed the assassination of the Austrian Archduke Franz Ferdinand by Serb nationalists, British newspaper headlines continued to be monopolized by the impending civil war in Ireland, though by the end of July it was widely recognized that Britain might be involved in a European war. The Austro-Hungarian government, subjected in the past to considerable provocation from Serbia and aware of her terrible weakness in having an enclave of Serbs within her borders, had clearly welcomed the assassination as an opportunity to crush a difficult neighbour; after making sure of German support, it issued an impossible ultimatum to Serbia, followed on 28 July by a declaration of war. Conscious of the need to preserve Russia's dignity as the Slav super-power, the Czarist government began mobilization on 30 July; German and then French mobilization followed on the 31st. That very morning *The Times*, leading proponent of an unimpassioned, realistic assessment of world politics, argued in favour of an immediate British declaration of war on Germany in order to forestall a German conquest of northern France. On 1 August Germany declared war on Russia; late the following day she sent a twelve-hour ultimatum to Belgium demanding the free passage of German troops; on the 3rd (August Bank Holiday Monday in Britain) she declared war on France and on the 4th German troops crossed into Belgium.

At the end of the previous weeks there was a run on the British banks as ordinary folk, hoping for the best, withdrew their holiday savings, and wealthy folk, fearing the worst, decided to seek greater safety for their deposits. Bank Rate, 4 per cent on Thursday 30 July, went to 8 per cent on Friday and 10 per cent on Saturday, when, also, the Government began a series of emergency proclamations covering such things as the use of wireless telegraphy and aviation. The Bank Holiday was extended to Thursday 6 August and Postal Orders made temporary legal tender. Stock-piling of food produced a sharp rise in prices on Bank Holiday Monday. While railway stations and coastal resorts were as busy as ever, crowds also gathered in central London, where shouts of 'Down with Germany' were heard.[41] In the House of Commons the Foreign Secretary, Sir Edward Grey, described Britain's ties of friendship and moral obligation to France and the likelihood of a German violation of Belgian neutrality, guaranteed by a treaty of 1839 to which Britain was a signatory. When the news of the German invasion came through on Tuesday, Asquith announced that an ultimatum expiring at 11 p.m. (midnight in Berlin) had been served on the Germans calling upon them to withdraw from Belgian territory. As the time-limit approached, people gathered in Trafalgar Square and Whitehall, singing and flag-waving and displaying 'marked tendencies towards Mafficking'. When the British declaration of war upon Germany was issued at the Foreign Office it was greeted with 'round after round of cheers'.[42]

But it is important to stress that the patriots did not have things all their own way. Although the militaristic trends of Edwardian Britain are clearly discernible, they existed side by side with an important sector of articulate opinion which was strongly anti-militarist. This sector included the bulk of the Labour Party and a major part of the Liberals, given a lead by two daily papers, the *Daily News*, edited by A. G. Gardiner, and the *Manchester Guardian*, edited by C. P. Scott, and a weekly, the *Nation*, edited by H. W. Massingham. War, said the *Daily News*, in reply to Sir Edward Grey's Bank Holiday speech, would quite probably lead to French absorption of Belgium and Russian dominance in the East.[43] A Labour demonstration against war on Sunday 2 August was addressed by Keir Hardie (founder of the I.L.P.), H. M. Hyndman (founder of the S.D.F.), George Lansbury (of the 'bleeding heart') and Arthur Henderson (secretary of the Labour Party). On 4 August the jingoes in Trafalgar Square had competition from an organized anti-war demonstration, and that evening Mrs Fawcett of the N.U.W.S.S. addressed a women's protest against war. Over the weekend distinguished leaders of opinion, including Gilbert Murray, the classical scholar, Basil Williams, the Oxford historian, two bishops, and Ramsay MacDonald, chairman of the Parliamentary Labour Party, called for Britain to preserve her neutrality.[44]

But impressive as was this opposition to war, still more impressive was the speed with which it dissolved, as the pacifists underwent thirteenth-hour conversions. After a brief phase of grudging acceptance of war as an immediate reality, the *Daily News* swung into enthusiastic support for it. So did the Labour Party and the trade unions, forcing Ramsay MacDonald, who maintained his anti-war stand, to resign the chairmanship of the Parliamentary Party. Edwardian nonconformists, pacifist during the Boer War, saw support for this one as a religious duty: 'The path of duty', said the Reverend John Clifford,

shone out in clearest light, and wherever it might lead us we had to go. It was the pillar of cloud by day and the pillar of fire by night. We must follow.[45]

Mrs Fawcett called upon the N.U.W.S.S. to put its organization at the disposal of the nation in its hour of need.[46] An important if disparate collection of socialists, Liberals, and philosophical pacifists did maintain an unflinching commitment against the war, but in general terms British society, by the beginning of the second week of August 1914, presented a picture of unity and enthusiasm for the war: 'England,' F. S. Oliver, businessman, social-imperialist and political *éminence grise*, reported cheerfully, if ungrammatically, to his brother in Canada, 'is already a different place than it has been for years past.'[47]

NOTES TO CHAPTER TWO

1. For this paragraph see J. B. Mitchell (ed.), *Great Britain: Geographical Essays*, 1962, pp. 3–16.
2. *Ibid.*, pp. 17–31.
3. *Lord Hervey's Memoirs* (ed. R. Sedgwick) 1963 edn, p. 100.
4. W. Dickinson, G. Donaldson and I. Milne, *Source Book of Scottish History*, vol. 1, 1955, p. 98.
5. Quoted by I. Jennings, *Cabinet Government*, 1959 edn, p. 16.
6. W. Bagehot, *The English Constitution*, 1868 and 1872.
7. See e.g. R. H. S. Crossman's introduction to the 1965 issue of Bagehot's *English Constitution*, and J. P. Mackintosh, *The British Cabinet*, 1960.
8. M. Ostrogorski, *Political Parties*, 1902.
9. This section leans heavily on a fascinating article by Neal Blewett, 'The Franchise in the United Kingdom 1885–1918', in *Past and Present*, December 1965. See the sources cited there.
10. See especially J. M. Keynes, *The End of Laissez-Faire*, 1920.
11. A. V. Dicey, *Lectures on the Relation between Law and Public Opinion in England in the Nineteenth Century*, 1905.
12. For full details see F. Bealey and H. Pelling, *Labour and Politics 1900–1906*, 1959, pp. 265 ff.
13. On all this see Bealey and Pelling, pp. 125 ff.
14. A. Marwick, 'The Labour Party and the Welfare State in Britain 1900–1948', *American Historical Review*, December 1967.
15. See M. Cole, *The Story of Fabian Socialism*, 1961, pp. 113–14.
16. C. Booth, *Life and Labour of the People in London*, series 1, vol. 1, 1901, p. 62.
17. B. S. Rowntree, *Poverty: A Study in Town Life*, 1901.
18. A. Marwick, *American Historical Review, loc. cit.*
19. R. Titmuss in M. Ginsberg (ed.), *Law and Opinion in the Twentieth Century*, 1959, p. 15.
20. Board of Education, *The Education of the Adolescent*, 1927, pp. 3 ff.
21. R. H. Tawney, 'The Abolition of Economic Controls, 1918–1921', *Economic History Review*, 1943, p. 1.
22. A. L. Bowley and A. R. Burnett-Hurst, *Livelihood and Poverty*, 1915, p. 5.
23. E. P. Thompson, *The Making of the English Working Class*, 1963, p. 10.
24. T. Escott, *England, Her People, Polity and Pursuits*, 1879, pp. 314–15.
25. C. F. G. Masterman, *The Condition of England*, 1909, pp. 57–58.
26. Bowley and Burnett-Hurst, p. 176.
27. The figures on which this section is based, drawn from Board of Trade and Census statistics, are presented in convenient form by A. L. Bowley, *The Division of the Product of Industry*, 1919, pp. 8–13.
28. L. C. Money, *Riches and Poverty*, 1905, 1913 edn, p. 49.
29. F. M. L. Thompson, *English Landed Society in the Nineteenth Century*, 1963, pp. 292–326.
30. D. Lloyd George, *War Memoirs*, 1933, pp. 35–41. J. A. Spender and C. Asquith, *Life of Asquith*, vol. 1, 1932, p. 287.
31. Figures from A. L. Bowley, *The Division of the Product of Industry*, 1919, and *Studies in the National Income*, 1942.

32. As when he declared, 'I can imagine no length of resistance to which Ulster will go, which I shall not be ready to support.' For details see R. Blake, *The Unknown Prime Minister : the Life and Times of Andrew Bonar Law*, 1955, p. 130.
33. R. C. K. Ensor, *England 1870–1914*, 1936, p. 398.
34. *Ibid.*
35. The best secondary account is I. Clephane, *Towards Sex Freedom*, 1936. See also National Council of Public Morals, *The Declining Birth Rate*, 1916, and *The Ethics of Birth Control*, 1925.
36. M. G. Fawcett, *The Women's Victory and After*, 1920. The best secondary account is R. Fulford, *Votes for Women*, 1957.
37. Booth, Final Volume, 1901, p. 54.
38. I. F. Clarke, *Voices Prophesying War 1763–1984*, 1966, pp. 105–161.
39. T. C. Horsfall, *National Service and the Welfare of the Community*, 1906, p. 71.
40. Quoted in D. Newsome, *Godliness and Good Learning*, 1961, p. 202.
41. *Annual Register 1914*, p. 184. *Labour Gazette* 1914, p. 323. *The Times*, 4 August 1914.
42. *Daily News*, 5 August 1914. *Daily Mail*, 5 August 1914.
43. *Daily News*, 4 August 1914.
44. *Ibid.*, 3, 4, 5 August 1914. *The Times*, 5 August 1914.
45. J. Clifford, *Our Fight for Belgium and What it Means*, 1917, p. 17.
46. *Common Cause*, 7 August 1914.
47. S. Gwynn (ed.), *The Anvil of War : Letters from F. S. Oliver to his Brother*, 1936, p. 30 (12 August 1914).

CHAPTER THREE

The Great War

I. OUTLINE

Contemporaries spoke of 'the Great War'; that the term was universally adopted from the moment that war broke out is in itself good evidence of the existence deep within British society of an expectation and acceptance of war as a coming event.[1] The phrase 'the First World War' was used by Colonel Repington when he published his war diaries in 1920.[2] For those who lived through it the war had all the horror or exhilaration of a mighty cataclysm: even those born long after 1918 still go on shedding tears for the pity of it. Before turning to a detailed examination of the four modes through which the war affected British society, I propose to glance quickly at the military war and at the more obvious emotional responses to which it gave rise.

War was nothing new in human experience, though Britain had not been involved in a major one since the time of Napoleon. Nor, expressed as a ratio of deaths to size of armies, was the death rate high in this war relative to that of the Napoleonic wars.[3] The difference was one of scale, both in terms of the destructive weapon-power yielded by advancing technology, and of the numbers involved: by 1918 six million ordinary citizens had directly confronted the horrors of war, and their sufferings, even if society never really grasped the true nature of life in the trenches, could not finally be pushed out of sight as could those of a neglected professional army recruited from the slums, especially when among the sufferers there were representatives of the sheltered, but articulate, middle classes. The enthusiasts of 1914 had expected

the war of tradition. Cavalry charged at the foe. When death came, it was a heroic death brought about by heroes on the other side.[4]

Instead there came atrocities, 'frightfulness' and wholesale slaughter which went on and on and on. Over the four and a quarter years of war, there was, each day, an average of fifteen hundred

British casualties. Just to contemplate a newspaper of the time with its column after implacable column of small black print listing the names of dead and wounded, is to come back into contact with a living nightmare.

Yet although society at home was aware of the statistics of slaughter, those statistics were softened by mushy war stories and the paper victories of government propagandists, so that it remained oblivious to the real tortures, physical and mental, of life in the front line. At home there appeared to be affluence; there certainly was profiteering. One young serving man, F. H. Keeling, pointed the bitter contrast:

Broadly speaking, the English either volunteer for this hell or else sit down and grow fat on big money at home. The contrast between the two fates is too great.[5]

Bitterness, too, was aroused over the contrast between the conditions of the fighting men and those of their generals, far behind the lines. C. E. Montague set it all down in his post-war classic, *Disenchantment*. He wrote of the evolution of a type of warfare which for the troops in the line imposed

a much diminished chance of survival, only the barest off-chance if they stayed there year after year. While they lived it was inflicting upon them in trenches a life squalid beyond precedent. And that same evolution had pressed back the chief seats of command into places where life was said to contrast itself in wonderful ways with that life of mud and stench and underground gloom.[6]

There was a highly-charged controversy, then and afterwards, over the competence of the British High Command. In *The General*, written towards the end of the war, Siegfried Sassoon, a serving officer on the Western Front, expressed a thought which had much support at the time, and gathered a great deal more subsequently:

'Good-morning; good-morning!' the General said
When we met him last week on the way to the line.
Now the soldiers he smiled at are most of 'em dead,
And we're cursing his staff for incompetent swine.
'He's a cheery old card,' grunted Harry to Jack

As they slogged up to Arras with rifle and pack.
But he did for them both by his plan of attack.

Some of the best recent historical studies of the First World War
have helped to rehabilitate the British military leaders[8] (although
few good words have been offered on behalf of the first British
Commander-in-Chief, Sir John French). What the critics of the
generals too often missed was the unchangeable fact that, like it or
not, Britain's military effort was inextricably meshed with that of
France, so that the British military leaders were never completely
free agents; the Germans *were* in France.[9] None the less even now
all of the charges of incompetence and flexibility have not been fully
rebutted.[10]

The war was fought in the Low Countries and France, where the
Allies successfully stemmed the first German invasion designed to
knock France out in one speedy blow; but not till the very end
were they able to push the Germans back into their own territory,
for instead of the war of glorious charges that had been expected,
technological invention had reached a stage when the defence,
possessed of magazine rifles and the belt-fed machine-gun, had an
overwhelming advantage. It was the tunnel war of the Western Front
that haunted the souls of men for decades thereafter. The war was
fought too along the frontiers of Germany, Austria and Russia.
The British expected much of the Russian 'steam-roller', but in fact
the Russians' one great victory, against the Austrians in Galicia in
the summer of 1916, was merely a prelude to her collapse. Early
attempts were made to break the deadlock on the Western Front,
deploy British naval supremacy and exploit the alleged weaknesses
of the Turks, who entered the war on the German side in October,
by opening a new front in the Eastern Mediterranean. In mid-
February the Turkish forts which blocked the Dardanelles were
bombarded: troop landings at Gallipoli did not follow until late
April. Whether or not this enterprise should have been embarked
upon is an open question; there is no doubt that it was carried
through in a disastrously desultory and incompetent fashion.
British, Australian and New Zealand troops found themselves
pinioned in the same static situation as obtained on the Western

Front, with the added torment of dysentery in summer and frost-bite in winter. In December 1915 and January 1916 they were evacuated.[11] The other effort in this part of the world, the Anglo-French landings at Salonika in Greece, where 600,000 Allied troops were bottled up for most of the war, was no more successful. Italy entered the war on the Allied side in May 1915: thus another immobile front was opened on the mountainous frontiers between Italy and Austria. Minor campaigns, in which T. E. Lawrence achieved a legendary fame rivalled in this war only by the airmen, were waged against Turkey in Palestine and Mesopotamia. There was only one major naval engagement, the Battle of Jutland in May 1916. Tactically this battle was inconclusive; strategically it resulted in the German High Seas fleet keeping out of action for the rest of the war; popularly it lowered faith in the traditional supremacy of the British Navy. The major achievement of the Navy was an economic blockade of the Central Powers: this the Germans attempted to break by submarine warfare, commenced in February 1915, interrupted for a time in an effort to appease American and neutral opinion, and resumed again in October 1916. German colonial territories in Africa were successfully attacked by the South African generals, Botha and Smuts, and the Japanese seized the opportunity to capture the German possession of Shantung in China.

The first British Expeditionary Force, which joined up with the French left wing, numbered less than 100,000 men, and the first phase of the war which can, roughly speaking, be taken as lasting till the battle of Neuve Chapelle (10–13 March 1915) was fought, as Britain's wars in the past had been fought, by the professional army. From the start Lord Kitchener, the Government's last-minute secondment to the office of War Secretary, was aware that military efforts on an altogether different scale were called for. On 7 August the first recruiting appeal appeared:

YOUR KING AND COUNTRY NEED YOU
A CALL TO ARMS

An addition of 100,000 men to His Majesty's Regular Army is im-mediately necessary in the present grave National Emergency. Lord

Kitchener is confident that this appeal will be at once responded to by all who have the safety of our Empire at heart.

TERMS OF SERVICE

General service for a period of three years, or until the war is concluded. Age of enlistment, between 19 and 30.

Recruiting offices were at once thronged by thousands of young men, eager to dedicate themselves to a glorious cause. Miners from South Wales were as much in evidence as university and public school men;[12] there were young radicals, like F. H. Keeling, as well as the products of conventional Evangelical homes. Keeling wrote:

I may possibly live to think differently; but at the present moment, assuming that this war had to come, I feel nothing but gratitude to the gods for sending it in my time.[13]

The ineptitude of the authorities prevented the first 100,000 from being obtained until 25 August. Three days later a call for a further 100,000 was issued and the age-limit raised to thirty-five. By mid-September there were half a million new recruits and the recruitment of a further half million was under way. In November an increase in the Army of another million was authorized and by the end of the following year a third and then a fourth million.

Neuve Chapelle was fought to the same simple two-point plan as all the other attempted offensives on the Western Front: first, a heavy bombardment was unleashed to smother the enemy's artillery, cut his barbed wire and kill the inmates of his front trenches; second, the guns lifted to targets farther in the rear, and the infantry leapt out of their own trenches and into the fire of his machine-guns, gaining, if successful, a few yards of territory at the expense of thousands of lives.[14] Neuve Chapelle, the second Battle of Ypres (22 April to 25 May, and known as 'Wipers' to the British soldier) and Festubert (9–25 May) were the last battles of the old army. Slowly the new men of Kitchener's armies began to move in, glad to be quit of their overcrowded camps where training facilities were often totally inadequate, unaware of the squalid horror ahead of them. The effects of trench life on the more articulate can be traced in the many collections of soldiers' letters. 'I hope this bloody war is going to end soon – of course there is no chance of that, but the sooner the better,' wrote Keeling in August 1915.[15] 'Any faith in religion I ever had is most frightfully shaken by things I've seen,' wrote another in March 1916.[16] Over all 1915 was an unhappy year for British arms and very heavy losses were suffered at the Battle of Loos, fought in the last part of the year. The British troops in France – still less than a million of them in January 1916 – began the new year under a new Commander-in-Chief, Sir Douglas Haig, a lowland Scot possessed of supreme confidence and an unquenchable belief in the Almighty's willingness to deal him a winning hand. Haig, after initial reservations, plunged enthusiastically into preparations for the great Anglo-French 'push' to take place on the Somme in mid-summer. The volunteer army was now at its peak; already conscription was in force and a new breed of soldiers were being trained. For the first time its was the major role, for the French had been gravely weakened by the long agony of Verdun. The Somme brought the second phase of the military war to an end, shattering the volunteer armies as the early battles of 1915 had shattered the professional army. On the first day of July 1916, the first day of the Battle of the Somme, nearly 20,000 British soldiers were killed. These were mainly men of simple old-world faith in God, King and Country. Before going over the top a young subaltern, J. S. Engall, described in a letter to his parents the impressive Communion service which he and dozens of other had attended the previous day:

I placed my soul and body in God's keeping, and I am going into battle with His name on my lips, full of confidence and trusting implicitly in Him. I have a strong feeling that I shall come through safely; nevertheless should it be God's holy will to call me away, I am quite prepared to go: and ... I could not wish for a finer death; and you, dear Mother and Dad, will know that I died doing my duty to my God, my Country, and my King, I ask that you should look upon it as an honour that you have given a son for the sake of King and Country.[18]

Engall did not come through safely. For those who did survive it was difficult not to doubt King, Country and God. While the

Somme battles raged on into the autumn the first conscripts began
to arrive in France, and it was upon them, a year later, that the
main burden of the most disastrous of all the disastrous episodes of
the war fell. The Somme 'push' had failed; the early months of 1917
went badly for the Allies; in the summer, therefore, Haig again
sought a break-through in the third Ypres campaign, the campaign
indelibly etched on the British consciousness as Passchendaele. Passchendaele was fought over low-lying ground whose normal drain-
age system had been destroyed by constant shelling, so that it had
become a vast swamp in which death by drowning was added to the
hazards of high explosives. The gains were negligible, the casualties,
between June and November 1917, a quarter of a million. In his
history of the war, which did so much to intensify the post-war
attack on the generals, Captain Liddell Hart concluded his account
of the campaign with a story which exactly captured the aftertaste
of Passchendaele. An officer from G.H.Q. pays his first visit to
the front after the battle has been going on four months: growing
increasingly uneasy as the car approached the swamplike edges of the
battle area, he eventually burst into tears, crying, 'Good God, did
we really send men to fight in that?' To which his companion
replied that the ground was far worse ahead.[18] Whatever the rights
and wrongs of Haig's initial intentions in launching the campaign,
he cannot be acquitted of criminal stubbornness in continuing with
it long after it was clear that it was achieving nothing. For the
sensitive there was little left after 1917 but anger and disillusionment. In November 1917 Paul Nash, a young artist in uniform,
wrote to his wife:

I am no longer an artist interested and curious, I am a messenger who
will bring back word from the men who are fighting to those who want
the war to go on for ever. Feeble, inarticulate will be my message, but it
will have a bitter truth, and may it burn their lousy souls.[19]

Already Siegfried Sassoon and Wilfred Owen were writing the
poetry of disenchantment. However, of the majority it would be
dangerous to say more than that they were wearied and a little
sceptical. As Charles Carrington put it, 'The soldiers were not

"disenchanted", for war had never offered them an enchanting prospect; they were just "fed up".'[20]

At the very end of the year the British did succeed in making a break-through at Cambrai, which brought (though without any official encouragement from the Government)[21] the ringing of bells from church steeples at home. The rejoicing was premature, and in March the Germans completely reversed the picture by achieving a forty-mile penetration into the Allied lines; there were further threatening offensives in April and May. But the Germans, too, were exhausted, and the second Battle of the Marne of July 1918 suggested that the initiative was now definitely back in the hands of the Allies. In September the Germans were pushed on to the defensive and the tunnel war at last broke out into a war of movement. By the end of September the German Commander-in-Chief, Ludendorff, had decided that an armistice must be sought. The collapse of Germany's allies hastened the end, and at 5 a.m. on 11 November the German armistice delegation accepted terms which involved a German withdrawal behind the Rhine and the surrender of large quantities of weapons and war materials: the armistice came into force at 11 a.m.

For that society of men in the front line there was only numbed relief, no jubilation. Richard Aldington imaginatively recreated the scene as noted by a junior officer, Ellerton.

The men were singing one of the worst of their drawling songs:

> 'It's a long, loong, traiil a-winding,
> Into the laand of my dreeams,
> Where the niightingaaales are siinging . . .'

Suddenly, round a bend in the road, appeared a Staff Officer on a chestnut . . . Ellerton hastily called the men to attention, but before they could unsling their rifles for the salute the Staff Officer waved his hand and shouted, 'Armistice was signed at six this morning, and comes into force at eleven. The war's over.' A languid cheer from the platoon, 'Oo-ray', and then as the Staff man rode on, they at once continued:

> 'It's a long, loong, traiil a-winding . . [22]

At home in Britain it was different. All the hysteria and jubilation of August 1914 burst out again[23] and continued for several days, to the extent of interfering with the circulation of Cabinet Papers. An unamused Cabinet put the blame on Australian troops, and Walter Long expressed the opinion, a rather graceless one considering the part the Australians had played in the war, especially at Gallipoli, that it was important to get them out of London as soon as possible.[24]

2. PROFIT AND LOSS: DESTRUCTION AND DISRUPTION

The destruction of British capital assets caused by the war was not of great economic significance. The destruction of human life probably was not either, though the effects in human and social terms were practically immeasurable. 745,000 of the country's younger men, about 9 per cent of all men under 45 were killed; 1·6 million wounded, many of them very seriously. In 1911 there were 155 males aged between 20 and 40 per thousand of the population in England and Wales; in 1921 there were only 141 per thousand. The balance of females over the age of 14 rose from 595 per thousand in 1911 to 638 per thousand in 1921, and the proportion of widows per thousand of the population rose from 38 to 43·25. Even if there is no exact measure of the personal agony concealed in these statistics, society in the Twenties and Thirties exhibited all the signs of having suffered a deep mental wound, to which the agony and the bloodshed, as well as the more generalized revulsion at the destruction of an older civilization and its ways, contributed.

The economic cost of the war had to be met somehow. In the first stages the British war effort was financed in the traditional way: borrowing – a procedure which, since the rich first lend their money, then get it back with interest, serves to increase inequality. Whatever other claims to fame Lloyd George may have, he was certainly no great war financier. It was not till Reginald McKenna's supplementary budget of September 1915, when an excess profits duty was introduced, supertax on incomes above £8,000 per annum was increased, and the income-tax was raised by 40 per cent, that the possibilities of direct taxation began to be exploited. While other measures, such as the 50 per cent increase in the tea and tobacco duties and the abolition of the halfpenny postage stamp and the sixpenny telegram, fell most heavily on the poorer sections of society, the general effect was towards further equalization of disposable income. In this sense the middle classes were most strongly affected: at the same time the extension of income-tax to working men earning more than £2 10s. a week, while adding to their immediate grievances, was a subtle blow at one of the rigid lines of demarcation between the Edwardian classes and masses. A further development in this fiscal democracy was the introduction early in 1916 of the War Savings Certificate, aimed specifically at the humbler members of the community: holdings were limited to a total of five hundred but, in an open gesture towards the democratic ideal, the original idea of imposing a means test on purchasers was abandoned because the War Savings Committee decided that this would involve the introduction of undesirable class-distinctions.[26] For the upper classes the incidence of death-duties, the level of which was steeply increased in 1919, was rendered more severe by the high casualty rate among young infantry officers of which this class provided a high proportion.

War taxation affected class relationships within society. Society as a whole was affected by the dislocation in Britain's world trading position brought about by the war. Cut off from Britain during the war, underdeveloped countries, hitherto fine markets for British products, were forced to build up their own industrial potential or find other sources of supply: at the end of the war they had ceased to be markets. Long-term technological trends, such as the development of oil-firing for the world's shipping, would in any event have brought difficult trading circumstances to Britain's old basic industries, but the war helped to telescope the process with a disastrous abruptness. To make matters worse the needs of war forced the country to expand and exploit to the uttermost the very trades, mining and the heavy metal industries, which in peace would be at a discount. Over and above this the war fouled up the delicate international financial mechanism which in Victorian and Edwardian days had functioned with relative smoothness. Various wartime expedients kept things going till peace came, when there was a rush to return to the methods of the pre-war world; unhappily that world had gone for good. The scene was set for economic depression and unemployment on a scale surpassing that of the first disruptions of the Industrial Revolution. On the long view the social and economic transformations of the First World War worked out to the advantage of the working classes, but mass unemployment took most of the savour out of the victory.

There is a similar paradox buried in another of the social 'losses' chalked up by the war, the halting of all progress in housing, health and education. Government plans for large increases in its education grants were announced in the Speeches from the Throne of 10 March 1913 and 10 February 1914, but, as the Board of Education subsequently reported, they were 'arrested by the outbreak of war'.[27] Within a year the Board was being subjected to heavy pressure from local authorities who argued that the national emergency required a suspension of the school attendance by-laws. County magistrates were keen that children should be released for 'national work', which frequently turned out to mean work on the farms of the county magistrates. In a letter to the Board of Education the secretary of one County Education Committee sadly explained the importance of paying heed to 'influential persons, including magistrates, chairmen of district councils, and so on' and the danger of alienating the 'sympathies of magistrates and employers of labour'.[28] There were other and more humane reasons for allowing children to forsake their studies. Families whose one wage-earner was on active service overseas were often placed in grave financial circumstances and pleas for the release of potential child wage-earners were hard to resist. The total wastage was enormous, as H. A. L. Fisher, President of the Board of Education, admitted in the House of Commons in August 1917. During the first three years of war 600,000 children to the certain knowledge of the Board had been put 'prematurely' to work; there were hundreds of others of whom the Board had no official knowledge.[29] At the same time the school medical services were severely curtailed, with a 28 per cent cut after 1916 in the number of children medically examined.[30] The situation described by the 1917 Departmental Committee on Juvenile Education was by no means a happy one:

Many children have been withdrawn at an even earlier age than usual from day schools, and the attendances at those evening schools which have not been closed show a lamentable shrinkage. . . . Excessive hours of strenuous labour have overtaxed the powers of young people; while many have taken advantage of the extraordinary demand for juvenile labour to change even more rapidly than usual from one blind alley employment to another.[31]

Children were withdrawn from school. So were teachers, many of them never to return. Many of the younger men who might have filled their places were also lost in action or had their studies interrupted by war.

Housing conditions were bad enough before the war. With the cessation of ordinary house-building and the congregation of hordes of people in the new munitions centres, they became infinitely worse. Housing at one such centre, Barrow, was officially described as 'a crying scandal'.[32] Reports multiplied of night-shift workers sleeping by day in beds occupied at night by day-shift workers – a common state of affairs certainly in the slum quarters of Edwardian cities, but less extensive and less commented on then. Short of 120,000 houses in 1913, the country needed 600,000 in 1918. And here we come to the paradox – a paradox which has its counterpart in natural catastrophe (one thinks of the rapid and magnificent rebuilding of San Francisco after the 1906 earthquake). So great was the problem of housing, so great also the problem of the educational and social neglect of young children, that politicians were forced to contemplate action on a scale beyond anything they would have tolerated in Edwardian times. The effect of the war, said the Committee on Juvenile Education, was to 'aggravate conditions that could hardly be made graver, and to emphasize a problem that needed no emphasis'.[33] Laying his Education Bill before the House of Commons in August 1917, Fisher said, among other things,

It is framed to repair the intellectual wastage which has been caused by the war; and should it pass into a law before peace is struck it will put a prompt end to an evil which has grown to alarming proportions during the past three years – I allude to the industrial pressure upon the child life of this country – and it will greatly facilitate the solution of many problems of juvenile employment, which will certainly be affected by the transition of the country from a basis of war to a basis of peace.[34]

To meet the shortage of teachers Fisher proposed a sharp rise in teachers' salaries. To meet the vast housing problem, too great for private enterprise to solve, State initiative would be essential: so concluded the Salisbury Committee on Housing in England and Wales, and the Royal Commission on Housing in Scotland, both of which presented their findings during the last eighteen months of the war.[35]

Apart from the temporary spasm of excitement which passed through society on the August days of 1914, the disruptive action of war was slow to take effect on the ordinary patterns of daily life. Led by W. H. Smith and Son, owners of the country's biggest chain of booksellers and newsagents, and by Harrods, the top department store of Edwardian England, the businessmen and shopkeepers adopted the phrase 'Business as Usual'.[36] The slogan was not altogether without point when war was widely expected to bring considerable immediate economic dislocation and unemployment. At the outbreak of war a special Cabinet Committee on the Prevention and Relief of Distress was established, followed speedily by the launching of the Prince of Wales's National Relief Fund. Within days 40 per cent of the women in the luxury trades were thrown out of work or on to short time.[37] But 'Business as Usual' became the cloak for an unwillingness to come to grips with the real needs of war and for an insistence on maintaining the rights of private profit against the interests of the community in its time of danger. By the middle of February 1915 the Government had abandoned its own endorsement of the slogan: a recruiting notice which addressed 'Five Questions to Patriotic Customers' demanded sharply, 'Have you realized that we cannot have "Business as Usual" whilst the war continues?'[38]

'No cricket, no boat race, no racing,' R. D. Blumenfeld, editor of the *Daily Express*, sadly confided to his diary after twelve months of war.[39] Eighteen months later a working man in Lancashire, harassed by the Government's new licensing regulations, was heard to murmur grimly as news filtered in from Russia, 'Russia was never troubled by revolution till she went teetotal.'[40] By the end of the war, Evelyn Wrench noted, the country had become so 'accustomed to restrictions of every sort ... that we found it difficult to jump back in our minds to the pre-war world in which we lived in July 1914.'[41] Restrictions and austerity in all walks of life were the most obvious product of the war's disruptive influence on domestic life. Austerity, in fact, did not become severe in Britain until 1917, when shortages of sugar, potatoes, margarine and coal were serious enough to bring a new phenomenon upon the civic scene, the queue.[42] Government attempts at voluntary rationing, local authority and co-operative society rationing schemes, and compulsory rationing for London led eventually in April and May 1918 to a nation-wide rationing system. At its lowest point, the weekly meat ration was fixed at three-quarters of a pound. All through the war recipes for such revolutionary delicacies as haricot-bean fritters, savoury oatmeal pudding and barley rissoles were much publicized; but it seems clear that they were aimed at middle- and upper-class households in which pre-war protein consumption had been high. Bread, after December 1916, was 'Government Bread'; in its later forms it contained various combinations of extraneous matter, such as potato flour or bean flour, some of which went 'ropey' in warm weather. Upon this bread the civilian, from late 1917 onwards, spread margarine manufactured under the direction of the Ministry of Food, and with it he drank the anonymous mixture, Government Control Tea. Yet there was certainly at no time widespread privation in Britain, and the effect of shortages and rationing was rather to level the standards of nutrition among social classes than to deprive the poorest: with government control of the purchase and distribution of meat, for instance, prime joints would frequently find their way to East End shops, while scraggy cuts, equally, might make a first appearance on the shelves of high-class West End butchers.[43]

Austerity, such as it was, was made worse by German bombing raids. First inkling that war was no longer just something that other people fought had come as early as 10 December 1914 when a German cruiser force shelled the Hartlepools, Whitby and Scarborough on the East Coast killing 137 and injuring 592 civilians.[44] Two aeroplane attacks at Christmas 1914 caused no damage: thereafter the Germans turned to the use of airships, and throughout the spring and summer of 1915 raids took place at an average of about one a fortnight. Unco-ordinated and not always very effective black-out schemes followed. After a slight lull in 1916 there came, on 13 June 1917, the worst raid of the whole war, when 162 people were killed and 432 injured: the autumn that followed was so full of menace that Londoners took to the practice of sheltering in the Tubes, while some of those who could afford it moved to safer residences at Bath or Bournemouth. The last raid of the war took place over Kent on 17 June 1918, when there were no casualties. Altogether between January 1915 and April 1918 there were 51 Zeppelin raids, causing 1,913 casualties, and between December 1914 and June 1918 there were 57 aeroplane raids, causing 2,907 casualties. Total civilian casualties were 5,611, including 1,570 fatalities, of whom 1,413 were killed in air attacks.[45] The town which suffered most of all was Dover, especially in the autumn of 1917 when the attacks came in waves lasting twenty to thirty minutes. Dug-outs were constructed and the caves at each end of the town were developed into shelters, so that by the end of the year there was accommodation for about 25,000 people. Householders who so desired were supplied with materials for building shelters in the chalky slopes of their own gardens.[46] Even the limited bomb attacks of the First World War demonstrated what has been shown again and again since, that such attacks often increase rather than decrease civilian morale. As Lord Curzon reminded the War Cabinet, 'Air raids here had not had the effect of depressing the population, but rather led to a demand for more energetic measures on the part of the Government.'[47] Here the destructive aspect of war merges with the psychological.

In the first months of upper-class enthusiasm for war it was, naturally, the leisure pursuits of the upper segment of society, as

Blumenfeld lamented, that suffered interruption. Professional football, the great spectator sport of the working and lower-middle classes, continued in the first winter of war in front of crowds bigger, if anything, than ever before. Prodded, however, by Lloyd George and bullied by patriotic Press Lords and religious busy-bodies such as Frederick Charrington, Evangelical zealot and leader of the campaign against football, society was made to feel that professional football was twice-cursed: it kept the man who played from the trenches, it kept the man who watched from the factory. Sandwich men who once had proclaimed, 'Repent, for the time is at hand,' now carried such messages as, 'Be ready to defend your home and women from the German Huns.'[48] The Football League capitulated in the spring of 1915, and from the following season football ceased.

Since the various sporting activities were resumed practically unchanged at the end of the war, the long-term effects on British society of these various minor disruptions can be accounted negligible. But the effect of the introduction in 1916 of military conscription was rather more significant. Something has already been said of the nature of life in the trenches. Conscription meant that first-hand experience of war was brought not just to a couple of million volunteers and professionals, but willy-nilly to twice as many ordinary unadventurous citizens – one in three of the adult male population. Conscription also produced the fascinating phenomenon of the anti-conscription movement. Liberal news-papers which at the last had swung round in support of the war, long maintained the position that conscription would be an unwarranted interference with British liberties. In October 1915 it was abundantly clear that the first recruiting campaigns were not providing the men needed on the Western Front, despite the magnificent Kitchener poster with the pointing finger and accusing eyes, reinforcing the moral imperative, 'Your country needs you.' Still sensitive to liberal opinion, the Government skirted open compulsion by instituting the Derby Scheme, whereby men were called upon to 'attest' that they would undertake to serve if and when called upon. The failure of the Derby Scheme was a con-vincing demonstration of the failure of the voluntary principle, as was probably the intention, and in January 1916 conscription for single men, followed in May by universal conscription, was introduced, causing much heart-burning among Liberals, Socialists and trade unionists.

In December 1914 a group of Liberals and Socialists had founded the Union of Democratic Control (U.D.C.), whose aim, first, was to secure a negotiated peace, and, ultimately, to secure for the post-war years a democratically–controlled foreign policy (as distinct from traditional 'secret diplomacy'). It was in the same month that three young men of military age, Fenner Brockway, Clifford Allen and C. H. Norman, founded the No-Conscription Fellowship (N.C.F.). Throughout both the prelude to conscription and the years during which it was in operation, this body fought a series of skirmishes against the might of the central government. Partly due to the agitation of the N.C.F., acting in conjunction with a handful of friendly Liberal and Labour M.P.s, the Conscription Acts included a proviso that the special tribunals, appointed under the terms of the Derby Scheme to consider appeals for exemption on grounds of economic or personal hardship, should also hear appeals based on 'a conscientious objection to the undertaking of combatant service'. A new term (usually of abuse), 'conscientious objector', had entered the English language. Few tribunals had much sympathy with the objectors, of whom there were about 16,000 altogether, and rather more than 6,000 were imprisoned at least once. The Government did make genuine attempts to meet the position of men who were prepared to undertake alternative service, but the 1,500 'absolutists' who refused all alternative service were treated with great harshness, being subjected to a dismal treadmill of arrest, court-martial, imprisonment (with hard labour), release, arrest, court-martial, imprisonment and so on. At least seventy men died from the privations suffered in prison.[49]

3. TEST, DISSOLUTION, TRANSFORMATION

The needs of war very directly challenged the sacred principles upon which Britain's economic policy had been conducted since the early nineteenth century. In the immediate upheaval of the declaration of war it was accepted by even the most confirmed liberals that emergency measures were necessary. But after the first burst of legislation extending the powers of the State, there was, throughout the period of 'Business as Usual', a long lull in which government policy was characterized by the attempt to retain at all costs the primacy of the free market. After Neuve Chapelle events increasingly forced the hand of the Government, but its measures, even after the formation of the first coalition in May 1915, continued to be fumbling and half-hearted. It was during this period, however, that a coherent body of intelligent opinion in favour of a clearly thought-out collectivist approach to the problems of war began to take shape. Pressure from this body of opinion was one factor in the collapse of the Asquith coalition. Many of the ideas canvassed in the Press and in Parliament in the late summer of 1916 were put into practice by the second coalition, formed by Lloyd George in December 1916.

The biggest single challenge to orthodox economics brought by the war was its costliness. In 1914 annual national expenditure was running at £197½ million; in 1920–21 it had risen to £1,184 million. The National Debt swung upwards from £650 million in 1914 to £7,435 million in 1919. In 1914 expenditure on the Army ran at £29 million and on the Navy at £51½ million. For the war period no separate figures are available, but as early as July 1915 the total daily cost was £3 million per day; by 1917 the war was costing the British people £7 million a day. In the year 1919-20 expenditure on the Army had risen to £405 million and on the Navy to £160 million. Traditional currency policy succumbed to the war emergency as early as 6 August, when the Currency and Banknotes Act authorized the Bank of England to increase the Fiduciary Issue (the issue of paper money in excess of gold held by the Bank) and empowered the Treasury to issue £1 and £10 notes (till these were ready postal orders were made legal tender). Some sovereigns and half-sovereigns continued to circulate till late 1915, and the Treasury notes were in theory convertible. But since the Treasury exerted a firm control over gold exports, the country was in effect off the Gold Standard. There were as yet few theoretical apostles of the managed economy, but a young economics don, who was eventually to become one of the very few individual men decisively to influence the course of Britain's twentieth-century history, wrote in the *Economic Journal* as early as December 1914:

If it prove one of the after-effects of the present struggle, that gold is at last deposed from its despotic control over us and reduced to the position of a constitutional monarch, a new chapter of history will be opened. Man will have made another step forward in the attainment of self-government, in the power to control his fortunes according to his own wishes.

The author of this humane aspiration was J. M. Keynes. Surreptitiously the Government put part of the aspiration into practice: in face of the unprecedented dislocation of the international exchanges, the pound was, for the duration of the war, pegged artificially at a value of 4·76 dollars.

The Stock Exchange was closed on 31 July 1914, and when it opened again in January 1915 it was kept under very severe restrictions. Yet opinion seems to have been more impressed by the Stock Exchange being open at all than by the limitations imposed upon it. Only the Fabian *New Statesman* stressed the importance of the innovation of government control of capital issues and direction of investment towards projects believed to be in the national interest.[50] Restrictions were also imposed upon foreign lending, yet except by a few socialistic observers such interference with the rights of private enterprise passed unremarked. Even interference with the holy writ of Free Trade caused little more disturbance. This particular breach in the dyke of classical political economy did not come till September 1915: it was a breach no bigger than a man's finger, but the waters, once allowed to pass through, would not easily be stayed. In introducing his budget proposals, McKenna remarked that they would 'satisfy neither the strict Free Trader nor the scientific Tariff Reformer', but then, he explained, the war had already interfered with the natural working of Free Trade. The sentences which marked the most momentous change in British economic policy since the Repeal of the Corn Laws in 1846 slipped out pretty innocuously, the more so since they called forth a fine example of House of Commons humour from the veteran Labour M.P., Will Crooks:

I put forward, now, however, a list of articles the importance of which may properly be restricted by means of duties, in time of war, on both the grounds I have mentioned, namely foreign exchange and luxuries. So far as the duties do not put an end to importation, they may be a source of revenue not to be neglected. The articles to which I refer are motor-cars and motor-cycles, and parts thereof, cinema films – (Mr W. Crooks: 'Poor old Charlie Chaplin') – clocks, watches, musical instruments, plate glass, and hats. ... On each of these articles I propose an *ad valorem* duty of $33\frac{1}{3}$ per cent, or its equivalent, in the form of a specific rate, that is to say, on weight instead of on price.[51]

The only defender of Free Trade was Thomas Lough, a former Liberal junior minister and chairman of a prosperous grocery chain, but despite his vociferous protests the breach was further widened early in 1916, though still the dirty word 'Protection' was avoided: a number of essential British industries were to be 'safeguarded'.

In the broader reaches of industry and trade, moves towards collectivist control were extremely hesitant: the very reluctance with which they were embarked upon emphasizes the critical influence of the war. The financial measures carried through in the days of emergency were above all in the interests of the banks themselves. The rather more compelling action whereby the Government took over control of the railways had in fact long been accepted as an essential ingredient in national security in time of war and had been legislated for in the Regulation of the Forces Act, passed at the time of the Franco-Prussian War (1871). The significant innovation was that the railways were now run as a unified system. Although officially the chairman of the new Railway Executive Committee was the President of the Board of Trade, the acting chairman, with real power, was Herbert Smith of the London and North Western Railway, and the other members of the committee were the general managers of the principal lines. Financially the Government created a pool which guaranteed the individual companies the net incomes they had enjoyed in 1913. The other important step taken in August 1914 was the appointment of a Sugar Commission to undertake bulk purchase of sugar: again this was above all in the interests of the trade itself, since prior to the war two-thirds of Britain's sugar had come from the enemy countries, Germany and Austria. The Government also undertook the direct bulk purchase of wheat, but, so strong was *laissez-faire* sentiment, it did so in secret.[53] Right through 1916 official opinion remained convinced of the superior virtues of free competition: 'methods of private trade,' a Departmental Committee of 1916 reported, 'were better adapted than the government scheme to avoid financial loss'.[54]

But already necessity and intelligent opinion were insisting upon the contrary. The three most significant pressures of necessity were the shortage of munitions, clearly apparent from the time of Neuve Chapelle, and ancillary shortages in such fundamental areas as the coal industry; the inflationary spiral in prices engendered by scarcity and profiteering; and shortage of food, inevitable in a country which in pre-war days had depended upon imports for 80 per cent of her wheat and 40 per cent of her meat. More generally, the moves towards tighter State control were informed by the fundamental principles of preserving the security of the realm (the Defence of the Realm Acts provided the machinery through which much of the control was exercised) and of maximizing the efficiency of the war effort. The problem of munitions supply led to a number of committees being appointed early in 1915: their labours culminated in the D.O.R.A. order of 24 March 1915 authorizing the Admiralty or Army Council to occupy premises for housing workmen and to requisition the output and take possession of factories and regulate their operation. In April 1915 the Munitions of War Committee was established under the chairmanship of Lloyd George, and this, after the first Cabinet crisis, became the Ministry of Munitions. The first major piece of legislation of the new Ministry was the Munitions of War Act of 2 July: Part I of the Act made provision for the settlement of labour disputes in munitions works; Part II provided for limitation of profits in these works; Part III, the result of a later amendment, set up special Munitions Tribunals to deal with offences under the Act. In 1917 government control was extended to include the supply of aeroplanes, agricultural machinery, sulphuric acid and fuel oils. By 31 March 1918 the Government owned 250 mines or quarries, and superintended around 20,000 controlled establishments.[55] Constant friction between management and labour in the South Wales coalfields led to the Government taking over control there in November 1916. Control of the coal industry throughout the entire country came about in the following March, when the new office of Coal Controller was created; as with the railways, however, the financial basis was that the coal-owners were guaranteed their pre-war level of profits.[56]

The question of high prices brings out clearly that the extension of State power in time of war was not merely an ineluctable impersonal process, but that ideological, idealist, or personal influences were at work as well. On 11 and 17 February 1915 Labour speakers in the House of Commons pressed the Government hard in a major debate on food prices. Asquith and Walter Runciman, President of the Board of Trade, seemed almost to parody their own cause of *laissez-faire*; the Prime Minister actually defended the failure to institute price control on the grounds that present conditions were no worse than those suffered by the working classes in 1871 after the Franco-Prussian war.[57] But the Conservative leader Bonar Law had, somewhat ambiguously, been reflecting along other lines:

I repeat that there is a limit to the profit which we can allow to be made out of this war, and if that limit is reached, I would be at one with those who say that the House of Commons ought to step in.[58]

Later in the year the Fourth Report of the Committee on Production made it clear that fear of profiteering was a strong motive in directing the thoughts of its members towards the possibilities of State control.[59] A Committee of Investigation into Coal Prices followed a similar logic.[60] Continued Labour agitation over food prices brought a steady government take-over of shipping space, and a working-class campaign against high rents, which was especially effective in Glasgow, led to the Increase of Rent and Mortgage Interest (War Restrictions) Act of 1916, which pegged rents at their 1914 level.

It was in the summer of 1915 that the long controversy over the rising cost of living merged with the problem of physical scarcity of food. The first report of the Milner Committee on Agriculture in June 1915 advocated a national agricultural policy.[62] Cocooned in the belief that it had meantime mastered the submarine menace, the Asquith Cabinet took no action. At the suggestion of the second report, presented in October, County War Agricultural Committees were appointed with powers to issue policy directives to farmers; but with the Edwardian aristocrat, Lord Selborne, at the helm, there was no lead from the Board of Agriculture. The plans, which when carried through eighteen months later gained great praise from the Lloyd George government, were fully developed in the autumn of 1915: there lacked only the political will to turn plan into practice. Throughout 1916 the voice of intelligent criticism of the Government's continued addiction to the principles of *laissez-faire* became louder and louder. F. W. Hirst left the editorship of the *Economist*, which now became a stout advocate of collectivism. During July and August *The Times* printed a series of articles, shortly republished in pamphlet form with an introduction by Lord Milner, on *The Elements of Reconstruction*. The anonymous authors contended for 'one national plan' and contrasted the old 'chaotic world of individualistic business run unchecked for private profit' with a proposed new 'system of amalgamated businesses in which the public interest is the controlling shareholder'.[63] In a collection of essays compiled in 1916, W. H. Dawson, the historian, condemned 'the deadly doctrine of *laissez-faire*', and Sir Joseph Compton-Rickett, Free Churchman, Liberal M.P. and former coal-owner, expressed the view that 'the growth of communal control and State ownership will probably secure the best of Socialism for us without its inherent weakness'.[64] In another work, C. W. Dampier-Whetham, the Cambridge science historian, roundly concluded that

the war has led to a widespread recognition that the economic theory of *laissez-faire*, on which for a century the country has relied, is a dangerous guide in the present condition of the world.[65]

While thinkers of the political Right and Centre were voicing support for collectivist intervention, spokesmen of the Left were consolidating their prepared positions. At the 1916 Labour Party Conference all sections of the movement rallied behind Philip Snowden's resolution calling for nationalization of railways, mines, shipping, banking and insurance.[66] By the autumn of 1916 the elements making for a reappraisal of the country's economic policy were held in densely saturated solution: precipitation was brought by the resumption in October 1916, of German submarine attacks. At once the Government took what an American contemporary noted as a 'decisive step'[67] in the expansion of State powers: the appointment of a Royal Commission

to inquire into the supply of wheat and flour in the United Kingdom, to purchase, sell and control the delivery of wheat and flour on behalf of His Majesty's Government, and generally to take such steps as may seem desirable for maintaining the supply.

On 16 October there was yet another parliamentary debate on food prices with Labour members again prominent. Runciman poured derision upon the suggestion that a Food Controller, or Minister of Food, be appointed.[68] Within a month he was eating his words:[69] but the problem was that the Government, assailed on all sides, could find no one to take on the job. Once the Lloyd George Ministry, formed in December, had settled in, there was no problem, save that Lloyd George's first choice for the job, Lord Devonport, proved to be completely incompetent. Only when Lord Rhondda took office as Food Controller in 1917 was effective price control introduced to which, in the last year of war, was added a system of rationing. By the end of the war more than nine-tenths of the country's imports were being bought directly by the Government. Informed observers tended to accept that many of the socialistic experiments would be retained after the war: sensing the prevailing currents and deciding to make the best of a bad job, the Anti-Socialist Union decided to change its name to the Reconstruction Society.[70] The opinion of the Federation of British Industries, founded during the war and itself a symptom of the accelerated movement towards larger units of production, was that in modern conditions 'the group, the society, and collective effort are authoritative'.[71] The Government verdict was that

the war has brought a transformation of the social and administrative structure of the state, much of which is bound to be permanent.[72]

One of the most vital areas in which the test of war had brought a striking transformation was in the exploitation of science and technology. In pure science, one of the most international of all man's activities, the major twentieth-century discoveries were made before 1914. In nuclear physics the discoveries of J. J. Thomson in the 1890s led on just before the war to the construction of a model of the atom by his distinguished protégé, Ernest Rutherford. In theoretical physics the continental scientists, Einstein and Planck, had formulated the Relativity and Quantum theories respectively. In the new psychology, Sigmund Freud had already accomplished his major investigations into the subconscious, though his work as yet was not well known in Britain. In biochemistry, much of the pioneer work had been done by Frederick Gowland Hopkins. If British governments prior to 1914 took little interest in Relativity, the subconscious, or the putative shape of the atom, this was scarcely surprising. What was lamentable was the failure to appreciate fully the significance of applied science and technology, so that leadership in many of the new industries had been allowed to pass to Germany. Thus, among its many emergency actions on the outbreak of war, the Government set up a Chemical Products Supply Committee

to consider and advise as to the best means of obtaining for the use of British industries sufficient supplies of chemical products, colours and dye-stuffs of kinds hitherto largely imported from countries with which we are at present at war.[73]

By the spring of 1915 the Government was so seriously worried by its 'embarrassment of . . . many necessities', its grave deficiency in production of optical glass, dye-stuffs, magnets, 'countless drugs and pharmaceutical preparations', tungsten and zinc, that it decided to establish a 'permanent organization for the promotion of scientific and industrial research'.[74] Formally appointed by an Order in Council of 28 July, this organization took the traditional form of a Committee of the Privy Council, assisted by an Advisory Council, which actually did the work. Meeting for the first time on 17 August, the Advisory Council was allocated £25,000 for its first year's work, £40,000 for its second. From 1 December 1916 the Committee of the Privy Council for Scientific and Industrial Research was reorganized as a separate government department with a minister, in the shape of the Lord President of the Council, responsible to Parliament. (The Lord President was, however, responsible for an awful lot of other things as well.) A few months later a further step in the centralized direction of scientific research was taken when the National Physical Laboratory was transferred from the Royal Society to this newly christened Department of Scientific and Industrial Research (D.S.I.R.). A further million pounds was made available for the work of the Department.[75] Under the terms of the National Insurance Act of 1911 a Medical Research Committee was set up in August 1913, but it does not seem to have accomplished anything till war put wind in its sails: its first report is for the year 1914-15. The reports thereafter are full of all the enthusiasm of writers who believe that at last science is on the march: the war, they declare, is 'a great stimulus' providing 'unequalled opportunities for study and research, of which the outcome may bring lasting benefits to the whole future population'. Attention was paid not only to the prevention and treatment of disease and injury, but also to the psychological problems posed by cases of 'shell shock' in the trenches and of 'industrial fatigue' on the domestic front: British applied psychology, Professor L. S. Hearnshaw has written, was 'brought to birth' by the First World War. Through the Medical Research Committee work of the utmost value on dysentery, typhoid, cerebro-spinal fever, and new antiseptics was carried out. With the ending of the war funds were drastically cut back, yet it was clear that the new institutionalization of science was accepted as a permanent development. From 1 April 1920 the committee assumed the more impressive title of Medical Research Council.[76]

Apart from the obvious forms of government sponsorship of science, the new and insistent needs of war tended to foster both new invention and the expansion of existing technology. Before the war the motor vehicle was a luxury item, usually manufactured abroad; it was, apart from the motor bus, scarcely used at all commercially. The War Office, however, had some understanding of its potential, and during the war it steadily took over all factories able to produce suitable machines, of which a great variety, ranging from lorries and ambulances to, eventually, tanks, were developed. The domestic motor-car industry, as such, came to a standstill; but the great expansion of productive capacity meant that at the end of the war there would be a strong commercial interest in the continued manufacture of whatever type of vehicle would best meet the needs of peace. Manufacturers, furthermore, had the encourement of the $33\frac{1}{3}$ per cent McKenna Duty on imported cars. Before the war both the Army and the Navy had their own air services, the Royal Flying Corps and the Royal Naval Air Service, with a Joint Air Committee under the Committee of Imperial Defence to secure co-ordination. German air attacks in 1915 provoked demands for a unified policy of defence and retaliation. After a number of unsatisfactory improvisations typical of the Asquith era, a new service, the Royal Air Force, was created, with control vested in an Air Council presided over by a Secretary of State for Air. In the early stages of the war, the main military function of aeroplanes was reconnaissance over the enemy lines, a few raids upon civilian centres also being undertaken. Such raids were greatly extended in 1917 while the defensive role of the air service was at all times constantly before the eye of the domestic population. By the end of the war there was widespread interest in the possible civilian uses of aircraft. In April 1918 the Government formed a Civil Aerial Transport Committee, while two leading manufacturers, anxious to exploit their new productive capacity, proclaimed their plans for the development of civil aviation. The stimulus to what was virtually a new industry was enormous. At the outbreak of war the British air services had possessed a total of 272 machines;

in October 1918 the R.A.F. had over 22,000 effective machines. During the first twelve months of war the average monthly delivery of aeroplanes was 50; in the last twelve months it was 2,700. Before the war Britain had been heavily dependent on other countries for aero-engines, so much so that in the Aerial Derby of 1911 only one of the eleven machines had a British engine. 'By the end of the war, however,' reported the British Association for the Advancement of Science, 'British aero-engines had gained the foremost place in design and manufacture, and were well up to the requirements as regards supply.'[77] Advances in performance were even more impressive. The aeroplanes sent out with the British Expeditionary Force in 1914 had a maximum speed of 80 miles an hour, a rate of climb from ground level of 300 or 400 feet per minute, and engines of 60 to 100 horse-power. In 1918 the fastest machines could reach 140 miles per hour and had a rate of climb from ground level of 2,000 feet per minute. The Handley Page V/1500, which had its first test flight in May 1918, was capable of developing over 1,300 horse power. The maximum flying height had been raised from 5,000 to 25,000 feet. Three days before the armistice, two Handley Page bombers stood fully equipped awaiting the order to start for Berlin.[78]

Wireless likewise proclaimed its potential during the war and underwent the same process of gigantic technical advance. From the earlier disc, arc or alternator transmitters the first valve transmitters were developed. (The electronic valve itself dated from just after the turn of the century.)[79] As supplies from the main pioneer companies in this field, Marconi, Edison, Swan and A. C. Cossor, were insufficient, contracts for radio valves were given to the main manufacturers of electric light bulbs, the General Electric Company Ltd, the British Thomson-Houston Company Ltd, and the British Westinghouse Electric and Manufacturing Company Ltd. The commitment of these companies to the nascent radio industry was, by the end of the war, so great that it was they who exerted some of the strongest pressure on the Government to permit broadcasting in the post-war years. The first actual broadcasters were in many cases men who had gained experience of wireless during the war: Arthur Burrows, employed by the

Government to monitor the wireless transmissions of the Central Powers, H. J. Round, who operated wireless direction-finding stations on the East Coast, and Peter Eckersley, a wireless equipment officer in the Royal Flying Corps.[80] Burrows saw most clearly the future uses of wireless for broadcasting speech and music instead of merely for telegraphic communication: in 1918 he forecast 'the concert reproduction in all private residences of Albert Hall or Queen's Hall concerts, or the important recitals at the lesser rendezvous of the music world'.[81]

The train of causation in the rise of these various new technologies is not a simple one: it involves the pre-war level of technical and social advance, developments in other countries (not necessarily themselves affected by the war), and cross-currents from the other modes through which the war affected society; but at the centre lies the basic issue of the challenge presented by wartime necessity to the 1914 reluctance to exploit the potential of science. The British had to develop these new capacities, or perish. In the instances of chemicals and electrics, the causation is rather simpler. In the former the German near-monopoly forced government intervention and subvention, most notably through the flotation of British Dyes Ltd, which only managed to survive to the end of the war by virtue of £1,700,000 of government money. The electrical industry, a pigmy in the pre-war world, had, if the war were to be won, to help shoulder the giant burden of fuelling the other war industries; between 1914 and 1919 the capacity of municipal and private generating stations increased by nearly 100 per cent.[82]

As well as the principles of economics and the organization of science, the war tested existing social institutions. Military recruitment brought out very forcibly the intolerably low standards of health and nutrition of a large section of the population, and helped thereby to bring about a demand for remedial action. Dr Addison explained the process to the House of Commons in introducing the second reading of the Ministry of Health Bill:

For years our attention has been drawn to the fact that we have in our children, in our elementary schools, armies who are physically defective or have defective vision, etc. We have them of every age and in every year, not a company or a brigade or a division, but an army. Every year they go and lose themselves in the mass of the population. We forget them until suddenly some great national event occurs which brings it up to us in its reality. That was the case in the war. Then we saw those generations of children we had heard of so often who were presented in the military age by hundreds of thousands of men who were physically unfit and could not pass the very moderate standard of physical fitness which the army required. Then it was revealed as a source of national weakness, which is very great in time of emergency, but it is just as much a source of national weakness in time of peace.[83]

Defective public health provision had meant a tragic squandering of the community's human resources. Heavy indulgence in alcoholic drink among the lower classes was another form of squandering of physical and moral resources (though a much lesser one) felt to be intolerable in time of war. Before the war public houses in London were open from five in the morning till half past midnight; in other English towns from 6 a.m. to 10 p.m.; and in Scotland from 10 a.m. to as early as 9 p.m. in some areas, 11 p.m. in others. The undesirability of recruits coming on duty in a state of intoxication was at once perceived by War Office and Admiralty, but the threat to domestic war production was not revealed in its full dimensions until Lloyd George's dramatic declaration in March 1915 that, of the three deadly foes facing the country, 'Germany, Austria and Drink', the deadliest was Drink. First, under the Defence of the Realm Act, the authorities in certain militarily sensitive areas were given power to impose restricted opening hours. But the major Acts, which within four years affected a revolution in British drinking habits, were the Intoxicating Liquor (Temporary Restriction) Act of 31 August 1914, and the Defence of the Realm (Amendment No. 3) Act of 19 May 1915. Under the provisions of the latter a Central Control Board was established for the purpose of controlling liquor licensing in all areas where excessive drinking could be held, in some way or other, to be impeding the war effort. By the end of the war, control extended to all the main centres of population, covering 38 million people out of a total of 41 million, though in rustic parts it was still possible to drink from dawn to dusk without let or hindrance. In the controlled areas two main measures prevailed. The first limited hours of sale to two and a half in the middle of the day and to three (or, in some cases, two) in the evening. The second followed an early appeal by the Secretary for War, Lord Kitchener, asking the public to refrain from 'treating the men to drink' and to give them 'every assistance in resisting the temptations which are often placed before them': by prohibiting 'treating', this measure, in the words of the Bootle chief constable, wiped out the 'public-house bummer'. Special restrictions were placed upon spirits, including a maximum potency of 70 degrees proof, culminating finally in a total prohibition of their manufacture. In some areas publicans were instructed not to permit the simultaneous purchase of a 'nip' of spirits and a 'chaser' of beer. A pint of beer or a glass of spirits in 1914 cost 3d., contributing one farthing to the imperial exchequer. By 1920 heavily discriminatory wartime taxation took spirits into the luxury class at four or five times the pre-war price. Beer, drastically reduced in gravity and known derisively as 'Government Ale', rose to 7d. a pint, of which half went in taxation.[84]

In 1908 William Willett, F.R.A.S., had forcibly argued that each summer the British needlessly wasted the early morning hours of valuable sunlight. His proposal that in summer all clocks should be put forward by an hour was, in peacetime, treated rather lightly. The manifest necessity to maximize the country's productive resources in wartime ensured that when Willett's idea was revived in May 1916 it was enthusiastically adopted. From 21 May to 30 September 1916 all British clocks ran one hour in advance of Greenwich Mean Time, giving longer and lighter evenings. A government committee appointed to investigate the effects reported enthusiastically upon increased efficiency and greater opportunity for healthful recreation; children, it was true, were causing their parents some trouble by refusing to go to bed, but the committee was clear that Summer Time should remain as a permanent institution, as indeed it did.[85]

4. POLITICS: TEST, DISSOLUTION BUT LITTLE
TRANSFORMATION

For failing to rise to the challenge of war, two governments were broken. The Liberal Party was gravely damaged, the Labour Party greatly strengthened, the personnel of the Conservative leadership significantly changed. In Ireland events moved speedily to a tragic climax. A new executive organ, the War Cabinet, was created, along with many new ministries. With the passing of the Reform Act of 1918, Britain for the first time became in the formal sense a democracy. The war, it may well be thought, had as striking an effect on politics and government as on economic and social institutions. In fact the real substance of politics changed but little. This was partly a tribute to the resilience of the British political system as it had developed up till 1914: more important, it was due to the way in which the State is linked to and shielded by the fate of society as a whole. Society survived: so perforce did the State: the soldiers in their mouldering trenches and the workers in the factories had, among so many achievements, preserved for future generations Britain's Edwardian power structure. For although certain front-line sectors of society were forced into change of a qualitative nature, politics, with its G.H.Q. positioning, got by with only a few superficial modifications.

It cannot be said that the politicians were particularly quick in perceiving the needs of the situations in which they found themselves. Indeed, between the two points in time at which one can state with fair certainty that a majority of intelligent opinion was convinced of the need for a drastic change in the political direction of the war and the two great political crises, there was in both cases an interval of several months. Asquith's one concession to the notion that war might require new methods of political decision-making was the establishment on 5 April of a War Council.[86] Little more than a successor to the pre-war Committee of Imperial Defence, the Council had no executive authority, and power, in the traditional manner, remained in the hands of the strong men in the Cabinet: Asquith, a man of fine legal mind, but distinctly lacking in energy, Kitchener, a god in the eyes of the public but a man devoid of organizational ability, and Churchill, a genius of boundless energy and endless organizational ingenuity, but detested by the Conservatives and by sections of the Labour movement.

By the beginning of 1915 important and progressive-minded Civil Servants like Sir Hubert Llewellyn Smith and U. F. Wintour, Director of Army Contracts at the War Office, were beginning to set down in writing their conviction of the need for a stronger approach to the problem of procuring munitions.[87] In March news of the enormous losses at Neuve Chapelle began to seep through, elaborated by horrifying tales of men hung up like washing on German barbed wire which faulty British shells had failed to cut. Discussion of the inadequacies of British war production began to dominate political speeches, newspaper articles and private conversations. Of the politicians, Lloyd George was the most active, taking the initiative in summoning the Treasury Conference (17 to 19 March) at which the main trade union leaders (the miners remained apart, the engineers came in later) agreed to the suspension of many trade practices thought to be impeding production. But this did not allay the atmosphere of crisis, which steadily intensified. In the middle of April there came Sir John French's final dispatch on Neuve Chapelle, which was somewhat less optimistic than his earlier ones. On 14 May there appeared in *The Times* the famous dispatch from the paper's military correspondent Colonel Repington. Repington is an unsympathetic figure, and he was concerned to inflate the munitions shortage in order to conceal the inadequacies of French's generalship, but he certainly touched a sensitive nerve when he wrote:

We had not sufficient high explosives to lower the enemy parapets to the ground, after the French practice. The infantry did splendidly but the conditions were too hard. The want of an unlimited supply of high explosives was a fatal bar to our success.

The response was anger in the community at large, and the appointment by the Government of a special Munitions Committee headed by Lloyd George. This was hailed by *The Times* as a solution 'for which *The Times* has repeatedly pressed'. The

Manchester Guardian called for 'some of the discipline and organization of Germany',[88] and other papers made much of the shining example set in this respect by the enemy country. From both *The Times* and the *Mail* there was much heated agitation for 'mobilizing the whole nation' or for 'national service'.

The wide and growing sense of crisis would almost certainly have brought a change of ministry within months. The shell scandal blown up by Colonel Repington made it inevitable within weeks. It was actually a violent and irreconcilable quarrel at the Admiralty over the ill-fated Dardanelles expedition, between the First Sea Lord, Admiral Fisher, whom the Conservatives admired, and the First Lord of the Admiralty, Winston Churchill, whom they loathed, which pinned it down to days. Only the back-bench Liberals seem to have been taken by surprise when on 19 May Asquith announced that he was proposing to reconstruct his ministry.[89] The bringing in of the Conservatives as equal partners in the First Coalition, though undoubtedly an unaccustomed development, was scarcely a revolutionary one. Of much greater significance was the entry into the Cabinet for the first time in British history of a Labour member, Arthur Henderson. Two other Labour men attained minor office: William Brace, a South Wales miner, became Under-Secretary at the Home Office, and G. H. Roberts, a printer, became a Government Whip. The new Cabinet, consisting of twelve Liberals, eight Unionists, one Labour member and Lord Kitchener (who sat as a non-party representative), was bigger by two than the old Cabinet. To curtail the need for costly by-elections one small step was taken towards modernizing the parliamentary system: a temporary Act (which in 1919 was made permanent) was passed, freeing ministers from the eighteenth-century requirement that upon appointment they must resubmit themselves to the electorate. In June, in token recognition of the need to reorganize political control of the war, the War Council was reconstituted as the Dardanelles Committee, the name itself expressing the significance of the Dardanelles expedition as the main centre of military controversy of the period. Yet the executive decisions remained in the hands of the large and unwieldy Cabinet. As early as September 1915 *The Times* was calling for 'a smaller Cabinet sitting every day',[90] and on 12 September Lord Esher presented a note to the Cabinet on the unsuitability of the system of Cabinet government to the prosecution of war: he recommended an Anglo-French 'Directing Cabinet'.[91] In November the Dardanelles Committee became the War Committee of six leading politicians, organized on a more formal basis; the Cabinet was still the ultimate authority. As there was no place for him in the six, Churchill, who in the May crisis had been shunted sideways to the Duchy of Lancaster, resigned from what he called 'well-paid inactivity' and joined his regiment in France.

'Nobody', the novelist Arnold Bennett, dining at the McKennas', was informed, '*could* be worse at the War Office than Kitchener. He wasn't even a brute.'[92] Kitchener indeed was now rivalling Sir John French as the Government's major embarrassment. Asquith's solution was twofold: he divested the War Secretary of his Staff functions, giving them, along with the title of Chief of the Imperial General Staff, to Sir William Robertson, 'Wullie', the one field-marshal in the history of the British Army to rise from the ranks, though not necessarily the more enlightened for that; French was replaced as Commander-in-Chief by Sir Douglas Haig. Although these changes undoubtedly meant that in purpose and organizational power the British military effort was considerably strengthened, Asquith's deferential attitude towards the two military strong men meant that political control over the military was weakened.

Criticism of Asquith's political leadership continued to mount. In March 1916 Christopher Addison, Liberal M.P. and crony of Lloyd George, noted in his diary:

There appears to be a movement among the Conservatives to try to get L.G. to take a strong line and they are even prepared to go the length of recognizing him as P.M.[93]

In April there was a first-class political crisis over the Government's handling of the conscription issue. It was already clear that the conscription of single men, provided for in the January Act, would be insufficient to meet the country's military needs. The Government, still shirking the imposition of full-scale universal conscription, therefore introduced a compromise measure which, inevitably, would be neither efficient nor fair. So strong was political feeling over the issue that the Government felt it the better part of valour to have the Bill discussed in a secret session of the House of Commons. So forceful was the opposition there that, as Asquith, reporting to the King on the succeeding Cabinet meeting, put it:

The Government has no alternative but to proceed at once with legislation for general compulsion.[94]

Arthur Henderson, Labour's representative in the Cabinet, though fully in support of this decision, found himself in an awkward position. A special Labour conference in January had, by 1,998,000 votes to 783,000, passed an anti-conscription resolution regretting

that the unity and solidarity of the nation have been gravely imperilled, and industrial and political liberty menaced, by the proposal to introduce such a system, against which it makes a most emphatic protest, and decides to use every means in its power to oppose.

The Executive of the Labour Party and the Parliamentary Labour Party decided that Henderson, Roberts and Brace must accordingly resign from the Government. The resignations were first tendered, then, following a meeting between Asquith and the two Labour bodies, the resignations were withdrawn, pending the annual Labour Party Conference. This conference reaffirmed its opposition to conscription, but the resignations issue was not pressed.[95] Henderson, however, expressed to his Cabinet colleagues the fear that the conscription decision would lead to serious labour troubles, especially in South Wales. He was joined by Runciman, who thought that there would be trouble from the railwaymen. But Lloyd George, perceptive in so many ways of the sentiments of the British working classes, believed that 'all these fears and forebodings are exaggerated'.[96] Lloyd George was right; but Asquith's prestige had suffered a serious blow, to the extent that one Cabinet member, Lord Robert Cecil, felt that the Government should resign and be reconstructed.[97]

The Dublin Easter rising, 1916, further diminished the prestige of the Ministry, and in May *The Times* called for drastic changes.[98] The drowning of Lord Kitchener, when the ship in which he was bound for Russia was sunk off the Orkneys on 5 June, strengthened the Government but weakened Asquith, since Kitchener had at least been the soul of loyalty. While the main line of attack on the Government was against its hesitancy and inefficiency in face of the pressing demands of war, there were individuals who argued that in apparently accepting without question the need for a fight to the finish, the Government was failing to meet the complex political and moral problems raised by the war. In November Lord Lansdowne circularized his Cabinet colleagues with a memorandum advocating the opening of moves towards securing a negotiated peace. Of more immediate significance, however, was the memorandum which Cecil circulated in reply. Admitting the gravity of the military situation, he referred to the confidence which the Government's military advisers had in the prospect of great success in 1917:

If therefore we can carry on for another year we have a reasonable prospect of victory. A peace now could only be disastrous. At the best we could not hope for more than the *status quo* with a great increase in the German power in Eastern Europe. Moreover this peace would be known by the Germans to have been forced upon us by their submarines, and our insular position would be recognized as increasing instead of diminishing our vulnerability. No one can contemplate our future ten years after a peace on such conditions without profound misgiving. I feel, therefore that we are bound to continue the war.

After this clear exposition of the official thinking of the day, Cecil went on to say what so many outside of political circles had been saying for months:

But I also feel that to attempt to do so without drastic changes in our civil life would be to court disaster. . . . We must see that the comfortable classes do not escape their share of privation. . . . The men who talk and write so blatantly about calling upon the people for fresh sacrifices should be made to understand something of what war means. Apart from this, we cannot expect the working class to undergo fresh burdens unless they feel that all are treated alike.[99]

Cecil wanted the Government at once to take over the coal industry, and, probably, the liquor trade; and he wanted a special Cabinet Committee of three to deal with civilian organization.

In the event it was over the form which the executive machinery of war government should take – a conflict which could easily resolve into one of personalities – that the final crisis came. At the end of November Asquith had decided that it would be desirable to set up 'side-by-side with the War Committee another Cabinet Committee to deal with domestic questions of national organization for the purposes of the war'.[100] But Lloyd George had already hit on a more drastic scheme. On Friday 1 December he put it to Asquith that the war should be run directly by a reduced War Committee, which would take day-to-day decisions without reference to the larger Cabinet; Asquith would continue to have the name and forms of the Prime Ministership, but he would be excluded from this committee, of which Lloyd George would be the chairman.[101] Lloyd George was without doubt chiefly motivated by a genuine anxiety over the incompetence with which the war was being waged; at the same time he must have been fully aware that his proposal in effect meant the supersession of Asquith by himself. Asquith was not greatly taken by the idea, but the impression he derived on Sunday 3 December that the Unionists would not back him made him decide that evening to give way. The next day, therefore, Lloyd George began making his plans, while Asquith was brought to furious second thoughts by an article in *The Times* (written not by Lord Northcliffe but by the editor, Geoffrey Dawson) saying that in the proposed arrangement he would be a nullity, and by the advice of his close political cronies. He might have done well to ponder the leading article in the same morning's *Manchester Guardian*, which in vigorous denunciation of the Asquith ministry declared: 'Nothing is foreseen, every decision is postponed. The war is not really directed – it directs itself.' In supporting Lloyd George's scheme, C. P. Scott, editor of the

Guardian, could see as clearly as Dawson that it effectually meant the eclipse of Asquith: his final remedy was the holding of a general election, scarcely practicable in time of war.[102]

Asquith now informed Lloyd George that his projected system was unworkable. The latter responded by resigning. The following day (Tuesday 5 December) the Conservative members of the Cabinet pressed Asquith either to resign himself or to accept their own resignations. Asquith, therefore, went to the King with his own resignation, his friends telling him that, since none of his rivals was strong enough to form a ministry, he would soon be back. In fact Bonar Law (brought to an appreciation of Lloyd George by the mediation of the Canadian newspaperman, Max Aitken), Lloyd George, and their close associates were now concerting their final moves. Though Lloyd George was clearly going to be the dominant figure in any alternative ministry, it was agreed that, if strategy demanded it, Bonar Law (who was summoned by the King that evening) should become Prime Minister. When Asquith refused to serve in any other government than his own – not a great testimony to his patriotism – the King, on Bonar Law's advice, invited Lloyd George to form a ministry, and he, after his 'doping seance' with the leaders of the Labour Party, in which he got their support in return for a series of more or less extravagant promises, accepted the King's commission the same evening (Thursday 7 December).[103]

The political crisis of December 1916 sprang directly from the failure of the existing government to meet the challenge of war. About the crisis and its relationship to the changing political structure a number of points can be made. First of all in this change of government, as in the earlier one of May 1915, the House of Commons played no part. In a time of national emergency it was not thought expedient to expose political divisions too openly, and no one endeavoured to do so; but here, none the less, was a long step in the march away from the mid-Victorian ideal of day-by-day parliamentary control over the executive. The formation by Lloyd George of a small War Cabinet (his original War Council upgraded to full Cabinet status) also involved the assertion of tighter political control by a smaller body of men. In openly accepting the need for greater collectivist control of the war effort, the War Cabinet moved far beyond the liberalism which had previously informed British political practices and into a kind of totalitarianism. Although in 1917 there was a resurgence of war-weariness and a questioning of the policy of all-out war, in which Lord Lansdowne now gave a public lead, this was a government which, whatever shifts it might make to accommmodate the stirring internationalism of its Labour supporters or of President Wilson of the United States, was unequivocally committed to unconditional defeat of Germany. Not all the efforts to exert strict control were successful: Lloyd George was never able to dominate Haig, and although he replaced Robertson by the militant Ulsterman, Sir Henry Wilson, the latter proved equally independent-minded: some experiments, such as the Food Ministry under Devonport and the Ministry of National Service under Neville Chamberlain, were notorious failures. Although the annual reports of the War Cabinet are characterized throughout by a self-congratulatory insistence on the extent of the governmental innovations which are taking place, the salient feature is the stress simultaneously laid on continuity with traditional practices and on the empirical nature of the various innovations. Only one committee was set up at the end of the war to investigate the question of the machinery of government: its report, it must be said, was a poor piece of work; no attention, anyway, was paid to its recommendations.[104]

More dramatic were the effects on the Liberal Party. Asquith, having rejected the attempts to include him in the new ministry, retired with his followers to the Opposition benches, and, in so doing, they, not Lloyd George, split the party, though it was Lloyd George who confirmed the split by perpetuating his coalition with the Conservatives at the end of the war. It is possible that without the war the Liberals might have found time to resolve the fundamental dichotomy already apparent in Edwardian times, between *laissez-faire* absolutists and radical social reformers, to trim their out-dated dogmas, and to open their ears to the aspirations of the working classes. But the war was a ruthless examination with a rigid time-limit: the Liberals failed.[105] Liberal decline was Labour opportunity: but the power to grasp that opportunity sprang mainly from the social participation of Labour in the war effort, which will be discussed in the next section. It was the Conservatives, above all, who profited from the upheavals of war. Their major pre-war rival was split in half; the most able of their former opponents joined forces with them and allowed them to share his halo as 'the man who won the war'. Emotionally and traditionally the Conservatives in any case were the party best fitted to profit by the tide of jingoist fervour which swept the country in the aftermath of victorious war. Lloyd George, in the final months before the Armistice, apparently believed the old Liberal Party to be finished, and so ignored Asquith's appeal on 2 November 1918 for a Liberal reunion. Instead he singled out a small group of amenable Liberals who would be endorsed as Coalition candidates in the first post-war election, while Bonar Law chose a balancing group of Conservatives: together these candidates were allotted a joint letter of support, signed by the two leaders, sarcastically described by Asquith as the 'coupon', in topical allusion to the recently introduced rationing system. The coupon, as Mr Trevor Wilson has pointed out, was simply the outcome of a tactical bargain between Lloyd George and the Conservatives, designed to secure for him a body of Liberal supporters when he was 'declaring war on the greater number of Liberal candidates'; it was not, as has been said, determined on the basis of attitudes taken up in the Maurice debate, the one occasion on which Asquith and his followers had divided the House against the Lloyd George government.[106]

Although the coupon was scarcely relevant to the major outcome, the election of 14 December 1918 has always been known since as the 'Coupon Election'. The alternative sobriquet is more apt; this, like the election of 1901, was a 'Khaki' election in which the dominant element was patriotic hysteria. Little real effort was made to secure the suffrages of the fighting men, and only one in four was able to cast a vote. Had more soldiers voted, so the *Daily Mail* Parliamentary Bureau in Paris reported, the beneficiary would have been the Labour Party.[107] Altogether between 50 and 60 per cent of the electorate recorded their votes, and rather more than half of those – 5,091,528 in all – voted for the Coalition, giving it 484 members, of whom 338 were Conservatives. As there were a further 44 Conservatives not formally associated with the Coalition, the total Conservative strength amounted to about three-fifths of the entire House of Commons. Labour, for the first time, became the largest Opposition party with 59 members. The Asquith Liberals, or 'Wee Frees', secured only 26 seats, though polling more than a million and a quarter votes. Asquith himself was defeated; so were Ramsay MacDonald and Philip Snowden; so also was the son of Lord Lansdowne, one of only eight Unionists to be defeated in this election: all of these defeats demonstrate the strength of jingoism as an issue in this election.

The Conservatives, then, were the victors, even if they had to endure the leadership of a one-time radical. In personnel their own party had undergone some interesting changes, mainly for the worse. Businessmen who had served the necessary parliamentary apprenticeship were an accepted part of the political *élite* of Edwardian Britain. The mass-entry of lesser businessmen begins with the political upheaval of December 1916. The press at the time had been agitating for 'a businessman's government', and Lloyd George obliged by bringing in Sir Albert Stanley, manager of the London Underground and General Omnibuses Combine, Joseph Maclay, a Glasgow shipowner, Lord Rhondda, a coal-owner, Lord Devonport, an ennobled shopkeeper, Sir Alfred Mond, a chemicals manufacturer, Sir Frederick Cawley, Albert Illingworth and Rowland Prothero. These changes were ratified and extended in the election of 1918, in which there was a great swelling in the ranks of local businessmen sitting on Conservative benches: of new members returned in the Conservative interest in 1910 the majority (65 per cent) of those returned for county constituencies were local (landed) figures, while those returned for boroughs were mainly non-local (i.e. landed or nationally eminent figures); in the counties after 1918 outsiders (usually small businessmen) were in the majority (54 per cent), while in the boroughs local men (almost without exception local businessmen) overwhelmingly predominated (82 per cent).[108] All over Europe revolutions were taking place; in Britain, still secure in her traditional ways of doing things, there was only a coupon election, and its fruit was an inexperienced and, by pre-war standards, an elderly parliament.

5. MILITARY PARTICIPATION

It will be a central argument of this section that the participation in
the war effort of the working classes and of women of all classes
brought both of these far-flung social groupings an 'extension of
social and political privilege' which can reasonably be termed
'significant'. The gains made by the working classes were threefold:
because of their strengthened role in the market their wages and
living standards rose; because of their increased participation in
activities and decisions that were, and were seen to be, important,
their political and industrial organization was toughened; because
the Government needed them, it gave them, mainly through the
processes of legislation, enhanced recognition and status. The
advance was by no means a steady one: many working-class families
endured intense privation due to high wartime prices, or the loss or
departure of a principal wage-earner; men, women and children
were often worked to the utmost level of endurance in overcrowded,
ill-equipped factories; it was from the working class (despite some
curious theorizing to the contrary at the end of the war) that the
bulk of the British armies that sweated, itched and died in Flanders
and France were drawn. In the battle to secure increased production
many cherished trade union rights were trampled into the mud.
But if the short-term picture is of many real and deep-felt grievances, the long-term reality remains one of genuine gains, despite
even the post-war depression, of which the workers again were the
major victims.

As early as February 1915 an upward movement in wages due
to constant employment, longer hours, and war bonuses was
apparent. Over the whole year there was an average rise in earnings
of 3s. 10d. per week. A year later the *Labour Gazette* was commenting:

No complete account can be given at this time of all the changes
in rates of wages which have been made since the beginning of the war,
as amongst unorganized work people many changes escape attention,
but so far as reported it appears that up to the end of December 1916,
nearly six million work people had received some advance. The amount
varied, but on average the weekly increase to these work people was

about six shillings per head, and in some of the industries directly concerned with the supply of war requirements ranged from ten shillings to twelve shillings per week.[109]

Relatively the gains were most marked among the submerged 'prisoners' (in Masterman's terminology) of pre-war days, the underemployed and the unemployed, the unfit and the casual and sweated workers. In 1915 and 1916 there was a sharp decline in the incidence of pauperism, and in the autumn of the latter year it was confidently reported that there was 'less total distress in the country than in an ordinary year of peace'. This was the passage which the Press like to quote. However, the same government report continued somewhat less optimistically:

Certain classes normally in regular employment, whose earnings have not risen in the same proportion as the cost of living – for example, the cotton operatives and certain classes of day-wage workers and labourers – are hard pressed by the rise in prices, and actually have to curtail their consumption, even though the pressure of high prices may have been mitigated, in some cases, by the employment of members of a family in munition works, and by the opening of better-paid occupations to women. Many people in receipt of small fixed incomes necessarily also feel the pressure; and it is obvious that while the total receipts of families past school age may have greatly increased, a family of the same class in which children are within school age may suffer exceptionally.[110]

But where the workers were prepared to strike, their demands were almost invariably met: the Government simply could not afford a cessation in necessary war production, and employers, with quick profits to be made, were often ready, in conditions of labour shortage, to offer special war bonuses. On Clydeside the first major engineers' strike, in February 1915, secured a penny an hour increase, with 10 per cent on piece rates, though this was only half of the demand made by the local Amalgamated Society of Engineers.[111] Strikes on the South Wales coalfield in July and August, after strong but empty talk on the part of the Government, gained for the men the rise they were demanding.[112] None the less working-class discontent with high prices and other irritations brought about by the war reached a peak in 1917 when the Government appointed Special Commissions of Enquiry into Industrial Unrest. The report of the Commissioners for the North-East was duplicated in all areas investigated save Scotland:

The high prices of staple commodities have undoubtedly laid a severe strain upon the majority of the working classes, and in some instances have resulted in hardship and actual privation. It is no doubt true that in some industries wages have risen to such an extent as largely to compensate for the increased cost of living, but there are workers whose wages have been raised very slightly, if at all, and some whose earnings have actually diminished.[113]

But in the last months of war and the first months of peace labour's strong bargaining power, product of a continued labour shortage, ensured further advances in wage rates. By July 1919 a bricklayer in full employment, who in July 1914 would have had an average weekly wage of 42s. 10d. was earning 79s. 2d.; in 1920 this had risen to 100s. 7d. His labourer's earnings at the same three points in time were 29s. 1d., 65s 2d. and 87s. 4d. In the engineering and ship-building trades a patternmaker's average wage rose from 42s. 1d. in August 1914 to 86s. 8d. in February 1920: a riveter earning 37s 9d. in August 1914 earned 74s. 9d. in April 1919, and was earning 80s. 5d. a year later; the corresponding figures for a labourer were 22s. 10d., 58s. 3d., and 63s. 11d. A compositor working in Sheffield (where wages were lower than in a larger town) was on average paid 36s. a week in July 1914, 72s. in 1918, and 89s. 6d. in July 1920. Engine-drivers earning about 42s. a week in 1914 were earning up to 90s. in August 1919; firemen had risen from 26s. to 66s. The trend towards greater proportionate increases in the poorer-paid employments can be clearly seen in the worst-paid of all manual occupations: the agricultural worker who averaged 13s. 4d. in 1914 was by 1920-21 earning 46s. a week. The average income of all working-class families between 1914 and 1920 rose by 100 per cent, which slightly more than cancelled out the rise in the cost of living. After 1920 price-levels fell, while, with some exceptions, the new wage-levels were successfully defended, so that by the early

Twenties the working classes, provided they were not unemployed, were in real terms about 25 per cent better off than before the war. At the same time the average working week fell from fifty-five hours to forty-eight. Most important of all, the working classes during the war had secured a taste of the honey of affluence: their 'reference group' altered: henceforth they would demand some of the amenities previously in the jealous preserve of the middle classes.

The first major act of the trade union leadership after the outbreak of war was to offer up a somewhat vague 'Industrial Truce'. Thereafter the main problem facing the Government was to secure practical trade union support for 'dilution', the introduction of semi-skilled, unskilled, or female labour, into jobs or parts of jobs formerly performed by skilled labour. At the Treasury Conference in March 1915 a group of trade union leaders, headed by Arthur Henderson, voluntarily agreed that unions engaged on war work should forgo the right to strike, that disputes should go to arbitration, and that there would be a relaxation of 'present trade practices'; it was understood that these concessions were for the duration of the war only, and that the Government for its part would see to it that the permanent standards of trade unionists were not endangered. On the surface these negotiations were scarcely favourable to the labour movement, but already the point had been made that if the war were to be fought to a successful conclusion the co-operation of labour leaders must be enlisted. This point was driven home by the appointment of the men who had represented labour at the Treasury Conference as a standing National Labour Advisory Committee to the Government, though this body was to prove of symbolic rather than practical importance. When the first Coalition Cabinet was formed there was a place in it for Arthur Henderson.

By collaborating with the Government the national trade union leaders, in effect, stepped aside from their role of protecting special working-class interests. While the development in status and power of the official labour organizations, both industrial and political, was one major consequence of working-class involvement in the national effort, the growth of new organs of semi-official and official protest was another. It was the Shop Stewards' Movement on Clydeside, and in Sheffield and other places, and the Reform Movement in South Wales which led the defence, often highly successfully, against the wartime curtailment of trade union privileges. The first major enactment of the Government which Henderson had joined was the Munitions of War Act, which aimed a heavy blow at established trade union liberties. Under the Act, dilution arrangements were enforced; after a series of storms on Clydeside the unofficial workers' leaders succeeded in working out with the Government an acceptable compromise scheme.[114] However, believing the Clyde leaders to have little support in the labour movement as a whole, the Government at the same time embarked on a determined policy of suppressing the trouble-makers, and in April 1916 ten of the leaders were deported to other parts of the country. The clause in the Munitions Act which caused most discontent among the workers was that dealing with 'leaving certificates':

A person shall not give employment to a workman who has within the previous six weeks . . . been employed on or in connexion with munitions work . . . unless he holds a certificate from the employer by whom he was last employed that he left with the consent of the employer.

Meantime the operations of the Conscription Acts, passed in any case against the expressed wishes of organized labour, were causing much friction, particularly over the administration of exemptions for certain classes of workers. In November 1916 the wrongful enlistment of a Sheffield engineer called Hargreaves brought an unofficial strike organized by the shop stewards. Finally the official leadership of the Amalgamated Society of Engineers had to take the matter up with the Government, winning a signal victory for labour in the Trade Card Agreement, by which decisions in the matter of exemptions from military service were to be left in the hands of the union itself.[115] For all that the individual workman might still feel his disabilities and grievances, this victory, achieved by a combination of unofficial and official action, must be accounted convincing evidence of the power and status enjoyed by labour at the end of 1916. This was confirmed by the Cabinet changes of December. Arthur Henderson received a seat in the new small War Cabinet over which Lloyd George now presided, John Hodge of the steel smelters became Minister of Labour, G. N. Barnes of the Engineers became Minister of Pensions, and three other Labour M.P.s, William Brace, G. H. Roberts and James Parker, all got minor posts.

During 1917, amid other causes of working-class discontent, there was a sharp clash over attempts to extend dilution to private work. Both this proposal and the long-hated leaving certificate were finally dropped. Labour's belief in itself and its determination to voice its grievances and aspirations were well demonstrated at the 1917 conference of the T.U.C., which, as the *Observer* commented at the time, marked the beginning of a change of mood throughout the entire Labour movement.[116] Arthur Henderson and Sidney Webb completed their draft of a new constitution for the Labour Party, which, while retaining something of the old federal quality, sought by making provision for the establishment of local constituency parties to give it a more homogeneous national basis, turning the ramshackle structure into something more like the efficient mass electoral machine necessary if Labour were to compete successfully with the other major parties. The new constitution came before the Labour Party Conference in January 1918, and, after a second conference, was finally adopted.[117]

Not only was the Labour Party now stronger organizationally, it had, through its war experience, become immeasurably better equipped philosophically to deal with the problems of domestic and world politics. The outbreak of the war had thrown the Labour world into utter confusion, and unfavourable comparisons are often drawn between the bold words of the Socialist International calling upon the workers of the world, by their united action, to bring any future war to a speedy close, and the patriotic support offered by the various socialist parties to their respective governments. In Britain only a minority, it seemed, remained true to their earlier principles: and even this minority was sharply split in two:

There were really two anti-war oppositions, the one led internationally by Lenin, revolutionary and entirely unconcerned with the merits of the case advanced by any capitalist government, and the other either out-and-out pacifist or working for peace by negotiation, but opposed to any attempt to invoke revolutionary violence as a means of ending the war by international working-class revolution.[118]

Fortunately, so a fashionable theory runs, the Labour movement was ultimately rescued from confusion and division by a group of middle-class and upper-class Liberals centred in such bodies as the Union of Democratic Control (U.D.C.), who presented the Labour movement with a coherent, fully-worked-out foreign policy: the break-through in this acceptance of Liberal policy, so the theory continues, came with Arthur Henderson's exclusion from the Cabinet.[119] In fact the statements and deeds of members of the 'revolutionary' British Socialist Party, even after it had purged itself of Henry Hyndman and the pro-war leadership of the I.L.P. and of the No-Conscription Fellowship (the 'non-revolutionary' bodies), and of the mass of the Labour and trade union movement (usually held to be 'pro-war') show that any rigid threefold classification is not viable. In 1916 the British Socialist Party affiliated itself to the Labour Party; it had a representative on the executive of the National Council against Conscription, a very middle-class body, which became the National Council for Civil Liberties; it co-operated closely with the No-Conscription Fellowship (N.C.F.), was affiliated to the Peace Negotiations Committee (also very middle-class) and in January 1917 it sponsored the parliamentary candidature at Rossendale of Albert Taylor, who stood on the platform not of 'revolution', but of 'peace by negotiation'; the B.S.P. formed, in the United Socialist Council, a close association with the I.L.P.[120] I.L.P. leaders, for their part, made some seemingly contradictory and equivocal pronouncements. Ramsay MacDonald, in the first issue of the *Socialist Review* after the outbreak of war, wrote that 'the socialist' . . .

sees that if diplomacy is to remain in the hands of those who now conduct it any opposition taken to conscription is to be hypocritical in theory and ineffective in practice.

There is nothing inconsistent in Socialists saying that their native land should be protected in its day of trial, or that when it finds itself in a war it should be helped to get out of it without disgrace and dishonour, if that be at all possible.[121]

Yet the leadership of the N.C.F. was provided by two younger members of the I.L.P., Brockway and Allen, and they, in turn, constantly stressed that their opposition to conscription and the war must be seen as part of a conscious, activist working-class, rather than merely pacifist, movement.[122] These several bodies, together with George Lansbury's Herald League, organized the famous Leeds Convention of 3 June 1917, whose significance lies not in its resolution in favour of the establishment of 'Workers' and Soldiers' Councils', but in its call for an immediate negotiated peace.[123] As for the Labour Party and the trade unions, there was, save perhaps for a few ageing leaders, no question of unreserved support for a war to the finish: Labour spokesmen justified support for the war not on a King-and-Country basis, but on the grounds of opposing 'Prussianism' and furthering democracy;[124] Labour conferences were hostile to conscription; essentially Henderson left the Cabinet in September 1917 because it was no longer possible to reconcile the Government's policy of a 'knock-out' victory with the deeper desire of the British Labour movement to participate in an International Socialist Conference at Stockholm which was to be attended by German as well as Allied and neutral delegates;[125] even Barnes, who replaced Henderson in the War Cabinet, and who later moved out of the Labour Party, strongly pressed Lloyd George to make a declaration of war aims and to support the idea of a League of Nations[126] when the latter still preferred the notion of unconditional surrender; local Labour organizations provided, from the time that body was founded, the basic support for the U.D.C.[127] Far from breaking down into three primary colours, the Labour reactions to the war covered a wide spectrum. If they were not sharply defined, that was because the war itself raised issues of fantastic moral complexity. Yet behind the confusion one can detect a certain unity of conviction: Labour men were unhappy about war waged solely as an instrument for the total defeat of Germany: they were in favour of an early peace and sought after international co-operation. Thus they turned early and eagerly to the many bodies advocating these and similar notions. The I.L.P., in common with various middle-class groups, produced its own theories about a post-war League of Nations.[128] Liberal foreign policy-makers did not capture the Labour Party: the Labour Party, having a deep, though muddled, commitment to peace and internationalism, captured the Liberals. In December 1917 a special Labour and Trade Union Conference enunciated its war aims.[129] Pushed by Labour and tugged by President Wilson of the United States, Lloyd George now for the first time felt it incumbent upon himself to state some war aims of his own. Britain did not aim, he declared, at 'the break-up of the German peoples', but while there was 'no demand for war indemnity' there must be 'complete restoration, political, territorial and economic, for the independence of Belgium, and such reparation as can be made for the devastation of its towns and provinces'; the future territorial settlement must be based on self-determination; and there must be some kind of 'League of Nations'.[130]

Labour, then, had reached the stage of having a definite foreign policy, and in this it had shown itself to be some months in advance of the Prime Minister of the United Kingdom. In defining its domestic policy the pre-war Labour Party had always avoided adopting any resolution which would clearly identify it as a socialist party. Now in the light of the successful socialistic experiments of the war period, in which Labour ministers had played such a leading part (Barnes, reacting to domestic policy as to foreign policy, was a strong upholder in the Cabinet of collectivist principles),[131] the party in its new constitution declared itself in favour of 'the common ownership of the means of production, distribution and exchange'.[132] Labour ministers in office had shown themselves to be as capable of governing as the country's 'natural' rulers. The future for Labour as a political party did not prove quite as rosy as it looked: still, the *Observer* was only a degree out on both counts when it predicted that in ten years' time Clynes (who had succeeded Lord Rhondda as Food Controller) would be Prime Minister of a Labour government.[133] The successes in war of trade union action and representation, both official and unofficial, combined with a general atmosphere of affluence, materially assisted the progress of the industrial wing of the Labour movement. From 4 millions in 1914, total membership rose to 6½ millions in 1918 and 8½ millions in 1920.

The changes which, in the end, brought a transformation in the social, political and economic status of women were slow to come. When considering the first phase of the expansion of women's employment into areas formerly reserved for men, it is important to remember that grinding industrial work had been the lot of very many women since the industrial revolution and indeed before: in 1914 these women were, on average, earning 11s. 7d. a week, one third of the average male weekly wage. For many of them the first wartime changes meant only slight modifications in the nature of their employment, though there were cases where girls and women previously employed as waitresses, shop assistants, clerks and domestic servants, as well as the unemployed from the dressmaking trade, and girls who formerly had scarcely ventured across the threshold of their homes, were brought into munitions and ordnance factories. So trivial was this movement, however, that by April 1915 it only just cancelled out the unemployment the war had created in the women's luxury trades.[134] The most notable characteristic of the early months of 1915, in fact, is the gap between the obvious desire of women, particularly in the upper and middle classes, to undertake war service, and the opportunity offered to them to satisfy this desire. In July 1915 Mrs Emmeline Pankhurst and the W.S.P.U., with the support of Lloyd George, organized a demonstration of 30,000 women on behalf of women's 'right to serve'. However, the acceleration in women's employment in which the first phase culminated owed more to economic necessity and the dilution clauses of the Munitions of War Act than to the agitation of ex-suffragettes. By the end of 1915 the new use of female labour was being extended to industries other than those directly involved in the manufacture of munitions, and the Board of Trade increased its staff of women factory inspectors by 50 per cent.[135]

Even so there was a tendency on the part of the Press and other observers to exaggerate the extent of the feminine invasion, since it was easy to deduce from the odd encounter with a female bus conductor or ticket clerk that a whole liberating army of women was on the march when in reality only a few outposts had been established. The London General Omnibus Company, indeed, did not start employing conductresses till March 1916. The first phase, then, went little beyond a limited expansion and upgrading of female industrial labour, made slightly more dramatic by the entry for the first time into hard physical work of a few adventurous members of the upper classes. The second and definitive phase was launched by the introduction of universal military conscription for men. On 8 June, two weeks after the passing of the Conscription Act, the Government began its first concerted national drive to fill the places vacated or about to be vacated by men. The process is clearly reflected in the statistics of women's employment. In July 1914 there had been 212,000 women employed in what were to become the munitions industries. The figure for July 1915, 256,000, shows only a small increase. But the expansion of later 1915, combined with the first impact of conscription, is seen in the next July figure, 520,000, an increase of over 100 per cent. A year later, assisted by the intensification of conscription and the introduction of Lloyd George's National Service Scheme the figure had swollen to 819,000. In the last year of the war there was a further increase of over 100,000. In all industrial occupations the total employment of women and girls over ten as between 1914 and 1918 increased by about 800,000, from 2,179,000 to 2,971,000. If professional employment, nursing at home and overseas, and service in the auxiliary police forces, the WAACS, the WRENS and the WRAFS, is included, well over a million women for the first time entered upon paid, and usually arduous, tasks. Transport showed the biggest proportionate increase – from 18,000 in 1914 to 117,000 in 1918 – a reflection of the much-publicized appearance of bus conductresses, women porters, etc. The one industry to show a decline was domestic service: there were 1,658,000 female domestic servants in 1914, 1,258,000 in 1918; the decline (400,000, or 25 per cent of the original figure) is significant, particularly in connection with the changing class structure, but, as can be seen, domestic service was far from being wiped out.[136] Contemporaries probably exaggerated the change: after describing in a letter to a friend the way in which housemaids were flocking into the munition factories, R. D. Blumenfeld added his conviction that they would never come back;[137] mass unemployment in the inter-war years partially falsified this forecast, and the full effects of developments initiated during the First World War were not felt till after the Second World War.

After transport the biggest proportional increases in women's employment were in clerical, commercial, administrative and educational activities. In banking and finance there was a fantastic rate of growth – the 9,500 female employees of 1914 had become 63,700 in 1917. Between 1914 and 1918 the number of women and girls employed in the whole of commerce and its allied occupations rose from 505,000 to 934,000. In national and local government (including education) numbers rose from 262,000 to 460,000.[138] It is in these statistics that we traverse a central theme in the sociology of women's employment in the twentieth century, the rise of the business girl, whether shorthand typist or executive secretary. Without doubt the spontaneous growth of large-scale industry and bureaucracy would have brought this development in time, but it was the war, in creating simultaneously a proliferation of government committees and departments *and* a shortage of men, which brought a sudden and irreversible advance in the economic and social power of a category of women employees which extended from sprigs of the aristocracy to daughters of the proletariat. The advance was noted as early as September 1915: 'no woman worker is in greater demand than the shorthand typist', reported the *Daily Mail*, remarking that wages in a year had risen from 20s. to 35s. per week.

The wartime business girl is to be seen any night dining out alone or with a friend in the moderate-priced restaurants in London. Formerly she would never have had her evening meal in town unless in the company of a man friend. But now with money and without men she is more and more beginning to dine out.

The writer further noted the public smoking of 'the customary cigarette'.[139]

During the war women of all classes shared in a similar kind of emancipation. It is true that the women who seized the new professional opportunities were women of the upper and middle classes. But many of them had in pre-war days been almost as much a depressed class, bound by the apron-strings of their mothers or chaperons, or by the purse-strings of their fathers or husbands, as were their working-class sisters. Through earning on their own account, they gained economic independence; through working away from home, sometimes far from home, they gained social independence; through their awareness that they were performing difficult but invaluable tasks, were living through experiences once open only to the most adventurous male, they gained a new pride and a new self-consciousness. Working-class women were less well placed at the end of the war to defend their gains, yet their experience in essence was not different from that of upper-class women. Of great significance was the escape from ill-paid, life-diminishing drudgery as dressmakers and domestic servants or low-grade industrial labour into work which gave both economic status and a confidence in the performance of tasks once the preserve of skilled men. Even those women who were still unable to break clear of the worst-paid trades were able to command at least a pound a week instead of the 9s. of pre-war days. At the end of the war female munitions workers were earning well over 40s. per week, while other women factory workers could count on about 25s. a week.[140] In his report for 1916 the Chief Factory Inspector made a point of what he called 'the new self-confidence engendered in women' by these various transformations. The *New Statesman*, too, reported:

They appear more alert, more critical of the conditions under which they work, more ready to make a stand against injustice than their pre-war selves or their prototypes. They have a keener appetite for experience and pleasure and a tendency quite new to their class to protest against wrongs even before they become 'intolerable'.[141]

The suffragette movement before the war had, for whatever

sophisticated motives (the main one being that 'votes for women' must come on its own merits, not as a part of a general extension of the franchise), set as its objective the same limited franchise for some women as was enjoyed by some men. The Women's Movement from 1915 onwards was a more unified movement than it had ever been previously. Indeed many leading women who had actively opposed women's suffrage before the war became so excited by women's new wartime role that they found it impossible to maintain their opposition: Mrs Humphry Ward, the novelist, is a good example.

The idea that women's participation in the war effort must inevitably lead to women's direct participation in politics through possession of the vote was voiced by a number of men formerly hostile to 'votes for women'. As J. L. Garvin, editor of the *Observer*, writing in August 1916, put it:

Time was when I thought that men alone maintained the State. Now I know that men alone never could have maintained it, and that henceforth the modern State must be dependent on men and woman alike for the progressive strength and vitality of its whole organization.[142]

Yet it was not for this reason alone that the question of giving women the vote became a pressing issue half-way through the war. In fact the manner in which the political emancipation of women was achieved demonstrates very clearly the categorical importance, as an agent of change, of working-class participation in the war effort. Just as the first overwhelming demands for man-power had triggered off the expansion of women's employment, so the question of the voting rights of men serving at the front dragged the question of women's suffrage into the foreground of political debate. By the terms of the Parliament Act of 1911 the normal life of any one parliament was limited to five years; there should, therefore, at the very latest have been an election in January 1916. But, quite apart from the question of the wisdom of holding a general election in time of war, there was the problem that by going overseas to fight, or to other parts of the country to make munitions, several million men had lost their occupation qualification and had hence disfranchised themselves; moreover, there was a very strong feeling that men with no voting qualification in pre-war days had now established an unchallengeable claim to one.

It was the prospect of a clean-up of the regulations affecting the existing male franchise that aroused the suffragists from the political truce that they had enthusiastically joined at the beginning of the war. How far the suffragists felt themselves to be from their ultimate objective is well brought out in the pages of their journal, *Common Cause*: to an article published in June 1916 describing how the war for the time being had put the suffrage issue to sleep a revealing footnote was added explaining that 'this article was written before the answers about a possible Redistribution Bill *threatened* [italics mine] to bring the question of the Suffrage into the sphere of immediate practical politics'.[143] Towards the end of the year the problem was turned over to a conference drawn from all parties and both Houses, to sit under the chairmanship of the Speaker of the House of Commons. From the Speaker's Conference there emerged the outlines of the Great Reform Bill of 1918. The Conference unanimously recommended that the complicated occupational basis of the existing franchise should be replaced by a simple residential qualification embracing, for the first time, all adult males over the age of twenty-one: this was embodied in the Bill. The Conference also unanimously recommended the introduction of proportional representation; but as the war wore on to a successful conclusion with Britain's major governmental institutions still relatively unscathed, such a drastic alteration in traditional political practices was scarcely to be expected. Unanimity was lacking on the recommendation 'that some measure of woman suffrage should be conferred'; because women formed a majority in the community, the Conference thought there should be an age-bar and a small property qualification (the same qualification as continued in being for Local Government elections) for women voters. So it was that in the Act, as finally passed into law on 6 February 1918, women under the age of thirty were excluded along with a minority of working-class women who neither qualified by virtue of their own or their husband's possession of the

local franchise. But the struggle for votes for women had been won
and the exceptions could not long endure. Political emancipation
was followed, as the suffragists always said it would be, by a spate
of social and economic legislation affecting women. During the
war numbers of married women had demonstrated the fallacy of
the old male belief that they were unreliable workers who would
rush off home at the drop of a nappie. Section 1 of the 1919 Sex
Disqualification (Removal) Act declared that 'no person shall
be disqualified by sex or marriage from the exercise of any public
function or from being appointed to any civil or judicial office or
post'. But although the topic was much discussed in the inter-war
years a *de facto* marriage bar was maintained in that unchanging
institution, the British Civil Service.[144] The 1919 Act did give
women restricted entry to the upper reaches of the Civil Service
(if unmarried), and opened jury service, the magistracy and the
legal profession to them; it was also made clear that there was in
law no barrier to their full membership of the ancient Universities
of Oxford and Cambridge.

Although the local franchise was still not fully democratic and
plural voting remained in existence, the Representation of the
People Act of 1918 was the greatest of all the great Reform Bills,
bringing the country for the first time within an approximation to
democracy in the formal sense. The explicit exclusion from voting
of Conscientious Objectors, who were held not to have participated
in society's great effort, points up effectively the force of the
military participation motivation behind the Act, as does the
inclusion of men under twenty-one who had served in the war.

6. THE TRAUMA

Trauma means wound; as used by psychologists it means a wound
in the mind. Something of the military and statistical nature of the
wound suffered by the British consciousness in the years after the
war has already been examined. The wounding effect can be traced
more specifically in religion, philosophy, politics and the arts.
But it has at all times to be remembered that while for some men
the war created an enormous wave of emotional revulsion, for

others it was a period of unprecedented emotional excitement, which sometimes reached hysterical proportions. This particular reaction was socially and historically of the greatest importance when it accentuated and ratified changes which were already taking place due to the other modes through which the war affected society. During the war there was a feeling abroad that this indeed was *the* Great War, a time when the very distillates of history were being consumed. Writing in August 1916, Sir Michael Sadler, the distinguished civil servant and educational reformer, saw the war as a time of 'gestation of a new social ideal'. Blumenfeld had already confided to his diary the thought that 'the war has simply turned the whole world topsy-turvy'; in October 1917 he was writing, 'That horrible ogre, Tradition, lies in the dust.'[145] Official reports and commissions nearly all have somewhere a note of optimism; change *is* taking place, or at least it ought to be. The historian W. H. Dawson, writing late in 1916, expressed the whole mood very well: 'We are living at a time when days and weeks have the fulness and significance of years and decades'.[146] The emotional impact of the war is essentially a twofold, and, in a sense, a contradictory one. The contradiction was partially resolved when those whose aspirations had been artificially heightened by the excitements of war found them disappointed; they then joined forces with the ranks of the bitter, the disorientated and the disillusioned.

'From the trenches, the prisoners' camp, the hospital and the home the question has been put in the stark brevity of mortal anguish: is there now a God?'; so declared a tract written in 1918.[147] While the war lasted the churches were crowded; on Armistice Day Birmingham Cathedral had to hold three separate services in order to accommodate all those wishing to express their thanksgiving in traditional form.[148] But the 'mortal anguish' provoked by the hideous irony of war, and, more critically, the reaction against the blatant wartime jingoism of the churches, soon brought a sharp acceleration in the decline (apparent before 1914) in church-going as a Sunday pastime.[149] The working classes had never been great church-goers – now they were increasingly joined in non-attendance by their social superiors. For those who had rallied to human reason as an alternative absolute to revealed religion, the senseless havoc of war, in conjunction with Freudian psychology and the Quantum and Relativity theories, was also a shattering experience. John Galsworthy, the novelist, put the matter jocularly:

Everything being now relative, there is no longer absolute dependence to be placed on God, Free Trade, Marriage, Consols, Coal or Caste.[150]

E. L. Woodward, the historian, put it more seriously:

Man was now left to himself, yet he was not even master of his own intelligence and will. It would appear that he was free only to laugh, and the echo of this laughter down the corridors of time was not a pleasant sound.[151]

The war meted out heavy punishment to that broad humane liberalism which for two centuries had been one of the most vital elements in British politics. Some years before the holocaust Winston Churchill had remarked in a letter to Lord Fisher that he did not believe that civilized nations would resort to submarine warfare.[152] Even as late as June 1917, when Lord Curzon put before the War Cabinet suggestions for bombing raids on German centres of population, there was opposition on the grounds that this meant imitating the German policy of 'frightfulness'. Three months later, however, this sensitivity had disappeared.[153] Many British liberals overcame their revulsion against the war by enthusiastically adopting the notion of the 'war to end war', the war on behalf of 'the liberties of Europe', the war which was 'the last supreme struggle of the old dispensation against the new'.[154] When peace and liberty failed to materialize after 1918, the blows to liberalism were all the heavier for having been postponed. E. L. Woodward described the war as having had a 'scorching' effect on the minds of British intellectuals:

The novels and poems of D. H. Lawrence, the early novels of Aldous Huxley, Lytton Strachey's *Eminent Victorians*, Mr Keynes's *Economic Consequences of the Peace*, bear evidence of minds 'scorched' by war and reacting against a nervous strain which was almost unbearable. The strain was caused not by any doubt about the issue of the war, but by the very fact of a European war and the breakdown of accepted standards.[155]

To attribute the cynicism of Lytton Strachey or the mystical hatred of industrial civilization of D. H. Lawrence solely, or in any sizeable degree, to the experiences of the war would be ludicrous. The serious attack on Victorianism began in the late Victorian period, developing under the leadership of Bernard Shaw, H. G. Wells, John Davidson, Roger Fry and many others in the pre-war years, but it was in the nature of the war, murderous beyond all proportion to moral or material gains made, to foster scepticism, irony, irreverence. Where, naturally, this was especially true was among the young writers and artists who fought during the war. Bitter anger and savage contempt for the older standards are the keynotes of the greatest of all British war novels, Richard Aldington's *Death of a Hero*, published in 1929. The work of the war poets is well known. Siegfried Sassoon's controlled and elegant poems show a steadily mounting awareness of betrayal by the older generation. Wilfred Owen, in much more jagged style, expressed movingly and bitterly the alienation of one generation from another, as, for example, in his 'Parable of the Old Man and the Young':

> So Abram rose, and clave the wood, and went,
> And took the fire with him, and a knife.
> And as they sojourned both of them together,
> Isaac the first-born spake and said, My Father,
> Behold the preparations, fire and iron,
> But where the lamb for this burnt-offering?
> Then Abram bound the youth with belts and straps,
> And builded parapets and trenches there,
> And stretched forth the knife to slay his son.
> When lo! an angel called him out of heaven,
> Saying, Lay not thy hand upon the lad,
> Neither do anything to him. Behold,
> A ram, caught in a thicket by its horns;
> Offer the Ram of Pride instead of him.
> But the old man would not so, but slew his son,
> And half the seed of Europe, one by one.

It is illuminating to compare the work of the war-battered Owen who was killed in the last year of the war with that of Rupert Brooke, who died in the first year of the same war, and even more illuminating to compare it with Owen's own rather conventional references in 1914 to 'the foul tornado, centred at Berlin' and 'the need of sowings for new Spring, and blood for seed'.[156] In such paintings as 'Void of War' and 'The World they have Built' Paul Nash, with devastating lucidity, conveyed his 'message ... from the men who are fighting to those who want the war to go on for ever.'[157] C. R. W. Nevinson, who had once toyed with the credo of futurism, which glorified the dynamic of war, in 1917 painted 'Illustration: Mitrailleuse', described by his elder, Sickert, as 'the most authoritative and concentrated utterance on the war in the history of painting'.[158]

The agony of these writers and painters was all too real; yet British literature and art were permanently enriched. The war did not create the vital new movement in the arts, but it fostered what was most rigorous and most essential in modernism: to deal with modern war, only the techniques of modern art were adequate. One product of the heightened emotional responses stirred by war was an increased appreciation of serious art forms among the public at large. In 1918 the crowds at the National Gallery were so considerable that on some days the turnstiles had to be put out of commission.[159] In the world of music there was a notable increase in attendances at symphony concerts and operatic performances, for, as Sir Thomas Beecham explained, 'the temper of a section of the people became graver, simpler and more concentrated': 'the thoughtful intelligence,' as the great conductor put it, 'craves and seeks these antidotes to a troubled conscience of which great music is perhaps the most potent.' While attempts to secure a ban on the playing of all German music were usually resisted, patriotic enthusiasm did provide Beecham with the opportunity to play the music of unfashionable French, Russian, Italian, and, above all, British composers.[160]

In the main, however, the type of entertainment for which there was highest demand, both from civilians with money in their pockets and soldiers with time on their hands, was that which provided speediest and easiest release from present reality. From the winter of 1914–15 the London theatres, described at the end of August as 'desolate and dreary wastes', entered upon a period of boom that outlasted the war. Visiting Edinburgh in the summer of 1918, Clifford Allen, the pacifist leader, noted in his diary:

Thursday, August 15th; Start for King's Theatre. Full up. On to Empire Theatre. Full up. On to some more pictures. Friday August 16th: ... Theatre ... succeeded in getting a seat at last.[161]

Everywhere melodrama, sentimentality, or, more usually, scantily-dressed revues, often with elaborate patriotic trimmings, predominated. For the future of the theatre there were two more serious developments. Wartime casting difficulties and wartime inflation, together with the popular rejection of serious theatrical productions, hit many suburban and provincial theatres before they had any opportunity to profit by the boom. Another medium, well adapted to prevailing appetites, standardized in cost, and unhampered by casting difficulties, the cinema, was ready to take over. There were over three thousand cinemas in pre-war Britain, but it was now that there came a first burst of conversions of theatres and music-halls into picture houses. The West End theatres which were able to benefit from the inflated wartime demand soon fell under the acquisitive hands of the property dealers. There followed a revolution in British theatrical management, paralleled elsewhere in the economy by the sudden blossoming of large-scale banking and industrial concerns. Before the war an important position was still held by actor-managers, such as Norman Marshall, who ran their own theatres according to their own clearly-conceived policies. During the war, as Mr Marshall has remarked,

theatres became just another asset on the list of assets held by business magnates, regarded as impersonally as the factories, the hotels, the chains of shops, the blocks of flats which also figured on the list. With the individual managers no longer in control, a frightful sameness descended upon the English theatre. The public was given what they wanted. At least, it seemed to be what they wanted, as theatres were packed, but they were given no chance of proving whether they wanted anything else.[162]

Yet some of the same factors that affected British music were also at work in the theatre. The plays of Ibsen, in their gloomy irony matching well the world tragedy of civilization in crisis, enjoyed a sudden popularity; and the Old Vic, drawing some of its audience from the proletarian environs of Waterloo Road, was packed out night after night for its Shakespearian productions.[163]

The new and converted cinemas of the war period began to attract the patronage of the middle classes. This development was fostered by the new respectability the film derived through being used, after initial resistance from the War Office and Admiralty, for propagandist purposes. A significant turning-point was the first showing on 27 December 1915 of the pioneer British propaganda film, *Britain Prepared*, at the Empire Theatre, Leicester Square, once the focal point of the theatre world of the gay Nineties. Before the war, as the chairman of the London branch of the Cinematograph Exhibitors' Association pointed out, the picture house was 'the poor man's theatre'. To meet the fears of the prudish, a Board of Film Censors had been established at the end of 1912, and pre-war cinemas employed specially trained supervisors to guard against the dangers implicit in an entertainment, freely attended by members of both sexes, that took place in the dark; 90 per cent of the films shown in British cinemas on the outbreak of war were American. The British film industry was handicapped by technical backwardness and, at a time when films were made out of doors, by the British climate: the grip of Hollywood tightened as the demand for escapist entertainment mounted and, coincidentally, scarce British resources were directed away from commercial film-making towards the requirements of war. Hollywood was only too well qualified to meet the demand for spectacular or sensual films. Magistrates and newspapers readily blamed the rise of juvenile delinquency, clearly a consequence of the upheavals of war, on the cinema. Yet intelligent critics recognized the intellectual and aesthetic potential of the film, and

Chaplin and Griffith in their different ways were already demonstrating what could be done with the medium. The Chaplin films shown on the Western Front received an enthusiastic response from British troops, a response upon which was built his subsequent massive popularity in Britain.[164]

In affecting society through the emotional responses of that society, the war created little that was new; but it ratified and exaggerated developments brought about through the other modes through which it affected society. This was true even of the intense anti-German hysteria which was one of the most obvious phenomena of wartime social psychology. William Temple (subsequently Archbishop of York) noted of his congregation at St James's, Piccadilly: 'They are prepared to believe any evil of the Germans without a particle of evidence.'[165] Violent hostility to Germany was an important feature of the 1918 General Election. But this kind of sentiment, on a less vicious scale, had existed in pre-war days. With the arrival of the days of disillusionment much of it was to disappear, leaving only a kind of embarrassed hangover behind. And if debased nationalism was to the fore in 1918, so too was a keyed-up optimism. Addressing the concourse in Victoria Square, Birmingham, on the evening of Armistice Day, the Lord Mayor, Sir David Brooks, declared:

Today is the greatest day in the history of our country, and it marks the beginning of a new era in human development. . . . We must take care to use this great opportunity aright so that the world may be better and not worse by reason of the overthrow of the old order.[166]

In the last entry in his war diary, Michael McDonagh wrote of the inauguration of 'an era of peace and security, after years of care and worry'; and even as the sweeping Lloyd George election victories were announced in the closing days of 1918, Evelyn Wrench, and many others, felt 'convinced that we were about to witness the greatest constructive job of social reform carried out in our life-time'.[167]

7. THE UPSHOT OF IT ALL

In examining the *modes* through which the war affected society, it has been in practice almost impossible to isolate one mode from the others. It is now time to take all four modes together and describe what, for lack of a better word, can be termed the 'consequences' of the war. We can perhaps make a basic distinction between the conscious, guided acts of politicians and other persons of influence – themselves of course influenced by the forces we have been examining – and the unguided consequences within society spring-ing out of the same forces. We can also detect changing attitudes and alignments among influential individuals and opinion-formers, creating in themselves pressures for guided change. Out of the wealth of examples which one could choose, this explanation by a wealthy publisher of 'Why a Tory joined the Labour Party' at the end of the war best hits off the various themes which have been elaborated during the course of this chapter:

Then came the war. It is impossible to say how greatly moved I was by the spectacle of loyalty and patriotism exhibited by the great mass of the nation. The workers poured out of the slums and rookeries in which they had been compelled to dwell, and fought with invincible courage and died with unquenchable heroism for a country that had treated them but poorly. Universal admiration was expressed for the valour of the British Army and Navy, and it was loudly proclaimed that Britain must be a land fit for heroes and that a 'New England' was imperatively needed. I myself, on recruiting platforms and elsewhere, had said so as loudly as any, and meant what I said. I realized that the war had changed the whole atmosphere of the world. There are certain great historic events, like the Protestant Reformation and the French Revolution, that have altered mankind for good. The war was one of these far-reaching forces.[168]

In economic policy there was undoubtedly a retreat from the massive collectivist experiments of the war period, though whatever businessmen and politicians might desire, things would never be quite the same again as they had been in 1914. The wartime expedient of running the railways as a consolidated national service rather than as a series of private profit-making agencies was widely held to have vindicated itself triumphantly, and in 1919 a Bill for the establishment of a Ministry of Ways and Communications with powers to buy up all railways, canals and docks was introduced. But as the exponents of private enterprise recovered their confidence, this putative ministry shrank to a mere Ministry of Transport. When government control finally expired in 1921, the 130-odd railway companies of pre-war days were grouped into the Big Four, the London and North Eastern, the London Midland and Scottish, the Great Western, and the Southern. Important safeguards for the community were preserved in the form of a new Railway Rates Tribunal, and in elaborate, though not very effective, conciliation machinery for dealing with labour disputes. A lesser but more complete example of persisting collectivism was the establishment of the Forestry Commission. Elsewhere there was a deliberate policy of decontrol and decentralization, at the same time, it may be noted, as the accelerated phase of private industrial combination apparent during the war reached a climax. In the first half of 1919 the forty-three chief banking concerns of 1914 became the Big Five, with a powerful hold on British trade and industry. Lever Brothers swallowed a few more of their smaller competitors; Vickers Maxim amalgamated with Metropolitan Carriage Works; a group of financiers acquired and greatly extended Guest, Keen and Nettlefolds.

The return to economic orthodoxy was most completely demonstrated in the reports of the Balfour Committee and the Cunliffe Committee. The former, while divided on the question of Free Trade, with a strong minority advocating a general 10 per cent tariff, was firm in its advocacy of a rapid demolition of State control; the latter cheerfully pinned its faith in the Bank Charter Act of 1844, and recommended an eventual return to the Gold Standard.[169] It recognized, however, that the internal circulation of gold sovereigns had gone for good, as indeed it had. In its decontrol policies the Government was actuated by the belief that it was doing the best thing for the stimulus of post-war industry. Exclusively wartime measures obviously had to go, and the sooner the better. However, the hope and encouragement socialists and others had derived from the wartime innovations could not be

permanently stilled; correspondingly the fears aroused among
last-ditch individualists could not be allayed either. A Conservative
Party leaflet of 1919 claimed to the credit of the Government that
in time of war it had 'carried on war industries', 'controlled
other industries', 'organized shipping' and 'organized food
supplies'. But a leaflet of 1920 declared:

Nationalization has never been tried on a large scale in this country,
and where it has been tried – in Germany and Bolshevik Russia – it has
proved a hopeless failure, compared with individual enterprise.[170]

Four major Acts of Parliament sum up the distance which the
war pushed the State in the direction of collectivist social legislation
undertaken on behalf of the lower sections of the community:
the Education Act of 1918; the Ministry of Health Act of 1919;
the Housing Act of 1919; and the National Insurance Act of 1920
(extended by the further Act of 1921). In introducing his Education
Bill into the House of Commons in August 1917, H. A. L. Fisher,
first professional teacher to hold political responsibility for
education as President of the Board of Education, referred to the
disruptive influence of the war, which had caused 'intellectual
wastage' and had raised the 'industrial pressure upon the child
life of this country' to 'alarming proportions', to the manner in
which 'deficiencies' had been 'revealed by the war' and to the way
in which the participation of the working classes in the war had
created an 'increased feeling of social solidarity' so that 'the same
logic which leads us to desire an extension of the franchise points
also to an extension of education'.[171]

The mass entry of women into factories, along with a slow-
stirring awareness of some of the factors governing industrial
efficiency, led during the war to a great improvement in standards
of factory welfare. The other extensions of State power encouraged
the notion of a concerted national attack upon the problems of
public health through a Ministry of Health. Discussion of such a
project began as early as 1916, and Lord Rhondda, as President of
the Local Government Board, took the matter up enthusiastically
in 1917. Again strong vested interests delayed matters, and the

Act as finally passed in 1919 left too much power in the hands of individual local authorities. None the less by abolishing the old Local Government Board, which had latterly proved itself a veritable hotbed of reaction, and centralizing in one ministry functions which had previously been scattered among several competing departments, the Act established the necessary minimum requirement for a co-ordinated attack upon the nation's health problems, and for a national attack upon the scandalous housing situation.

The Housing and Town Planning Act of 1919, more than any other single piece of legislation, symbolizes the extent of the revolutionary influence of the war upon social policy. House-building had practically ceased during the war, creating a gap so wide that a mighty dynamo was required to get a spark across it. Commissions of investigation, provoked by the need to appease working-class grievances, had brought out the iniquity of existing housing conditions. The Government itself stood committed to building 'Homes fit for Heroes'. Heroes, and others, in a time of galloping inflation, had become used to the idea of controlled rents. That private enterprise could provide the necessary 600,000 houses was dubious; that it could provide them at the sort of rents people expected to pay was out of the question. While the Salisbury Committee on Housing in England and Wales, which reported in October 1917, had tentatively canvassed the idea of intensified State action, the Royal Commission on Housing in Scotland had already indicated the only solution, a massive public initiative in house-building. Public direction and control of other areas of the economy in time of war had accustomed the public to the notion of such an initiative, and, for the time being, had silenced the upholders of the older orthodoxy.

The Act, therefore, called upon the local authorities to conduct within three months, and from time to time thereafter, surveys of the housing needs of their areas, to draw up plans for dealing with these needs, and to submit the plans for approval to the Ministry of Health. The first critical feature of the Act was the undertaking that when these plans had been approved all losses incurred in carrying them out, save for the tiny contribution yielded by the penny rate which the local authorities were to levy, would be borne by the Exchequer. The State, in other words, was assuming direct financial responsibility for a large sector of the future homes of the working classes. The second distinctive feature of the Act was the method adopted for determining the rents to be charged in the new houses. The existing controlled rents of working-class houses were to be taken as a general guide, but rents could be varied both above and below this line according to the amenities of the house and, more important, the tenant's capacity to pay. Though it was expected that by 1928 it would be possible in most cases to charge an economic rent, the principle of subsidized accommodation for those most in need was to be maintained. That costs under the Act were sometimes needlessly high was the fault of the way in which it was operated rather than of the Act itself: in providing for the building of local authority housing up till 1921 at a rate equivalent to 70,000 houses a year, let at rents ranging from about 5s. a week in rural areas to about 12s. a week in parts of London, the Act was not unsuccessful. In that the Minister had powers to insist that the new houses should have fitted baths the Act did give a modest impetus to the movement towards a general diffusion of common material standards. This for the time being was more important than the long-term consideration that as long as there were both private and public housing, the boundary of the municipal housing estate would also be a boundary of social class. Dr Addison, the first Minister of Health, did not entirely circumvent private enterprise. The Housing (Additional Powers) Act, which followed rapidly behind the major Act, permitted a small lump-sum subsidy for houses built by private enterprise, provided they conformed to certain standards as to size. Although the finger which the State in 1915 had laid on fast-rising rents had opened out into two copious hands, the original problem had not disappeared. Acts of 1919 and 1920, while permitting substantial increases in controlled rents, extended the scope of control to cover houses built before the summer of 1919 which had rateable values of up to £105 in London, £90 in Scotland and £78 elsewhere.

For the first two years of war, military pensions, a pressing problem in this war of unprecedented casualties, were provided,

much as they had been in previous wars, by a *mélange* of private
philanthropy and loose State supervision. Again war forced a sharp
shift in policy, marked by the Pensions Act of late 1916 and the
establishment of a Ministry of Pensions. These measures were
governed as much by the disruptions and flux in domestic employment as by the military situation, for the 1911 National Insurance
Act was now extended to cover all persons employed in trades
relating to the war effort. In February 1917 a more generous scale of
war disablement and widowhood pensions was introduced, with
rates varying, for privates, from 27s. 6d. per week down to 5s. 6d.
with allowances for children. A first breach in the insurance
principle canonized in 1911 was opened by the 'Out-of-Work
Donation' instituted at the end of the war. Without being called
upon to make any contribution, ex-servicemen and women and
war workers were entitled to benefits of 24s. (raised to 29s. four
days before the General Election) for each week they were without
employment, with 6s. for a first child under fifteen and 3s. for each
additional child; payments, however, were restricted to a maximum of twenty weeks out of the first fifty-two following upon demobilization, or termination of war employment. Clearly the Government's primary motive was a desire to mitigate the economic
dislocation expected in the aftermath of war. The National Insurance
Act of 1920 extended the idea of including nearly all wage-earners
within its embrace, though at the same time it reasserted the insurance principle – the embrace was to be that of a Victorian father.
Included were all wage-earners save for non-manual workers earning more than £250 per annum, Civil Servants, soldiers, school-
teachers, farm labourers and domestic servants. A contribution of
10d. per week for men, shared, as in the 1911 Act, among employee,
employer and the State, yielded an unemployment benefit of 15s.
per week for a maximum of fifteen weeks in any one year, provided
that a minimum of twelve contributions had been made, and
provided that though capable of work the applicant had been
genuinely unable to find any. The confines of the scheme may seem
more obvious than the breadth of commitment in fact assumed by
the State. But in 1921 two crucial alterations were made: following
upon the precedent of the Out-of-Work Donation, dependants'

allowances were introduced, and 'Extended Benefit' was granted beyond the original fifteen weeks: an expedient to meet the onset of post-war unemployment, this was theoretically treated as an 'advance' against future contributions; in reality an irreparable hole had been blown in the insurance structure, constantly widened as the irresistible tides of mass unemployment poured in after 1921. In the development of British Unemployment Insurance policy it is true that the economic circumstances of the inter-war years are at least as important as the wartime experience (it is significant that there were no equivalent developments in Health Insurance): yet it is to be doubted that the new State commitment would have been accepted so readily had not the collectivist experiments of the war served to acclimatize the community to this type of policy. Within the central reaches of government there were administrators now fully convinced of the virtues of a broader collectivist approach to social policy. The first initiative for extending Unemployment Insurance to all trades (as the 1920 Act more or less did) came from the Civil Servants within the Ministry of Labour, while the Cabinet, as late as August 1919, was still very reluctant to commit itself.[172]

In writing of 'the Failure of Social Reform, 1918–1920' Dr Abrams has stressed how little practical effect the burst of legislation at the end of the war actually had, especially when overlaid by policies of economy and retrenchment. Yet even if guided social policy could be forced into reverse, so that its main significance lay in its establishment of new precedents and new expectations, the deeper unguided changes which had taken place within society could not be. When society settled down again in the early Twenties, important alterations in the social structure became apparent, and, because of the disruption by the war of the old reference groups accepted by the lower classes, more were on the way. Already it was clear that a whole new code of social *mores* had come into being. And, however powerful the attack on established canons, however wide the gulf separating the older generation from the young, that code showed that British society was becoming increasingly homogeneous, both as between men and women and as between social classes. The technological basis of this was not immediately apparent while the war was in progress; but as radio valves and motor vehicles were developed for military purposes, so there was ultimately a stimulus to their use for civilian purposes; broadcasting and motor transport in the Twenties and Thirties were to draw society still more closely together. That apart, the greater wealth available to working men during the war gave them a taste for the amenities characteristic of a modern technological society.

During the war great attention was paid to what was felt to be a deterioration in national morals. The tale that girls all over the country were about to become mothers of 'War Babies' was widely circulated in 1915 (it figures in Ford Madox Ford's literary chronicle of the war, *Parade's End*, published in four volumes from 1924 to 1928). In fact the year 1915 saw the highly moral combination of a very low illegitimate birth rate and an extremely high marriage rate, 19·5 per thousand inhabitants, the latter being evidence of the heightened emotional activity and response brought by the war. In 1916 (and subsequent years) there was a sharp rise in the illegitimate birth rate, explained by the Registrar General in terms of 'the exceptional circumstances of the year, including the freedom from home restraints of large numbers of young persons of both sexes'.[173] It may well be too that at a time when life itself seemed so cheap, older standards, for many, seemed scarcely worth preserving.[174] Those standards had been maintained (in public at least) by the middle and upper classes, though within the family unit contraception was already being practised. The lower orders have never been so trammelled, but they did not have easy access to contraceptives. What happened during the war was that promiscuity moved up the social scale, and contraceptives, made available to service men for prophylactic purposes, spread down it. In war the market for prostitution was good, some of its higher-class practitioners attaching themselves to the new night-clubs which were displacing the luxurious brothels of Edwardian days. On the wider view, however, the social and economic changes associated with the war – the moral climate that accepted extra-marital relationships of an emotional rather than a commercial character, and the improved economic circumstances of women of the lowest classes – brought a permanent diminution in the number of professional prostitutes in Britain (to around 3,000 in the case of London during the inter-war years).[175]

In the early stages of the war chaperons disappeared; they shrank from the hazards of travel in war conditions; they had other work to do, knitting for troops overseas, canteening for troops at home; and hosts, in times of scarcity, were reluctant to cater for them.[176] Men, too, were scarce. Young women, therefore, had to appear in public unescorted, ordering meals in restaurants, smoking cigarettes, often travelling long distances to their various arduous patriotic duties. They began to rely, to an extent that older contemporaries found appalling, upon the heavy use of cosmetics, arousing the tolerant Arnold Bennett to comment on the prevalence of 'painted women'.[177] Their skirts at the same time grew shorter. Any direct attribution of this to women's assumption of labours for which trailing skirts were unsuitable would be false, since the first fashion changes appeared in December 1914, six months before there was any important expansion of women's employment (there had been hints of change as early as 1910): it must be attributed to the will to serve rather than to the service itself.[178] Altogether the changes in appearance were symbolic of the new self-confidence among women of all classes. Men's clothing also changed, it may be noted. The older badges of class, top hats, wing collars, dropped from sight. The common wartime level of discreet shabbiness tended to set the trend for the post-war years.

Ragtime and jazz had reached Britain shortly before the war. During the dancing craze which affected fevered high society in the middle years of the war, they were used as the basis for such sophisticated and complicated new dances as the foxtrot. Because of the difficult nature of the steps, so a dancing-master declared, couples began to spend entire evenings together rather than risk dancing with a clumsy outsider.[179] A more potent reason, however, for flouting the older conventions that one should never dance twice successively with the same partner was the shadow of the Western Front, constantly demanding the parting of sweethearts. Out of wartime hedonism, wartime darkness and dullness, wartime liquor restrictions, and the wartime presence of young officers on leave, there sprang up a new growth, much commented upon in the Press, the night-club, whose main functions were the provision of liquor and facilities for gambling. Night-clubs were patronized by only a small segment of society; gambling affected all classes. From such evidence as there is, it seems clear that while drinking and, in the long term, prostitution declined, gambling, as a leisure pursuit of the British people, increased. The reasons are to be found partly in the enforced shortage of the alternative opiate, drink, but mainly in the strange war environment in which the greyness of immediate domestic existence was combined with the false excitement of living through one of history's turning-points, and the horror of war's reality was combined with a high level of spending money. The suspension of normal spectator sports only diverted, did not suppress, the need; in the immediate post-war years there came the poor man's racecourse, the greyhound track. And if the gay life of the Twenties, so often seen as a reaction against the war, but in fact originating in the frenetic activities of the war years, was confined to the small upper set, the poor, in the years after the war, found their own tastes catered for in new structures which were thrown up throughout the country, public dance-halls.

NOTES TO CHAPTER THREE

1. See especially Lloyd George's speech at the Queen's Hall on 19 September 1914, reprinted as *The Great War*, 1914.
2. C. à C. Repington, *The First World War*, 2 vols, 1920.
3. For illuminating statistics see N. B. Dearle, *The Labour Cost of the World War to Great Britain*, 1940, and M. Greenwood, 'British Loss of Life in the Wars of 1794–1815 and 1914–1918', *Journal of Royal Statistical Society*, vol. CV, part 1, 1942.
4. E. Wrench, *Struggle 1914–1920*, 1935, pp. 112–13.
5. F. H. Keeling, *Keeling Letters and Reminiscences* 1918, p. 290 (27 February 1916).
6. C. E. Montague, *Disenchantment*, 1922, p. 31.
7. S. Sassoon, *Counterattack and Other Poems*, 1918, p. 26.
8. One thinks particularly of J. Terraine, *Douglas Haig, the Educated Soldier*, 1963. Arthur Marder, *From Dreadnought to Scapa Flow*, vol. II, 1966, shows Sir John Jellicoe not to be the nincompoop he was once made out to be.
9. This is one of several important themes in Terraine, *op. cit.*
10. The most powerful critic of the generals of an older generation is Liddell

Hart. See his *The Real War*, 1930, republished as *History of the World War 1914–1918*, 1934. The most recent academic work in the same tradition is P. Guinn, *British Strategy and Politics, 1914–1918*, 1965.

11. The best recent account is R. Rhodes James, *Gallipoli*, 1965.

12. Board of Trade, *Report on State of Employment in United Kingdom*, July 1915.

13. Keeling, p. 209.

14. The best account of what it was like to fight in the war is C. Carrington, *Soldier from the Wars Returning*, 1965, which admirably blends first-hand experience with the balanced judgement of a historian.

15. Keeling, p. 238 (11 August 1915).

16. L. Housman (ed.), *Letters of Fallen Englishmen*, 1931, p. 150.

17. J. S. Engall, *A Subaltern's Letters*, 1918, pp. 119–20.

18. Liddell Hart, p. 434.

19. P. Nash, *Outline: An Autobiography and Other Writings*, 1949, pp. 210–11.

20. C. Edmonds (i.e. Charles Carrington), *A Subaltern's War*, 1929, p. 205.

21. Cabinet Minutes, 22 November 1917, P.R.O., CAB 23/4, 280.

22. R. Aldington, *Roads to Glory*, 1930, pp. 43–44.

23. For a fuller description see my *The Deluge: British Society and the First World War*, 1965, pp. 258–61.

24. Cabinet Minutes, 14 November 1918, P.R.O., Cab 23/8, 502 (I).

25. The figures, drawn from the Census reports of 1911 and 1921, are presented in convenient form by A. L. Bowley and M. Hogg, *Has Poverty Diminished?* 1925, p. 3.

26. *National War Savings Committee: First Annual Report*, P.P., 1917–18, XVIII. Cd. 8516, p. 7.

27. *Report of Board of Education for 1914–1915*, P.P., 1916, VIII, Cd. 8274, p. 1.

28. Board of Education, *Correspondence relating to School Attendance 1915*, P.P. 1914–1916, L, Cd. 7803, p. 9. See also Cd. 7881 and Cd. 7932.

29. *House of Commons Debates*, 10 August 1917.

30. *Report of Board of Education for 1916–17*, P.P., 1918, IX, Cd. 9045, p. 5.

31. P.P., 1917–18, XI, Cd. 8512, p. 5.

32. *Commission of Enquiry into Working Class Unrest*, P.P., 1917–18, XIV, Cd. 8663, p. 31.

33. P.P., 1918, XI, Cd. 8512, p. 5. On 'catastrophe' see S. H. Prince's study of the Halifax (Nova Scotia) disaster of 1917, *Catastrophe and Social Change*, 1920.

34. *House of Commons Debates*, 19 April 1917.

35. P.P., 1918, XXVI, Cd. 9087, P.P., 1917–18, XIV, Cd. 8731.

36. *Daily Chronicle*, 11 August 1914. *The Times*, 26 August 1914.

37. I. Andrews and M. Hobbs, *Economic Effects of the War upon Women and Children in Great Britain*, New York, 1918, p. 23.

38. *The Times*, 17 February 1915.

39. R. D. Blumenfeld, *All in a Lifetime*, 1931, p. 27 (20 August 1915).

40. *Daily Mail*, 3 April 1917.

41. Wrench, p. 333.

42. See e.g. *Observer*, 8 April 1917. W. Beveridge, *British Food Control*, 1928, p. 195, postdated the advent of the queue by over six months.

43. Marwick, *The Deluge*, pp. 191 ff.

44. *The Times*, 17, 18 December 1914.

45. Official figures, printed in *Observer*, 12 January 1919.

46. S. Coxon (ed.), *Dover During the Dark Days*, 1919, pp. 170–84.

47. P.R.O., CAB 23/3, 154 (3) (5 June 1917).

48. M. McDonagh, *In London During the Great War*, 1935, p. 44 (16 December).

49. For a fuller treatment see Marwick, *The Deluge*, pp. 76–85.

50. *New Statesman*, 23 January 1915.

51. *House of Commons Debates*, 21 September 1915.

52. *Board of Trade Journal*, 1914, p. 808.

53. P.P., 1915, LXXXVI, Cd. 8438.

54. P.P., 1916, XIV, Cd. 8358.

55. *Official History of the Ministry of Munitions*, 8 vols, 1918–22, *passim*. H. L. Gray, *Wartime Control of Industry*, New York, 1918. S. J. Hurwitz, *State Intervention in Great Britain*, New York, 1949. E. V. Morgan, *Studies in British Financial Policy*, 1914–25, 1952. Marwick, *The Deluge*, pp. 151–86, 246–54.

56. Sir R. A. S. Redmayne, *The British Coal-Mining Industry During the War*, Oxford, 1923, *passim*.

57. *House of Commons Debates*, 11 February 1915.

58. *Ibid.*

59. *History of Ministry of Munitions*, vol. II, Part 2, pp. 68–70.

60. P.P., 1915, X, Cd. 7866.

61. In General see A. Salter, *Allied Shipping Control*, Oxford, 1925.

62. P.P., 1915, X, Cd. 8048.

63. *The Elements of Reconstruction*, 1916, pp. 38–39, 43.

64. W. H. Dawson, (ed.), *After War Problems*, 1917, pp. 10, 116–20.

65. W. C. Dampier-Whetham, *The War and the Nation, a Study in Constructive Politics*, 1917, p. v.

66. Labour Party, *Annual Conference Report*, 1916, p. 135.

67. Gray, *Wartime Control*, p. 205.

68. *House of Commons Debates*, 16 October 1916.

69. *Ibid.*, 15 November 1916.

70. *Daily Express*, 20 May 1918.

71. The Federation of British Industries, *What it is and What it does*, p. 3.

72. *Report of War Cabinet for 1918*, P.P., 1919, XXX, Cd. 325, pp. 214–15.

73. P.P., 1916, VIII, Cd. 8336, p. 8.

74. *Ibid.*, pp. 7–8. P.P., 1914–16, L, Cd. 8005.

75. Cd. 8336, pp. 3, 8–9. P.P., 1917–18, XI, Cd. 8718, pp. 3, 49. P.P., 1918, IX, Cd. 9144, p. 3.

76. P.P., 1914–16, XXXI, Cd. 8101. 1916, XIV, Cd. 8399. 1917–18, XVII, Cd. 8825. 1919, XXVI, Cd. 412, pp. 5, 7. 1920, XXI, Cd. 1088, p. 5. L. S. Hearnshaw, *A Short History of British Psychology 1840–1940*, 1964, p. 245.

77. *Report of British Association*, 1919, p. 15.

78. *Ibid.*, p. 258. See Marwick, *The Deluge*, pp. 232–34.

79. See, in particular, J. D. Bernal, *Science in History*, 1954, 1965 edn, p. 554.

80. *Report of British Association*, 1919, pp. 158, 269–70. A. Briggs, *The Birth of*

Broadcasting, 1962, p. 37. S. G. Sturmey, *The Economic Development of Radio,* 1958, pp. 34–35.

81. Quoted by Briggs, p. 38.
82. J. M. Rees, *Trusts in British Industry, 1914–21,* 1922, pp. 160–61. *Report of British Association, 1919,* pp. 18, 165.
83. *House of Commons Debates,* 28 February 1919.
84. Marwick, *The Deluge,* pp. 62–68.
85. *Ibid.,* p. 138.
86. J. P. Mackintosh, *The British Cabinet,* 1960, pp. 329 ff.
87. *History of Ministry of Munitions,* vol. I, pt. I, pp. 58–59, 70.
88. *The Times,* 12 May 1915. *Manchester Guardian,* 12 May 1915.
89. C. Addison, *Politics from Within,* 1924, vol. I, p. 58.
90. *The Times,* 1 September 1915.
91. P.R.O., CAB 37/134.
92. A. Bennett, *Journal 1896–1926,* 1933, p. 156 (11 March 1916).
93. Addison, p. 246.
94. P.R.O., CAB 37/146/24. Photographic copy of original letter preserved in the Royal Archives, made available by gracious permission of Her Majesty the Queen.
95. Labour Party, *Report of Annual Conference, 1916,* p. 8.
96. P.R.O., CAB 37/146/24.
97. *Ibid.*
98. *The Times,* 2 May 1916.
99. P.R.O., CAB 36/160/21. Photographic copy of original letter preserved in the Royal Archives, made available by gracious permission of Her Majesty the Queen.
100. P.R.O., CAB 37/160/30. Photographic copy of original letter preserved in the Royal Archives, made available by gracious permission of Her Majesty the Queen.
101. This sentence and what follows is based on T. Jones, *Lloyd George,* 1951, pp. 83–87, and the sources cited there. For a view more favourable to Asquith see R. Jenkins, *Asquith,* 1964.
102. *Manchester Guardian,* 4, 6, December, 1916.
103. Jones, *loc. cit.*
104. P.P., 1918, XII, Cd. 9230.
105. An excellent recent account is T. Wilson, *The Downfall of the Liberal Party,* 1966.
106. See T. Wilson, "The Coupon and the British General Election of 1918", *Journal of Modern History,* March 1964.
107. *Daily Mail,* 30 December 1918.
108. J. M. McEwan, 'The Coupon Election of 1918 and the Unionist Members of Parliament', *Journal of Modern History,* 1962, pp. 294 ff.
109. *Labour Gazette, 1915,* pp. 67, 105, 142, 354–55. *1916,* p. 4–5.
110. Board of Trade, *Report of Departmental Committee on Prices;* P.P., 1916, XIV, Cd. 8358, p. 5.
111. W. R. Scott and J. Cunnison, *The Industries of the Clyde Valley during the War,* Oxford, 1924, pp. 139–41. W. Gallacher, *Revolt on the Clyde,* 1936, pp. 38–39.

112. M. B. Hammond, *British Labour Conditions and Legislation during the War*, New York, 1919, pp. 231–34.

113. P.P., 1917–18, XIV, Cd. 8662, p. 2.

114. D. Kirkwood, *My Life of Revolt*, 1935, pp. 117–18. See also G. D. H. Cole, *Workshop Organisation*, 1923 and B. Pribicevik, *The Shop Stewards' Movement and Workers' Control 1910–1922*, 1959, p. 35.

115. H. Wolfe, *British Labour Supply and Regulation*, Oxford, 1924, pp. 38–40, 44–45.

116. *Observer*, 21 October 1917.

117. Labour Party, *Report of Annual Conference 1918*, pp. 102, 140.

118. G. D. H. Cole, *History of the Labour Party Since 1914*, 1948, pp. 29–30.

119. See e.g. C. Cline, *Recruits to Labour*, 1961. G. R. Cohen, *Disarmament in British Labour Policy*, 1959. Elaine Windrich, *British Labour's Foreign Policy*, 1957. H. H. Hanak, 'The Union of Democratic Control during the First World War', *Bulletin of Institute of Historical Research*, November 1963.

120. B.S.P., *Conference Reports*, 1916, 1917.

121. *Socialist Review*, October–December, 1914.

122. A. Marwick, *Clifford Allen: the Open Conspirator*, 1964, pp. 35–45.

123. United Socialist Council, *Workers' and Soldiers' Councils*, 1917.

124. *British Labour and the War*, 1915.

125. P.R.O., CAB 23/13, 199A, 201A. CAB 23/3, 202, 207, 211, 212.

126. P.R.O., CAB 23/13, 308A.

127. According to U.D.C. publications, by the end of the war 300 Labour bodies were affiliated.

128. I.L.P., *Report of Annual Conference*, 1915, p. 88, 1916, p. 20.

129. Published as *The War Aims of the British People*, n.d. (1917?).

130. Published as D. Lloyd George, *The Allied War Aims*, 1918.

131. P.R.O., CAB 23/15, 607A.

132. Labour Party, *Report of Annual Conference 1918*, pp. 102, 140.

133. *Observer*, 30 June 1918.

134. *Report of Chief Inspector of Factories and Workshops, 1914;* P.P., 1914–16, XXI, Cd. 8051, pp. 32–33. Andrews and Hobbs, p. 24.

135. *Report of Chief Inspector of Factories and Workshops, 1915;* P.P., 1916, IX, Cd. 8276, p. 14.

136. *Report of Committee on Women in Industry, 1919;* P.P., 1919, XXXI, Cmd. 135.

137. Blumenfeld, *All in a Lifetime*, p. 61 (8 May 1916).

138. Cmd. 135.

139. *Daily Mail*, 14 September 1915, 17 April 1916.

140. A. L. Bowley, *Wages and Income in the United Kingdom Since 1860*, Cambridge, 1937, p. 192.

141. P.P., 1917–18, XIV, Cd. 8570, p. 7. *New Statesman*, 32 June 1917.

142. *Observer*, 13 August 1916.

143. *Common Cause*, 30 June 1916.

144. *Marriage Ban in the Civil Service;* P.P., 1945–46, X, Cmd. 6886.

145. Sir M. Sadler in A. P. Newton (ed.), *The Empire and the Future*, 1916, p. 4. Blumenfeld, pp. 51, 95.

146. W. H. Dawson (ed.), *After War Problems*, 1917, p. 7.
147. W. B. Worsfold, *The War and Social Reform*, 1919.
148. A. Briggs, *History of Birmingham*, vol. II, 1955, p. 225.
149. For some figures see B. S. Rowntree, *Poverty and Progress*, 1940, p. 420. In general see G. Spinks (ed.), *Religion in Britain since 1900*, 1952.
150. J. Galsworthy, *A Modern Comedy*, 1929.
151. E. L. Woodward, *Short Journey*, 1941, p. 123.
152. I owe this reference from the Buccleuch papers to Mr Martin Gilbert.
153. P.R.O., CAB 23/3. 154 (3). CAB 23/4, 228 (5).
154. *Daily News*, 5 August, 8 August, 14 August, 1914. *Daily Chronicle*, 8 August 1914. A. D. Lindsay, *The War to End War*, 1914.
155. Woodward, p. 122.
156. W. Owen, 1914, *Collected Poems* (ed. C. Day Lewis), 1963, p. 129. 'The Parable' is printed on p. 42.
157. See above p. 60.
158. C. R. W. Nevinson, *Modern War*, 1917, pp. 22–23.
159. *Report of Director of National Gallery for 1919*, P.P., XXI, 1919, 21, p. 6.
160. T. Beecham, *A Mingled Chime*, 1944, pp. 133, 152, 156–57, 161–62. See also Ernest Newman in *Observer*, 12 December 1918.
161. Marwick, *Clifford Allen*, pp. 50–51.
162. N. Marshall, *The Other Theatre*, 1947, p. 15.
163. T. H. Meech, *This Generation, 1900–1926*, vol. II, 1928, p. 176.
164. For details see Marwick, *The Deluge*, pp. 140–43.
165. F. A. Iremonger, *William Temple*, 1948, p. 171.
166. Briggs, *Birmingham*, p. 225.
167. McDonagh, p. 333. Wrench, p. 425.
168. J. A. Lovat Fraser, *Why a Tory joined the Labour Party*, 1921, p. 4.
169. P.P., 1918, XIII, Cd. 9035, pp. 25–26, 44–53, 67–68. P.P., 1919, XIII, Cmd. 464, p. 3.
170. National Union of Conservative Associations, *The Government Record in War and Peace*, 1919, *Labour and the Labour Party*, 1920.
171. *House of Commons Debates*, 10 August 1917.
172. P.R.O., CAB 23/10, 615 (3).
173. *Annual Report of Registrar General 1915*, P.P., 1917–18, V, Cd. 8484, p. vii. *1916*. P.P., 1917–18, V, Cd. 8869, p. xix.
174. See esp. Clephane, p. 196. R. Strachey (ed.), *Our Freedom and Its Results*, 1936, p. 251.
175. *New Survey of London Life and Labour*, 1934, vol. IX, p. 297.
176. C. S. Peel, *How we Lived Then*, 1929, p. 70.
177. Bennett, *Journal*, p. 229 (28 April 1918).
178. See Marwick, *The Deluge*, pp. 111–12.
179. *Daily Mail*, 4 September 1918.

CHAPTER FOUR

From World War to World Crash

Britain's social development was affected in obvious ways by war; it could not remain unaffected by the problems of peace. On the surface the First World War was a famous victory for France and for the British Empire. It is indeed noteworthy that while all through the inter-war years and during and after the Second World War lamentations were frequently voiced over the parlous state of the British economy, few doubted the strength and solidarity of the Empire. The voices, of course, were the voices of a ruling class and its Press, enthusiastic in the cause of wage reduction and orthodoxy and retrenchment in government policy, but ignorant of the deeper realities of the world power situation and contemptuous of the forces of nationalism and self-determination.

The reality of the world situation after 1918 was rather different from the appearance. In Europe it seemed that the defeat of Germany had removed the pressing threat to the balance of power which had been one of the major causes of the war. In fact Germany was still a united nation with enormous potential in population and resources, even if for a moment she was suffering extremes of privation and economic dislocation: the appearance of exhaustion was symbolized by the fantastic inflation of the mark in the early Twenties; the reality was visible beneath in the relative ease with which the mark was stabilized. France still had a smaller population, a lower birth rate and fewer industrial resources; she had suffered a terrible bleeding of manpower and great physical devastation in a war fought principally on her soil. To the east of Germany, Russia, for all the wild fears of the 'Communist contagion', could not, while she assimilated her revolution, pose for at least a decade the same kind of threat to German security that the pre-war Czarist régime had done. The new Poland proved able to hold its own against revolution-torn Russia in 1920; its rulers mistakenly assumed that despite its lack of natural frontiers it could also stand alone against Germany. The Austrian Empire had disappeared: the gaggle of weak 'successor states' which had replaced it provided greater opportunity than ever before for the German 'Drang nach Osten'. Serbia, the spunky trouble-maker of pre-1914 days, had expanded into Yugoslavia: but enlarged territories scarcely compensated for the bleeding and devastation of war. So the irony emerged that the war fought by the Allies to preserve the balance of power had resulted in its destruction. In 1918 they had only two choices: to reconcile Germany or to use their temporary supremacy to crush her completely.

In the wider world the relative power of the British Empire was diminished by the enormous accession of strength the war brought to the two peripheral powers, the United States and Japan. The proud two-power standard upon which the Edwardian Navy had been based had now to give way to a one-power standard, and even that seemed menaced by the exaggerated fears over the ill-health of the British economy. During the economy debates in the Cabinet in February 1922, Winston Churchill, as Colonial Secretary, warned that

if it became widely known that we had abandoned the one-power standard, our diplomatic position throughout the world would be weakened, and it would indicate to the Dominions that a new centre had been created for the Anglo-Saxon world.[2]

The putative 'new centre' was the United States, whose increased naval power had been recognized at the naval conference held in Washington in the winter of 1921–22. The naval ratios agreed upon there were: the United States and Britain as 5, to Japan's 3, to 1·6 for France and Italy. At the London conference of 1930 the American and British ratio to Japan was amended slightly in favour of the latter to read 10 to 7: France and Italy refused to accept the decisions of this conference. The favourable position Britain had occupied in pre-war days as an island fortress was altered also by the potential of air power revealed and strengthened by the war. In fact British statesmen had a tendency to exaggerate the threat of air attack; but as long as their fear existed, it would serve as a constraint upon their foreign policy.

The British Empire can be thought of as consisting of two concentric rings. Within the privileged inner ring in pre-war days were the white self-governing Dominions, Canada, Australia and New Zealand, whose development had been relatively tranquil, despite the possibility of friction in Canada between the French- and British-speaking elements; also in this ring was the Union of South Africa (established in 1910), which differed from the other three in that the bulk of its population was non-white, and further-more in that the activist element in the white settler class was Dutch in origin. Within the outer ring were the vast range of colonial dependencies. India was unique in that under her Viceroy she theoretically had self-government; but the Government was that of the white 'Anglo-Indian' ruling class, aided by certain native princes. The word 'Commonwealth' had already been coined: its implied meaning of 'free association of independent nations' was fostered by a coterie of enthusiasts in Britain, the Round Table Group; the term could certainly not be applied beyond the white Dominions, and even they had certain limitations on their inde-pendence. In August 1914 the British Government had declared war in complete confidence that the entire Empire would follow: the Dominions had unquestioningly sent their contingents, the Australians and New Zealanders distinguishing themselves at Gallipoli, the South Africans in German West Africa and the Cameroons, and the Canadians at Vimy Ridge. The military par-ticipation theory applied to them as to the British working classes. In the later stages of the war, and at the Peace Conference, heed had to be given to the independent views of the Dominion leaders. As General Smuts, speaking for South Africa, triumphantly de-clared in 1919:

We have received a position of absolute equality and freedom, not only among the other states of the Empire, but among the other nations of the world.[3]

In that same year the British Government recognized the enhanced status of the Dominions by creating a separate Dominions Office within the Colonial Office: from 1925 there was a separate Sec-retary of State for the Dominions.

There was yet another direction in which the nature of British Imperial power was being transformed, as events reached a climax in that age-old colonial dependency, Ireland. In the election of December 1918 Sinn Fein candidates stood in every constituency: seventy-three of them were elected as against six of the old Nationalist Party. Meeting in Dublin in January 1919, the seventy-three Sinn Feiners proclaimed themselves the Dail Eireann, the parliament of the independent Irish Republic. Ireland now had two rival governments, and throughout the year sporadic clashes took place between the police and military forces of the British Crown and the agents of the Dail, declared illegal by the British in September 1919. The Republican government was not strong enough to wage open war on British rule, but it hoped, by stepping up its guerrilla attacks in 1920, to make continued British rule too uncomfortable and too expensive to maintain. For its part the British Government was reluctant to admit the seriousness of the war in Ireland, and preferred to reinforce its police rather than its military forces. New recruits were not be to found in Ireland; but in Britain, as in other European countries, there was a pool of ex-soldiers trained to arms and out of sorts with a civilian life where rampant democracy seemed to be eating away the old authoritarian principles. In Italy, Germany, France and Central Europe such men flocked into the various nascent fascist organizations. In Britain they were recruited into the 'Auxiliary Division' of the Royal Irish Constabulary and into the 'Black-and-Tans' – so called because in the shortage of police uniforms they wore a combination of khaki and police caps and belts. From the summer of 1920 British Irish policy was entrusted to a tough-skinned Canadian adventurer, Sir Hamar Greenwood: it was his belief that the 'Black-and-Tans' and 'Auxis' should be left to fight it out with the Irish Republican Army, which was itself not fully under the control of the Dail. In a manner which has become all too familiar in recent history, the scale of horror, atrocity and reprisal escalated. Cooler heads among the Republicans realized that no ultimate victory could be won, while in Britain Conservative, Liberal, Labour and nonparty spokesmen began to voice their revulsion against the bloodshed and violence being committed in the name of British power in

Ireland. In 1920 the Labour Party published a detailed report on events in Ireland which did much to alert a wider public opinion.[4] Meantime the Ulster leaders, formerly stern opponents of any alteration in the *status quo*, had come to realize that it might be better to accept some compromise accommodation from the British Government. Thus they agreed to the partition embodied in the Government of Ireland Act of December 1920, which declared that Northern Ireland (the six Ulster counties whose exclusion from Home Rule had been proposed in 1916) and Southern Ireland should each have its own parliament, that both should be represented at Westminster, where final supremacy remained, and that reunion should be possible if both separate parliaments wished it. Although the Republicans declared their total hostility towards this partition, it did in fact mark an important stage towards a final solution. In opening the newly-elected Northern Ireland Parliament in June 1921, King George, who shared the disquiet of many leading Britishers over the condition of Ireland, made a personal appeal for 'forbearance and conciliation'. Two days later Lloyd George invited the Republican leader, Eamonn de Valera, and Sir James Craig, Carson's successor as leader of the Ulstermen, to a conference in London. The conference began on 12 July *after* the British Government had agreed to suspend military operations. The difficult and protracted negotiations were just the sort to fit Lloyd George's talents: by holding out the prospect of the ultimate disappearance of partition, while at the same time threatening the resumption of total war, he finally persuaded the Irish delegation to sign, without reference to Dublin, the 'Treaty' of 6 December 1921, which safeguarded certain basic British interests. Although the treaty applied to the whole of Ireland, the Northern Ireland Parliament was guaranteed the right if it so wished (which it did) to opt to retain the status established by the Act of 1920; as a sop to the Irish negotiators a boundary readjustment was promised, but this never took place. More important, the new 'Irish Free State' was to remain within the British Empire as a self-governing dominion, while Britain was to maintain naval establishments in a number of Irish ports. There was bitter opposition in Ireland to a treaty in which the British seemed to have conceded the shadow in order to retain the substance, and from June 1922 to May 1923 a fierce internecine war was fought between pro-treaty and anti-treaty factions. Yet there could be no doubt as to the shrinkage in the territorial area of the United Kingdom and of the area over which the writ of the British Government still ran; nor could there be any real guarantee of the continued loyalty to the British connection of the new Free State. In the meantime the new dominion, described in the treaty as having 'membership of the group of nations forming the British Commonwealth of Nations', joined with the other recent member, South Africa, in pressing for some clear definition of this 'Commonwealth'.

In 1921 General Smuts produced a memorandum entitled 'The Constitution of the British Commonwealth', and five years later the new South African Prime Minister, Hertzog, came to the Imperial Conference determined either to secure a clear definition of the Commonwealth or to secede. This movement towards definition was reinforced by a constitutional crisis which blew up in 1926 concerning the respective powers of the Governor General, the representative of the British Crown in Canada, and the Canadian Prime Minister. In an attempt to meet various pressures, Lord (the former A. J.) Balfour, presiding over the Imperial Conference 'with a smile like moonlight on a tombstone', offered a definition of the relationship between Britain and the Dominions which spoke of

autonomous communities within the British Empire, equal in status, in no way subordinate one to another in any aspect of their domestic or external affairs, though united by a common allegiance to the Crown, and freely associated as members of the British Commonwealth of nations.[5]

Further discussion of the question at the 1930 Imperial Conference led to the Statute of Westminster of November 1931, which formally recognized the complete legislative independence of the Dominions, and specified the Crown as the 'symbol of the free association of the members of the British Commonwealth of nations'. Not all the Dominions, however, were in a tearing hurry to ratify the statute; Australia did not do so till 1941, New Zealand till 1947. The critical fact for Britain's foreign policy was that she could no longer hope to declare war on behalf of the entire Empire; henceforth she would be specially careful to carry Dominion sentiment forward with her. At the same time Britain's grip on India was steadily weakening as the Nationalist Congress Party grew in strength, and her relations with her colonial dependencies in Africa were complicated by the continuing influx of white settlers into the Central and Eastern territories. The most coherent and articulate settler population was to be found in Southern Rhodesia: while in legal theory the responsibility for ruling this country remained with the British Government, *de facto* power was allowed to pass to the settler class; it would not easily be won back. Despite, then, the 'mandates' which Britain secured over former German and Turkish colonies, permitting the red on the map to spread over an area hitherto unsurpassed, Britain's world position was in reality less secure than it had been in the Edwardian era. And, furthermore, through the disruptions of war, her position, both as a leading industrial nation and as a world financial centre, had been seriously diminished.

The statesmen who met at Versailles in January 1919 to draw up the terms of settlement with Germany had no easy task. From the very start of the war a crusading spirit had been detectable in the pronouncements of many British public figures; as the war lengthened into a bloody struggle of attrition, the original objective for which Britain had embarked upon the war in the West, the maintenance of a barrier against growing German power, became buried beneath a storm of slogans: 'war to end war', 'world safe for democracy', 'national self-determination'. At the same time murderous slaughter in the first war truly fought by entire nations had whipped up passions which ran utterly contrary to the spirit of such slogans. Lloyd George was personally concerned to avoid making Germany a permanent outcast, yet he had himself been caught up in the popular mood which was set upon exacting crushing reparation from the defeated and, for the time being, hated enemy. He had to face the claims of Orlando, determined that Italy should secure in full the territories used as a bribe to bring her into the war, whether or not these claims could be accommodated to

idealistic slogans, and the demands of Clemenceau, determined
that France, twice a victim of German invasion in fifty years,
should be secured against any future aggression. Clemenceau's
demand was for a Germany confined behind the Rhine: instead the
Rhineland was established as a demilitarized zone, and Britain and
America were to give France a joint guarantee against German
aggression, but the refusal of Congress to ratify this arrangement
gave Britain an excuse to pull out. Thus as the post-war years
began the Germans were not alone in smarting under a sense of
grievance; so also did the French. The worst feature of the Versailles Treaty was its explicit attachment to Germany and her allies
of 'war guilt' and of responsibility for paying reparations for the
whole cost of the war, the only formula by which Britain, who had
not suffered the direct physical damage of France and Belgium,
could herself profit. (Such 'profit' was a delusion since Germany
could only pay in industrial goods which would directly compete
with British industry.) In practice Germany received more in loans
than she ever paid in reparations, but that did not stop her from
feeling aggrieved, especially when her forced disarmament seemed
to perpetuate an inequality of status relative to the other powers.

The noblest feature of the Treaty was the Covenant of the
League of Nations, embodied in the first twenty-six clauses. 'Out
of evil cometh forth good,' a Conservative Party leaflet declared
enthusiastically, though in reality Conservatives in Britain were
generally sceptical about the possibilities of the League. So, to
begin with, were many Liberals and Labour supporters, who saw
the League as merely a continuance of the wartime alliance instead of the genuine all-embracing body they had advocated during
the war. But in the early Twenties the Labour and Liberal
Parties enthusiastically adopted the League of Nations as the
supreme agency for maintaining peace: too many of their members,
however, mistaking the wish for peace for the will to peace, preferred to forget that the ultimate rationale of collective security is a
willingness to declare war on a disturber of the peace.[6] Conservative foreign policy-makers continued to prefer limited agreements
related to specific areas of friction rather than the blanket coverage
of the League. The League of Nations 'failed' not because it was

in itself an unsound idea, but because the various nations, Britain especially, were not really prepared to make it work. America's refusal to join, certainly, was a heavy blow, and rendered effective League of Nations action beyond Europe impractical; but it need not have stymied League of Nations action within Europe, where much of the potential trouble lay.

Germany was not crushed by the Treaty, and by the mid-Twenties was well on the way to recovery. Conciliation (or 'appeasement', to use the contemporary word which has now lost some of its savour) was thereafter the only possibility. Allied reparations claims were twice revised, in the Dawes Plan of 1924 and the Young Plan of 1930. Germany entered the League of Nations in 1925 and at the end of the same year signed the Locarno treaties guaranteeing the existing Western European boundaries. What was lacking was any initiative towards necessary revisions of the Versailles Treaty. As it was, Germany had already turned to the country the Western powers seemed determined to make a permanent European outcast: Russia. On Russian soil the Germans began the build-up of a modern military machine.

2. THE ECONOMY, THE STATE AND THE WORKING CLASSES

The single most significant characteristic of Britain in the inter-war years was the malfunctioning of the economy, giving rise to industrial depression and a high level of long-term unemployment. It must be said of the politicians of the time that, however unsuccessful they may have been in dealing with the problem, they were very fully aware of it, even obsessed by it. Although the wartime level of demand, together with rising prices, rising wages, and a general atmosphere of boom, continued until the summer of 1920, from the moment the end of war appeared in sight the politicians were prepared for the worst: in expecting the worst they helped to bring about the worst, but they cannot be accused of unconcern over the country's major misfortune. The Government's carefully planned demobilization schemes caused soldiers' demonstrations and riots because they were completely inequitable, but the principle on which they were based was that by first releasing certain 'key' occupations a smooth transition to peace without the unemployment which had occurred at the end of the Napoleonic wars might be achieved[7] (if British governments have often been short on economic sense, they have never been slow to quote history). The 'Out-of-Work Donation' betrayed a similar expectation of unemployment, and in August 1920 a Special Cabinet Committee to find remedies for unemployment was appointed.[8]

The years following the war were marked by great industrial unrest, so much so that observers, both at the time and since, detected a 'revolutionary' intent on the part of British working-class leaders. In fact neither the working classes nor their leaders deserted their pragmatic and conservative traditions: their activities in this period were aimed, first, at consolidating the gains of the war period while the auspicious circumstances of the post-war boom lasted, and secondly, at defending themselves from attacks upon their new position once economic depression set in. The boom reached its peak in the spring of 1920 with a lunatic burst of speculation. The index number of prices, standing at 192 in 1918, 206 in 1919, and 265 at the April peak of 1920, collapsed to 155 in 1921 and 131 in 1922. The slump had set in, and despite a temporary recovery during the French occupation of the German Ruhr coalfield in 1923–24 and the appearance of modest progress between 1924 and 1929, it persisted till it was engulfed in the still greater economic crash of 1929–31. As an island trading power Britain was especially dependent on the efficient working of the international trading system, which, we have seen, had been seriously disrupted by the war. The war had accelerated the twentieth-century technological revolution, establishing the primacy of new fuels such as oils and electricity, and discounting heavy industry in favour of light engineering and its offshoots. While partially sharing in this revolution, Britain during the war had been forced to continue the building up of her heavy industries; at the end of the war her entrepreneurial class, firmly rooted in the traditions of Victorian prosperity, showed a marked reluctance to move into the new areas of industrial enterprise. The 'New Industries' – electricity, rayon, motor vehicles, patent foods, luxuries – had amounted to 6·5 per cent of Britain's total industrial output in 1907; in 1924 they contributed 12·5 per cent, and as late as 1928 still only 16·3 per cent.[9]

As J. M. Keynes expressed it in the *Nation*:

The mishandling of currency and credit by the Bank of England since the war, the stiff-neckedness of the coal-owners, the apparently suicidal behaviour of the leaders of Lancashire, raise the question of the suita-bility and adaptability of our Business Men to the modern age of mingled progress and retrogression. What has happened to them – the class in which a generation or two generations ago we could take a just and worthy pride? Are they too old or too obstinate? Or what? Is it that too many of them have risen not on their own legs, but on the shoulders of their fathers and grandfathers?[10]

Apart from the inadequacies of British business enterprise, how-ever, there was another fundamental cause of economic malaise: the existence of a short-fall between the total amount of national ex-penditure necessary to keep fully employed all the resources of the community, and the amount of expenditure actually taking place. According to the canon of nineteenth-century classical political economy, as embodied in Say's Law, a natural adjustment of interest rates would soon bring the economy into equilibrium and abolish this short-fall. In the disturbed conditions of the post-war world this failed to happen, for, as Keynes later described it, there was a high 'propensity to save'. In other words the old nostrum of thrift, which equated saving with investment, was no longer valid: the thrifty classes were saving, but they were not investing, hence the short-fall in the total amount of money cir-culating in the community, the short-fall which brought about stagnation and unemployment. This analysis of the problem was only worked out fully in the 1930s by Keynes,[11] and to that extent the governments of the 1920s may be excused for not under-standing what was happening. At the same time Keynes and others were already protesting forcefully over existing economic policy. Not only did the Government pay no heed to these critics, it proceeded single-mindedly to implement a policy which did no good whatsoever; indeed, it did a great deal of harm. Following the recommendations of the Cunliffe Committee, it severely cut the supply of money by raising the Bank Rate (in April 1920) to 7 per cent and by drastically reducing the fiduciary issue. Driven by a legion of terrified businessmen, in August 1921 it set up an Economy Committee under Sir Eric Geddes.[12] Early in 1922 the 'Geddes Axe' chopped away a substantial section of public expenditure, thus further reducing the spending power of the community. Factors far beyond government control had begun the vicious process: government policy turned it into a circle.

Financial orthodoxy and national vanity were responsible for one other very serious error. In 1925 Churchill, now Chancellor of the Exchequer, was prevailed upon to return the country to the Gold Standard at the pre-war parity of pound to dollar, regardless of the fact that the pound had meantime dropped in relative value by at least 10 per cent. Sir Roy Harrod has described the background to the move in the following terms:

In the second half of 1924 sterling began to rise in a sinister manner in the foreign exchange market. The originating impulse was obscure; it may have been connected with Federal Reserve Policy; America had a minor trade recession in that year, and the Federal Reserve System, in accordance with its now well-established practice, proceeded to pump in credit in order to stimulate trade; this may have been the initial cause of the weakening of the dollar against sterling. Be that as it may, there is no doubt about what was responsible for the continuing major upward movement, a return to the old Gold Standard was definitely in the air now, and bulls were buying sterling at a discount in order to make a profit when the old parity should be re-established. The important thing to notice was that the rise in sterling did not reflect a reduction in British costs or a rise in American prices.[13]

British industry, therefore, was presented with a gratuitous handicap in that foreigners were now expected to pay 10 per cent more for British exports (4·25 dollars for every pound's worth, instead of 3·85 dollars). Many industrialists felt that the only way out was to reduce costs through wage cuts equivalent to the ten per cent.

Many of the more doleful tunes of the decade were rehearsed by Lloyd George at a Cabinet meeting of 5 August 1919, when he initiated a review of the 'whole position of the country' now that the peace treaty was concluded. Apparently in one of the moods of mystical depression which seized him from time to time, the Prime Minister declared that Britain was now a debtor country. In this he was immediately controverted by Bonar Law:[14] strictly speaking Bonar Law was correct (our wartime allies owed us more than we owed the Americans – and anyway we defaulted on part of our American payments), but it was the gloomy view of Lloyd George which tended to govern subsequent economic policies. There were, Lloyd George continued, two problems facing the country: strikes, and, more serious, declining productivity. The Bolsheviks, he said, launching upon one of the flights of fancy which, unhappily for the country, had a firm hold over his mind, had captured the trade union organizations. At the same time labour had legitimate grievances, among which Lloyd George stressed profiteering and bad housing. As a remedy for the former, the Prime Minister touched on the possibility of a programme of nationalization: he immediately met strong hostility from the other members of the Cabinet, who clearly preferred his vague references to stimulating agriculture and watching expenditure. Then Lloyd George came to some remarks which bring us to the very heart of the storms which were to rage over British domestic history between 1919 and 1922:

... they could not take risks with labour. If we did, we should at once create an enemy within our own borders, and one which would be better provided with dangerous weapons than Germany. We had in this country millions of men who had been trained to arms, and there were plenty of guns and ammunition available.[15]

Risks, the Prime Minister continued, in a curious but typical modulation of key, could be taken with external foes, but not with the 'health and labour of the people'. This was a critical discussion, and recognized as such, for it was decided that not a hint of what had been discussed should be allowed to appear in the Press.

The storm centres of working-class agitation can be precisely identified: the readjustment to peacetime conditions, leading, after 1920, into the wider problem of mass unemployment; the coal industry, where the miners were puzzled and embittered to find that, having been in the highest-paid segment of the working class in pre-war days, and having been the industrial workers upon whom the British war effort had seemed to depend, they were now entrapped in a declining industry; and, of transient importance only, the fear that a government which in 1918 had adopted the war aims of the Labour movement might now involve the country in a war against Soviet Russia. Even the avowed British revolutionaries seem to have had little idea of how to turn these situations to revolutionary advantage: strong only in words, they were sometimes verbally joined by other working-class leaders whose moderate objectives were never really in doubt. However, the Lloyd George government was convinced of the reality of the Bolshevik threat; it was the Government, therefore, not the workers, which carried into practice the Marxist doctrine of the Class War.

The year 1919 opened with soldiers' demobilization riots, followed immediately by the forty-hour strike in Glasgow. The wartime Clyde strikes had been spontaneous and broad-based: now when the Clydeside workers' leaders called for a general strike on Monday 27 January, to press their very practical demand for a forty-hour week as a means of absorbing returning servicemen, they were fully supported in all the principal factories: three mass demonstrations took place on the 27th, the 29th and the 31st. The third the Government anticipated by concentrating troops, tanks and machine-guns on the city, though the actual 'Battle of George Square' was fought with policemen's truncheons and lemonade bottles.[16] On 1 February the tanks moved in upon the deserted battlefield: the strike continued for a further ten days. The Press was filled with all kinds of alarmist tales, though the Red Flag raised by the strikers was a symbol not of revolution but of working-class solidarity. The attitude of the Government was clearly phrased in Cabinet by Churchill:

The disaffected were in a minority, and, in his opinion, there would have to be a conflict in order to clear the air. We should be careful to have plenty of provocation before taking strong measures. By going gently at first we should get the support we wanted from the nation, and then troops could be used more effectively.[17]

A dozen of the leaders were arrested, but only against two could a successful charge be made out, and that scarcely implied any deep subversion of the established order: Willie Gallacher and Emmanuel Shinwell were imprisoned for 'inciting to riot'. Looking back ruefully many years later, Gallacher unwittingly exposed the reality of the situation: 'We were carrying on a strike when we ought to have been making a revolution.'[18] In fact nothing which had been published on the early history of the British Communist Party suggests that native British Communists had the faintest idea of how to set about having a revolution.[19] The Government, none the less, sent a secret military circular to all commanding officers in Britain asking whether their troops would respond to orders necessary for preserving public peace, and whether they would participate in strike-breaking.[20] A few days later a permanent anti-strike organization, in the form of committee of the Cabinet, was established, under the headship of Sir Hamar Greenwood, later the spearhead of British terror tactics in Ireland.[21]

The first of the post-war mining crises also broke in January 1919. The threat of a national miners' strike was averted by the appointment of a special Statutory Commission to investigate the condition of the coal industry. This commission, presided over by the Hon. Justice Sankey, consisted of four members appointed by the Government, four members appointed by the Miners' Federation of Great Britain, two members agreed between the Government and the miners (R. H. Tawney and Sidney Webb – both members of the Labour Party), and three members appointed by the coal-owners. During its hearings the commission, to an extent which clearly worried the leaders of private industry, powerfully reinforced the general case for nationalization, a large number of expert witnesses revealing clearly how the wartime experience had changed their thinking on this topic.[22] Yet the verdict finally presented in the form of four separate reports was only a degree or two clearer than mud. Sankey himself favoured State ownership: so did Tawney and Webb, acting in concert with the miners' representatives; the three mine-owners, together with two of the Government representatives, were categorically opposed to nationalization; the other government representative, Sir Arthur Duckham, advocated 'district unification'. Before going off to the Paris peace conference Lloyd George had seemed to be in favour of nationalization; on his return he appeared to be so preoccupied with international rather than domestic matters that he readily yielded to the chorus of hate his colleagues raised against the suggestion. What apparently weighed most with the Cabinet was Churchill's assurance that should the miners seek united trade union action through the 'Triple Alliance' of miners, railwaymen, and general workers, 'militarily' the Government was in a good position to fight.[23] Accordingly on 18 August Lloyd George announced his rejection of nationalization: this was not a scandalous disregard of the commission's hazy verdict – merely a stupid one. The miners were permanently alienated, though for the time being, it is true, they were unable to whip up enthusiasm for further strike action.

The limelight had passed to London and Liverpool, where for the second time within a year there were police strikes. Between Friday 1 August and Sunday 3 August there was extensive rioting in Liverpool as the lawless elements in that great seaport exploited the absence of the usual law enforcement officers. The riots may well be significant as showing how large a proportion of society remained indifferent to the principles of law and order, but they do not provide any evidence of revolutionary intentions on the part of organized labour.

The *Morning Post* reported:

After the first outbreak in the neighbourhood of the Rotunda Theatre, where a shop was attacked and looted, had been answered by the reading of the Riot Act, a body of soldiers fired a warning volley, pointing their rifles over the heads of the crowds. Thereafter they paraded the districts where the mob were threatening activity, without, however, actually interfering. Their passivity being cunningly sensed, no sooner were they out of reach than shop windows were smashed, and the law breakers, many of them young women, pressed forward to help themselves to the contents. Four tanks, which moved in yesterday to support the men of the Notts and Derby and the South Staffordshire Regiments who composed the occupying military force, stood silent sentinels on St George's Hall platform, while within a stone's throw away scenes of lawless effrontery were witnessed.[24]

Altogether 2,600 troops were brought in, as well as the four tanks, H.M.S. *Valiant* and two destroyers which stood off Liverpool port. After a round of shots one civilian died of wounds, and there were bayonet charges on the Sunday night. Despite its own careful eyewitness reports (corroborated in other newspapers) the *Morning Post* in its leading articles continued to assert that the Liverpool violence and the various minor strikes throughout the country could be explained only by the two words, 'attempted revolution'.[25]

Faced with a proposed cut in wages, the railwaymen, anxious like everyone else to safeguard the gains of the war period, called a national strike on 30 September. Before the strike began the Government had reconstituted the Cabinet Strike Committee, and had divided the country into twelve divisional areas, each with a Commissioner and Staff.[26] D.O.R.A. still being in force, a State of Emergency was declared immediately the strike broke out. On Friday 3 October the Home Secretary appealed to all citizens to join in the formation of 'Citizen Guards' 'in face of the menace by which we are confronted today'.[27] However, the railwaymen's case was essentially a reasonable one, and it was reinforced by a deputation of the Transport Workers' Federation, led by Arthur Henderson and J. R. Clynes, who were able to assert some of the influence which had accrued to them because of their participation in the political direction of the war. The strike ended on 5 October, when the Government, which still controlled the railways, decided to abandon this proposed wage cut.[28]

There were several other strikes of a similar nature; then, half-way through 1920, there came a series of events which seemed to indicate that Labour was prepared to use its industrial power to influence the foreign policy of His Majesty's duly elected Government. Two questions are involved: was this action 'potentially revolutionary'[29] and did it have any effect? The object once again was a concrete one: to stop Britain being involved in a war on behalf of Poland against Soviet Russia. Unconstitutional perhaps, but a very different thing from aiming at the overthrow of established government. Indeed, although windbags like J. H. Thomas might like to stress the seriousness of Labour's intentions by talking of a 'challenge to the whole Constitution of the country', the term 'unconstitutional' is scarcely really relevant: decisions in modern British society are made as much through the pressure of relevant interest groups, such as the Federation of British Industries or the medical profession, as by appeal to abstract constitutional theory. Did it have any effect? The first event was the refusal on 10 May 1920 of a gang of London dockers to coal the *Jolly George,* believing it to be carrying munitions bound for Poland. The incident does not seem to have disturbed the Cabinet, which was absorbed on 10 May in Coal Prices, the Amritsar Massacre and the Mural Decoration of the Foreign Office, and, on 12 May, in Ireland, India, Turkey and Asphyxiating Gas.[30] On Sunday 8 August a series of Labour demonstrations against the possibility of British intervention on behalf of Poland were organized, followed on 9 August by the setting up of a Council of Action to implement a joint Labour Party-T.U.C. decision to use 'the whole industrial power of the organized workers' against war.[31] There was in fact no British intervention against Russia. But the Cabinet papers for the period between the *Jolly George* incident and the final Labour outburst make it clear that whatever Labour thought or did the Government was by no means hell-bent on supporting Poland. All that the Labour agitation, in conjunction with that of the Asquith Liberals and sections of the Press, achieved was the strengthening of the hand of the Government in its dealings with the French, who were much more belligerent on this issue.[32] In a conference with the French which took place during the same weekend as the first Labour demonstrations, Lloyd George stressed that

the working classes were frankly hostile to intervention and this view was shared by Conservative opinion, as was clearly indicated in the Press.[33]

By 10 August any danger of intervention was really over, for the
Cabinet decided that the Russian terms for an armistice with the
Poles were reasonable, and since 'Labour was in a very irritable
frame of mind at present', a disavowal of any interventionist intentions might be issued.[34] That the trade union movement has
not since contemplated action of quite the same type is not so
much because it has meantime become less revolutionary, but
because it now has other means of asserting its power.

In October the miners and the unemployed jumped almost
simultaneously back into the headlines. To meet the still rising
cost of living, the miners went on strike briefly, and successfully,
to secure a 2s. increase per shift. When, at the height of the crisis,
a strike of the entire Triple Alliance seemed likely, the Government, though refusing permission to the Chief of the Imperial
General Staff to move troops into the mining areas, reassumed
through the Emergency Powers Act the totalitarian authority
which it had possessed during the war.[35] More violent, though
less serious, was the first major post-war incident involving the
unemployed, known to history as the Battle of Downing Street.
A deputation of London mayors led by George Lansbury, with the
workless marching behind in their thousands, had demanded an
interview with Lloyd George to discuss the unemployment problem in their boroughs. A peaceable demonstration erupted into
violence when the police suddenly decided to clear Whitehall by
means of mounted baton charges, which caused many ugly incidents.[36] Throughout 1921 there were further violent scenes
associated with the unemployed. Yet although a headship to the
agitation was given by the Communist-sponsored National
Unemployed Workmen's Movement, the demands made were
always specific and practical, so that when open conflict with the
police did break out it was usually over the elementary right of
the unemployed to free assembly, or, in some instances, over the
slightly more ambitious demand for a meeting hall in which to
ventilate their grievances.[37] Presented with organized action on the
part of the unemployed, successive governments steadily expanded
the benefits and conditions of the Unemployment Insurance
scheme; the National Health Insurance scheme meantime lan-

guished, there being no organized body to press for changes in it.

On 31 March crisis again came to the coal industry. As government control ended the coal-owners posted new terms, which in most cases involved substantial wage cuts for the miners; for with the first shipments of Germany's reparation payments in coal Britain's export market, which had been enjoying a feverish and unreal boom, collapsed. The miners, cheated, as they believed, of nationalization, argued strongly for a national wages agreement drawing upon a national wages pool, so that the relatively prosperous mines could subsidize the uneconomic ones; determined upon the total return to unrestricted private enterprise, the owners would have none of this. The *Daily Herald* published tables of what the owners' terms meant in practice. Cuts were particularly heavy in South Wales (also in North Wales, the Forest of Dean, the North-East, and Scotland):

present average per week		*owners' offer*		*reduction*	
Colliers	£4 9s. 3d.	£2 13s. 6½d.		£1 15s. 8½d.	
Hauliers	£4 0s. 9d.	£2 5s. 9d.		£1 15s.	
Labourers	£3 13s. 11½d.	£1 18s. 11½d.		£1 15s.	[38]

That in citing such figures, as it continued to do throughout the crisis, the *Herald* in addition always made reference to the miners' pre-war wage is a revealing commentary on how the attitude of the miners was conditioned by the relative prosperity they had formerly enjoyed. That the coal-owners could unilaterally plan such Draconian cuts in the living standards of their workers is a still more revealing commentary on their adherence to the master–man concept of the early Industrial Revolution. The issue was first of all one of wages, with the owners determined to pass the whole burden of the depression in the British coal industry on to the miners, and the miners arguing that through national agreement (and, if need be, national reorganization) existing standards could be maintained. Declaring that the attack on their standards was merely a prelude to a general attack on working-class living standards, the miners felt justified in again expecting the support of the Triple Alliance. So in a sense the ground was laid for clear confrontation between Capital and Labour, to take place outside the constitutional parliamentary framework; but again the objectives were specific and limited. If from time to time exuberant working-class leaders spoke a language which sounded revolutionary, their phrases always, on examination, proved to have relevance only to immediate economic claims or, at most, to be a response to the many provocative actions of the Government. It is in this context that the famous remark of the miners' secretary Frank Hodges must be placed:

When the country knew that the Government was adopting such tactics, then the leash which checked revolutionary action would be loosed and there would be upheaval and rebellion.[39]

Quite possibly the only long-term answer to the problems of the mining industry was a ruthless rationalization involving the retraining of many miners for other industries; equally possibly a thoroughly modernized, highly productive mining industry producing for the domestic industrial market could have provided a vital stimulus to the flagging British economy. But only an enlightened ownership, or a strong government, could have carried out either programme. In the meantime it was clear to many observers, some far from the Labour camp, that the miners had a reasonable case, and that that case had nothing to do with revolution. As the Labour correspondent of the *Daily Express* percipiently remarked:

One thing should be made clear. The issue at present is wholly industrial. The trouble is over wages and nothing else. Questions of political and constitutional policy have not yet entered into the matter. The movement at present is not a 'Red' one – but the manner of its development depends on circumstances.[40]

Later, at a Cabinet presided over – in the absence of Lloyd George – by Austen Chamberlain, 'misgivings' were expressed over the way the crisis had been brought about by sudden wage cuts:

During the war the miners had shown that they were immensely patriotic, and it would be a calamity if Labour generally obtained the impression that the Government was siding in this matter with the employers.[41]

Unhappily every Cabinet meeting which Lloyd George himself presided over furnished further evidence to support the conviction long held within the Labour movement that he was their Public Enemy Number One.

Immediately upon the commencement of the coal strike, and long before any decisions had been taken in regard to joint action by the Triple Alliance, the Government, under the terms of the Act of 1920, declared a State of Emergency.

Through lobby correspondents, the Cabinet allowed it to be known that the mining strike was to be treated as 'the gravest menace the country has had to face since war was declared' and the miners' action 'as the first move in a deliberate challenge to constitutional government'. On Monday 4 April the Cabinet discussed the disposition and availability of the armed forces, authorized the Secretary of State for War to prepare for the mobilization of the Territorials and the call-up of the Army Reserve, and appointed a sub-committee to consider the idea of creating a special force of 'loyal ex-servicemen and loyal citizens'.[42] That evening the first Order in Council under the Emergency provided for government control, if necessary, of land, food, coal-mines, traffic and supplies, and for the prohibition of the buying and selling of firearms and the holding of public meetings. Approval for the special Defence Force was given at a 'Conference of Ministers' on 6 April, though the meeting at which the leaders of the Triple Alliance agreed to sympathetic action on behalf of the miners did not take place till 8 April. Now a second Royal Proclamation called out the Army Reserve, Class B of the Royal Fleet Reserve and the Air Force Reserve, and plans for the new Defence Units to be attached to the Regular Army for 'temporary military service not exceeding ninety days' were announced.[43] Over the succeeding weekend enrolment of the Defence Units began, encampments being formed in parks, on the outskirts of the main cities, and in disused military camps. The following week there were movements of troops, transports and tanks, while troops equipped with machine-guns moved in on the Fife coalfield. Military manœuvres in the coalfields were brought about less because of the threat of a Triple Alliance strike than as a reaction to the miners' insistence that the safety men, whose responsibility it was to keep the mines from being flooded, should also join the strike: this was the miners' strongest card, and where managerial staff remained behind to man the pumps they were liable to attack from angry strikers; serious rioting broke out in Lanarkshire, Fife and South Wales.[44]

The Triple Alliance strike was set for midnight of Tuesday 12 April, unless, as J. H. Thomas and a deputation of railwaymen and transport workers put it to the Prime Minister, negotiations with the miners were resumed. The Triple Alliance case was this:

We are not proclaiming a revolution, we are standing shoulder to shoulder for fundamental trade union rights. If these are denied to us now they will be denied to the whole of the trade union movement later. The fight must be won; it will be won; British trade unionism will triumph against the united effort of British organized capital in its attempt to destroy the trade union achievements, legitimately gained by years of hard work and sacrifice.[45]

Thus pressured, the Government did in fact institute negotiations with the owners and the miners, and the Triple Alliance strike was called off. But there remained the basic stumbling-block of the question of a National Agreement on miners' wages, something for which Lloyd George had by now conceived an almost pathological hatred: 'the national pool,' he told his colleagues, 'merely signified control in a most virulent form.'[46] With the breakdown of negotiations on this issue the Triple Alliance strike was rescheduled for midnight on Friday 15 April. But instead of being a day of triumph for British trade unionism, 'Black Friday' saw the collapse of the attempt at united action. The reason was twofold: the proposed strike, despite all government endeavours to label it a 'general strike', was essentially a sympathetic strike, which meant that it had no organized central direction and no clear decision on whether the battle was to be fought on terms considered acceptable to the miners, or terms thought reasonable by the supporting members of the Triple Alliance, for increasingly the railwaymen's and the transport workers' leaders became alarmed at the prospect of granting the miners *carte blanche*. These leaders, secondly, were essentially men of moderate outlook who were unduly sensitive to the theoretically unconstitutional implications of a strike which went beyond the confines of one grievance in one industry. Out of a meeting of Coalition M.P.s on 14 April, attended by Frank Hodges, there emerged a possible compromise which Lloyd George immediately seized upon: on the fatal Friday he offered the miners a temporary arrangement on wages, provided the National Agreement question was shelved. The Triple Alliance leaders urged the miners to discuss this proposal. The miners, who felt that they had been duped once too often by Lloyd George, refused. The Triple Alliance leaders cancelled the strike. The miners fought on alone, finally on 1 July being forced back to work, to local agreements and, in most areas, to substantial cuts in wages.

Recruitment to the Defence Units, after a slow start, was meantime proceeding apace; it was suspended on 18 April when the total force numbered 70,000, with a further 10,000 men registered.[47] Among the recruits were many ex-officers, many university students, many disgruntled members of the middle classes alarmed by the uppishness of the workers, and also, to point the tragic humour of the whole episode, many striking miners.[48] At the Old Bailey on 8 April, the Recorder of London (Sir Forrest Fulton, K.C.), in binding over a defendant said to have served in the Air Force, remarked:

I entertain very grave doubts as to whether I ought not to send you to prison. I am influenced by the fact that we are living in a very perilous time and that your services may, for all I know, within the next few days be again required by His Majesty. The present condition of things is very alarming, and we may require the services of such men as you to defend the country against a foe perhaps quite as serious as the Germans whom we spent four years in fighting; therefore I cannot but be reluctant to send you to prison, where you would be of no kind of use to His Majesty.[49]

Ian Hay, one of the more egregious authors of the mushy accounts of the Western Front which had proliferated during the war, stressed the similarity of the mining crisis to that of August 1914:

This week the country has been confronted by a situation equally grave. Once again the appeal has gone out, and today we have another hundred thousand in being – a new hundred thousand. Here they are encamped all over the country – and here they seem likely to remain for a while. The threatened general strike, it is true, has collapsed, but there is plenty of trouble left to go on with. The miners are out for a fight to the finish. It may be a long and bitter fight. And behind the dust – the coal dust – of this particular conflict other forces are at work. Unemployment and unrest are widespread, and there is a tendency here and there towards sabotage and 'direct action'. Naturally the professional mischief-makers are taking advantage of the situation to ply their furtive trade and exploit honest hot-heads. Inflammatory speeches are being made and seditious literature circulated in every favourable district. It is just as well, then, that the forces of law and order should be mobilized and equipped to protect all of us – both the just and the unjust – from sudden upheaval. That is why the defence force was embodied. That is why they will carry on until the hot-heads have come to themselves again and the mischief-makers have been relegated to their holes.[50]

Against this kind of attitude, and such statements as that of Lloyd George on 8 April that 'the country is facing a situation analagous to civil war'[51] can be put the fumblings and hesitations of the Triple Alliance, which resulted in their strike being twice called and twice called off.

Given the slump conditions, it is not surprising that strikes in various other industries during 1922 were unsuccessful in resisting wage cuts; it should be remembered, too, that along with wages the cost of living was dropping from the post-war peak. At the end of 1922 the Labour Party began to show signs of shaking itself out of the lethargy which had afflicted it since 1918. There was a steady drop in the incidence of strikes. The centre of militant working-class activity tended, therefore, to move back to the unemployed. On Armistice Day 1922, 25,000 London unemployed tacked themselves on the official ceremony, carrying at their head a large wreath inscribed: 'From the living victims – the unemployed – to our dead comrades, who died in vain.'[52] It was at the end of 1922 that the first Hunger Marches began, organized by Wal Hannington in the South and by Harry McShane in Scotland. Again there was no lack among the prosperous classes of people prepared to see in marches, demonstrations and 'Unemployed

Sundays' the sinister hand of revolutionary intent: references to unemployed marches in *The Times* are indexed during the Twenties under the heading 'Russia: government propaganda'. Members of the National Unemployed Workers' Committee Movement took an oath 'to never cease from active strife against this system until capitalism is abolished, and our country and all its resources belong to the people'.[53] But the active Communist element remained a minority among the unemployed, and the unemployed themselves were to some extent cut off from their fellow workers lucky enough to be employed. In any event Hannington, McShane and their associates seem to have concentrated their energies on specific abuses within the administration of the unemployment insurance scheme and within the Poor Law (which concerned those who did not qualify for insurance or who had exhausted their benefits). Rates of poor relief were at the discretion of the local Boards of Guardians: the N.U.W.C.M. directed its fire at the niggardly ones, while the more generous ones, such as the Poplar Board, ran foul of middle-class opinion. In protest against the heavy burden being imposed on borough rates and against the attempt of the Government to control expenditure on poor relief, George Lansbury and the Poplar Council refused to pay their precept to the London County Council. The thirty councillors were imprisoned for over a month, but, as did some of the protests of the unemployed, their gesture brought its reward: an Act was passed spreading the costs of relief more equitably over London as a whole.[54]

The first Labour Government came and went. Unemployment remained above the $1\frac{1}{2}$ million mark. In 1925 came the return to the Gold Standard, and with it a resuscitation of all the bitter conflicts within the coal industry. As a consequence of a brief revival of prosperity during the French occupation of the Ruhr, the miners had gained an increased 'addition' to their standard wage. On the last day of June, less than two months after the return to the Gold Standard, the owners announced the abolition of the 'addition'. Again, rather than accept a cut in wages the miners turned to strike action. There was no longer a Triple Alliance, but, instead, thanks to the efforts of some of the newer trade union leaders, particularly Ernest Bevin, the General Council of the Trades Union Congress, founded in 1920 in place of the old Parliamentary Committee of the T.U.C., and itself a product of Labour's high mood of confidence at the end of the war, had meantime grown in strength and wisdom.[55] It promised the miners its support in their 'resistance to the degradation of the standard of life of their members', and ordered an embargo on the movement of coal as soon as the miners went on strike at midnight on Friday 21 July. In contrast to the feverish activity of the Lloyd George ministry, the Baldwin government was scarcely prepared for this demonstration of working-class solidarity, and so felt forced to intervene. In order that existing wages could be maintained meantime, it undertook to subsidize the industry while a Commission of Inquiry under Sir Herbert Samuel investigated the whole problem of wages and costs. Labour now had a victorious 'Red Friday' with which to try to expunge memories of the humiliating 'Black Friday'.

Baldwin undoubtedly had some sympathy with the plight of the miners, but he also shared something of the continuing upper-class fear of working-class insurrection:

I am convinced that if the time should come when the community had to protect itself, with the full strength of the Government behind it, the community will do so, and the response of the community will astonish the forces of anarchy throughout the world. I say it merely as a warning.[56]

To make the warning meaningful the Government brought back into working order the anti-strike organization which had originally been conceived in face of the industrial troubles at the end of the war, and which had had a skeleton existence ever since. No special Defence Units were recruited, but the Government offered its blessing to the privately-sponsored Organization for the Maintenance of Supplies, which, though it had no military role, was drawn largely from the same groups as had joined the Defence Units. If the Government felt it necessary to justify these moves, it had only to turn to the speeches of the fiery miners' leader, A. J. Cook. Of Cook it was once said, unkindly but not altogether unfairly,

'Before he gets up he has no idea what he is going to say; when he's on his feet he has no idea what he is saying; and when he sits down he has no idea what he has just said.' Referring to the government subsidy, Cook declared, 'Take it from me there would otherwise have been a revolution. I fear there will be trouble next May.'[57] Like other British 'revolutionaries' of the period Cook combined a mystical faith in the might of the working class with a complete disregard for any kind of revolutionary planning and an even more complete disregard of the necessary role of weapon-power in any successful revolution:

I don't care a hang for any government, or army or navy. They can come along with their bayonets. Bayonets don't cut coal. We have already beaten not only the employers, but the strongest government in modern times.[58]

On 14 October a raid was conducted on the headquarters of the Communist Party and on the houses of twelve of its leading members. How closely related this was to preparations for the impending coal crisis is difficult to say: five were sentenced to a year's imprisonment, which certainly kept them out of circulation over the period when trouble was to be expected, but the other seven received six months' imprisonment, which meant that they were released in good time for the commencement of the General Strike. But in any case if the Communist Party had any clear idea of how the coal crisis was to be converted into a revolution, no one has ever revealed the faintest hint of what it was. What was more important was that the General Council of the T.U.C., having notched up its initial victory, now sat back in the complacent hope that the Commission would come up with some acceptable solution. The Commission reported in March, giving little joy either to owners or miners. Stressing the parlous economic state of the industry, it recommended a two-stage operation. As an immediate remedy for the 'disaster ... impending over the industry' the miners must accept cuts in wages; but the long-term problem could only finally be solved by a sweeping reorganization.

Four parties were involved in the General Strike. In the forefront were the miners, who were fighting against cuts in wages and for reorganization of the industry and the principle of national wage agreements, and the coal-owners, determined to impose cuts and to resist reorganization and the national wage principle. Behind miners stood the remainder of the British trade union movement, represented for this purpose by the Industrial Committee of the General Council of the T.U.C.: as in 1921, the members of this committee could see that the miners' cause was the cause of all British trade unionists, but, also as in 1921, they were chary of action which could be labelled unconstitutional and, above all, of giving the miners *carte blanche*. In a dangerous situation of this sort, responsibility for decisive action lay fairly and squarely with the fourth party, the Government. It is true that the Baldwin ministry persevered right up till the last with round after round of discussions with the other three parties, but in so far as it made no attempt to impose the recommendations of the Samuel Commission upon the principals it was favouring the economically stronger party, the owners, and accepting the class-war thesis (of which Lloyd George, formerly, and Baldwin's own right-wing colleagues in 1926, were leading exponents) that a show-down with Labour was inevitable and necessary. In this sense the Baldwin ministry itself invited the General Strike.

On Saturday 1 May miners everywhere, refusing to accept the new wage cuts, were out on strike. The Executive Committees of the various separate unions now met and agreed to hand their powers over to the T.U.C. General Council. This was the first real preparation which the unions made for a national strike – two days before it began. What, anyway, did the decision mean? Did it entrust to the General Council powers to negotiate on behalf of the miners, or did it mean that the General Council had to fight things out till a settlement acceptable to the miners was reached? The miners believed the latter, the General Council the former. No one noticed at the time, but it was the same difference of interpretation that had caused 'Black Friday'. Satisfied that everything was in train for a national strike, the miners' representatives left London. This created an unfortunate delay when the General Council, still locked in last-minute conclave with the Government, wished to consult the miners on a new compromise proposal. None the less channels between the Government and the Industrial Committee still seemed open late into the night of Sunday 2 May. Then news reached the Cabinet that the *Daily Mail* printers, acting on their own account, had refused to print an editorial describing the threatened strike as a 'revolutionary movement'. On this pretext the Government broke off the negotiations which the General Council were only too anxious to continue: it thus precipitated the General Strike as an actual event, commencing at midnight on 3 May.[59]

From the trade union point of view three characteristics stand out from the nine days of general strike. Since all the classes of workers that the General Council called out did in fact come out, it was a successful demonstration of working-class solidarity in the cause of the miners. Given the complete lack of any advance planning, the relatively successful organization of the strike was a tribute to the improvisational qualities of both national and local trade union leaders. Thirdly, in the minds of the members of the General Council of the T.U.C. there was no question of a direct challenge to the British Constitution. As the *British Worker*, the news-sheet brought out to counterbalance the Government's *British Gazette*, reiterated, 'The General Council *does not* challenge the constitution'; it was 'engaged solely in an industrial dispute'; 'there is no constitutional crisis'.[60] Left-wing political activists, who were only too keen to participate in the running of the strike, were resolutely kept out.[61] For the community as a whole, the days passed remarkably uneventfully, partly because of the untypically benign weather, but not completely uneventfully – stories of policemen and strikers playing football together (and why shouldn't they, given the essentially limited objectives of the strikers?) have been allowed to obscure the fact that in many places there were repetitions of the Battle of Downing Street type of incident which had been endemic between police and workers in 1920 and 1921.[62]

Successful within its limits, the strike posed the General Council the same problem that had faced the Chartists after their great Convention of 1839, the problem which must always face a weak party in conflict with a strong one: 'What do we do now?' The General Council had hoped all along that it would not become involved in a strike; once in, it hoped that such chaos would be created so quickly that the Government would be forced to reopen negotiations. Worried by the drain on trade union funds, and by arguments that their action was unconstitutional (in the House of Commons Sir John Simon announced that under the Trade Disputes Act of 1906 a general strike was illegal[63] and, despite the fact that Sir John was speaking through a hole in the back of his neck, trade union leaders were impressed), the moderate trade union leaders were anxious to find some middle man who could reopen negotiations without too much loss of face for the unions. That man was Sir Herbert Samuel. Acting entirely on his own initiative Samuel prepared, as a possible basis for a settlement, a précis of the Royal Commission report, usually referred to as the Samuel Memorandum. The Government, insisting upon unconditional surrender, would give no undertaking in respect of the Memorandum, and the miners rejected it outright; none the less so anxious were the T.U.C. leaders to see the strike ended that they unilaterally declared the memorandum an acceptable basis for bringing the strike to a close. Officially the General Strike ended on 12 May; but realization that no real concessions had been gained on behalf of the miners and bitterness over attempted victimization by employers brought a second spontaneous General Strike on 13 May, involving more men than had the nine days' strike.[64] In the few days of the second strike there were manifestations of bitter class feeling. 'Here,' Professor Mowat has written, 'smouldered the fire of possible violence and civil war'[65] – save only, however, that the violence was uncanalized, the men leaderless.

The General Strike was not so much a defeat for the organized working class (the strike was not of its seeking) as a victory for the class-war doctrines of right-wing Conservatives. The Baldwin government without doubt was entitled to the credit which it claimed in the aftermath of the strike, except that it had completely lost sight of the vital quantity at the base of the crisis: any hope of redeeming the economic chaos and virulent industrial relations rampant in the British coal-mining industry had gone for good. Within the trade union movement disillusionment with the collapse of the strike, combined, in all probability, with pressure from employers, produced a sharp fall in membership, which in 1927 stood at less than 5 millions for the first time since 1916.

Besides these considerations, the Trades Disputes Act enacted by the Government after the strike, though a source of political controversy and bitterness to activists in the Labour movement, was probably of less significance. The Act declared general strikes illegal (convincing evidence that previously they were *not* illegal) and altered the basis of the trade union contribution to the finances of the Labour Party: the individual trade unionist now had to 'contract in' to payment of the political levy instead of 'contracting out' if he did not want to pay it. Apathy was no longer on the side of the angels, and Labour Party funds naturally dropped. None the less it is difficult to prove that the party suffered drastic damage: it was not, after all, prevented from winning its major victory in 1945.

Working-class history since the war had not been characterized by concerted, coherent militant action. The many sporadic outbursts that there had been were due to the way in which the high hopes of the war period were disappointed and the main burdens of adverse economic circumstances were passed directly on to the workers. The General Strike was not different in kind from a number of similar incidents in the coal industry: in fact it was 'Black Friday' all over again, save for the intrudent nine days, forced by the Government's mishandling of the situation and kept in being by the deep class loyalties of the British working class. Most of the leading trade unionists had little sympathy with the notion of a general strike; the events of 1926 confirmed them in this feeling. It was those members of the Labour movement, like James Maxton of the I.L.P., who saw the strike as a beginning rather than as an ending, who now began to lose touch with the mainstream of Labour thinking. In the late Twenties there developed a movement towards industrial co-operation, associated with the talks held between Sir Alfred Mond, for management, and Ben Turner for the T.U.C. Thus, after the dislocations of the first post-war years, there was something of a resumption of the wartime trend towards social harmony. At the same time Ernest Bevin, who was now clearly emerging as the greatest trade union leader of his generation, reached a decision which could have great potential influence in improving the lot of the working classes: he decided that, instead of undertaking independent, and futile, industrial action, the T.U.C. must exert a more direct influence on the Labour Party.[66]

3. POST-WAR SOCIETY

The depression in the coal-mining and in the other old heavy industries created a new population drift, away from the areas which in 1914 held the main concentrations of industrial power, towards the south-east where the new light, science-based industries were to be found. While the population of London and the Home Counties increased by 18 per cent between 1921 and 1937, that of the Midland Counties increased by only 11 per cent, that of the West Riding, Notts and Derbyshire by only 6 per cent, the Lowlands of Scotland by only 4 per cent (although the Scottish birth rate was higher than the English) and that of Lancashire by less than 1 per cent. The population of South Wales declined by 9 per cent, and that of Northumberland and Durham by 1 per cent.[67] London and its motorized traffic problem had caused concern before the war, and it already had its extensive environs inhabited by 'suburbans'; but it was in the Twenties that the great development of the major commuter areas such as Hendon, Morden and Wembley began, so that the total population of Greater London rose to over 8 millions. Before the war it was London with its sweated trades which housed the most downtrodden, poverty-stricken elements in the community, while the miners and the skilled workers in the heavy industries had been the most prosperous members of the working classes. Now a new pattern established itself: a prosperous, bustling South producing a tremendous range of new consumer goods; and a decaying North.

Britain in the 1920s, as the industrial history of the decade makes abundantly clear, was very much a class-conscious society. None the less there were striking variations from the structure that had obtained before 1914. At the top the landed class, which had been the dominant component of the political *élite* of Edwardian times, moved into political, though by no means economic and social, eclipse. Much attention, in the first years of peace, was focused on the extensive land sales which took place: 'England is changing hands' became a piece of standard journalese. By March 1919 about half a million acres were on the market, and by the end of the year over a million acres had been sold. In 1920 sales were still greater, the Duke of Rutland leading the field with the sale of about half of his Belvoir estate, 28,000 acres in all, for £1½ million. It was claimed by one firm of estate agents that within a single year land equal in area to an English county had passed through their hands. In part these sales were simply the continuation of a policy initiated at the beginning of the century whereby the land-owner sought to consolidate his income by selling off outlying holdings; financial impoverishment was not necessarily involved. At the same time high taxation, introduced before 1914 but greatly extended during and at the end of the war, did force some of the sales. Landowners were also influenced by the fact that, because of wartime exploitation of agriculture, land values had greatly risen, while rents had not; by selling, the landowner could put the increased value into his pocket. Economically, therefore, the position of the landowner was far from being as serious as the columns of the society newspapers suggested: indeed their incomes were often healthier than they had been for many years. But their great landed empires were curtailed and their feudal dominance over the countryside was almost at an end, as their own tenants took the opportunity presented by the land sales to set themselves up as owner-farmers. Urban land was sold as well as country estates, clearing a path for the small domestic landlord and for a new type of property developer, whose interest in West End theatres was so much deplored by theatre men of the old school. Now that the upkeep of large establishments was becoming so difficult, town houses were often sold also; aristocratic high society was being pushed back from the centre of the London political stage.[68] Landed society was even being manœuvred from the centres of local power, as the cult of the expert, fostered during the war, began to take over from that of the aristocratic amateur.[69]

The new balance of political power within the upper class was symbolized by the passing over of Lord Curzon in favour of the 'countrified businessman' Stanley Baldwin for the Prime Ministership in 1922, and by the establishment in the same year of the influential 1922 Committee of Conservative back-benchers, most of them businessmen. It was, naturally, a matter of deep regret to aristocrats like Lord Henry Bentick who believed that the Conservative Party was being 'thoroughly commercialized and vulgarized', and Plutocracy 'ennobled, decorated, knighted and enriched'.[70] The upper class, then, was still, as in Edwardian times, a composite class, but primacy had slipped from the hands of the landed interest into those of the businessmen. This was the class which occupied the literary attentions of Aldous Huxley and John Galsworthy, indefatigable chronicler of the continuing fortunes of the Victorian business family, the Forsytes. Making a not very funny joke at the expense of social investigators who talked of the 10 per cent below the poverty line, Galsworthy said that he was concerned only with the 10 per cent above the property line.[71] The gay high-life of the 'roaring Twenties' was the creation of the sons and daughters of this privileged class. Yet if inequality in the division of income and wealth was still very marked, it was not quite as great as before the war: in 1910 1·1 per cent of the population took 30 per cent of the income; in 1929 1·5 per cent took 23 per cent of the income, and two-thirds of the wealth was owned by 2½ per cent of the population. Bowley and Stamp, in their analysis of the national income as it was in 1924, pointed out that, while in 1911 individuals with incomes above £5,000 drew 8 per cent of the aggregate national income, in 1924 those earning £9,500 (the equivalent, given the rise in prices between 1914 and 1924) drew only 5½ per cent. They then proceeded to a very cautious summing-up:

When the full effects of taxation are taken into account the real income available for saving or expenditure in the hands of the rich is definitely less than before the war. The sum devoted to luxurious spending is (allowing for the rise of prices) definitely less than in 1911, but it is still sufficient to bulk large in the eyes of the public, since it is concentrated in small areas, enlarged by the spending of visitors from overseas and advertised by the newspapers.[72]

Moving to the middle classes, the most significant fact is the increase in the salaried class. In 1911 less than 1·7 million were included under this heading, while in 1921 the figure was over 2·7 millions, an increase from 12 per cent to 22 per cent of the occupied population.[73] Itself a social phenomenon of outstanding importance, this increase reflected the growth of four important groups within the community: the professions, for whom rising material and welfare standards brought a new demand; the Civil Servants and clerical administrators needed by the growing bureaucracy; the managerial class required for the running of large-scale modern industry; and those women who held on to the opportunities opened to them during the war (in 1931 there were 5½ million women in employment, 37 per cent of the female population between 14 and 65). The other noteworthy feature is the decline in servant-keeping among middle-class households, often exaggerated, but none the less real. Despite the opinions expressed by various observers during and at the end of the war, many women were forced back into this occupation as the munitions factories closed down. But the overall decrease which appears in the statistics mainly came out of middle-class households. In the commuter areas of London the number of resident servants per 100 families declined from 24·1 to 12·4, whereas in the essentially upper-class West End it only moved from 57·3 to 41·3. In the whole of Liverpool the decline was from 13·5 to 8·3; in suburban Wallasey from 22·4 to 14·5.[74]

The decline in servant-keeping helped to weaken the barriers between the middle and lower classes. In the year 1919–20 the 'tax line' had all but disappeared, for there were 7¾ million tax-paying citizens, six times the number in 1914, though this total fell again when the exemption limit was shortly raised to £150 per annum. When Bowley conducted a second social survey in 1924 with the express purpose of finding out whether working-class poverty had diminished since 1913, the problems of deciding which were working-class households and which were not had subtly changed:

In general, our principle has been 'when in doubt, rule out'. In the previous inquiry the inclination seems rather to have been the other way.[75]

Definition by instinct has become a little more difficult, but the feeling is that the clearly definable working class has got a little smaller. This feeling is borne out by the figures in the 1921 census: the total number in the 'wage-earner' category, the main core of the working class, has fallen to under 15 millions, other variables being at least cancelled out by the increase in the population. The working class in 1914 was large and it was poor. In the Twenties it was not quite so large and it was not quite so poor. Referring to his earlier pronouncement that 'to raise the wages of the worst-paid workers is the most pressing social task with which the country is confronted today', Bowley continued:

It has needed a war to do it, but that task has been accomplished, so far as rates of wages are concerned, though employment has not been permanently possible for all at those rates.[76]

For many, in the Twenties, the second part of this somewhat laconic utterance was more significant than the first. Real wages for full-time employment were up by 20 per cent, the average working week down from fifty-five hours to forty-eight hours. But in certain areas there was continuous unemployment on an unprecedented scale. Where 11 per cent of the families in Bowley's previous survey had been in primary poverty, the new wage rates should have reduced this figure to 3·6 per cent: because of unemployment the actual figure was 6·5 per cent. In the mining village of Stanley, where in the boom conditions of 1913 6 per cent of the families had been in primary poverty, the figure was now 7·5 per cent.[77] Bowley's standard, having been formulated before the war, was an extremely bare one; the new generation of social commentators talked rather in terms of 10 per cent of the population (not just the working classes) being below the 'poverty line',[78] which was not always clearly defined.

The ideas of State responsibility for the poorer sections of community had received a considerable setback since the high days of talk of a 'fit land for heroes to live in'. None the less the social services continued to be elaborated, in a manner which was still piecemeal, but which yet went well beyond what Edwardian

orthodoxy would have considered fit or proper. Against the fundamental menace to social security, mass unemployment, no government had any effective defence. Palliatives only, in the form of
unemployment insurance, were available. As a result of the
legislation of 1920 and 1921 the unemployed man (if he had made
twelve contributions) received 15s. a week for himself, 5s. a week
for his wife and 1s. for each child, for a period of fifteen weeks,
followed by a 'gap' (originally five weeks, later three weeks) after
which he could claim 'extended benefit' for a further five weeks
(later raised to twelve weeks) at the same rates, when a 'gap' again
intervened. For a man who failed to qualify, or lost his qualification, who had no savings to supplement his benefits or take him
through the gaps, there remained the Poor Law. At the beginning of
1921 the Labour Party unsuccessfully proposed in Parliament the
abolition of the workers' contribution to unemployment insurance
(leaving the entire burden to be borne by employers and the State)
and at the end of the same year it demonstrated against the
niggardly dependants' allowances.[79] In its nine months' spell of
office in 1924 Labour was no more successful than any other
government in solving the basic economic problems underlying
unemployment, and, although it raised benefits to 18s. and abolished
the 'gap', it made no fundamental alterations in the structure of
unemployment insurance. On the Right, where the phrase 'the
dole' was coined, there was criticism of a scheme held to be lavish
and demoralizing. Shortly after their return to office the Conservatives appointed a departmental committee, under Lord Blanesburgh, to study the problem of unemployment insurance.[80] In
evidence before this committee the Labour Party and the T.U.C.
jointly put forward two sets of recommendations, one ideal, one
immediate. The ideal recommendations were that the unemployed
should be paid full maintenance, the entire cost should be borne
by the State, and the Poor Law should be abolished. The immediate programme involved raising benefits to 20s. per week, a
further extension of the classes covered by unemployment insurance (without, however, there being any question of the middle
classes as a whole being brought in), the replacement of extended
benefit by continuous benefit paid as of right, a reduction in the

employee's contributions and an increase in those of the Exchequer, and, finally, the establishment of training centres for the unemployed.[81] The Committee, which included one Labour representative, Margaret Bondfield, did recommend the replacement of 'extended benefit', by 'transitional benefit', claimable as of right for an unlimited period, provided only the claimant demonstrate once every three months that he had formerly been in good standing in terms of contributions; but it also recommended reductions in standard benefits from 18s. to 17s. Against the opposition once again of the parliamentary Labour Party these recommendations were enacted towards the end of 1927, and they governed the operation of unemployment insurance till the scheme was recast in 1934. The Blanesburgh Committee forcibly expressed the Victorian reaction of the rate-paying classes to the spectre of 'Poplarism':

We understand that the poor law Acts and regulations made thereunder prohibit, except in special cases, the unconditional outdoor relief of able-bodied persons, and although the Minister of Health has found it necessary, during the extreme post-war depression, to assent to a widespread use of regulations permitting unconditional relief in special cases, we think, both from the point of view of the parties to the unemployment insurance and on general grounds, that in so far as it deals with the able-bodied unemployed, poor law relief should retain the deterrent effect which now attaches to it, or may be applied thereto.[82]

Here was the authentic Gladstonian voice, appropriate to the middle of the previous century, but a poor guide in the world of the 1920s. Under the provisions of the Local Government Act of 1929 the separately-elected office of Poor Law guardian was abolished, but the transfer of Poor Law functions to Public Assistance Committees of the local authorities represented a change which was of greater administrative than social significance. Even in the 1930s there were individual instances of able-bodied men being committed to the workhouse. One addition to the social security framework which illustrates very well the piecemeal nature of the reforms of the period, was the Widows', Orphans', and Old Age Contributory Pensions Act of 1925, which was really an elaboration of National Health Insurance, providing a basic 10s. pension at 65 for those covered by Health Insurance (contributions were now increased). Side by side with the new pensions, the 1908 non-contributory pension, payable at the age of 70, continued in existence (at, since 1919, the level also of 10s. a week).

Apart from its important commitment to housing, the Ministry of Health, as it emerged from the 1919 Act, had little more than supervisory power over public health and, indeed, over miscellaneous allied problems such as the Poor Law, which it inherited from the Local Government Board. One apparently hopeful sign was the appointment in 1920 of the Dawson Committee. But although it has been fashionable among historians anxious to trace the steady evolution of the modern Welfare State to stress the significance of the recommendations of this committee[83] they are noteworthy mainly for their negative quality: anything in the nature of a free health service is ruled out. On one count, however, the Dawson Report did reflect the best informed opinion: it stressed the importance to any public health scheme of the establishment of health centres.[84] Yet no government could ignore the simple fact that in a world of rising costs the voluntary hospitals were finding the gravest difficulty in carrying on unaided. The Lloyd George Cabinet feared that if the voluntary hospitals were allowed to collapse there would be an 'irresistible demand' for them to be taken over by the State or by the local authorities: the demand, the Cabinet notes, was especially strong from the Labour Party.[85] The full predicament of the voluntary hospitals was very clearly brought out by yet another committee of investigation, this time presided over by Viscount Cave. The Cave Committee recommended a government subvention to the voluntary hospitals of £1 million.[86] The Government not only cut this sum to £500,000, it also stated openly just how narrow a concept it held of medical provision:

The Government accept the view of the Cave Committee that the voluntary system must be maintained, and they have reluctantly assented to a special contribution from State funds because in the judgement of the Cave Committee the voluntary system would be gravely imperilled if the present temporary difficulties are not surmounted. But on the merits of the case they cannot admit that it is incumbent on the Government to find money to make up the present deficit in the voluntary hospitals, and they can only contemplate the provision of State assistance for a very limited period and solely as a means of giving the voluntary hospitals a breathing space, during which they can establish their position, as the conditions resulting from the war disappear, and an opportunity of improving their organization and developing their revenues.[87]

By a familiar process, the Government in granting its niggardly, temporary sum also felt obliged to appoint a supervisory agency, the Voluntary Hospitals Commission. Under the terms of the 1929 Local Government Act the local authorities were encouraged to develop and build their own hospitals, an important move in itself, though it did tend to encourage the destructive rivalry between local authority and voluntary hospitals. Halting cripple though the Unemployment Insurance Scheme undoubtedly was, it kept steadily ahead of the even feebler Health Insurance scheme. Like benefits, the free services of the 'panel' doctor, strictly speaking, were available only to the insured employee and not to his dependants. Because of the way in which the scheme was administered through the 'approved societies' some participants received only a basic general practitioner service (popularly regarded as inferior to the service provided by the same doctor to his fee-paying patients, though on the whole the necessarily intangible evidence would seem to contradict this opinion), while others, fortunate in having their insurance managed by one of the larger, better-organized companies, received 'additional benefits' in the form of dental or ophthalmic treatment. In worst case of all was the 'bad risk', the man congenitally in ill health: if the approved societies refused to take him on their lists, as they usually did, his insurance was administered directly by the local Insurance Committee, which meant that although he above all needed the best attention he actually got only the bare minimum. The 'bad risk' is the most convincing single witness on behalf of publicly administered insurance as compared with insurance administered by private companies.

In 1918 the Labour Party annual conference had unanimously adopted a resolution calling for 'the organization and development of a unified Health Service for the whole community':[88] the resolution was an important one, though too marked by the prejudices of the time (especially in its emphasis on local authority control) fully to justify, though by no means wholly to invalidate, Professor Robert Brady's comment on the National Health Service of 1948:

The programme which Bevan inaugurated on the vesting day, July 5, 1948, was almost a verbatim copy of the one laid out by a Labour Conference thirty years earlier.[89]

Greater importance, in fact, attaches to a series of special Labour conferences and policy documents of the 1920s, which have hitherto been ignored by both historians of the Labour Party and by historians of the Welfare State. From the deliberations of an Advisory Committee on Public Health there appeared in 1922, under the joint imprint of the Labour Party and the T.U.C., the most complete blueprint for a future National Health Service yet put on paper by any interested body.[90] Although the proposed 'Public Medical Service' was to be administered by the local authorities, they, in turn, were to be under the firm supervision of the Minister of Health. Furthermore it was recognized that 'the country should be divided into areas of sufficient size to allow of complete medical organization' – though in practice these areas were equated with the existing counties and county boroughs (excluding, therefore, boroughs and districts). At one with the Dawson Report, the memorandum stressed the importance of health centres. It was, however, somewhat hesitant on the controversial topic of nationalization of all hospitals, advocated by Labour conferences in pre-war days, and it ignored the views of an influential minority on the Advisory Committee that all doctors should be placed on a salaried basis. Yet it was emphatic in stating that the service should be 'free and open to all', making possible the abolition of the existing insurance structure. The intense practicality, indeed caution, of Labour thinking on the problem of a National Health Service is made clear by the transitional stage envisaged in the memorandum and by the conferences held by the party with representatives of the medical and nursing professions, the Approved Societies, the Insurance Committees and the major hospitals.[91] Since Labour was only briefly and weakly in office none of this important work had any immediate direct effect, and indeed figured only sketchily at party conferences and in propagandist literature. Where Labour did assert direct influence (and this was true of all aspects of social policy) was through its representatives on the local authorities, especially after the local elections of 1919 gave it control of Bradford and twelve London boroughs, majorities in Durham, Glamorgan and Monmouth and substantial minorities in other areas. In local government, however, Labour policy was not so much to create new social initiatives as to seek the implementation of the legislation which had sprung out of the war period.[92] The inadequacy of the country's health provision, allied with the low standards of nutrition resulting from inadequate wages and prolonged unemployment, was reflected in the low vitality and poor health of much of the nation. The school medical services in England and Wales found that a steady level of from 17 to 20 per cent of the children examined required medical treatment.[93]

Under the two Addison Housing Acts about 214,000 houses were built in England and Wales before the programme was aborted by the savage surgery of the Geddes economies. In 1923 Neville Chamberlain, Conservative Minister of Health, introduced a bill designed to help private enterprise solve the housing problem – a measure typical of the Victorian collectivism of this ministry and of this minister in particular: an annual state subsidy of £6 for twenty years was provided for houses of a maximum size of 950 square feet; theoretically local authorities as well as private builders could avail themselves of the subsidy, but in practice most of the 436,000 houses built before the subsidy was terminated in 1929 were built by private enterprise, and almost all of those for sale. Despite the restrictions on size, designed to place the houses beneath the contempt of the rich, they did not come within the reach of the manual working class: they served rather to swell the growing white-collar commuter areas. In pure economic logic the idea of annual subsidies to local authorities is a clumsy one, since before it can begin building the local authority must first borrow the capital cost: a great part of the subsidy therefore goes on servicing the interest on the loan, that is to say straight into the pocket of the money-lender. With this in mind the Labour Party had adopted as its official housing policy the idea of low-interest loans from the central government[94]. Yet the official policy was completely ignored in what was none the less the outstanding achievement of Labour in office in the 1920s: the 1924 Housing Act, conceived and executed by the most brilliant of the Clydeside I.L.P. figures, John Wheatley. Unlike so many pieces of British social legislation in the twentieth century it was far more than a statement upon paper of certain laudable aspirations. Wheatley put in hours of patient negotiation with both sides of the building industry, in which he judiciously mixed threats and cajolery, smoothing the way for the higher levels of productivity which the Act would require.[95] Up till 1933 when the scheme was abolished, the local authorities built over half a million houses, all of which had to be let at controlled rents; each house qualified for a forty-year subsidy of £9 per annum, with a higher subsidy for houses in rural areas where conditions were often more scandalous than in the cities, and where the authorities were often too poor to do much about it. Impressive though Wheatley's achievement was, it is clear that the new houses tended to be occupied by the better-off members of the working and lower-middle classes; at best what happened to the very poor was that they could now move into the older houses vacated by the new Wheatley tenants. In many areas, therefore, housing conditions remained very bad. The 1931 Census revealed that in England and Wales 35 per cent of the population lived more than two to a room; 15 per cent more than three to a room; 6 per cent more than four to a room. The position in Scotland was rather worse.

Scotland could, however, still boast of a rather better educational system than England, where such promise as the Fisher Act had contained was stifled by the economy campaign of 1922. Educational opportunity in England in the 1920s was openly governed by social class, and, as a natural consequence, served to reinforce it. However, this consideration was swamped, even in the minds of those who might on ideological grounds have been expected to care, by the more oppressive fact that the educational provision for the lower classes was appalling. In 1923 rather more than 1,600,000 children between the ages of 11 and 14 (72·5 per cent of this age-group) were being educated in elementary schools which did not even claim to provide 'advanced instruction';[96] in other words they were simply receiving a repetition of the same rudimentary material until the blessed day of legal release, which was at the end of the term in which the pupil reached the age of 14. A further 5·5 per cent were receiving 'advanced instruction', either in the same schools as they had entered at the age of 5 or in the separate 'central schools' which certain local authorities had been establishing since shortly before the war. About 0·5 per cent were in attendance at junior technical schools. Only 7 per cent succeeded in reaching the grant-aided secondary schools, which, for a working-class child, meant passing the 'Free Place Examination' usually held at the age of 11. The remainder of the age-group (about 14 per cent) was divided among those who still managed to escape schooling altogether (as much as 22 per cent in the critical final compulsory year of 13–14) and those who attended the various private schools, including the famous English 'Public Schools' which catered for about 6 per cent. The average percentages cited above fail to bring out one other consequence of the inadequate concern for education of English governments, the immense variation in educational opportunity from one local authority area to another.[97]

Over the obvious inadequacies of the system there was considerable agreement among informed critics of all parties and opinions. Even the Lloyd George ministry, sensitive to electoral prospects if to little else, shrank from the full cut of £18 million in educational expenditure recommended by the Geddes Committee, reducing the figure to £6½ million. It also dropped a mischievous plan to raise the school *entry* age to 6.[98] Educational psychologists and the teachers' organizations concentrated their attacks upon the manner in which elementary education continued to the age of 14 or later, *parallel with* secondary education for a favoured few. R. H. Tawney, the Oxford historian, teacher at the London School of Economics and active member of the Labour Party, succeeded in getting the party to adopt the policy-statement *Secondary Education for All,* which stressed the conception of secondary education as *succeeding upon* elementary education (which was to be renamed primary education). The aim was

that all normal children, irrespective of the income, class, or occupation of their parents, may be transferred at the age of 11 + from the primary or preparatory school to one type or another of secondary school, and remain in the latter till sixteen.[99]

In office Labour's education policies were entrusted to C. P. Trevelyan, a former Liberal who had moved into the Labour Party by means of the I.L.P. (itself the most advanced of all political groupings in its pronouncements on education):[100] in 1924 he relaxed the economic restrictions which had been placed on the public education system, and, more important, appointed a Consultative Committee under the chairmanship of Sir W. H. Haddow. The Haddow Report did not appear until December 1926: its major proposal was the abolition of the old conception of elementary education and its replacement by primary education, followed, at the age of 'eleven plus', by secondary education, a term which was to cover both the traditional form, whose practitioners were now to be renamed 'grammar schools', and a new, less academic form of secondary education, to be given in 'modern' schools. The committee further recommended that, after an interval of five years, the school-leaving age should universally be raised to 15.[101] First grants towards implementing these proposals were allocated in September 1929, but in the economic crisis of 1931 the whole programme was suppressed.

Neither in *Secondary Education for All* nor in the Haddow Report is there any proposal for interference with the privileged private sector. Certainly the Headmasters' Conference, representing the public schools had, while still flushed with the wine of war-time social harmony, proposed that a public school education be made available to all ex-elementary school boys capable of profiting from it; but the proposal itself was vague, and nothing at all was done to implement it. Baldwin, himself a Harrovian was making a peculiarly British kind of jest, that is to say no kind of jest at all, when in a notorious speech at his old school he said:

When the call came for me to form a government, one of my first thoughts was that it should be a government of which Harrow should not be ashamed. I remember how in previous governments there had been four, or perhaps five, Harrovians, and I determined to have six.[102]

It is not surprising that the 1926 Labour Party conference rebelled against official party policy, and called for more 'Workers' Control' in education.[103] Under the Conservatives, however, a new refinement in the class structure of English education was created: in 1926 certain fee-paying schools, then outside the public system, were allowed to qualify for 'direct grants', which meant that they, and therefore their fee-paying pupils, got a State subsidy without the loss of status implied in coming under the jurisdiction of the local authority. At the top of the educational scale the universities had an obvious class quality in that they recruited only from a tiny minority of the population; only four or five out of every thousand products of the English State elementary schools reached a university.[104] The founding of new 'red brick' university colleges (that is, colleges which prepared students for degrees awarded by London University) at Nottingham, Southampton, Exeter, Hull, Leicester and one university entitled to award its own degrees at Reading extended the opportunities of the middle class, though in the mid-Twenties the student population in England was still under 30,000 (including 8,000 women), or less than 8 students per 10,000 of the total population; the federal University of Wales had 2,750 students, or 12 per 10,000 of the Welsh population; the four Scottish universities had just over 10,000 students, or 21 per 10,000 of the Scottish population.[105] The initiative for the founding of new universities was essentially local, but the establishment in 1919 of the University Grants Committee as an autonomous agency for channelling State finance to the universities did result in a raising of standards, and the launching at the same time of State scholarships and (in subsequent years) of local authority grants increased social mobility within the educational structure. Even so there remained class distinction as between different universities: Oxford and Cambridge ranked above the newer foundations in much the same way that the old-established public schools ranked above all other institutions of secondary education.

Given such narrow educational provision, the intellectual atti-tudes and artistic activities usually associated with the age were necessarily those of a small minority, though popularizers and disciples did ensure that such names as Einstein and Freud were more widely known than ever Darwin's had been in the nineteenth century. Einstein enjoyed something of a boom in the British Press in the early Twenties, though the appreciation of the philosophical implications of the scientific laws he defined went little beyond the platitude, 'Everything is relative'. Two works of popular exposition enjoyed great success: *Stars and Atoms* (1927) by Sir Arthur Eddington and *The Mysterious Universe* (1930) by Sir James Jeans. In Jeans's conclusion that the 'Great Architect of the Universe now begins to appear as a pure Mathematician'[106] can be detected an early hint of the belief, soon to come, that mathematics was the essential basis of the serious investigation of any political, social or academic problem. In fact, although there were great practical achievements in atomic physics and in astronomy, British physics, in keeping with a national characteristic we have already noted, was weak on the theoretical side.[107] In 1924 Cambridge University, somewhat late in the day, gave recognition to the significance of the researches of Frederick Gowland Hopkins by creating an Institute of Biochemistry. Despite Hopkins's own deep sense of social com-mitment the immediate results for society as a whole were slight, though in high society there developed a fad for vitamins. Although Marie Stopes aroused the wrath of conservative opinion by her public advocacy of contraception, she stood essentially in the tradition of the great nineteenth-century claimants for women's rights: she sought for women emancipation from frequent child-bearing, but certainly not from marriage ties; her greatest work was, indeed, entitled *Married Love*. More grist to the mills of those who wished themselves to behave promiscuously or who wished to shake their heads over the promiscuity of others was to be found in the works of Havelock Ellis, author of *Studies in the Psychology of Sex,* published before the war, and Ernest Jones, Freud's greatest English disciple.

In the creative writing of the period three characteristics call for the attention of the historian. First, for all that the course of modernism can be traced back to the end of the previous century, this decade stands out in clear relief as an age of experimentation in new techniques, as an age which approximates as closely to a clean break as any age in literature possibly can. It may well be true that the war itself had not the slightest effect on James Joyce and Virginia Woolf in their development of the stream-of-consciousness technique of novel-writing; and Joyce in his last two novels, *Ulysses* and *Finnegan's Wake,* certainly pushed technical innovation practically to breaking point. But the fact that they were followed by a host of imitators of one sort or another suggests once again that, although the new technique might have been conceived by a few leading creative spirits in pre-war days, it was the changed society thrown up by the earthquake of war which gave them wide acceptance. The other points of historical interest in regard to the literature of the period concern its subject matter and the frankness with which it dealt with sexual matters: those writers who in the main clung to the traditional modes of expression tended either to deal directly with the war experience, or else with the cynical, pleasure-loving, apolitical upper-crust society of these 'roaring Twenties' (in the phrase of one of the youngest novelists of the time, Evelyn Waugh). Into the former division fall Ford Madox Ford's great tetralogy expressing restrained criticism of the military and political conduct of the war and quietly lamenting the passing of the Whiggish values of the English landed class, the novels and stories of Richard Aldington, and the autobiographical work of C. E. Montague, Siegfried Sassoon and Robert Graves. The hedonism of the roaring Twenties was most clearly chronicled in the early novels of Aldous Huxley. Huxley was more open in his descriptions of sexual encounters than any respectable Edwardian writer had been, and the fashionable preoccupation with Freudian psychology is very apparent. What a later generation termed four-letter words appeared in D. H. Lawrence's *Lady Chatterley's Lover* and in Aldington's *Death of a Hero*: however, while indi-

viduals might essay such frankness of expression, established opinion of the day found it unacceptable, and Lawrence's novel was
banned altogether, while Aldington's appeared only in expurgated
form. In the work (at this time) of T. S. Eliot, the greatest English
poet of the twentieth century (he was born an American), were to be
found a new use of language deriving from the experiments of
John Davidson and other Edwardians, elements of sexual frankness
and, overall, a spirit of total despair and desolation. In his novels
Huxley made great display of his wide learning in many languages
and several cultures; Eliot loaded his *The Waste Land* with an
immense apparatus of recondite allusions. The reaction here,
possibly, was against the advance of political democracy and against
the levelling of standards with which upper-class newspapers were
so constantly preoccupied.

English painting in the Twenties became much more definitively
'modern', though generally highly derivative and showing little of
the creative intensity of the continental schools. The situation was
happier in Scotland, where the Glasgow school had provided an
authentic modern tradition and where the Royal Scottish Academy
was not the bastion of reaction that its English counterpart had
become. Although Stanley Baldwin, no Bohemian leader of the
avant-garde, participated in the unveiling of Jacob Epstein's
memorial 'Rima', the Press conducted a vicious campaign against
its alleged obscenity. Throughout most of the Twenties British
architecture remained relatively uninfluenced by the great continental giants, Le Corbusier, Mies van der Rohe and Walter
Gropius, though there were some determined efforts to publicize
the basic theories of the first-named and his visions of a type of city
suited to the age of advanced technology.[108] Some, albeit unimaginative, use was being made of the basic material of the new architecture, ferro-concrete, but the major influence remained that of
Voysey who, at the turn of the century, had pioneered a freer, less
cluttered domestic style than that of the Victorians. Music, somehow, did better. Building on the opportunities created by the composer Elgar and the conductor and impresario Beecham, Vaughan
Williams, Arnold Bax and William Walton helped to maintain for
English music an international position it had not held for two

hundred years. Drawing heav:ly on older English musical traditions, these composers at the same time made use of the technical innovations of the great founder of modern diatonic music, Arnold Schoenberg.[109] The overall impression conveyed by the more distinguished intellectuals and creative workers of the time is of innovation, scepticism, and rejection of old standards and old absolutes. In the writing of history the end of the old liberalism was reflected in the reaction against the 'Whig Interpretation of History' based first of all on Lewis Namier's painstaking, even (in an elementary form) numeral studies (Namier himself likened his researches to the processes of non-Euclidean geometry)[110] of the later eighteenth century, which seemed to show politics as motivated by personal and family ambitions, rather than by the grand chorus of liberty broadening down from precedent to precedent. In studies of the Industrial Revolution a high-minded preoccupation with the sufferings of the poor gave place to a stolid recounting of the steady economic progress to be associated with industrial change.[111]

In greater or lesser degree the historians, poets and painters of the time were affected by the society in which they lived and the great holocaust through which they had passed. How far did they in turn affect society? One possible channel of communication was greatly developed in the Twenties, that provided by the mass media, newspaper, film and radio. In the world of newspapers the positive effect of a continued expansion in total circulation was partly offset by increasing commercialization and increasing concentration of ownership. This period saw the completion of the process whereby the Press became big business dependent upon advertising revenue, the decimation of the old provincial Press which had played a leading role in Liberal politics in the nineteenth century, and the consolidation of three major newspaper empires, those of Lord Beaverbrook, Lord Rothermere and the Berry brothers.[112] The first newspaper to reach a daily circulation of one million was actually the *Daily Herald,* which, between its foundation by George Lansbury in 1911, and 1922 when it was officially taken over by the T.U.C. had led a precarious and free-booting existence. Although at the end of the war it attracted the pens of such distinguished figures as Bertrand Russell, C. E. M. Joad (both philosophers) and Robert Graves, as an official Labour paper it became steadily duller, and was never really commercially completely viable (partly because of the reluctance of businessmen to advertise in it). In 1929 the wealth and expertise of Odhams Press was placed behind the *Herald*. The real success of the time, however, was Beaverbrook's *Daily Express*, whose lively presentation took it ahead of the relatively staid *Daily Mail*. By putting Einstein into the headlines, and endeavouring to hurl Epstein into the sewage system, the popular Press did at least bring a wide audience into a form of contact, however distorted, with some of the major intellectual trends of the time. The newspapers played a part, too, in that standardization of aspiration and behaviour which was a critical element in class change in post-war society. For the rest, much of their influence was towards trivialization and the building up over a period of time of one major news story (the word is apt) at the expense of a rounded presentation of all matters of moment. By combining, in his solo flight of the Atlantic, personal courage and endurance with one of the major wonders of science, the American flier Charles A. Lindberg had an obvious claim to become the hero of the Western world: that he did so was essentially due to the enormous publicity given to him by the world's Press.

A much more potent influence on the lower orders of society was the film, overwhelmingly an American product. As was remarked in the *New Survey of London Life and Labour*, conducted during the Twenties and early Thirties:

The influence of the films can be traced in the clothes and appearance of the women and in the furnishing of their houses. Girls copy the fashions of their favourite film star. At the time of writing, girls in all classes of society wear 'Garbo' coats and wave their hair *à la* Norma Shearer or Lilian Harvey. It is impossible to measure the effect the films must have on the outlook and habits of the people. . . . It is estimated by the Cinematograph Exhibitors' Association that the aggregate weekly attendances at London cinemas now amount to a third of the population. Certainly today the cinema is *par excellence* the people's amusement.[113]

The new permissiveness, and the effective boundaries still imposed on it, were best illustrated in the films of Cecil B. de Mille, who, it has been said, devoted his earlier works to showing people in great detail and at great length what they ought *not* to do. The great American film makers, Griffith, Flaherty and de Mille, greatly extended the scope and scale of the silent picture. Then, just when the first great cinema boom in Britain seemed to have subsided in 1926–27 into a period of slump, the invention of 'talkies', followed by the building of huge luxury picture houses, brought a revival which lasted for another generation.[114] The cinema was exceptional among all the products of twentieth-century technology in that it reached the poorer elements in the community first, before spreading upwards to those who at first affected contempt for it. It also provided the occasion for a major piece of collectivist intervention of the type which, while temporarily out of fashion in economics and industry, was very much to the fore in social matters. Alarmed over the Hollywood stranglehold, the Conservatives in 1927 passed the British Cinematographic Films Act which by 'establishing a system of quotas and subsidies' was designed to break the Hollywood monopoly and encourage the production of British films. The Act also set up a specialist committee to advise the Board of Trade on matters concerning the film industry.

Radio broadcasting, the one completely new mass medium of the 1920s, had rather less effect than the other two: by 31 March 1927 only 2,269,644 receiving licences had been issued,[115] and the radio receiver was still something of a luxury toy. But undoubtedly the potential of broadcasting was enormous, and that again provoked collectivist action on the part of a Conservative government. First governmental reactions, however, point up very neatly the manner in which the revolution in social and technical processes provoked by the war had gone unmatched by any comparable reformation of political attitudes. Despite the interest aroused by the famous Melba broadcast from Chelmsford in June 1920, the Marconi Company was shortly banned from making further broadcasts, though there was nothing to stop would-be listeners from tuning their sets to the stations of our more adventurous European neighbours.[116] When, in January 1922, permission was given for the resumption of broadcasts, the Post Office insisted that there must be a pause every seven minutes to allow for the reception of official messages. On 11 May 1922 broadcasts of one hour a day began at 2LO – Marconi House in the Strand. The single personality who most influenced 2LO policy and helped to establish some of the basic principles on which British broadcasting subsequently developed was Arthur Burrows (who during the war had been employed by the Government to monitor the wireless transmissions of the central powers). Burrows argued that while there should be a large number of items of 'a really popular character' the attempt should also be made to 'lift' the public above its 'present standard of musical appreciation'.[117]

The Marconi Company was not alone in its interest in broadcasting. Other companies which desired to exploit the new capacity developed for war purposes included the British Thomson-Houston Company, the Metropolitan-Vickers Electrical Company, the Western Electric Company, the Radio Communications Company and the General Electric Company. It was pressure from these six companies plus the example of the colossal radio boom which took place in the United States at the beginning of the Twenties which brought about the 'treaty' between the companies and the Post Office which established the British Broadcasting Company. The British Broadcasting Company began transmissions at the end of 1922 and in April 1923 it moved to its famous home at Savoy Hill. Essentially concerned with the private profit to be made through the expanding sales of radio sets, the company none the less, under the direction of Burrows and of the Calvanistic Scot, John Reith, set high standards. But from August 1923, when a Departmental Committee on Broadcasting presented a glowing appreciation of the potential of the new medium, thoughts in government circles began to turn towards more positive intervention. As the Broadcasting Committee of 1925 declared:

Broadcasting has become so widespread, concerns so many people, and is fraught with so many far-reaching possibilities, that the organization laid down for the British Broadcasting Company no longer corresponds to national requirements or responsibility. Notwithstanding the progress which we readily acknowledge, and to the credit of which the Company is largely entitled, we are impelled to the conclusion that no company or body constituted on trade lines for the profit, direct or indirect, of those composing it can be regarded as adequate in view of the broader considerations now beginning to emerge.[118]

So in the 1926 the private company was replaced by a public corporation. The establishment of the British Broadcasting Corporation marks a melding of the new economic doctrines fostered by the war experience and the new technology stimulated by the war's demands.

A similar though less complete evolution took place in the aircraft industry. The first daily air service between London and Paris was inaugurated in August 1919 by Holt Thomas's Aircraft Transport and Travel Company. While newspapers spoke excitedly of 'the dawn of a new commercial era in the history of aviation'[119] passengers, 'resigned but apprehensive', would be packed into the small aeroplanes like 'sardines in a tin'.

One would walk into the little office where the clerk . . . was seated and ask: 'How many have you got for today?' 'Two,' he would answer, with an air of satisfaction. 'And how many for tomorrow?' . . . 'Three,' he would reply, with an even greater pride.[120]

By January 1920 three British companies were operating in the cross-channel skies. Yet for all the romance which attached to aviation, especially when memory of the daring exploits of the war pilots was enhanced in 1919 by the Atlantic crossing of John Alcock and Arthur Whitten-Brown and the flight from England to Australia of the Smith brothers in a Vickers 'Vimy' (an adaptation of the watime bomber) civil air transport simply could not pay its way. The Government first granted temporary subsidies to the air companies, then in 1924 founded British Imperial Airways, which had a government subsidy and a number of government-appointed directors.[121] Not all technological developments got even this amount of encouragement. True, the Central Electricity Board was set up in 1926 to co-ordinate the supply of electricity through a national 'grid', an important step towards complete nationalization. But, despite the encouraging report of the Water Power Resources Committee of 1921, little was done to develop this important potential source of electric power. A major reason was that possible sites for schemes were almost exclusively to be found in Scotland and Wales: Scottish and Welsh pressure groups were not yet strong or coherent enough to force the Parliament at Westminster out of the long-standing lethargy and contempt with which it treated Scottish and Welsh problems, especially since, on the other side, there was to be found the powerful opposition of the landowners and of the coal-owners; 'though,' as a government committee later commented, 'coal is virtually non-existent north of Fifeshire.'[122] Britain's first major hydro-electric scheme at Foyars in Scotland had been opened in 1896 by the British Aluminium Company, for its own industrial purposes; a second scheme was opened at Kinlochleven in 1909. In 1922 the Grampian Electricity Supply Company secured powers to develop the public supply of hydro-electricity, but in fact did nothing with them: in 1927 this ineffectual private company was taken over by the Scottish Power Company Limited which, in 1930 and 1933 respectively, opened schemes at Rannoch and Tummel. Meantime the first public supply stations had already, in 1926, been opened at Bonnington and Stonebyers by the Clyde Valley Company.[123] Prejudice against State action, save where the national interest was at stake was so evident that even an English politician could perceive it, was still strong enough to prevent matters being taken any further than this. Apart from one small scheme in the 1930s (see below Chapter Five (1)), in no case

has any Governmental agency taken any supporting action in relation to hydro-electric development, nor, so far as we have discovered, has any Government ever framed any plan or programme for the development of these resources. So far as Northern Scotland is concerned – and it is there that the great bulk of the undeveloped resources of the United Kingdom are situated – the last occasion on which Parliamentary approval for a hydro-electric scheme was granted was in 1922. Of the six Northern Scottish schemes promoted since 1929, all have been rejected. In contrast with the immense achievements abroad in water-power developments . . . the record . . . is not an inspiring one.[124]

The motor manufacturing industry was able to expand impressively without any government assistance, save that provided by the continuance of the wartime tariff policy. In 1920 there were 550,000 motor vehicles (including motor bicycles) on British roads; in 1922 there were 952,000 licences and in 1930, 2,218,000. This last figure (remarkably similar to the number of radio licences) represents only about one vehicle to every five families, so the consequences are significant in straddling the gap between the upper and the middle classes, rather than the gap between the middle and working classes. More important socially at this time was the development of the motor bus. Most local authorities had a long tradition of 'municipal socialism' and by 1929 (though the number of trams and of electric trolley buses also increased) 100 municipalities were running a total of 4,737 buses.[125] Longer distance routes were usually privately operated. Bus and car together contributed to the development of new industrial centres, new residential areas, new roads, walled in by a new semi-urban 'ribbon' architecture, and new methods of outdoor advertising. Isolated villages were brought into the orbit of centralized British life. Furthermore the manufacturing side of the motor industry made the fullest use of new mass production techniques which slowly spread to other industries, bringing forth a great flood of new consumer goods and ultimately making it necessary, if the new growth were to be sustained, for the purchasing power of the masses to be raised.

Class divisions and gross inequalities in wealth and opportunity remained: but the trend initiated during the war towards greater homogeneity in social behaviour continued. Lavish private dances, the exclusive splendours of Ascot and Henley were the prerogative of the upper classes: but the lower classes had their dance halls and greyhound tracks. Practically every working-class girl, the Merseyside Social Survey reported, had a special dress for her Saturday evening dancing.[126] As well as film-going, spectating at football matches, formerly also an essentially lower-class activity, became an acceptable pursuit for the wealthy, especially after the English Football Association acquired the prestigious new stadium built for the 1923 Empire Exhibition at Wembley. Heavy drinking among the working classes was in decline, as was church attendance among the middle classes. All classes had shared in the recent disruptions in the patterns of moral behaviour, all shared an awareness that, in some quarters, standards which were not those of the reign of Queen Victoria were being advanced, though squeamishness was still a British characteristic. Sir Roy Harrod narrates how a hearty Cambridge undergraduate in 1922 found 'unseemly and immoral' a reference to contraceptives made by Keynes when delivering a paper on Malthus.[127] But at least there was something of an approach to equality of moral standards as between the sexes.

Mass production and mass communication contributed to standardization of fashion and of environment. The buildings raised for the Wembley Exhibition revealed little trace of modernism save in the use of steel and concrete, but in photographs and newsreels of the multitudes milling around among the pavilions one is at once struck by that sameness of appearance that was the trade mark of the post-war world. On the other hand the exhibition catalogue struck a note of confidence when it said:

The chief characteristic of modern decoration was a vividness of colour, which is perhaps due to the influence of the Russian ballet.

In the 'Palace of Arts' a hall, dining-room and bedroom were set up – all selected on the basis of public competitions promoted by the magazine *Country Life*. Of the bedroom, the catalogue continued:

The furniture is in English walnut, outlined in gold, and the beds stand on black ebony plinths.

The bedroom also included:

Three electric lamp standards, painted and decorated wood.
Hand-tufted Axminster carpet, coloured border.
Hanging carved gilt lamp.
Curtains, blue and green striped.
Blinds, gold and blue shot net.
Sofa, upholstered in blue and green striped silk.[128]

The *Daily Mail* Seventh Ideal Home Exhibition, held at Olympia, London, in March 1923, had three distinctive features closely related to the trends of the time: a bungalow town, a wireless section and an Egyptian handicrafts section.[129] The last was a facet of the craze for all things Egyptian which followed upon the publicity given by the mass media to the unearthing at Luxor of the tomb of the Pharaoh Tutankhamen. In an earlier age the discoveries of a Sir Charles Lyell, the theories of a Ruskin reached the ears only of a limited coterie; now such things were projected into a circulation, however debased, which involved the whole community.

4. THE DILEMMA OF DEMOCRACY

The post-war decade was the first in which Britain, even in the formal sense, was a full democracy: in 1928 those women who had still been left outside the pale of the constitution in 1918 were enfranchised. Ironically it was also a time in which the British parliamentary system, which had worked so well for three-quarters of a century, began to seize up. Although there was much violence in the country, particularly in the immediate post-war years, there was no real threat, despite the wilder pronouncements of right-wing politicians and journalists, of working-class revolution. Lacking a revolutionary spear-head, the organized working class required an effective political leadership, capable of operating through the parliamentary system; yet while the Labour Party undoubtedly made substantial gains in this period, it never achieved a position of real power, partly because of its own weaknesses and partly because it had to compete with the Liberal Party as the rallying point of anti-Conservative opinion. Theoretically an anti-capitalist party, Labour showed itself more willing to adapt to the existing system than to grapple with the problems of capitalist crises. When Labour and Liberals competed in their claim to be the effective progressive party, only the Conservatives could benefit: yet they, the country's 'natural leaders', were afflicted by a sore unwillingness to lead. Was this, then, an era of political pygmies, as Robert Boothby, the Tory radical, declared:

The Genoa Conference crashed, and with it all the hopes of a generation. Lloyd George went home to be overthrown. Rathenau went home to be assassinated. The era of the political pygmies was at hand.[130]

Britain's problem was part of Europe's irony: the war, allegedly fought to make the world safe for democracy, had in fact made the world desperately dangerous for democracy. Britain's dilemma was the world's dilemma: how to reconcile strong leadership with democratic forms. MacDonald, Baldwin, Chamberlain, Snowden: all were democrats to the core; all were Gladstonian in their faith in liberal institutions. They were well aware of the economic problem, but because in the middle Twenties full recovery seemed only round the corner the true nature of the dilemma was concealed from them. They stuck by the old virtues of traditionalism, liberalism and pragmatism in an age in which, by themselves, these were not enough.

But first Lloyd George remained in office long enough to discredit anything that might be described as dynamic leadership. His was the ministry that promised a fit land for heroes to live in, and produced a Waste Land; his was the ministry of the Geddes economies – the Committee and its chairman being very much a personal choice of the Prime Minister himself;[131] his was the ministry of the black-and-tan war in Ireland. Nothing could shake the Coalition's huge majority, though almost every by-election showed positive signs of disillusionment on the part of sections of the electorate. As early as October 1919 *The Times* had declared:

In by-election after by-election the country has shown, either by crushing defeats of Coalition candidates or by huge reductions of Coalition majorities, its dissatisfaction and resentment.[132]

Eventually the Cabinet came to worry less about the economic situation, and more about the electoral consequences of its retrenchment policies; and it is scarcely surprising that by 1922 many Conservatives came to think of Lloyd George as a millstone round their necks, the more so as they began to feel the surge of their own independent power flowing through their veins. At the Carlton

Club Meeting of 19 October 1922 the Conservatives voted to withdraw from the Coalition: having allowed himself first to become the prisoner of his Conservative majority, Lloyd George was now their victim. In the General Election which followed the Conservatives received a secure majority (367 seats to 142 for Labour and 117 for the two groups of Liberals), but the new Government formed under the prime ministership of Bonar Law lacked some of the more experienced Conservative leaders who had resisted the decision to break with Lloyd George. Bonar Law himself was a sick man; the rising star seemed to be that of the Chancellor of the Exchequer, Stanley Baldwin, who had been a leader of the campaign against Lloyd George. Baldwin was no hard-faced man, but he was one of those non-self-made men of whom Keynes had complained, inheriting his fortune along with his Victorian business and his Victorian attitudes. After only a modest apology for the political apprenticeship which the older order had demanded of aspiring businessmen, Baldwin was pushed forward to junior office in 1917 by Bonar Law, to whom he was related by marriage. Baldwin affected a countrified manner, delighting in posing among his pigs, and, unlike Law, he had had the standard upper-class education at Harrow and Cambridge. After the horror of the four-year crisis in modern civilization, and the empty pyrotechnics of the late Prime Minister, who was a social climber and a Welshman, Baldwin portended tranquillity and solidity. Amiable and somewhat indolent, he was strongly motivated by the best features of nineteenth-century Anglican Christianity. In a much-quoted speech at Oxford he declared:

There is nothing else for this generation to do than devote itself as no other generation has done in the past to its millions of people who have not got our advantages.[133]

His simple moral eloquence proved well adapted to the first age of radio communications. When ill health forced Bonar Law's retirement in May 1923, it was Baldwin whom King George V invited to assume the prime ministership, believing, despite Law's resolute silence on the matter, that he was the outgoing Prime

Minister's own favoured candidate. Baldwin then became leader of the party. This was entirely in keeping with the hierarchical principles on which British Conservatism was based, there being no question of the party electing a leader in advance of the King's decision. In fact Baldwin's only rival had been the Foreign Secretary, the Marquess Curzon, but Balfour, now filling the role of Conservative elder statesman, had pointed out to the King that, at a time when the Labour Party was the official Opposition, it would be awkward to have a Prime Minister in the House of Lords. This advice probably did not critically affect the outcome; but the event none the less effectively established the principle that no peer would in future hope to hold the prime ministership, and symbolized the decline of aristocratic influence within the ruling class.

In another age Baldwin might well have been a successful Prime Minister. He was an astute tactician, and, within the limits imposed by this quality, honest. After only eight months in office, despite his secure majority, he offered himself and his government to the hazards of a General Election. He had realized that the best way of fully unifying his party and forestalling any bid Lloyd George might make to revive the Coalition idea was to declare himself in favour of Tariff Reform. His theory of democracy demanded that he should submit this change of plan to the electorate. A more dynamic leader would simply have changed the policy and eschewed the election. In the sense that there was a combined Free Trade vote of 191 Labour members and 159 Liberals (now more or less reunited) to 259 Conservatives, Baldwin lost the election; but in the longer term he strengthened his party, finally driving Lloyd George away from the Conservative bastions of power back to the failing Liberal Party. The outcome was the first Labour government, which took office in January 1924. In keeping with his acceptance of the traditions of fair play as the essence of the British parliamentary system, Baldwin was all for letting Labour have its chance to govern. During its uneasy nine months of office the Labour government was able to achieve little. It fell because, under pressure from its Left wing, it concluded a commercial treaty with the Soviet Union: the actual issue on

which the critical vote of confidence was taken was that of the
Attorney General's dropping of the case for sedition that he had
instituted against a Communist journalist, J. R. Campbell, again
because of pressure from the Left. The issue was trivial, and the
original prosecution sadly misconceived, but while gross sins of
omission could be readily forgiven, by Conservatives and Liberals
alike, the apparent interference of Leftist politicians with the
due processes of law could not be tolerated, and so Conservatives and Liberals combined to vote the Government out of
office.[134]

Baldwin and the Conservatives returned to power. In 1922 they
had secured 28·2 per cent of all votes cast; in 1923, 38·1 per cent;
in this election of 1924 they received 48·3 per cent; and in 1929
they were to receive 38·2 per cent.[135] Conservative dominance of
the British scene is first of all attributable to the strongly conservative nature of a large section of the British public. The anti-
Conservative vote, certainly, was divided: but it was far from clear
that Liberal voters, given no Liberal candidate, would vote Labour.
At the same time the Conservatives had been given a gigantic
electoral head-start in the exceptional election of 1918. Able at all
times to present themselves as the party of stability and the party
of patriotism the Conservatives always benefited from any political
upheaval, real or alleged, falling short, as was always the case, of a
complete collapse of the whole system. The 1924 election is
remembered for the Zinoviev letter scare. From internal evidence
it is probable that this was not, as it purported to be, a letter
from the President of the Communist International to the British
Communist Party. In that it neatly suggested that the recent
Russian trade treaty had advanced the prospect of revolution in
Britain, its publication, obviously, could only serve the cause of
the Conservatives; but there is no conclusive evidence that it was
in fact the work, officially or unofficially, of the Conservative Party,
though in the mind of the Left this was exactly the kind of
tactic which the Conservatives, with their powerful will to power,
might be expected to adopt.[136] Actually the 'Red Letter' had
little effect on the result, which was mainly brought about by
a switch of Liberal support to the Conservatives.[137] In that it

could be represented as an unconstitutional challenge to the due processes of democracy, the General Strike, too, assisted the Conservatives.

As leading proponents of the empirical tradition, the Conservatives were happy to proceed with modest advances in the realm of collectivist social reform. In 1928 they gave the 'flappers' the vote, something which came easier from an accepted ruling party than it might have done from a party still making its way as the Labour Party was. Young men with the right educational background, however critical they might be of the party leadership, still went into the Conservative Party, the party with the tradition of ruling, and the party which seemed most likely to go on ruling. In the constituencies the local party organizations had a great deal of independence, which, since the party was seldom affected by great ideological disputes, was not a source of any great trouble to the central organization. Baldwin did have to meet more hostility from within his party than was usually the case with a Conservative leader; none the less the hierarchical instinct inculcated at the great public schools ensured that loyalty continued, as has been said, to be the Conservatives' 'secret weapon'.[138] It was natural that large businesses, however much they might dislike individual items of Conservative policy, should regard the party as the best available defence of their special interests: the party, therefore, was well off financially. Constituency parties were run by local people of wealth and influence, and it was an accepted convention that a candidate should pay his own campaign expenses. The major organs of the daily Press, with the exception of the *News*, the *Chronicle*, the *Manchester Guardian* (all liberal) and the limping *Daily Herald*, were all Tory in outlook, though Rothermere (*Daily Mail*) and Beaverbrook *(Daily Express)* were bitterly hostile to Baldwin personally. In so far as this opposition was based on principle it was that the Government was too 'socialistic' and insufficiently imperialist. At the other pole some of the survivors of the lost generation, forming a group nicknamed 'the Y.M.C.A.', began to argue that some of the economic lessons of the war period might be put to fuller use in dealing with the current industrial depression:

The war period shattered preconceived economic notions, proved possible theoretic impossibilities, removed irremovable barriers, created
new and undreamt-of situations. Yet by far the greater part of the
legislation which today governs trade and industry dates from before
that period. We are surely entitled to ask whether it is now adequate to
meet the vastly changed condition of the modern economic era.[139]

But if the Conservative Party was not completely united, it was
still in much happier case than its two rivals.

The most reliable way of assessing the decline in Liberal fortunes
is to look not at the percentage of total votes cast, which is affected
by the number of candidates put forward, but at the average
percentage vote per candidate. In 1922 this was 38·4, in 1923 37·8,
in 1924 30·9 and in 1929 27·7. (Over the same period the comparable
Conservative percentage fluctuated between 39·4 and 51·9, and the
Labour percentage between 38·2 and 41·0.)[140] The Liberal problem was that, with Labour bidding for the working-class vote,
and the Conservatives clearly the most efficient defenders of upper-
class interests, they lacked any clearly marked socio-economic
grouping from which to draw support. Asquith inspired great
personal loyalty, but the war had destroyed him as a political
leader: by an irony implicit in the crisis of 1916 his wing of the
party was actually the more reactionary one. Lloyd George too
had loyal followers, but the basic sentiment he aroused in the
uncommitted was mistrust. Actually some of the finest constructive
political thinking of the period came from Liberals, spurred on by
J. M. Keynes who detested the Tories but who, being a highly-
cultured patrician, equally at home as Fellow and Bursar of King's
College, Cambridge, and as a member of the artistic Bloomsbury
set, with a certain faith in the future of capitalism, had little inclination to become embroiled with Labour. In 1921 Ramsay Muir,
Philip Guedalla (both historians), William Beveridge (pioneer of
Edwardian social reform, who in the Twenties became Director
of the London School of Economics), Ted Scott (son of the editor
of the *Guardian*), Walter Layton (civil servant and university
teacher) and E. D. Simon (businessman and Lord Mayor of Manchester) launched the Liberal summer schools as a means towards

scientific analysis of problems of public policy. H. W. Massing-ham, a devoted upholder of the *laissez-faire* Liberal tradition, was replaced as editor of the *Nation* by Sir Hubert D. Henderson, an economist who shared much common ground with Keynes.[141] Keynes himself kept up the high level of polemic he had begun with *The Economic Consequences of the Peace*, denouncing the return to the Gold Standard in his *Economic Consequences of Mr Churchill*. The grand culmination was the Liberal 'Yellow Book' of 1928, *Britain's Industrial Future*, which a year later became the basis of the Liberal election manifesto, *We Can Conquer Unemployment*. The three major proposals of the Yellow Book were: a full-scale attack on unemployment through massive schemes of public works; the establishment of an Economic General Staff (a phrase coined by Beveridge) to engage in continuous study of current economic problems, co-ordinate statistical information, call the attention of the Government to coming economic difficulties and suggest remedies; the replacement of a theoretical attachment to unadulterated individualism by an acceptance of a mixed economy in which public concerns would play an increasing part.[142] Unhappily many active Liberals, particularly those who held down seats in the House of Commons, found the Keynesian remedies too sharp an affront to the principles on which they had been reared. The inflexibility and backward-looking character of the existing political structure is still more luridly shown up in the White Paper brought out by the Treasury in attempted refutation of the Yellow Book: no amount of expenditure on public works, the White Paper insisted, could have any possible effect on the level of unemployment.[143]

Winning only fifty-nine seats in 1918 and losing most of its ex-perienced leaders, the Parliamentary Labour Party in the first years of peace did not cut a very inspiring political figure. Despite the new constitution of 1918 the party retained much of its old federal character; more than this, no changes in organization could oblit-erate the different attitudes which different members of the party brought to fundamental problems of Labour politics. Formally the party was now committed to a socialist objective, but there remained a substantial trade union section which thought in 'labour' rather than 'socialist' terms. Between this section and the Left, which was eager for a transformation in the economic and moral basis of society, there was a middle ground occupied by the more able leaders of the pre-war years and by some of the new Liberal recruits. The I.L.P. continued in existence and the opening of the Labour Party to individual membership did not, in the first instance, short-circuit the flow of members to it: on the contrary, in 1919–20 and again in 1922–23 the I.L.P. enjoyed two great expansions in membership.[144] But ultimately the problem for the I.L.P. was that it came more and more to look a mere miniature of the Labour Party (lacking only the really stolid trade union elements) rather than a distinctive wing. In the early Twenties when the 'labour' section dominated the Parliamentary Labour Party, active and able men of varying shades of opinion found a congenial home in the I.L.P. When the Parliamentary Labour Party emerged from the obscurity of ineffectual opposition and seated itself on and behind the Treasury Bench it seemed at first as though the I.L.P. might have established itself as the power behind the throne; but it could not be both this *and* a party of Leftist dissent. The true soul of the I.L.P. lay in genuine and impassioned working-class protest: the true source of prestige and power was in the official Labour Party, so it was in that direction that able but practical-minded former I.L.P. members began to turn. Yet the I.L.P. still did not monopolize the Left: some left-wingers came to scorn the intellectual, and sometimes pacifist, associations of the I.L.P. and preferred to mount their attacks directly from the flanks of the Labour Party; for men of still sterner views there was, from 1920, the Communist Party. Great practical difficulties rose in the 1920s over parliamentary candidatures: the I.L.P. had a habit of first running candidates it claimed as its own, then expecting the Labour Party to foot the bill. However, the stages by which the I.L.P. ceased to be an important force in British politics were gradual; it is perhaps unwise to write them off as inevitable.[145]

Labour made substantial gains in the 1922 election, and it was largely due to the revived strength of the I.L.P. that MacDonald was re-elected chairman and *leader* (an innovation noted at the time by the *Manchester Guardian*)[146] of the party – though he also had considerable trade union support. Under its new leadership Labour provided a more efficient parliamentary opposition; it was also, because of the arrival of a body of seventeen I.L.P. members from the West of Scotland, a more colourful one. In Scotland the I.L.P. still *was* the Labour Party: Labour constituency organizations were little more than empty husks, with the real germ of energy and power remaining in the local branch of the I.L.P.[147] The majority of Scottish I.L.P. M.P.s, therefore, had a clear-sighted and level-headed attachment to the Labour Party. Although the term 'Clydesider' was often applied indiscriminately to all West of of Scotland Labour M.P.s, it was really only meaningful if applied to a much smaller group of five: James Maxton, school-teacher son of two school-teachers and, later, when wartime imprisonment lost him his job, a worker in the shipyards, emotional, dedicated to the cause of the working classes rather than to any one political organization, lean and long-haired ('he not only preached the revolution, he looked it', it was said of him), a soft-boiled Marxist, attacked, of course, by the hard-bitten Marxists of the Communist Party; John Wheatley, a chubby owl behind his pebble-lens spectacles, once a miner, now in his fifties the proprietor of a prosperous publishing business; Campbell Stephen, jolly and rotund of countenance, a former advocate, clergyman and school-teacher; and George Buchanan and David Kirkwood, both from the engineering shops – though Kirkwood was actually a shop manager.[148] This was the group which in June 1922 staged a dramatic scene in the House of Commons. Maxton undoubtedly spoke from a sense of total emotional involvement when he attacked as 'murderers' government supporters of economies in milk supplied under child welfare schemes and in hospital accommodation for children; only recently he had seen his own young wife struggle vainly for life after a desperate battle for the life of his son. For refusing to retract the word 'murderer' Maxton, followed by Wheatley, Stephen and Buchanan, was suspended from the House.[149] MacDonald and the party leadership were thoroughly embarrassed by the incident, though there was never any question at this time of a break between the leadership and the activists. The advent of the first Labour government, however, brought into focus both the potential fissures within the party and the inadequacies of the leadership. All the major tactical decisions made in face of the unenticing parliamentary situation created by the 1923 election were sensible when viewed both from the Gladstonian standpoint of a parliamentary system demanding the good faith of those who work it, and from the standpoint of serving the long-term interests of the Labour Party. Labour had to take office if it were to demonstrate its fitness to govern; to demonstrate its contempt for the Liberals and its determination to supersede them, it had to avoid any formal Liberal-Labour agreement; finally, to demonstrate its faith in democracy, it made its minority position in the country and in Parliament the excuse for eschewing any tough or controversial legislation. Unhappily such niceties were out of place amid the grave problems of the 1920s. Clifford Allen, chairman of the I.L.P., argued for a different conception of the workings of democracy whereby Labour in office should proceed to introduce legislation regardless of its lack of a 'mandate', leaving it to democracy to pass judgement *post facto* at the next election. He also argued that at least the Government should use its position to launch a number of scientific studies of the major problems facing the country, with a view to remedial legislation during a subsequent Labour government.[150] His advice, despite his close personal association with Ramsay MacDonald, fell on deaf ears. In fact the gravest weakness of the Government was that its members, after having for years talked the vague language of evolutionary socialism, had no clear idea of the extent of the country's economic troubles, and no real notion of how to deal with them. It was noteworthy that the Government's most successful legislation was carried through by its most leftist member, John Wheatley. MacDonald, indeed, had gone very far in choosing a government of respectable appearance. 'It's a lum hat government like a' the rest' is the well-known judgement passed by one disappointed proletarian. Yet whatever the composition of Labour governments, whatever the composition even of the Parliamentary Labour Party, it remained essentially a working-class party by virtue of its local organizations, which were staffed by an utterly different class of people from those of the other two political parties. It remained too, essentially an 'outsider' party. This is highlighted by the readiness of MacDonald to make the Campbell case an issue of confidence by which his Government would stand or fall. MacDonald's own remarks during the Campbell debate ('It has been a high adventure')[151] were all very well: the party's problem remained to reconcile high adventure with practical government.

The lack of achievement of the first Labour government hastened the development of a more firmly defined discontent with the party leadership based on the leftist element of the I.L.P. Within the I.L.P. itself the power of this element was greatly strengthened when in 1925 Clifford Allen resigned from the chairmanship of the party, to be replaced by Maxton. But as the I.L.P. came to seem more and more extremist, its ability to affect the Labour leadership became less and less. It was widely thought in the Labour Party that MacDonald, in apparently accepting the genuineness of the Zinoviev letter, had not handled that issue at all well; but there was no one else in the party who could rival Mac-Donald's handsome presence and Scottish rhetoric. He above all had the qualities traditionally associated with a successful politician. On some issues Maxton and his associates were at one with the Labour Party conference as when, in 1928, a resolution calling for unemployment benefits of £1 a week was adopted.[152] For all that the party prided itself on being more democratic internally than its opponents, MacDonald made it clear that in practice not even a Labour prime minister could hold himself bound absolutely by conference decisions: this as an issue was to recur again and again.

The ineptitude that characterized the leadership of the parliamentary parties was to be found also in the Communist Party, effective in spear-heading extra-parliamentary pressure movements such as the Unemployed Workers' Movement, but naïve beyond belief in its political tactics and an utter dead loss as a possible instigator of revolution. Various fascist movements were apparent, but there was no unified fascist organization in Britain in the Twenties. Some of the steam which did so much damage in other countries Britain had funnelled off into the Black-and-Tans at the beginning of the decade. But the very existence of non-parliamentary parties strengthened the determination of both Mac-Donald and Baldwin to maintain to the last detail the forms of British parliamentary democracy, even if, in the meantime, the economy went to hell. The fires were to be stoked high on Wall Street in 1929. The world economic crisis which followed, in its British aspect illumined clearly all the weaknesses, and indeed all the virtues, of the British political structure of the 1920s. As a result of the 1929 election Labour took office again, now the largest party in the Commons, but still lacking in an overall majority. Its average percentage vote per candidate had scarcely risen, and its victory, such as it was, could to a great extent be attributed to the large number of candidates the Liberals threw into the field, to the disadvantage of the Conservatives rather than Labour. In view of the clear breakdown of the two-party system and of the problems the country none the less faced, it was not unconstructive for politicians to talk of the House as acting as a united 'Council of State' and of an end to 'party bickering'.[153] The alternative again was for the Labour government to ignore its lack of a popular majority and get on with the business of governing; but such a notion was no more acceptable to the party leadership than it had been in 1924. Nor indeed was the party leadership any better equipped to deal with the economic issues which beset it: Snowden, if anything, was more Gladstonian than ever. John Wheatley (who died in 1930) believed that Labour should not take minority office – but again this was scarcely a feasible choice for a party which wished to be taken seriously by the electorate.

By the late 1920s it was becoming apparent that there was, and could be, no universal recovery from the economic dislocations of the war. The face of the world economy was disturbed by a self-destructive division between debtor and creditor nations, and scarred by a fundamental dislocation in world trade relationships, which worked to the particular disadvantage of primary producers. Widespread industrial depression and conditions of political instability, especially in Central Europe, led to a clamping down on credit and general hoarding of capital. Before 1914 London had functioned triumphantly as the world's greatest financial centre on ridiculously small gold reserves, because in a time of confident expansionism the demand for gold was low; whenever assets did begin to drain from London, new ones could always be attracted by an increase in the Bank Rate. However,

One result of the 1914–18 war had been to reduce London's overall international creditor status. On short-term account the substantial creditor position built up after 1907 was converted, after 1918, into a heavy short-term debtor position.[154]

Wartime borrowing and sales of overseas assets had also adversely affected London's long-term creditor position.[155] For all that, the Bank of England went on behaving as if London was still the unshakable centre of the world money market, with a special obligation to go on supplying loans to underdeveloped countries within the area where sterling still ruled supreme (what in the Second World War became the sterling area). After the American Stock Market crash of 1929 crisis spread to Europe, where the various central banks ceased all lendings abroad and began to call in their own overseas assets; all banks, that is, but the Bank of England, which, taking up a bold nineteenth-century stance, endeavoured to overcome the world liquidity shortage single-handed, regardless of the fact that meantime, because of the poor state of the British domestic economy, confidence in London was steadily ebbing. One nineteenth-century remedy was denied to the Bank: although the gold reserves began to dwindle in 1920, the Bank Rate was not raised since this would depress an already severely depressed domestic economy; but failure to raise it increased the doubts of foreign investors.[156]

Snowden's 'business as usual' budget of 1931 showed as crass an unawareness of the needs of the hour as had Lloyd George's first war budget. In May the year-long splutterings of financial disaster in Central Europe touched off a final chain reaction of bank collapses, resulting in further withdrawals from London, and a loss of assets which Britain could recall. Brash complacency was now replaced by feverish panic. At the insistence of the Liberals in Parliament, a timorous breed compared with those Liberals outside who acknowledged Keynes as their mentor, the May Committee was appointed to investigate methods of pruning government expenditure, the high level of which, by orthodox pre-1914 standards, was also a cause of impaired foreign confidence. The moment Parliament rose for the summer recess, the May Report was published: it was couched in such gloomy terms that the outflow of funds was greatly accelerated. Were this trend allowed to continue unresisted it would soon lead to a devaluation of the pound and an enforced abandonment of the Gold Standard, which would represent heavy blows to what remained of London's position as an international financial centre. For the British domestic *economy* as a whole the situation was little more serious than it had been throughout most of the Twenties, though domestic stagnation had been one of the long-term causes of the ultimate *financial* crisis. Devaluation and abandonment of the Gold Standard would not of themselves directly damage British industry; indeed by providing a desirable whiff of inflation they would almost certainly help to revive it. On the other hand, the total collapse of London as an international money market would mean the wiping out of a substantial portion of Britain's invisible exports (banking and insurance services) which for long had helped to keep the Balance of Payments just in equilibrium. Few doubted that the pound must be 'saved'.

The necessary prerequisite was a restoration of foreign confidence, a difficult task for a minority Labour government. The earlier vague talk of collaboration between the parties, therefore, reached the stage where the Labour Cabinet authorized its chief ministers to enter into discussions with the Opposition leaders over the nature of the emergency measures which would have to be introduced.[157] As early as July the weekly journal of the I.L.P. (now effectively reduced in Parliament to a hard core of activists led by Maxton, and more or less constantly at war with what it saw as the compromising policies of the Labour government) carried a front page article headed 'Towards a National Government'.[158] The atmosphere of final political crisis was conjoined to that of potential economic disaster when, on 11 August, Ramsay Mac-Donald made a sudden return to London from a holiday in his native Lossiemouth. Within the Cabinet discussion centred on the size and nature of the economies which would have to be made to effect the necessary restoration of confidence. Meantime the Bank of England was endeavouring to raise loans from American and French banks. Provisionally the Cabinet was prepared to approve economies of £56 million, though there was strong resistance to a suggested cut in benefits paid to the unemployed, reinforced when the General Council of the T.U.C. came out strongly against any such attack on those who were already the worst-off members of the community. The Conservative leaders thought that greater economies would be necessary, and, in fact, on the evening of Sunday 23 August news reached what proved to be the final meeting of the Labour Cabinet that J. P. Morgan's of New York would only grant a loan if the Government proved its determination to face up to the problem of high government spending by imposing a 10 per cent cut in unemployment benefits. A majority of the Cabinet were prepared to accept the inevitability of such a cut; but a minority, including such key figures as Henderson (Foreign Secretary), Graham (President of the Board of Trade), Clynes (Home Secretary) and Adamson (Secretary of State for Scotland), were not. The Government could not go on.

But government there must be, and the outcome – a National Government, headed by MacDonald, who took with him from the Labour Party Snowden, Thomas and Lord Sankey, but as firmly rooted in Conservative support as Lloyd George's Coalition had been – was a great tribute to the British virtues of compromise and pragmatism; and also to MacDonald's willingness to risk eventual oblivion for what he believed to be his public duty. The bulk of the Labour Party would have nothing to do with the new Government: a few began to speak darkly of 'treachery'. Maxton, though a constant critic of the ministry which had just expired was clear that the Prime Minister had done 'what he believed right. Accusations from the Labour Party about treachery seem to me quite out of place.'[159] R. D. Denman, one of the few Labour M.P.s to give his support to the new MacDonald régime, gave his impressions of the parliamentary situation immediately after the formation of the new Government:

Labour M.P.s had no doubts at all that we dissentients would be swept away by waves of infuriated electors. In the House we remained quite friendly and I used to sit amongst them at lunch and listen to the immense majorities the 'cuts' would assuredly give them ... the most friendly were full of pity for my short-sighted folly.[160]

The new Government did carry through ruthless economies, got its foreign loans, and went off the Gold Standard. In terms of the basic issue of confidence there was, however, all the difference in the world between a weak Labour ministry being forced off gold, and the action of a National Government which had the weight of respectable opinion behind it. The financial crisis was weathered, without any serious damage to the international position of the London money market; the domestic economy, on the other hand, was very adversely affected by the accompanying deflation and retrenchment characterized by Keynes as 'replete with folly'. For as long as Britain went on playing a nineteenth-century financial role in the world drastically altered by the disruptions of total war she would be beset by the problem of how to maintain the necessary reserves without at the same time creating conditions of industrial stagnation.

Despite a promise that the National Government was a purely temporary expedient, to be followed as soon as the crisis had passed by a return to normal party alignments, MacDonald, pushed by Conservatives eager to secure a clear field for the introduction of Tariff Reform, and himself conscious that without Labour support his government had little claim to the title 'National', decided in October to seek popular endorsement. The election reduced Labour to a pathetic 46, while the National Government piled up the immense total of 556 seats, a signal demonstration, it could be said, of popular support. As ever, in this time of crisis, it was really the Conservatives who gained. Effectively Britain was in for a spell of one-party government, a poor outcome to a decade of democratic posturing, and one which lacked even the saving grace of providing the country with dynamic leadership.

NOTES TO CHAPTER FOUR

1. Recent authorities for the topics with which this section deals are: W. K. Hancock, *Survey of British Commonwealth Affairs : Problems of Nationality,* 1937, and *Problems of Economic Policy,* 1942; N. Mansergh, *Survey of British Commonwealth Affairs: Problems of External Policy,* 1952, and *The Irish Question,* 1964; D. Gwynn, *The History of Partition,* 1950; J. C. Beckett, *The Making of Modern Ireland,* 1966; F. H. Hinsley, *Power and the Pursuit of Peace,* 1963; F. S. Northedge, *The Troubled Giant : Britain Among the Great Powers, 1916–1939,* 1966; D. C. Watt, *Personalities and Policies,* 1966; W. N. Medlicott, *British Foreign Policy Since Versailles,* 1940; P. A. Reynolds, *British Foreign Policy in the Inter-War Years,* 1954; W. M. Jordan, *Great Britain, France and the German Problem, 1919–1939,* 1943. So far only the first part of the Twenties is covered by the *Documents on British Foreign Policy, 1919–1939,* series I.

2. P.R.O., CAB 23/29, 9 (22) (2) (15 February 1922).

3. Quoted by W. K. Hancock, *Problems of Nationality,* p. 80.

4. Labour Party, *Report of the Labour Commission in Ireland,* 1921.

5. Quoted by A. P. Newton, *One Hundred Years of British Empire,* 1940, p. 394. The description of Balfour is by Kevin O'Higgins.

6. See H. R. Winkler, 'The Emergence of a Labour Foreign Policy in Great Britain, 1918–1929', *Journal of Modern History,* vol. 28, 1956, pp. 247 ff. The Conservative leaflet is National Union of Conservative Associations, *The League of Nations to Prevent War,* 1919.

7. S. R. Graubard, 'Military Demobilization in Britain following the First World War', *Journal of Modern History,* 1947.

8. P.R.O., CAB 23/22, 48 (20).

9. A. E. Kahn, *Great Britain in the World Economy,* 1946, pp. 106–9.

10. The *Nation,* 13 November 1926.

11. Especially in the *General Theory of Employment, Interest and Money,* 1936.

12. P.R.O., CAB 23/29, 7/22 (2) (5).

13. Harrod, *Keynes,* p. 357.

14. P.R.O., CAB 23/15, 606.

15. *Ibid.*

16. W. Gallacher, *Revolt on the Clyde,* 1936, pp. 217–42. K. Middlemass, *The Clydesiders,* 1966, p. 30.

17. P.R.O., CAB 23/9, 521 (2). 28 January 1919.

18. Gallacher, p. 221.

19. The most recent works are H. Pelling, *The British Communist Party,* 1958, and L. Macfarlane, *The British Communist Party : Origin and Development to 1930,* 1966.

20. *House of Commons Debates,* 29 May 1919.

21. P.R.O., CAB 23/9, 529 (3).

22. P.P., 1919, XI Cnd. 359, pp. 79–89, 174, 181–2, 222–40. XII Cnd. 360, pp. 474, 1001.

23. P.R.O., CAB 23/15, 607A.

24. *Morning Post,* 4 August 1919.

25. *Ibid.,* 6 August 1919.

26. P.R.O., CAB 23/12. 626 (1) (2).
27. *The Times,* 4 October 1919.
28. There is a good general account in W. H. Crook, *General Strike,* 1931, pp. 350–1.
29. C. L. Mowat, *Britain between the Wars,* 1955, p. 41.
30. P.R.O., CAB 23/21, 26 (20) and 27 (20).
31. G. D. H. Cole, *History of the Labour Party Since 1914,* 1948, pp. 103–7.
32. P.R.O., Cab 23/22, 41 (20).
33. P.R.O., CAB 23/22, 46 (20).
34. P.R.O., CAB 23/22, 10 August 1920.
35. P.R.O., CAB 23/22, C. 56/20 (2) (3).
36. W. Hannington, *Unemployed Struggles 1919–1936,* 1935, p. 16. *The Times,* 19–20 October 1920.
37. Hannington, pp. 33 ff. *The Times,* 13 August, 7 September, 13 September, 1921.
38. *Daily Herald,* 1 April 1921.
39. *Ibid.,* 3 April 1921.
40. *Daily Express,* 1 April 1921.
41. P.R.O., CAB 23/25, 18 (21).
42. *Glasgow Herald,* 2 April 1921. P.R.O., CAB 23/25, C.17 (21).
43. P.R.O., CAB 23/25, Conference of Ministers, 6 April 1921. *House of Commons Debates,* 8 April 1921.
44. *The Times,* 31 March–7 April, 1921.
45. *Ibid.,* 14 April 1921.
46. P.R.O., CAB 23/25, 19 (21).
47. P.R.O., CAB 23/25, 23 (21).
48. *Glasgow Herald,* 13 April 1921.
49. *Daily Herald,* 9 April 1921.
50. *Glasgow Herald,* 19 April 1921.
51. *House of Commons Debates,* 8 April 1921.
52. Hannington, p. 77.
53. *Ibid.,* p. 81.
54. R. Postgate, *Life of George Lansbury,* 1952, pp. 216–20.
55. A. Bullock, *Life and Times of Ernest Bevin,* vol. 1, 1960, pp. 147–9.
56. *House of Commons Debates,* 6 August 1925.
57. *The Times,* 14 September 1925.
58. Crook, *General Strike,* p. 295.
59. There is an excellent account in Mowat, *op. cit.,* pp. 298 ff.
60. *The British Worker,* 4–11 May 1926.
61. See e.g. A. F. Brockway, *Inside the Left,* 1943, p. 120.
62. Cp. J. Symons, *The General Strike,* 1953, pp. 201–5.
63. *House of Commons Debates,* 6 May 1926.
64. Symons, p. 214.
65. Mowat, p. 310.
66. Bullock, *Bevin,* pp. 345 ff.
67. P.P., 1939–40, IV, Cmd. 6153 (Barlow Report), pp. 36–37.
68. C. F. G. Masterman, *England After the War,* 1922, pp. 45–46. F. M. L. Thompson, *English Landed Society in the Nineteenth Century,* 1963, pp. 330 ff.

69. J. M. Lee, *Social Leaders and Public Persons*, 1963, p. 80.

70. H. Bentinck, *Tory Democracy*, 1918, pp. 2–3.

71. J. Galsworthy, *A Modern Comedy*, p. x.

72. A. L. Bowley and J. Stamp, *The National Income*, 1924, pp. 57–59.

73. *Ibid.*, pp. 11–12.

74. *New Survey of London Life and Labour*, vol. 11, 1931, p. 465. D. Caradog Jones (ed.), *Social Survey of Merseyside*, 1934, vol. 11, pp. 301, 306 ff.

75. A. L. Bowley and M. Hogg, *Has Poverty Diminished?*, 1925, p. 3.

76. *Ibid.*, p. 20.

77. *Ibid.*, p. 36.

78. e.g. H. Tout, *The Standard of Living in Bristol*, Bristol, 1938, esp. pp. 25–36.

79. *House of Commons Debates*, 24 February, 26 October, 1921.

80. See A. Marwick, 'The Labour Party and the Welfare State 1900–1948', *American Historical Review*, December 1967.

81. Trades Union Congress and Labour Party, *Unemployment Insurance: Principles of Labour Policy*, n.d.

82. Ministry of Labour, *Report of Departmental Committee on Unemployment Insurance*, 1927

83. e.g. H. Eckstein, *The English Health Service*, 1958, p. 115.

84. P.P., 1920, XVII, Cmd. 693.

85. P.R.O., CAB 23/22, Conference of Ministers, 21 July 1920.

86. P.P., 1921, X, Cmd. 605.

87. P.P., 1921, XIII, Cmd. 1402, pp. 2–3, Cmd. 1335, p. 11.

88. Labour Party, *Report of Annual Conference 1918*, p. 124–5.

89. R. Brady, *Crisis in Britain*, 1949, p. 356.

90. Trades Union Congress and Labour Party, *Memoranda Prepared by Advisory Committee on Public Health*, n.d.

91. Reports of Conferences reprinted as Labour Party, *The Hospital Problem*, 1924, and *The Labour Party and the Nursing Profession*, 1927.

92. e.g. Labour Party, *Continued Education under the New Education Act*, 1919.

93. A. Carr-Saunders and D. Caradog Jones, *Social Structure of England and Wales 1927*, p. 147.

94. Labour Party, *Report of Annual Conference 1920*, p. 181.

95. For an admirable account based on ministerial archives, see Middlemass, *Clydesiders*, pp. 145–58.

96. Board of Education, *The Education of the Adolescent*, ('Haddow Report'), 1927, pp. 46–54.

97. *Ibid.*, esp. pp. 50–51.

98. P.R.O., CAB 23/29, 13 (22) (3a) (24 February 1922).

99. Labour Party, *Secondary Education for All*, n.d., p. 7.

100. See e.g. *New Leader*, 12 October 1923.

101. 'Haddow Report', pp. 70–100.

102. Quoted by S. Haxey, *Tory M.P.*, 1939, p. 180.

103. Labour Party, *Report of Annual Conference 1926*, pp. 164–5.

104. Carr-Saunders and Caradog Jones, 1927, pp. 127–8.

105. J. Dover Wilson, *Schools of England*, 1928, p. 343.

106. J. Jeans, *The Mysterious Universe*, 1930, p. 134.

107. J. G. Crowther, *British Scientists of the Twentieth Century*, 1952, p. 138.

108. See the introduction by Frederick Etchells to *The City of Tomorrow* (trs. by C. E. Jeanneret-Gris), 1929.

109. See generally E. Mackerness, *Social History of English Music*, pp. 261 ff.

110. L. Namier, *Structure of Politics at the Accession of George III*, 1929, p. vii.

111. e.g. the works of Arnold Toynbee (the elder, not to be confused with A. J. Toynbee, author of *A Study of History*) and the Hammonds gave place to those of Clapham and Ashton.

112. For the press in this period see Francis Williams, *Dangerous Estate*, 1952, P.E.P., *The British Press*, 1948, *Report of Royal Commission on the Press, 1947–49* and *Report of Royal Commission on the Press, 1962*.

113. *New Survey of London Life and Labour*, vol. IX, 1934, p. 47.

114. For the British cinema in this period see Commission on Educational and Cultural Films, *The Film in National Life*, 1932, and *Report of Moyne Committee*, P.P., 1936–37, IX, Cmd. 5320.

115. *B.B.C. Report and Accounts, 1955–56;* P.P., XI, Cmd. 9803, app. I, p. 98.

116. This account is based on Briggs, *History of Broadcasting*, pp. 45–88, 93–142.

117. Quoted by Briggs, p. 79.

118. P.P., 1926, XX, Cmd. 2599, p. 240.

119. *Morning Post*, 26 August 1919.

120. R. Harper, *The Romance of a Modern Airway*, 1931, pp. 9–10.

121. See esp. A. Plummer, *New British Industries in the Twentieth Century*, 1937, pp. 156 ff. Also J. D. Scott, *Vickers*, 1962, pp. 174 ff.

122. *Hydro-Electric Development in Scotland;* P.P., 1942–43, IV, Cmd. 6406, p. 6.

123. *Ibid.*, p. 3.

124. *Ibid.*, p. 5.

125. Plummer, pp. 103, 109.

126. *Social Survey of Merseyside*, III, p. 278.

127. Harrod, *Keynes*, p. 328.

128. British Empire Exhibition, *Catalogue*, 1922.

129. Daily Mail, *Seventh Ideal Home Exhibition*, 1923, *Catalogue*, 1923.

130. R. Boothby, *The New Economy*, 1943, p. 13.

131. P.R.O., C.63/21/(2), C. 68/21 (4).

132. *The Times*, 12 October 1919.

133. Quoted by A. W. Baldwin, *My Father : the True Story*, 1955, p. 138.

134. There is an excellent account in R. Lyman, *The First Labour Government 1924*, 1957, pp. 237–45.

135. D. Butler, *The Electoral System in Britain*, 1963, p. 173.

136. There are good accounts of the episode in Mowat, pp. 187–94, and Lyman pp. 257–61. See also L. Chester *et. al.*, *The Zinoviev Letter*, 1967.

137. Butler, p. 172.

138. Earl of Kilmuir, *Political Adventure*, 1964, p. 300. The best secondary studies of the Conservative Party are in R. T. Mackenzie, *British Political Parties*, 1955, and S. H. Beer, *Modern British Politics*, 1965. See also Guttsman, *The British Political Élite* and I. Bulmer-Thomas, *The Party System in Great Britain*, 1953, and the special articles in the *Political Quarterly*, 1961.

139. R. Boothby, H. Macmillan, J. Loder and O. Stanley, *Industry and the State*, 1927, p. 35.
140. Butler, p. 177.
141. Harrod, *Keynes*, pp. 334–7.
142. Liberal Party, *Britain's Industrial Future*, 1928, pp. 453–88.
143. P.P., 1928–29, XVI, Cmd. 3331.
144. For a brief account see A. Marwick 'The Independent Labour Party in the 1920s', *Bulletin of the Institute of Historical Research*, 1962. For an excellent detailed treatment see R. E. Dowse, *Left in the Centre*, 1966.
145. As Dr Dowse appears to do.
146. *Manchester Guardian*, 21 November 1922.
147. A. Marwick, 'James Maxton', *Scottish Historical Review*, 1964, p. 29.
148. For the Clydesiders see Marwick, 'Maxton', and R. K. Middlemass, *The Clydesiders*.
149. *House of Commons Debates*, 20 June 1922.
150. C. Allen, *Putting Socialism into Practice*, 1924.
151. *House of Commons Debates*, 8 October 1924.
152. Labour Party, *Report of Annual Conference 1928*, p. 115.
153. The first phrase was used by MacDonald and by Sir Laming Worthington-Evans, and the second by Snowden. See R. Bassett, *1931 Political Crisis*, 1958, pp. 45–46. In general see R. Skidelski, *Politicians and the Slump*, 1967.
154. D. Williams, 'London and the 1931 Financial Crisis', *Economic History Review*, 2nd series, vol. 15, April 1963, p. 519.
155. E. V. Morgan, *British Financial Policy*, pp. 322–6. Williams, p. 520.
156. Williams, p. 520.
157. The fullest discussion is in R. Bassett, *1931 Political Crisis*, 1958.
158. *New Leader*, 24 July 1931.
159. *Ibid.*, 4 September 1931.
160. R. D. Denman, *Political Sketches*, Carlisle, 1948, p. 6.

CHAPTER FIVE
After the Crash

After 1931 the organized Labour movement in Britain was thrown into retreat. But upper-class liberalism refound its voice; it could no longer speak through the Liberal Party, also finally shattered as a parliamentary force in 1931, so it emerged in the intra- and extra-parliamentary groupings that were a characteristic of the decade; it also emerged, humbly, in some of the policies of the National Government and, to pin down the fact by which the Thirties are often remembered, in the swing of the intellectuals towards the Communist Party. The great financial crisis intensified the depression in the old heavy industries, but the new industries continued to expand: this was particularly so of the chemical industry, affected on the economic front by the giant merger of the Twenties between Brunner Mond, United Alkali, British Dyestuffs and Nobel Industries, which created Imperial Chemical Industries, and on the scientific front by the discovery in the Thirties of the sulphonamides and of methods of synthesizing man-made fibres[1]; to a lesser extent it was true also of the electrical industry, where among other developments a modest start was made to the harnessing of the country's potential hydro-electric power.[2] Altogether the 1930s do mark a clear stage in the growing, though still utterly inadequate, scientific orientation of British industry. In 1930, 422 British firms were spending £1,736,000 on research and development; in 1935, 484 firms were spending £2,696,000; and in 1938, 566 firms were spending £5,442,000. Scientific graduates and other technically qualified personnel employed wholly or mainly on research and development in 1930 by 384 firms numbered 1381; in 1935 432 firms employed 2,566 persons in this category; and in 1938 520 firms employed 4,382. In 1927 the 16 private research associations which qualified for grants from the Department of Scientific and Industrial Research (D.S.I.R.) had a subscription income of £117,000, 20 associations in 1935 had an income of £235,000, and 22 in 1938 an income of £326,000.[3]

Under the surface of events changes in the long-term evolution of British society continued, but the surface picture, the living reality for millions of British people, was certainly a gloomy one. Regardless of the fact that the cyclical depression had begun in 1920, this is the period known as '*the* Depression', justifiably enough since it was in the Thirties that unemployment reached its peak of just under three millions, that the problem of the long-term unemployed, formerly mainly to be found in the post-1926 coal industry, became especially pressing, and that the icy winds touched members of the middle classes as well as manual workers. Whatever the National Government may have achieved in the way of restoration of 'confidence' it was not able to do anything about steadily mounting unemployment, which reached 2,955,000 in January 1933; in August, it was just under 2½ million; it did not go below 2 million till July 1935. A year later as Britain moved into a kind of 'recovery' it was 1·6 million, where it remained, 12 per cent of the insured population, till the outbreak of war. By the beginning of 1932 the total of long-term unemployed (out of work for a year or more) was over 300,000; early in 1933 (when the total was at its highest) the long-term unemployed numbered 450,000.

Of 100 men queuing up at the Exchange in September 1929, only 5 or 6 had been persistently unemployed. Of 100 men queuing up there three years later, when the depression was at its worst, 20 had had no work for a year or more.[4]

The tragedy was that as 'recovery' took place, it was the long-term unemployed who were left stranded on the economic slag heap. In 1936 there were still 250,000 long-term unemployed, involving a family total of 875,000 human beings, men, women and children. The incidence of middle-class unemployment was relatively slight, but there was insecurity, absence of choice in employment, and, especially among small businessmen, occasional hard stories, such as that of

. . . a married man, 37 years old, with a wife of 40 and a boy of 9 at school. This man became a clerk at 16, served in the war, and then set up in business, first with his brother, later on his own. He was at first very successful, and lived in a substantial house on the outskirts of Liverpool, but ultimately he failed and went bankrupt. He then became a storekeeper for a telephone company and held this responsible post for six years until he was dismissed in November 1932. For a week he tried to gain his living as a salesman for a tailoring company, but gave up and he has done no work since November 1932. The U.A.B. pays him the comparatively high amount of 36s., but as he pays 18s. 6d. for his four-roomed house on one of the new estates, there remains only 17s. 6d. to feed, clothe and warm three persons, 2s. 6s. a day all told. There was one other child. At the clinic they told his wife that the child was in need of extra nourishment, but – as he alleged – when the officer came round and saw a house of middle-class character, he said that no extra nourishment could be allowed. The child died. The home is still middle-class, as is the appearance and clothing of the household; but the furniture has gradually gone, an £85 piano fetching £35, a £30 bedroom suite £9, an £18 sewing machine £3. There is nearly £4 owing on the rest; there are debts for groceries – although relations help. All insurances have been realized. This man applied to one of the voluntary societies for a loan, but was refused, 'though in better times I used to give them a guinea'. He conceals the fact of his having been out of work from all his friends, if possible, and from his neighbours, and even the boy is not allowed to know the real position. . . .

If he had a little capital, they might start a business or a boarding-house, but there is nothing save this last straw to which they cling, their respectability.[5]

Yet for many of the more powerful members of the business community the National Government's round of economies did not go far enough. The Federation of British Industries in October 1932 recalled, somewhat unnecessarily, that

The F.B.I. has for many years past urged upon successive Governments the need for a drastic curtailment of public expenditure. This is now a vital and urgent economic necessity. . . . A change of policy and of outlook is now requisite. We must curb our desire to find a short cut to Utopia and rest content with the standard of life which we can afford.[6]

Industry's answer to the Depression was a policy of what was called 'rationalization'. Since one of Britain's basic problems was that she was overweight in regard to her traditional industries, and another the small size of too many of her units of production, there was good economic sense in amalgamating and closing down unremunerative plant. But neither private industrialists nor the Government gave sufficient thought to the social consequences, which were disastrous. Government encouragement was given to the founding of the British Iron and Steel Federation and the National Shipbuilders' Security: rational moves both, but ones that could result in dangerous private monopolies. The greater efficiency created within the iron and steel industry did allow for a remarkable expansion in light steel production; but at the same time older centres at Mossend in Scotland and Dowlais in Wales were completely shut down. At Jarrow the shipyards, upon which the bulk of the male population depended for a livelihood, were shut down by the National Shipbuilders' Security; when local efforts were made to launch an alternative light steel industry, they were stifled by the British Iron and Steel Federation. Jarrow, to quote the title of Ellen Wilkinson's passionate account, became *The Town that Was Murdered*.[7]

None the less the crisis did force a reappraisal of economic attitudes. The big shift in government policy, the adoption of full-scale protection, certainly, was something for which many businessmen had been agitating for years. In a world which had long since gone wildly economic nationalist, there was little else Britain could do but follow suit. Yet so strong were Free Trade prejudices among such pillars of the National Government as Philip Snowden that the matter had to be approached in the judicious manner of a dog sniffing round a lamp-post. Immediately after the election Walter Runciman, one-time Free Trade stalwart, introduced what was called an Abnormal Importations Bill, giving the Board of Trade power for six months to impose duties up to 100 per cent *ad valorem* on manufactured articles which were entering the country in 'abnormal' quantities: without further inquiry, though one had been promised in the election, 50 per cent duties were imposed upon pottery, cutlery, typewriters, woollens, cottons, paper, gloves, bottles, cameras, electric goods and radio parts. The Minister of Agriculture was then given similar powers in regard to imported fruits and vegetables. The direct attack on the lamp-post commenced with the appointment of a Balance of Trade Committee whose perfunctory inquiry was followed by the Import Duties Bill of 1932. Tearfully Neville Chamberlain invoked the spirit of his father as he described the Bill's three major points: a general 10 per cent tariff on practically all goods coming into the country; the establishment of an Import Duties Advisory Committee to decide upon further duties; the exemption from these provisos of members of the Empire, pending final decisions at the coming Ottawa Imperial Conference.[8] Other revolutions in economic policy were also under way. Immediate necessity and empiricist theorizing based on the war experience were at first more important than the sophisticated 'new economics' of J. M. Keynes. Keynes, along with Labour's most powerful spokesman, Ernest Bevin, had, as a member of the most important government committee to investigate economic policy in the Twenties, the Macmillan Committee, been able to mount a convincing criticism of orthodox financial policy, though the Macmillan Report was presented too late to have any effect on the great crisis. The full presentation of Keynesian thought did not appear till 1936, when the *General Theory of Employment, Interest and Money* was published: only then was the complete emphasis given to what Keynes and many others had earlier grappled towards, the need for governments to maintain 'an aggregate volume of output corresponding to full employment as nearly as is practicable'. This was to be attained by 'a somewhat comprehensive socialization of investment' – though Keynes continued to insist that 'apart from the necessity of central controls to bring about an adjustment between the propensity to consume and the inducement to invest, there is no more reason to socialize economic life than there was before'; by 'a low rate of interest' – but only, Keynes stressed, in a manner which was to prove relevant to Britain's post-1945 experience, to 'the point which corresponds to full employment'; and by increasing the propensity to consume 'among the poorer sections of the community'[9] – or, to use the phrase which had been on the lips of a generation of ordinary socialists ever since J. A. Hobson pub-

lished his *Imperialism* in 1901, by abolishing 'under-consumption'.
When the National Government took the country off the Gold
Standard, despite the fact that it had been formed to preserve the
Gold Standard, it was following a remedy implicit in Keynes's
writings since the 1925 *Economic Consequences of Mr Churchill*. The
necessary dose of inflation was maintained by the. unbalanced
Budget of 1932, though Keynes denounced the severe retrenchment
practised at the same time. What Keynes and Bevin had most
forcefully argued for on the Macmillan Committee was the need
for low interest rates to facilitate industrial expansion;[10] the Bank
Rate was reduced to 2 per cent, where it remained till the outbreak
of war (though, as we have seen, in times of financial crisis a low
Bank Rate could conflict with the international financial role
which the country had not cast off). The biggest innovation, and
one which far outranks in long-term significance the explicit abandonment of Free Trade, was the establishment in July 1932 of the
Exchange Equalization Fund with assets of £150 million in Treasury bills plus small quantities of gold and foreign currency. The
Treasury drew upon the fund to offset speculative dealings in sterling and unusual movements of capital, thus holding the exchange
value of the pound to a pre-selected level. As it affected the Bank of
England, this was, as Sir Roy Harrod has pointed out, '*de facto* a
partial nationalization and a more important event than the formal
nationalization of 1945'.[11] In September 1936, Britain, the United
States and France together signed a Tripartite Agreement to
maintain the stability of their three currencies which was nothing
less than a joint acceptance of the notion of a managed currency
adumbrated during the war. As part of a direct effort to lift British
industry and agriculture out of the slump, the Government instituted a policy of subsidies and quotas. Before it collapsed the
Labour government had introduced an Agricultural Marketing
Act which was put to work by its successor and extended in a
further Act of 1933: under the framework of these Acts a series of
Marketing Boards, not altogether unlike the Agricultural Committees of the First World War, were established to grade and
price agricultural produce, and give the farmer a guaranteed market.
Farmers also received livestock and acreage subsidies. After 1933

the Milk Marketing Board maintained a pool price for producers and provided subsidized milk for mothers and children. A similar policy was extended to the shipbuilding industry by the British Shipping (Assistance) Act of 1935, designed to encourage the scrapping of older ships and the building of new. A year previously, the North Atlantic Shipping Act had provided a subsidy of £9·5 million and government support for the laying down of a great new transatlantic liner, the *Queen Mary;* at the same time it was stipulated that the two great shipping lines, Cunard and White Star, should be merged.[12]

Together all of these measures represented the abandonment in regard to domestic industry of the attempt made in the previous decade to return to the purer private enterprise and Free Trade conditions of Edwardian times. Much of the demand for them came from industry itself. In a report submitted to the Government in February 1934 the Federation of British Industries had called for a system of quotas. It also demanded that the government take 'power to regulate foreign exchange, should such a course be necessary to protect British interests'.[13] While financiers might take a different standpoint, industrialists came steadily also to accept the virtues of being off the Gold Standard (this vital division of interest *within* the British 'capitalist' class is too often ignored). Whereas the International Chamber of Commerce in October 1938 reaffirmed its faith in 'the ultimate restoration of gold as the international measure of value, and in the fundamental economic function of a gold standard', the Federation of British Industries 'unhesitatingly' expressed a contrary opinion:

The difference between being 'on' a gold standard and being 'off' a gold standard may be stated shortly by saying that a country which is a member of a gold standard group is committed to a policy of tying up its *domestic* level of employment, prices and industrial activity to that of other members of the gold standard group. A serious domestic crisis in any one of them will affect the exchanges of the remainder. Since under a gold standard they are all compelled to maintain their exchange rates stable they will be forced to restrict for this purpose the domestic supply of credit. This will cause unemployment, a loss of profit and a decline in industrial activity.

On the other hand, a country which is 'off' the Gold Standard can afford . . . to ignore almost entirely any external crisis and the consequent depreciation of its exchange. It can concentrate on a policy of cheap money and thereby help to maintain business confidence and the level of domestic activity and employment. This latter is the policy which has been pursued by the British Treasury and the Bank of England ever since the breakdown of 1931.[14]

The leaders of the F.B.I., it can be seen, had been dipping into Keynes.

Pressures from various directions, therefore, as well as the need to respond to economic crisis, were pushing government policy a little way in the direction of a managed economy. Given their context, the policies were sensible, save that they did not go nearly far enough. Yet in the pronouncements of the F.B.I., as indeed in those of many socialists, there is a kind of complacent nationalism: only establish the right kind of exchange controls, the necessary quotas and subsidies, and Britain will be able to prosper independently of the rest of the world. For the time being, despite temporary imbalances, Britain, because of her overseas investments and her services as an international financial centre, was a creditor country. But a power like Britain could never really be independent of the rest of the world; once she was stripped of her overseas assets (as happened in the Second World War) this growing optimism of the Thirties that British governments could control Britain's economic fate was ruthlessly exposed. It was right that the Government should give direct stimulus to British industry, and true that it should have given more; yet what was done lay too much along the lines of preserving the existing industrial structure: rationalization was no substitute for massive new initiatives. One new industry which had already shown that it could not survive without government intervention was the aircraft industry, and economics were as strong a motive as politics in the establishment of the British Overseas Airways Corporation, a major act of nationalization to be placed alongside the establishment of the B.B.C. Earlier the conditions of natural monopoly (or chaos) afforded by London's transport problems had led the Labour government to plan the establishment of another, though smaller, public corporation, the London Passenger Transport Board. As with farming policy, this item was taken over by the National Government and put into practice in 1932. The Depressed Areas Act of 1934, making £2 million available for creating employment in depressed areas, marked a reversal of the Treasury policy enunciated in 1929; the grant itself was piddling, and the effects slight. Finally, as a possible prelude to more effective action a Royal Commission, under the chairmanship of Sir Montague Barlow, was appointed in 1937 to investigate the entire question of the distribution of the industrial population. Before its report could be published, however, war intervened.

The slight but noticeable change in economic policy did help to pull the country as a whole out of the depths of 1931 and 1932, though little of value was done to relieve the deeper pools of misery. The gross national product recovered its 1929 level in 1935, and proceeded to increase steadily thereafter. Exports made only a slight recovery after 1932, but Britain took a larger share of a shrunken world trade. By 1936 imports were back at the 1929 level, and they cost 32 per cent less. For the Labour movement this was a time of retreat. The economic effects of the crisis were most seriously felt by the working classes, and there was an immediate recrudescence of the type of militant activity that had appeared at the end of the war, involving a number of clashes with the police. On 15 January 1932 the Territorials were called out to guard Rochdale Town Hall and in October rioting in Belfast resulted in two workers being fatally injured and many others seriously wounded.[15] Demonstrations and hunger marches certainly served to dramatize the plight of the unemployed and may, as in the case of the dropping of Part II of the Unemployment Insurance Act of 1935, have had a slight effect on the Government,[16] but this was of minor importance compared with the decline of the real strength of the organized Labour movement as shown in the trade union membership figures: from the crisis till 1933 there was a steady drop to 4,392,000, which was only just above the 1914 level; on the eve of war membership had climbed back painfully to 6,000,000. Given this erosion of its industrial base as well as the overwhelming loss

of seats in the 1931 election, it is not surprising that the Labour
Party exhibited some signs of loss of confidence. Whatever its
failures in office during the Twenties, it had in opposition developed
some ambitious long-term social policies. Now all the emphasis
was switched from planning for the future to endeavouring to safeguard the existing social services: while attacking the educational
economies of the National Government as 'reversing the policy
followed by all its predecessors since 1902'[17] Labour concentrated
on the need for maintenance grants, rather than on any ambitious
expansion of educational provision; in housing, the emphasis was
placed on slum clearance rather than house building; in health,
despite the efforts of the Socialist Medical Association (founded in
1931) to revive the ideas of the Twenties, the Labour Party
Executive went no further than a very cautious report of 1934 which
was not considered worth printing as a separate pamphlet, and
which thereafter was totally ignored until the outbreak of war.[18]
Labour was too involved in the bitter polemic of this decade of
political commitment to do much really constructive social
planning.

2. THE BITTER SOCIETY

One consequence of prolonged economic depression was a growing
awareness of, and preoccupation with, the social and political evils
of the day among groups and individuals who in the Twenties had
often stood aloof from such matters. Social investigators ceased to
extol the rise in basic wage rates achieved over the war period and
the diffusion of material standards through technological advance,
and began to denounce the persistence and aggravation of areas of
privation and poverty. Men of moderate political opinions, or of
none, began to talk the language of revolutionary violence; liberal
intellectuals joined or flirted with the Communist Party. In the
arts, a concern with the abstract and the universal gave way to an
emphasis on social problems and political commitment: in the
classic phrase of Hugh Gordon Porteous, written in 1933, 'Verse
will be worn longer this year, and rather Red.'[19]

There are a number of comments to be made on the social

investigations of the Thirties. First, there were a lot of them. Second, although they bring out forcefully the deplorable conditions in which sections of the population were still living, taken in conjunction with national income statistics they do also demonstrate that there was a modest advance in living standards for the *majority* of British people: it was in part the contrast between the lot of the majority, and that of the substantial minority, which created the intensity of feeling for change. Third, these reports were given wide prominence in the Press: relativity, Tutankhamen, individual heroisms and group hysterias had been featured in the Twenties; now the spotlight was on the equally stark realities of British domestic life. Over the sharpest period of crisis wage rates fell by 4 per cent, an average figure which concealed a very slight advance in the new industries and a very steep drop (around 15 per cent) in the old industries. A clear pick-up of 2 per cent was apparent in 1936, and by 1938 wage rates had almost returned to the 1924 level.[20] Such a situation so long after the war (which could be held by employers to have inflated wages unduly) reveals how strong was the power of the employer relative to that of the working class. But because of the sharp slump in prices real wage rates jumped by at least 10 per cent between the end of the Twenties and the mid-Thirties, and real earnings, because of a continued upgrading of labour and more extensive use of piece-work, by a little more. Averages only tell a little of the story, when, as an official Ministry of Labour inquiry of October 1935 brought out, weekly earnings could vary from well over 80s. at the top to less than 50s. at the bottom, with the average at around 70s.[21] In Bristol in the South-West, centre among other things of the growing aircraft industry, Herbert Tout's survey, *Standard of Living in Bristol*, found that 12 per cent of working-class families with a total average weekly income of 117s. 7d. were living in comfort. 68 per cent had a 'sufficiency' of 75s 10d. per week. But Tout also found that 10·7 per cent of working-class families were below the 'poverty line'.[22] This poverty line, slightly more generous than that applied by Edwardian investigators, was essentially based, with some modifications, on the findings of a British Medical Association Committee appointed in 1933 'to determine the minimum weekly expenditure on foodstuffs which must be incurred ... if health and working capacity are to be maintained'. The figure arrived at, 5s. 1d. per person, allowed only for bare existence without obvious deficiency, but would not support moderately heavy labour, nor would it allow of proper physical development for a child.[23]

In a study made on behalf of the Market Supply Committee of the Ministry of Agriculture and the Rowett Research Institute at Aberdeen, Sir John Boyd Orr employed slightly more ambitious standards, starting from the standpoint of a diet which would produce 'a state of well-being such that no improvement can be effected by a change in the diet'. He then, on the basis of a rather small sample, divided the population into six groups, classified by income and weight of family responsibility. With a fine awareness of the probability of statistical error not shared by all the investigators of the time Boyd Orr gave his results in rounded, and indeed symmetrical form. Group 1, estimated to spend 4s. per head per week on food, comprising 10 per cent of the whole population, were deficient in intake of calories, protein, fat, calcium, phosphorus, iron, and vitamins A and C. Group 2, spending 6s. per week on food, and comprising 20 per cent of the population, were deficient in all constituents considered save protein and fat. Group 3, spending 8s. and comprising 20 per cent, were adequate only in calories, protein and fat. Groups 4, 10s. per week, 20 per cent of the population, and 5, 12s. per week, 20 per cent of the population, were deficient only in calcium, Group 6, spending 14s. per week per head on food, and comprising 10 per cent of the population, was the only one meeting all of Boyd Orr's requirements.[24] Although Boyd Orr's findings were criticized in detail, it was undoubtedly true that his lower groups were particularly susceptible to such major scourges as tuberculosis, and to rickets, anaemia and dental caries. Members of his group 1 consumed only 1·8 pints of milk per head per week, 1·5 eggs, and spent only 2½d. on vegetables, while in group 6 the corresponding figures were 5·5, 4·5 and 1s. 8d. When all qualifications had been made, it seemed clear that 10 per cent of the country's population were being seriously undernourished, and, still more serious, that within this group were 20 to 25 per cent of the country's children. Boyd Orr's findings also indicated that it was not the working classes alone who suffered from dietary deficiencies. In the same year as his *Food, Health and Income* was published, the Medical Officers of Health for Cardiff, Newcastle upon Tyne and Cuckfield Rural District Council conducted surveys in their own areas which substantially reinforced Boyd Orr's discoveries about the chronic malnutrition among low income groups, as did the more comprehensive and less extrovert survey conducted by Sir William Crawford, published as *The People's Food*. Finally, the Army in 1935 had found that 62 per cent of all recruits were below the required (and rather modest) physical standard.[25]

Apart from the *Social Survey of Merseyside*, which had been launched in 1928, though not completed till 1934, and the *New Life and Labour of the People of London*, which spread over a still longer period and applied mainly to the Twenties, the most extensive survey was that conducted by Rowntree in York in 1935–36, repeating his pioneer work of 1899. In that study he had found 43 per cent of the working class in poverty – 15·5 per cent in primary poverty. On the same standard in 1935–36 6·8 per cent of the working class were in primary poverty. However, Rowntree now felt it necessary to revise his poverty line upwards, and, being more generous than the B.M.A. committee, hit on a figure of 43s. 6d. plus rent as a minimum for man, wife and three children: 31 per cent of the working class fell below this line.[26] You paid your money and you took your pick: but whatever social survey you read, the lesson of dire poverty – whether to the extent of 30 per cent, or just 10 per cent of the working class – was strongly etched into it somewhere. All the surveys were agreed about three of the basic preconditions of poverty: old age; unemployment; having, or belonging to, a large family. Studies of a wider and more intriguing nature were undertaken by a new organization employing the methods of social anthropology, Mass Observation.

In 1934 the publication of twenty-five first-hand accounts of what it was like to be unemployed laid bare, for those with eyes to read, the dismal progression from 'optimism to pessimism and from pessimism to fatalism'.[27] But the most complete survey of the life of the unemployed was conceived by Archbishop Temple of

York – one of many leaders of opinion for whom the crisis of 1931 had provided the psychological snap turning him from palliatives to fundamentals[28] – and carried through under the auspices of the Pilgrim Trust: *Men Without Work*, published in 1938, is a classic of objectivity and sensitivity which revealed the plight of the long-term unemployed as truly a desperate one. In the mining town of Crook in 1936, 71 per cent of the unemployed had had no work for five years or more; in the cotton town of Blackburn the figure was 51 per cent. Of Leicester it was remarked that 'when a man gets out of work in the boot and shoe trade, if he is over 50, there is little hope of his getting back again'. Long-term unemployment had its psychological as well as its physical consequences:

An instance taken at random from this group in the Rhondda sample is a collier, aged 37, who served three years in the war and has now done no work whatever for five years. He is described as wiry and very fit, a 'great walker, who always does his physical "jerks" '. But unemployed men are not simply units of employability who can, through the medium of the dole, be put into cold storage and taken out again immediately they are needed. While they are in cold storage, things are liable to happen to them. In the case of this man what has happened was that the 'will to work' had been affected; he 'seemed quite unconcerned about work'. And the other thing which it seems from the records may have happened (though in such cases it is impossible to say for certain) is that the health of one of his children has been seriously impaired by the low level at which the family has to live.[29]

In the main the investigators found a hunger for work, and an intense resentment that work was not to be found; in Blackburn, however, where normal wage levels were low, as many as 38 per cent of those interviewed reported themselves as happy on the dole. Unemployment in this area also had the paradoxical effect of recreating a kind of family life which had not existed since women went out to work in the cotton mills of the early Industrial Revolution.[30]

When there was such a widespread preoccupation with the problems of poverty and unemployment it was rather hard to wish away the existence of social classes. In the 1930s Carr-Saunders and Caradog Jones brought out a new edition of their *Social Structure of England and Wales*, based this time on the returns of the 1931 Census. In neither volume was there any glossing over the extent of poverty or inequality in the country, but in the 1920s the authors had forcefully insisted that 'the belief in the existence of social classes ... is the result of studying social theory of doubtful value and of neglecting social facts';[31] in the new edition 'social facts' clearly forced the authors to replace this belligerent utterance with the milder question: 'Is it not a misreading of the social structure of this country to dwell on class divisions when, in respect of dress, speech, and use of leisure, all members of the community are obviously coming to resemble one another?'[32] Undoubtedly it is less easy to build for the end of the inter-war period the same kind of model of the class structure as was attempted for the end of the Edwardian period. The upgrading of workers, the growth of the salaried class, the diminution in the vast incomes of the uppermost class, had continued slowly through the inter-war period. The socio-economic classes of the official census-takers are of little use to anyone looking for a model of the class structure; other authorities differ in their analysis. Since subsidized housing was intended only for the working classes, a clear acceptance of the reality of class divisions on the part of the Government, it was necessary for the Government to hazard (in Schedule 11 of the Housing Act of 1936) a definition:

The expression 'working class' includes mechanics, artisans, labourers, and others working for wages, hawkers, costermongers, persons not working for wages, but working at some trade or handicraft without employing others, except members of their own family, and persons other than domestic servants whose income in any case does not exceed an average of £3 a week, and the families of such persons who may be residing with them.

Dudley Seers has defined the working class of 1938 as including all manual workers and all non-manual workers earning less than £250 per annum, making up 84 per cent of the population.[33] But this figure is highly unsatisfactory since it includes almost 3 million

salary-earners in industry, teaching, the Civil Service and distribution. Such other writers as W. G. Runciman, when talking of the
working class, have confined this term to the manual workers.[34]
This is on the whole fairly satisfactory for the Thirties, since many
of the fringe occupations – such as hawkers or dressmakers – which
loomed so large in the Edwardian period had now largely disappeared. In defining the working class by those earning £4 per
week or less – 8·6 million families, 73·5 per cent of the total number
of families – the Coles[35] probably inflated the figure very slightly
by including some minor salary-earners who had now identified
themselves with the lower middle class. The middle class, then, one
might regard as slightly larger than their 2½ million families, or 21·3
per cent of all families. This would leave around 5 per cent as a
reasonable estimate for the upper class, now thoroughly compounded out of industrial wealth, some of it recent, too much of it
inherited, and the indestructible remnant of the landed aristocracy.

Taxation, save in the case of death duties at the very top of the
scale, did little to smooth out economic inequality: indeed the 1934
Budget, the one Chamberlain, in an astonishing revelation of
literacy, described as having brought the country from *Bleak House*
to *Great Expectations,* reduced the incidence of direct taxation.
Certainly the social services, since they were almost entirely restricted to the lower classes, did involve a redistribution from rich
to poor, possibly (by one calculation) as high as 5 per cent of the
national income. The major change in the social services, relating
naturally to the pressing problem of mass unemployment, though
on its own terms rational (as was the Poor Law Amendment Act
of 1834) was not well calculated to allay the bitterness of working-
class discontent: indeed the 'Means Test' which was enthroned in
the Unemployment Insurance Act of 1934 aroused the same kind
of hatred as the 'Bastilles', the workhouses of one hundred years
previously. The high level of public expenditure on relieving the
position of the unemployed had been one of the central issues in the
great political crisis. Soon after it was formed the National Government not only imposed the controversial 10 per cent cuts in insurance payments, but established by Orders in Council that
transitional benefits would be paid only when the applicant had

undergone a test proving that he had no other means of support. To avoid setting up yet more administrative machinery the Government left the assessment of means to the Public Assistance Committees of the local authorities, despite the fact that the benefits continued to come from the central government. The 1934 Act (passed shortly after the 10 per cent cuts were restored) made a clear distinction between Unemployment Insurance benefits to which full entitlement had been established and what was now to be called Unemployment Assistance, which replaced all other benefits, including transitional benefits and benefits paid under the Poor Law by the Public Assistance Committees. Unemployment Assistance was to be administered by an independent Unemployment Assistance Board, with its own offices throughout the country. The new rigid scales of relief and the new regulations for the Means Test laid down in advance by the Board aroused an outcry inside and outside Parliament, which delayed the implementation of the Act and mitigated its full rigour.[36] None the less the new Means Test roused a hostility never to be forgotten, essentially because it was based on the principle that the entire household, and not just the single unemployed individual, had to undergo assessment based on the amount that would be received if all the members of the family were unemployed and in receipt of the fixed U.A.B. allowance: the Board then inquired into the various incomes of the members of the family: out of the earnings of a wife, husband, father or mother, everything over the first 5s., or one half of the total earnings, whichever was less, must be counted towards the maintenance of the unemployed member; sons, daughters, brothers and sisters had to contribute two-thirds of the first 20s. they earned, and three-quarters of the remainder. Not only was the inquisitorial nature of the Means Test resented, but also the strain which it placed on family relations.

Nothing was done about the other two major sources of financial insecurity: old age and large families. The extension of subsidized milk and meals only nibbled at the problem of widespread malnutrition. Worst of all was the condition of the nation's public health provision, which apart from being totally inadequate in medical terms, seemed well calculated to foster social divisions.

There were no changes in the Health Insurance structure and the panel system. After the passing of the 1929 Local Government Act there was an expansion in local authority hospital provision, but (apart from infectious diseases hospitals where the authority could use its discretion) the authority was required to charge patients according to their means. As the voluntary hospitals tended to adopt the same practice, many people of middling incomes joined hospital contributory schemes, which in the 1930s rose to a membership of around 7 millions (not counting dependants), at which point the voluntary hospitals were deriving about half their income from these schemes.[37] Some of the rest of their income came from 'flag days', for private charity was still an integral part of British social provision. Voluntary hospitals continued to try to avoid taking chronic cases, and local authority hospitals preferred only to take patients from their own areas, despite the inconvenience, of course, that might be caused due to the accidents of geography. Unlike the harsh facts of poverty, the intricacies of Health Insurance and hospital provision were not amenable to simple exposition, so it was left to the specialist research organization, Political and Economic Planning, to publish the most critical exposure of Britain's health services.[38]

Bad housing conditions which persisted despite the building boom and the slum clearance programmes of the Thirties were more readily detectable. A government survey published in 1936 gave the statistics of overcrowding (i.e. three adults to two rooms, five adults to three rooms, or worse) in England and Wales: over the two countries taken as a unity the figure was only 3·8 per cent, which was probably the basis for various optimistic pronouncements about the satisfactory state of English housing provision (few pretended that the Scottish situation was satisfactory); but in an ageing industrial town such as Sunderland in the North-East the figure could rise to over 20 per cent.[39] R. M. Titmuss's *Poverty and Population*, published in 1938, brought out the deeper consequences of unequal housing provision: industrial areas in the North had infant mortality rates as high as 134 per thousand, whereas prosperous towns in the South-East had rates as low as 32 per thousand.[40] Or, as *Men Without Work* expressed it:

One thing which will remain in the memory of anyone going round among the Liverpool unemployed will be the appalling housing conditions and the low domestic standards which are to a large extent a consequence of them . . . there is the 'general labourer' of 33 living with a wife and four children (a daughter of 6 at school, another daughter crippled, a daughter of 2, and a son just born) in two rooms, small, dark, damp, with the plaster decayed, nowhere to wash, gas used all day at a cost of 2s. 6d. a week because there is no daylight – a necessity which substantially increases the gap between their net income of less than 34s. and the 38s. or so required by our 'poverty line' standard.[41]

Most condensed utterance of all was this:

'The thing that keeps me away from home,' as a middle-aged man, the father of two children and fond of them, said, 'is the smell.'[42]

Even where new housing estates were being made available to the poor, this was not always an unmixed blessing: higher rents and increased expenditure on bus or tram fares could involve a reduction of money available for food, and a reduction in already deplorable standards of nutrition[43] – 'malnutrition could be found in council houses as well as slum tenements.'[44]

Facts such as these, in varying degrees, entered the consciousness of the creative writers of the time. Assuming the pseudonym of George Orwell, Eric Blair, an Etonian from the genteel (if impoverished) upper-middle class, deliberately shared the life of the down-trodden poor and presented his factual findings in *The Road to Wigan Pier*, published in 1937. J. B. Priestley, who at the end of the Twenties had enjoyed an enormous success with his cheerful, optimistic picaresque novel, *The Good Companions*, by 1930 was in *Angel Pavement* encompassing the predicament of the ageing clerical worker. The collapse of Twigg and Dershingham puts Herbert Smeeth out of a job; and in the concluding passages of the book Smeeth explains the situation to his wife:

And if you think I'm going to get another job as good as that, or a job worth having at all, in a hurry, you're mistaken Edie. I know what it is, with office jobs; and it'll have to be an office job because that's what I've always done. I'm nearly fifty and I look it. I dare say I look older. . . .[45]

It was not within Priestley's experience or special talents to write a proletarian novel, but in 1933 he set out on a fact-finding *English Journey* which resulted in a deeply felt description of the state of the nation.

There was, first, Old England, the country of the cathedrals and minsters and manor houses and inns, of Parson and Squire; guide-book and quaint highways and byways England: 'Visit ancient York with its 1,300-year-old Minster; and Durham where lies the Venerable Bede. Wander through the historic streets of Norwich, once the second city of England. Look down from the battlements of Conway Castle. Visit Lichfield Cathedral, renowned for its three beautiful spires, and put yourself back in the Middle Ages at Warwick. Every county of great Britain speaks to you of your ancestors. . . .'

As our railway companies tell the readers of American magazines, most of whose ancestors never saw a county of Great Britain. But we all know this England, which at its best cannot be improved upon in this world. That is, as a country to lounge about in; for a tourist who can afford to pay a fairly stiff price for a poorish dinner, an inconvenient bedroom and lukewarm water in a small brass jug. It has few luxuries, but nevertheless it is a luxury country. It has long ceased to earn its own living. . . .

Then, I decided, there is a nineteenth-century England, the industrial England of coal, iron, steel, cotton, wool, railways; of thousands of rows of little houses all alike, sham Gothic churches, square-faced chapels, Town Halls, Mechanics' Institutes, mills, foundries, warehouses, refined watering-places. Pier Pavilions, Family and Commercial Hotels. Literary and Philosophical Societies, back-to-back houses, detached villas with monkey-trees, Grill Rooms, railway stations, slag-heaps and 'tips', dock roads, Refreshment Rooms, doss-houses, Unionist or Liberal Clubs, cindery waste grounds, mill chimneys, slums, fried-fish shops, public houses with red blinds, bethels in corrugated iron, good-class drapers' and confectioners' shops, a cynically devastated countryside, sooty dismal little towns, and still sootier grim fortress-like cities. This England makes up the larger part of the Midlands and the North and exists everywhere; but it is not being added to and has no new life poured into it. . . . What you see looks like a debauchery of cynical greed. As I thought of some of the places I had seen, Wolverhampton and St Helens and Bolton and Gateshead and Jarrow and Shotton, I remembered a book I had just read, in which we are told to return as soon as possible to the sturdy Victorian individualism. But for my part I felt like calling back a few of these sturdy individualists simply to rub their noses in the nasty mess they had made. Who gave them leave to turn this island into their ashpit? ...

The third England, I concluded, was the new post-war England, belonging far more to the age itself than to this particular island. America, I supposed, was its real birth-place. This is the England of arterial and by-pass roads, of filling stations and factories that look like exhibition buildings, of giant cinemas and dance-halls and cafés, bungalows with tiny garages, cocktail bars, Woolworths, motor-coaches, wireless, hiking, factory girls looking like actresses, greyhound racing and dirt tracks, swimming-pools, and everything given away for cigarette coupons. ... Care is necessary ... for you can easily approve or disapprove of it too hastily. It is, of course, essentially democratic. After a social revolution there would, with any luck, be more and not less of it. You need money in this England, but you do not need much money. It is a large-scale, mass-production job, with cut prices. ...

Unfortunately it is a bit too cheap. That is, it is also cheap in the other sense of the term. Too much of it is simply a trumpery imitation of something not very good even in the original. There is about it a rather depressing monotony. Too much of this life is being stamped on from outside, probably by astute financial gentlemen, backed by the Press and their publicity services. You feel that too many of the people in this new England are doing not what they like but what they have been told they would like. (Here is the American influence at work.)

Finally, Priestley was brought back to 'the England of the dole':

I saw again the older men, who, though they knew they were idle and useless through no fault of their own, felt defeated and somewhat tainted. Their self-respect was shredding away. Their very manhood was going. Even in England, which is no South Sea Island, there are places where a man feels he can do nothing cheerfully, where gay idling is not impossible. But the ironist in charge of our affairs has seen to it that the maximum of unemployment shall be in those districts that have a tradition of hard work and of very little else. Life on the dole in South Devon, let us say, may be bad enough, but life on the dole on Tyneside is a great deal worse. I saw these older workless men as a series of personal tragedies. The young men, who have grown up in the shadow of the Labour Exchange, are not so much personal tragedies, I decided, as collectively a national tragedy.

Priestley recalled the appearance of German prisoners of war just after the Armistice:

They have a certain look, these prisoners of war, most of whom had been captured two or three years before. It was a strained, greyish, faintly decomposed look. I did not expect to see that kind of face again for a long time; but I was wrong. I had seen a lot of those faces on this journey. They belonged to the unemployed men.[46]

From the 'England of the dole' there did emerge one genuine proletarian novel, *Love on the Dole* by Walter Greenwood, which enjoyed considerable success (eventually being filmed). Set in Manchester and Salford the novel describes the sufferings, material, moral and psychological, of the Hardcastle family when depression hits the local engineering works. Among many enemies is the 1931 Means Test:

Harry learnt that, in the opinion of the Public Assistance Committee, his father's dole and Sally's wages were sufficient to keep him. No more dole would be forthcoming.[47]

The voice of working-class anger can be heard in many of the little magazines of the period, which followed a deliberate policy of opening their pages to working-class contributors. More impressively, the intensity of working-class bitterness was apparent in strikes and demonstrations and in the evidence presented by such accounts as *Men Without Work*: in the coalfields especially there was widespread resentment over the victimization of strike leaders, and even the ordinary inactive working man with his deep-rooted conviction that at all costs he must keep up his burial insurance had a sense of where the enemy lay:

'The Means Test and the capitalists,' said this man, 'prevent me from having a decent life, but at least I will have a decent death.'[48]

But mainly the voice of commitment was the voice of the Liberal intellectual. Stephen Spender, scion of a great Liberal family, defined the process perfectly in his book *Forward from Liberalism* (1934), in which he declared, 'I am a Communist because I am a Liberal.'[49] A rising novelist, Graham Greene, was both a wry commentator on this leftward pilgrimage, and, apparently, involved in it. Of the Liberal intellectual, Mr Surrogate, in *It's a Battlefield* (1934), Greene writes:

All along one shelf stood the record of his intellectual progress: *Forward to Free Trade, Back to Protection,* in their English and American editions; only with the *Capital Levy* had his writing reached the Continent and German and Czecho-Slovakian publishers. His eye followed with pride the record of his increasing humility: *The Nationalisation of Industry, with an Appendix on Scales of Compensation,* was followed by the brief triumphant title, *No Compensation.*

A profounder commitment is expressed through the character of the Police Commissioner in the same novel: the Commissioner is musing on the fate of Drover, a bus driver who has killed a policeman during an anti-Fascist demonstration in Hyde Park:

... the Commissioner was more than ever thankful that justice was not his business. He knew quite well the cause of the discrepancy: the laws were made by property owners in defence of property; that was why a Fascist could talk treason without prosecution; that was why a man who defrauded the State in defence of his private wealth did not even lose the money he had gained; that was why Drover could not so easily be reprieved – he was a Communist.[50]

Beginning with an evocation of the apolitical Twenties, *Nobody Talks Politics* (1936), a novel by the social anthropologist Geoffrey Gorer, then moves to the feverish Thirties when *everybody* talks politics, finally advocating, as the only way out, a Communist revolution. W. H. Auden described in verse the scene that Priestley and so many others had described in prose:

Get there if you can and see the land you once were
proud to own.
Though the roads have almost vanished the expresses
never run:
Smokeless chimneys, damaged bridges, rotting wharves
and choked canals. . . .[51]

C. Day Lewis pointed to the fashionable remedy:

It is now or never, the hour of the knife,
The break with the past, the major operation.[52]

It was not domestic depression alone which turned Liberal
intellectuals towards left-wing extremism. In the aftermath of the
great world economic crisis overseas horizons frowned even more
darkly than those at home. In September 1931 the militarist régime
in Japan launched its attack on Manchuria; in January 1933 the
Nazi dictatorship of Adolf Hitler was established in Germany; in
October 1933 Germany withdrew from the World Disarmament
Conference and shortly afterwards proceeded to an open repudiation
of the disarmament clauses imposed upon her at Versailles; in
December 1934 the Fascist régime of Benito Mussolini invaded
Abyssinia; in March 1936 German troops reoccupied the demilitarized Rhineland; in July 1936 General Franco raised the
standard of Fascist rebellion against the Republican government
of Spain. It was this last event above all which outraged liberal
sentiment in Britain, especially when Hitler and Mussolini began
open support for Franco, using Spanish towns as testing grounds
for their new weapons of aerial offence.[53] When Russia began
assisting the government forces, that only seemed to clarify the
alternatives facing the world. The British government, fearful
that the Spanish conflict might escalate into world war, resolutely
upheld a policy of non-intervention; it also refused to allow the
Spanish government to buy arms in Britain. For these policies it
was fiercely denounced by Liberals and socialists, and, indeed, by
many Conservatives. The Spanish Civil War extended and intensified the hatreds against the established government engendered by its failure to solve the problems of economic depression.

Young men, and not so young, went out to fight in the International Brigades on behalf of the Spanish Republicans. As the Government continued (despite the German absorption of Austria in March 1938 and Hitler's manifest designs on Czechoslovakia) proudly to follow a policy of appeasement towards the dictators, coupled with a coldness towards the Soviet Union, bitterness increased and its base broadened.

Inside Britain various Fascist groups had been active all through the Twenties,[54] but until the resignation of Sir Oswald Mosley from the Labour government in 1930 because of his disgust at its faltering attempts to handle the worsening economic situation, they lacked that *sine qua non* of Fascism, a leader. The British Union of Fascists, with Mosley as Fuehrer, was established in 1934. From Hitler the British Fascists borrowed an open anti-Semitism, and, like Fascists everywhere, they posed as the country's front-line defence against Communism. Fascist marches took place in East London, where Jewish shops were the prime target; there were frequent open clashes with Communist and leftist sympathizers. Mass rallies, too, were held, and at these hecklers were treated with vicious savagery. So pronounced did extra-parliamentary activity become in the early Thirties that measures were passed to deal with it: the Incitement to Disaffection Bill of 1934 and the Public Order Bill of 1936. To many observers whose sympathies were steadily moving to the Left, it seemed that the British police were disquietingly tolerant of Fascist demonstrators, and unnecessarily harsh with Communist ones. In January 1934 four Communists successfully brought home a case for damages against the Chief Commissioner of the Metropolitan Police.[55]

After the troubled and unsatisfactory history of the Twenties the Communist Party now enjoyed a certain prestige and a slight expansion in numbers.[56] Other political organizations also shuffled to the Left. As early as 1930 the leaders of the I.L.P., who were to be responsible for taking it out of the Labour Party in 1932, had decided that the only possible response to the rise of Fascism in Europe was the adoption of a rigid neo-Marxist line.[57] For a time there were attempts at joint action between the I.L.P. and the Communist Party, but the reactions of rank-and-file members of the I.L.P. to what they regarded as Communist duplicity were so vigorous that the attempt collapsed.[58] Later in the decade, as the international situation got worse, there were attempts at forming Worker's Fronts (of extreme leftists only), United Fronts (of all leftists), and Popular Fronts (to include dissident Conservatives). Within the Labour Party there appeared in the room of the I.L.P. the Socialist League, whose publications openly predicted that a future Labour government would require to depart from normal constitutional procedures to frustrate the right-wing reaction its measures would necessarily evoke.[59] While the move to the Left was essentially emotional, it was given an intellectual and empirical thrust by the publications of the Left Book Club, founded in March 1936 by Victor Gollancz, a publisher, Harold Laski, a distinguished political scientist whose opinions, roughly, were in accord with those of the Socialist League, and John Strachey, another Liberal intellectual turned Communist. Within a year the Left Book Club had a membership of 50,000.[60]

3. THE POLITICS OF 'AGREEMENT' AND THE SOCIOLOGY OF 'PROGRESS'

> I sit in one of the dives
> On Fifty-second Street
> Uncertain and afraid
> As the clever hopes expire
> Of a low dishonest decade.[61]

Auden's epitaph on the Thirties has stuck. Whatever assistance the Conservative-dominated National Government may have given to economic recovery, whatever advances it may have made towards a welfare state and a planned economy, it failed to conquer unemployment. Whatever arguments might be adduced on behalf of the policy of appeasement, it failed. The formation and perpetuation of the National Government could be seen as at once a triumph for the British virtue of compromise and a bold new departure in political behaviour, but it brought neither national unity, nor bold leadership. MacDonald, worn down by a lifetime of hard work, was only a shadow of his former self; such talents of leadership and initiative as Baldwin may have possessed seemed to rust completely during his four years as second-in-command before he took Mac-Donald's place as Prime Minister in June 1935. The ministerial strong-man was Neville Chamberlain, who looked every inch the self-righteous narrow-minded pedant that he was, longing for the age 'before the days of motors and telephones'.[62] Yet since on the surface this leadership seemed quite successful – it did, after all, win the General Election of 1935 – it was able to count on the usual loyalty of the bulk of the Conservative Party.

In this age of violence the Labour Party was handicapped by being led by a pacifist, George Lansbury, who owed his position to the fact that he was the one front-rank personality to survive the 1931 débâcle. In 1935 he was replaced by one of the few second-line leaders who had similarly managed to survive – Clement Attlee, a mild-seeming middle-class former social worker, former major, former I.L.P. activist of the Clifford Allen type, now firmly set as a moderate. His second-in-command, and closest rival for the leadership, Herbert Morrison, was the son of a London policeman: with the appearance and manner of a slightly conspiratorial cockney sparrow, Morrison had already on the London County Council shown himself to be a formidable political boss; MacDonald had so admired his administrative talents as Minister of Transport in the ill-fated Labour government that he had tried to persuade him to join the National Government. As a Labour politician Morrison was on the Right of the party (or rather, it might be said that he stood on the former middle ground that was really now the Right of the party, since the old exclusively 'labour' elements were fading away) and he managed to persuade the party to accept his doctrine that nationalization by a future Labour government should take the form of the establishment of public corporations, like his own brain-child, the London Passenger Transport Board – that is, there should be no nonsense about 'workers' control'.[63] The third Labour leader of note, though he was not yet even an M.P., was Ernest Bevin, indisputably working-class in background and outlook, and also an occupant of the middle ground, though personally he already detested Morrison. Once the immediate scare of the crisis was over, it is not surprising that the Labour Party began to advance rapidly in by-elections, though the National Government majority was too enormous to overcome in the General Election of 1935: in this Labour won 154 seats against 387 for the National Government. Labour's average percentage vote per candidate was now back where it had been in the 1920s. Under its new leadership the party did not perform very impressively as an Opposition: its utterances on Spain, rearmament and foreign policy generally were confused. Officially the party opposed all attempts at forming a Popular Front, and spent a great deal of energy hunting down left-wing heresies: in 1938 four of the party's most gifted figures, Sir Stafford Cripps, Charles Trevelyan, G. R. Strauss and Aneurin Bevan were expelled for participating in Popular Front activities. Meantime Baldwin and the Conservatives reaped the glory of a series of events concerning the royal family: the Silver Jubilee of George V, the Funeral of George V, the Accession of Edward VIII, the Abdication of Edward VIII, and the Coronation of George VI: Baldwin then discreetly retired, giving place (in May 1937) to Neville Chamberlain.

The bitterness aroused by the National Government we have already noted: but there is another side to the Thirties which is of equal importance in understanding the age, and its place in the long-term development of British society: we may term it the 'agreement' aspect of the Thirties. First of the forces making for this 'agreement' was the revulsion against the continuance into the post-war world of the economic orthodoxy of 1914, provoked by the great crisis, a revulsion confined to men of no one political persuasion. Harold Macmillan, one of the bright young men of the 'Y.M.C.A.', provided a shrewd analysis:

. . . Great indeed were the changes which the shock of the crisis brought about in the minds of men with regard to economic and political theories. Formerly they had been content to accept, as the basis of their political thought, the economic theories that had been evolved in an earlier epoch of national and world history, when the basic circumstances of economic life were wholly different. Throughout the whole of the post-war period there had been growing an uneasy consciousness of something radically wrong with the economic system; and this uneasiness had overshadowed political controversy both within and between all the political parties for many years. One of the consequences of the crisis was to confirm these suspicions and liberate men's minds from a continued subservience to the economic orthodoxy of the pre-war world.

The 'liberation' took the form of a sudden devotion to the notion of economic planning. As Macmillan himself put it:

'Planning' is forced upon us ... not for idealistic reasons but because the old mechanism which served us when markets were expanding naturally and spontaneously is no longer adequate when the tendency is in the opposite direction.[64]

In February 1933 Thomas Jones, former Assistant Secretary to the Cabinet, wrote to his daughter:

Last night I was from 5.30 to 10 p.m. at Harold Macmillan's to discuss the question of founding an economic Institute on the lines of similar American institutions (Brookings, etc.) Present besides our host, Sir Josiah Stamp, Sir Felix Pole, Lord Allen (Clifford Allen, I.L.P.), Hartley Withers, Oswald Falk (financier), Lionel Hichens, and Sir Ernest Simon. Various groups are at work in London on 'the idea' that there ought to be a group of independent economists at work on big urgent problems, etc., there are groups at Chatham House; there is P.E.P. (Political and Economic Planning) run largely by Blackett and Sieff of Marks and Spencer...[65]

P.E.P. had been inaugurated at a dinner held in a London restaurant on 15 March 1931, some months before the final political crisis, but far enough into the fateful year for those assembled to find their motivation in the 'pressure of world events' and of 'national and international crises'. It was a 'fusion of a number of separate groups which had been studying and discussing certain aspects of economic and social problems'.[66] One such group centred on the *Week-End Review*, whose socialistic editor, Gerald Barry, had published on 14 February 1931 'A National Plan for Great Britain', calculated to secure 'a maximum of achievement with a minimum of insoluble *disagreement*'.[67] Independently a director of the Bank of

England and former Conservative candidate, Sir Basil Blackett, prepared a long document (apparently for the inaugural meeting of P.E.P.) on the need for 'orderly and co-ordinated planning'; a year later he summed up his opinions in the book *Planned Money*.[68] A third figure of note was Israel M. Sieff, vice-chairman and joint managing director of one of the most enlightened retail businesses of the age, Marks and Spencer. Around the nucleus P.E.P. collected together

more than a hundred working members who are by vocation industrialists, distributors, officers of central and local government, doctors, university teachers, and so forth, who give part of their spare time to the use of their special training in fact-finding and in suggesting principles and possible advances over a wider range of social and economic activities.[69]

Roughly twice a year throughout the Thirties P.E.P. issued detailed studies of economic and social problems which far outshone all but the most exceptional government-sponsored report of the Twenties; each fortnight it published the broadsheet *Planning*. P.E.P., however, foreswore all political and propagandist activity.[70]

A second set of forces making for agreement in the Thirties had its origins more directly in the First World War. One of the most important and ironic facets of British history in the inter-war years is the manner in which the 'peace movement' in all its aspects grew in force, till in the Thirties it became an important magnet for men whose entire mental and moral make-up unfitted them for a genuine grasp of its fundamental principles. What the disparate elements of the peace movement, who ranged from absolute philosophical pacifists to advocates of collective security through a strong League of Nations, had in common was a profound conviction as to the utter wrongheadedness of the international politics which led into the First World War. In a letter to Lord Allen of Hurtwood (the former Clifford Allen, he had been recruited by Ramsay MacDonald to the National Labour strength in the House of Lords), the Lord Chancellor, Lord Sankey, expressed the prevailing mood of British political leadership of the time: 'I should think there were very few people who would not now admit the war of 1914 was a tragic mistake.'[71] The two most important organizations respresenting the rejection of the old approach to international politics were the National Peace Council and the League of Nations Union. The former had been founded at Bristol in 1905, following upon the National Peace Congress held at Manchester on 22 and 23 June of the previous year. The war had thrown it into total confusion and till the early Thirties it languished; then in July 1933 the twenty-third National Peace Congress held at Oxford (the first for three years) enjoyed an enormous success. At the final public demonstration on 10 July a 1,600 capacity crowd at the Town Hall and a full overflow meeting heard speeches by H. A. L. Fisher, the former Minister of Education, now Warden of New College, Sir Stafford Cripps, Walter Citrine and Vyvyan Adams, a young Conservative M.P.[72] During the Congress those speakers, and a number of others including Sir Arthur Salter, Macmillan, Allen and Sir Norman Angell, who as a Labour M.P. had reserved judgement on MacDonald's actions in August 1931, had begun exploratory conversations upon the possibility of forming some organization to unite the centre-progressive forces. The result was the Liberty and Democratic Leadership Group. The very title expresses the fact that the most profound motive of all affecting the sponsors of political agreement was a fear for the future of democracy. Again, as in the Twenties, it sometimes seems as if the leaders of British opinion were too preoccupied with the forms of democracy and too little with the substance of government. It is noteworthy that J. B. Priestley, after condemning the conditions he found on his English journey, could not restrain a couple of cheers for British democracy:

... I had listened to almost every other kind of political and social theorist. They had always talked quite freely. They never suddenly looked over their shoulders or suggested that we should whisper in a corner. I had heard people say in a loud cheerful tone that they thought Soviet Russia a much better country than England. I had heard Jews denounce Fascists, and Fascists denounce Jews. I was not met in any town by the local representatives of the secret police.[73]

However, the real case of the apostles of agreement was that, faced with the experiments of militant Fascism and Communism, British democracy must demonstrate that it too was capable of vigorous attack on its own economic and social problems. The first manifesto of the Liberty and Democratic Leadership Group declared:

Democracy is again at stake. The struggle for liberty is once more a vital issue. Political movements are rapidly spreading, whose members are prepared to use violent methods both for the pursuit and retention of power.[74]

A vaguer motivation behind the movement for planning and political agreement may be found in the increasingly scientific orientation of British society. The growing importance of science and of the scientific method served to deflect intelligent minds from the shibboleths of party politics towards the problems of concerted action for the rational planning of the nation's resources. In his 1933 presidential address to the British Association for the Advancement of Science, Sir Frederick Gowland Hopkins emphasized, as a scientist, the need to employ the resources of science for the solution of social problems. He added:

In parenthesis allow me a brief further reference to 'planning'. The word is much in front just now, chiefly in relation with current enterprises. But there may be planning for more fundamental developments; for future adjustment to social reconstructions. In such planning the trained scientific mind must play its part. . . .

I have recently read Bacon's *New Atlantis* afresh and have been thinking about his Solomon's House. . . . When civilization is in danger and society in transition might there not be a House recruited from the best intellects in the country with functions similar (mutatis mutandis) to those of Bacon's fancy. A House devoid of politics, concerned rather with synthesizing existing knowledge, with a sustained appraisement of the progress of knowledge, and continuous concern with its bearing upon social readjustments.[75]

The parallel between these sentiments and those of the centre politicians is too striking to need special emphasis.

The Liberty and Democratic Leadership Group became the Next Five Years Group, and in July 1935 published *The Next Five Years; an Essay in Political Agreement*, intended as a programme which could be put into immediate effect during the five-year life-span of one parliament. The programme was divided into two: 'Economic Policy' and 'International Relations'. The fundamental principle of economic policy was to be that 'the community can and must deliberately plan, and control – not in detail but in broad outline – the economic development to which innumerable individual activities contribute'. Reorganization of industry, to the extent of nationalization in such sectors as transport, electricity, industrial insurance, mining royalties and armaments was deemed essential. Central direction of finance and credit was to be ensured by public control of the Bank of England and of the joint-stock banks. A chapter entitled 'Social Justice' advocated the extension of cheap milk facilities, the introduction of food subsidies, the raising of the school leaving age to 16, with part-time education to 18, and the development of a more steeply progressive tax structure.[76] Shortly afterwards the Group entered into an arrangement whereby it secured the benefit of the research facilities of P.E.P.[77] In 1937, while P.E.P. independently published its critical surveys of the British social services, the Group announced a *Programme of Priorities*, which, among other things, came out boldly for a 'Public Medical Service',[78] just at the time when the Labour Party seemed to have been deflected from its former interest in this problem.

At one stage it seemed possible that Lloyd George might throw in his lot with the Next Five Years Group. In the event he went ahead with his own 'Council of Action for Peace and Reconstruction'. As with the Next Five Years Group, the idea behind this essentially middle- and upper-class organization was that it should directly influence the National Government. As the Free Church leader, Dr Scott Lidgett, one of the last representatives of the old alliance between political Liberalism and religious nonconformity, emphasized at the inaugural meeting of the Council:

they were not out to support or oppose the National Government as such. He was a supporter of the Government in principle on its general record. They were equally not out to support or oppose the policies of rival political parties.[79]

However, after the election of 1935 many former supporters of the National Government began to dabble with the Popular Front idea. They shared obvious common ground with the socialist historian and political scientist G. D. H. Cole, when, in advocacy of what he called a People's Front, he declared that he was

less concerned about the need for passing Socialist measures in the immediate future than about the need for saving democracy from total eclipse.[80]

Official Labour hostility reduced the Popular Front notion to a mere chimera. The supporters of political agreement were anyway essentially establishment men, rating good intentions too highly and ignoring the realities of the struggle for political power. Yet, right or wrong, they were very perspicacious about the future course of events:

The historic controversy between individualism and socialism – between the idea of a wholly competitive capitalistic system and one of State ownership, regulation and control – appears largely beside the mark if regarded with a realistic appraisal of immediate needs. For it is clear that our actual system will in any case be a mixed one for many years to come; our economy will comprise with great variety of degree and method, both direct State ownership and control, and management by public and semi-public concerns, and also a sphere in which private competitive enterprise will continue within a framework of appropriate public regulation.[81]

The second part of *The Next Five Years* had been devoted to 'International Relations'; Lloyd George had stressed 'Peace' as well as 'Reconstruction'. The basic principle advanced by the Next Five Years Group was that 'we can and must master international anarchy and get rid of the war system by organized collective action'.[82] There was, as never before in British history, a unanimity

among the articulate that peace was better than war (if the sentiment sounds trite it has only to be compared with the opinions
voiced in the years before 1914). It was in fact out of the 'peace
movement', in its widest sense, that middle opinion had crystallized.
Books are still being written about Britain's 'appeasement' policy
of the 1930s.[83] Our concern here must be mainly with the relationship of that policy to the broader forces of British social history,
though, since much of this book is concerned with the association
between war and social change, it is obviously relevant to know
something of how the Second World War came about. There can
be little doubt that the foreign policy by which British society was
represented in the late Thirties did her little credit: in the sense
that war did actually break out in September 1939, and that within
a year Britain was waging war alone, that policy failed; furthermore,
judged by standards of common sense, consistency, morality, it
does not come out very well. But it is less clear that other policies
(unless pursued steadily from the time of Versailles onwards)
would have averted war: they might have done, or they might
have provoked an earlier (and possibly, though not necessarily,
lesser) conflict, or they might have postponed the war (for, in a
famous dictum of Churchill's, a war postponed may be a war
avoided). Behind all the denunciations of appeasement lie the
assumptions that morality in international affairs can be considered independently of the power to enforce it, and that in earlier
and better times Britain had followed policies that were both 'hon-
ourable' and realistic. In fact throughout the nineteenth century
British governments, secure in their world position, had been in the
habit of waiting on events, praying that there should be as little disturbance as possible of 'the inglorious traffic of industry and an ever
increasing prosperity', and turning only at the very last resort (as
in August 1914) to massive and single-minded military intervention. In the very changed world of the inter-war years the basic
endeavour was still the maintenance, at minimum cost to Great
Britain, of the natural harmony between nations assumed by Gladstonian Liberals. Unhappily the capability for last-resort military
action had been drastically reduced by the losses of the war, and
the will to take such action was even more seriously weakened by

the feeling, fostered by political 'agreement', that a repetition of 1914–18 must at all costs be avoided.

Britain's foreign policy was an outward projection of the defective structure of political influence and decision-making, modified (sometimes for the worse) but essentially untransformed by the First World War. Baldwin and Chamberlain and their associates were very much the prototypes of the political pygmies supported on the shoulders of the business enterprise of past generations, indicted by Boothby and Keynes. Though they shared in the stirrings of social conscience which, in social survey after social survey, had borne such a rich harvest, this was at the expense of the development of an internationalist mind: thus Chamberlain, with genuine exasperation, could talk of the Czech crisis of September 1938 as 'a quarrel in a far-away country between people of whom we know nothing'. Like the artists and intellectuals described by E. L. Woodward, the politicians too had been 'scorched' by war: they would not lightly risk playing with fire, nor, although as trammelled as any statesmen at any time by the needs of national security and the demands of national prejudice, would they give close attention to the theory of the balance of power which was widely regarded as having been a contributory cause of the great holocaust of 1914. While, in this period of crisis in democracy, they put too much weight upon what they believed to be the wishes of the electorate, and too little upon the duties of political leadership, they had no understanding of the strength of the militant Fascist ideologies that had been loosed by war and nurtured by economic disaster. Thus they continued in the Thirties the confusion and inconsistency towards Germany which had marked British policy since Versailles. It is often argued that the advent to power in 1933 of Hitler and the National Socialists, men who were not amenable to the appeals of rational diplomacy, should have clarified British policy in the direction of an unwavering toughness. How clearly apparent Hitler's irrationality was, or should have been, is difficult to determine. A study of contemporary opinion in Britain suggests that, apart from the journals of the far Left, given anyway to the ready discovery of villains and heroes, Hitler was not seen as anything more than the leader of a successful 'revolution', who, if

given appropriate recognition, could be treated as a rational statesman. Hitler, of course, was not the only ruler, or potential ruler,
who refused to meet the standards of a diplomacy which predicated
peace as its highest possible achievement.

By 1933, since no attempt had been made to give authority or
power to the League of Nations, Europe had reverted to a state of
'International Anarchy'.[84] The necessary reserves of power for the
preservation of international order were to be found only in the
United States and in Russia: but America, by her own decision,
had washed her hands of European affairs and Russia, by a fatal
misapprehension only too typical of Conservative leadership in the
inter-war years, was excluded from them. European anarchy, and
Britain's inadequate reaction to it, were exposed and exploited
(though not invented) by Hitler. To Neville Chamberlain, Prime
Minister from October 1937, fell the task of attempting, through a
policy of appeasement unmitigated by any consideration other
than that war was the ultimate horror, the superhuman task of
forcing the sands of time to flow against gravity. It is strange that
in our own age of sophisticated historical analysis so much stress
is still placed on Hitler as the man who caused the war, and Neville
Chamberlain as the man who failed to avert it: one might as well
believe that babies are brought by storks. Chamberlain, it is true,
was not a likeable personality: into his noblest endeavours he
always succeeded in importing an aura of the shady and the furtive;
his appearance was against him, too – more than any other statesman of the decade, he looked like one of the diplomats in Kurt
Jooss's famous ballet of 1932, *The Green Table*.

The state of British public opinion cannot be cited as an excuse
for British foreign policy, but nor, as a vital part of the general
continuum of confused thinking, can it be wholly ignored. Hore-
Belisha, Secretary for War, exactly echoed the thoughts of the
Cabinet when he recorded on 30 August 1938 that

he was against any threat being made that we would declare war if
Germany attacked Czechoslovakia unless there was an overwhelming
public demand first, and on the facts no such overwhelming public
demand exists.[85]

Actually 'the facts' were not at all clear. Judgement on what the British public wanted (to follow a vague substantive by an even vaguer verb) is usually based on two events: the East Fulham by-election of October 1933 and the 'Peace Ballot' of 1935. (A debate in the Oxford Union is sometimes also thrown in for good measure; given the existing state of the English education system the connection between this debate and the British electorate is pretty tenuous.) Neither provides very conclusive evidence. At East Fulham, where the Conservatives had the seemingly impregnable majority of 14,521, a fire-eating reactionary, Alderman W. J. Waldron, was defeated by the convincing margin of 4,840 votes by an attractive young Labour candidate, J. C. Wilmot. In his pronouncements on foreign policy Wilmot stressed disarmament and international co-operation through the League of Nations. But domestic questions, particularly bad housing in Fulham and the poor record generally of the National Government, appeared to play a much bigger role. East Fulham was a protest vote against an uninspiring government and its unattractive candidate, and, less certainly, his jingoism; if it was for anything in foreign policy, it was not pure pacifism, but support for the League of Nations, which could, though Wilmot, like other members of the Labour Party, must be indicted for not spelling this out in his campaign, require military action.[86] A similar, and slightly more positive, conclusion emerges from the results of the Peace Ballot, a protracted house-to-house canvass conducted by an offshoot of the League of Nations Union. Although the *Daily Express* commanded its readers not to participate in the 'Blood Ballot', $11\frac{1}{2}$ million people recorded their votes: 11 million favoured continued British membership of the League of Nations, 6,784,368 (against 2,351,981) were prepared 'if necessary' to support military sanctions against an aggressor.[87]

However, after years of neglect, the League of Nations was in poor shape to be used as the main instrument for deterring the major potential disturber of the peace, Germany. Japan was condemned for her invasion of Manchuria (September 1931), but no action was taken against her (as a matter of hard geographical fact, what action, save perhaps by the United States, *could* be taken against her?). In 1933–34 Hitler began a programme of open rearmament – which presumably could only have been prevented by an attempted reoccupation of Germany, a not very enticing prospect. In December 1934 Italy invaded Abyssinia, and after she had been condemned as an aggressor economic sanctions (though incomplete sanctions, for oil was excluded) were imposed on her. But this attempt to provide collective security on the cheap was a failure. Furthermore, if Germany was the major potential enemy, *realpolitik* suggested that however morally approbrious Italy might be it would be common sense not to antagonize her too much: so, with Neville Chamberlain leading the way, sanctions were abandoned. On 7 March 1936 German troops reoccupied the Rhineland – declared a demilitarized zone under the terms of the Versailles treaty. Dr Donald Watt has recently exposed the myth that, had military action been taken against Hitler, he would have immediately withdrawn, and would thus have been 'stopped' without an open military conflict.[88] In any case, in the light of the contemporary belief that Germany had been harshly treated at Versailles, it was a particularly unattractive issue on which to rattle the sabre: the Rhineland after all was a part of Germany. Undoubtedly from this point onwards resistance to Hitler would have to take the form of a declaration of general war, the very last thing British politicians wanted to be responsible for. Thus the German conquest of Austria in March 1938 went unopposed, and so in fact did German designs on Czechoslovakia, the occasion for Chamberlain's prodigious efforts, culminating in the Munich settlement, to meet German 'grievances' (allegedly centred on the German minority within the Czech borders) in advance of German military action. In terms of abstract justice, perhaps Hitler should have been met with force: the British case was that, apart from involving millions of innocent people in the terror of war, this, because of the hard facts of geography, could not even do the Czechs much good. As Lord Halifax, British Foreign Secretary, had phrased it:

to fight a European war for something that you could not in fact protect and did not expect to restore was a course which must deserve serious thought before it was undertaken.[89]

The real significance of Munich was that Britain had not only conducted, but had been seen to conduct, a search for peace that scarcely stopped short of national humiliation. By the same token, Hitler thereafter was publicly exposed as a dictator who could not be appeased. Attention switched from the unreal issue of defending neighbouring peoples from Nazi aggression, to the basic one of meeting head-on the threat to the civilized world posed by an expansionist Fascist Germany. Still held at arm's length by the British Government, Soviet Russia was left with little alternative but to conclude the Non-Aggression Pact with Germany which left the way clear for the Nazi invasion of Poland. There were now few in Britain to doubt that, however gloomy the prospect, there was no alternative to a declaration of war on Germany (3 September 1939).

NOTES TO CHAPTER FIVE

1. J. Jewkes, *et al.*, *The Sources of Invention*, 1958, pp. 329–31, 334–7, 339–42. R. Calder, *Profile of Science*, 1951, pp. 231–4.
2. P.P., 1942–43, IV, Cmd. 6406, p. 4. A recent book which develops these points is H. W. Richardson, *Economic Recovery in Britain, 1932–1939*, 1967.
3. Federation of British Industries, *Industry and Research*, 1963, p. 7.
4. Pilgrim Trust, *Men Without Work*, 1938, pp. 7–8.
5. *Ibid.*, pp. 10–12, 14–15, 92–93.
6. Federation of British Industries, *Public Expenditure*, October 1932.
7. E. Wilkinson, *The Town that Was Murdered*, 1936. See generally, D. L. Burn, *The Economic History of Steelmaking, 1867–1939*, 1940.
8. *House of Commons Debates*, 4 February 1932.
9. J. M. Keynes, *The General Theory of Employment, Interest and Money*, 1936, pp. 373–9.
10. P.P., 1930–31, XIII, Cmd. 3897.
11. R. Harrod, *The British Economy*, 1962, p. 60. For the Exchange Equalization Fund, see W. Ashworth, *An Economic History of England, 1870–1939*, 1960, p. 400–1.
12. Ashworth, pp. 403 ff. S. Pollard, *The Development of the British Economy, 1914–1950*, 1962, pp. 115, 138–42.
13. Federation of British Industries, *British Commercial Policy*, February 1936.
14. *British Industries*, March 1939, p. 67.
15. *The Times*, 16 January, 11–12 October, 1932. Statistics in regard to balance of payments, etc. are conveniently presented in London and Cambridge Economic Service, *The British Economy: Key Statistics 1900–1966*, 1967.
16. *House of Commons Debates*, 5 February 1935.

17. Labour Party, *Report of Annual Conference*, 1932, p. 250.
18. *Ibid.*, 1934, pp. 256–8.
19. Quoted by J. Symons, *The Thirties*, 1960, p. 9.
20. A. L. Bowley, *Studies in the National Income*, 1942, pp. 62–63.
21. Ministry of Labour, *Inquiry into Weekly Wages in Certain Industries*, October 1935.
22. H. Tout, *Standard of Living in Bristol*, 1938, pp. 25–36.
23. British Medical Association, *Inquiry into Minimum Weekly Expenditure*, 1933.
24. J. Boyd Orr, *Food, Health and Income*, 1936, p. 21.
25. *Ibid.*, pp. 32–49. *Annual Report of Medical Office of Health, Cardiff*, 1936, pp. 143 ff. Cuckfield Rural District Council, *Annual Report of Medical Office of Health*, 1936, pp. 5, 10–12. G. McGonigle and J. Kirby, *Poverty and Public Health*, 1936. W. Crawford, *The People's Food*, 1937. For an admirable summary see J. Burnett, *Plenty and Want*, 1966, pp. 239–57.
26. B. S. Rowntree, *Poverty and Progress*, 1941, pp. 96–102, 156–9.
27. H. L. Beales and R. S. Lambert (eds.), *Memoirs of the Unemployed*, 1934, p. 26.
28. W. Iremonger, *William Temple*, p. 441.
29. Pilgrim Trust, *Men Without Work*, pp. 51, 67, 70, 83.
30. *Ibid.*, pp. 83–84.
31. Carr-Saunders and Caradog Jones, *Social Structure*, 1927, pp. 71–72.
32. *Ibid.*, 1937, p. 66.
33. D. Seers, *Changes in the Cost of Living and the Distribution of Income Since 1938*, 1949, p. 11.
34. W. G. Runciman, *Relative Deprivation and Social Justice*, 1966.
35. G. D. H. and M. I. Cole, *The Condition of Britain*, 1937, p. 64.
36. See above p. 222.
37. 'Guillebaud Report'; P.P., 1955–56, Cmd. 9663, p. 64.
38. P.E.P., *Report on the British Health Services*, 1937.
39. Ministry of Health, *Report of Survey on Overcrowding in England and Wales*, 1936.
40. R. M. Titmuss, *Poverty and Population*, 1938, p. 80.
41. *Men Without Work*, pp. 94–95.
42. *Ibid.*, p. 95.
43. McGonigle and Kirby, *Poverty and Public Health*.
44. J. Burnett, *Plenty and Want*, 1966, p. 242.
45. J. B. Priestley, *Angel Pavement*, 1930, p. 602.
46. J. B. Priestley, *English Journey*, 1934, pp. 397–409.
47. W. Greenwood, *Love on the Dole*, 1933, p. 261.
48. *Men Without Work*, p. 183.
49. S. Spender, *Forward from Liberalism*, 1937, p. 202.
50. G. Greene, *It's a Battlefield*, 1934, pp. 39, 229.
51. W. H. Auden, *Poems*, 1930.
52. C. Day Lewis, *The Magnetic Mountain*, 1933.
53. For the Spanish Civil War see H. Thomas, *The Spanish Civil War*, 1961. For British reactions see K. W. Watkins, *Britain Divided*, 1961.
54. A good account is C. Cross, *The Fascists in Britain*, 1961.

55. *Llewellyn, Elias, Jane and Hannington v. Lord Trenchard,* King's Bench, December 1933, January 1934. *The Times,* 24 January 1934.
56. Pelling, *Communist Party,* pp. 73 ff.
57. Dowse, *Left in the Centre,* p. 181. Marwick, 'The I.L.P. in the 1920s'.
58. Marwick, 'Maxton', p. 40.
59. See e.g. S. Cripps, *Can Socialism Come by Constitutional Methods?* 1933.
60. Symons, pp. 99–110. Mowat, p. 526.
61. W. H. Auden.
62. Quoted by I. Macleod, *Life of Neville Chamberlain,* 1961, p. 151.
63. See C. F. Brand, *The British Labour Party: A Short History,* Stanford, 1964, p. 169.
64. H. Macmillan, *The Middle Way,* 1938, pp. 7–8, *Reconstruction,* 1933, p. 18.
65. T. Jones, *Diary with Letters,* Oxford, 1954, p. 87.
66. P.E.P., *Planning,* 24 March 1936, 25 April 1933.
67. *Week-End Review,* 14 February 1931. The italics are mine.
68. B. Blackett, *Planned Money,* 1932. The document is printed at pp. 14–17.
69. P.E.P., *Report on the British Health Services,* 1937, title page.
70. *Planning,* 24 March 1936.
71. Quoted Marwick, *Clifford Allen,* p. 127.
72. First National Peace Congress, *Resolutions & C.,* 1904, Second National Peace Congress, *Resolutions & C.,* 1905, pp. 19–20, Fifth National Peace Congress, *Resolutions & C.,* 1909, p. 27. National Peace Council, *Annual Report 1933–1934,* 1934, p. 5. For some stimulating reflections on the significance of the 'peace movement' see D. C. Watt, *Personalities and Policies,* 1965, pp. 117–35.
73. Priestley, *English Journey,* p. 412.
74. Liberty and Democratic Leadership Group, *Liberty and Democratic Leadership,* 1934.
75. *The Advancement of Science 1933,* pp. 23–24.
76. *The Next Five Years, an Essay in Political Agreement,* 1935, pp. 1, 92–96, 177–211.
77. A. Marwick, 'Middle Opinion in the Thirties: Planning, Progress and Political "Agreement"', *English Historical Review,* 1964, p. 295.
78. Next Five Years Group, *A Programme of Priorities,* 1937, p. 6.
79. *The Times,* 2 July 1935.
80. G. D. H. Cole, *The People's Front,* 1937, p. 15.
81. *The Next Five Years,* p. 5.
82. *Ibid.,* p. 2.
83. For an illuminating survey see D. C. Watt, 'Appeasement: the Rise of a Revisionist School', *Political Quarterly,* 1963. More recently there have appeared M. George, *The Warped Vision: British Foreign Policy 1933–1939.* Pittsburgh, 1965, W. R. Rock, *Appeasement on Trial,* 1966, and M. Gilbert, *The Roots of Appeasement,* 1966. The best accounts are the chapter entitled 'Appeasement' in A. J. P. Taylor, *English History,* pp. 389–438, and F. S. Northedge, *The Troubled Giant,* pp. 368–630.
84. Cp. G. L. Dickinson, *The International Anarchy,* 1914.
85. R. J. Minney, *The Private Papers of Leslie Hore-Belisha,* 1960, p. 138.
86. This account is based on reports in the local press. See *West London and*

Fulham Gazette, 13, 20, 27 October 1933 and *Fulham Chronicle,* 13, 20, 27 October 1933.

87. In general see A. Livingstone, *The Peace Ballot, The Official History,* 1935.
88. D. C. Watt, 'German Plans for the Reoccupation of the Rhineland: A note', *Journal of Contemporary History,* vol. 1, no. 4, 1966.
89. *Documents on British Foreign Policy,* 3rd series, II, p. 256.

CHAPTER SIX

The Second World War

I. PROFIT AND LOSS: DESTRUCTION AND DISRUPTION

The Second World War was longer and much more destructive than the First, yet it did not hit the country with anything like the shock of the earlier war. Events in Manchuria, Abyssinia and Spain had shown just what brutalities might be expected, though destruction of civilian life and property, greater by far than anything that had been hinted at in the First World War, proved in the end to be less than all pre-war estimates suggested. British troops were at least spared the worst tortures of a tunnel war and the senseless slaughter of major set-piece battles: combatant casualties were half those of 1914–18, amounting finally to about 300,000 dead. Meantime 60,000 civilians and 35,000 merchant seamen were killed, so that there could be no bitter feeling of inequality of sacrifice this time. Often, indeed, civilians were at greater risk than serving men, as Evelyn Waugh noted in the great trilogy *Sword of Honour*, which even outshines Ford Madox Ford's comparable work for the First World War:

'Take cover,' said the voice.

A crescent scream immediately, it seemed, over their heads; a thud which raised the paving-stones under their feet; a tremendous incandescence just north of Piccadilly; a pentecostal wind; the remaining panes of glass above them scattered in lethal splinters about the street.

'You know, I think he's right. We had better leave this to the civilians.'[1]

The declaration of war brought none of the excitement, none of the 'ebullitions', as the *Observer* put it, which had marked the August days of 1914: no rounds of cheers, no dancing in the streets, yet 'the sense of moral release was inexpressible'.[2] If there was to be less bombastic patriotism, the protracted and public search for peace in the Thirties had ensured that there was a deeper sense of inescapable national purpose. Within hours of the declaration of war the sounding of air-raid warnings over London seemed to demonstrate that the long-held fears of a bombing war were only too justified: but that warning proved a false alarm, and for the time being there was no other. The various disruptions of normal domestic life during the period of the 'phoney' or 'invisible' war arose from a preconception of what the war would be like, rather than from the war as it actually materialized. The Government persisted with the blackout first imposed on 1 September, despite the doubling of road casualties which the measure brought in its train. In the streets, there appeared 'gas detectors' and in buildings, parks, everywhere, sandbags.[3] Cinemas and theatres closed; but after a fortnight of war the former were open again; then over the following weeks the theatres, more slowly and cautiously, began to reopen. A wholesale slaughter of cats and dogs at the beginning of the war (75,000 in London alone, it was estimated) because of the anticipated food shortage, created by May 1940 a crying need for more cats to keep rats and mice under control.[4]

The second phase of the war began with the German invasion of Scandinavia in April 1940, followed by the failed attempt to land British troops at Narvik in Norway, the German invasion and conquest of France and the evacuation of British (and some French) troops from Dunkirk (29 May–3 June 1940). After the fall of France and the rejection of Hitler's last peace offer there came his attempt to prepare the way for invasion by the destruction of British air power. Victory by the British fighter pilots, assisted by radar, in the Battle of Britain, helped to ensure that, whatever devastations British society might suffer, the centuries-old barrier of geography would not be directly breached. Men and women in the factories were involved, especially those who were battling to increase aircraft production: those who lived in the South could see the battle going on above them, and the rest of the country could listen in to the somewhat ghoulish commentaries broadcast by the B.B.C. Yet in this war of mass participation the Battle of Britain, uniquely, was essentially fought by an *élite*. It was when Hitler switched from the attack on strategic targets to the mass bombing of civilian centres that he unleashed not only destruction, but the full forces of social change associated with modern total war. By the summer of 1941 the main bomb attacks were over (though, later, the flying bomb attacks of June 1944 briefly did much damage), but the Battle of the Atlantic, the fight to keep British supply lines open in face of submarine attacks, which was as vital to the nation's survival as the Battle of Britain, went on for years, reaching its peak only in 1942. By all the standards upon which men are accustomed to assess a nation's greatness the period of successful defiance of Hitler's Germany in 1940 and 1941, when the British people stood alone, was indeed, in Churchill's clarion phrase, Britain's 'Finest Hour'.[5] Whereas by 1945 every major European nation had suffered direct invasion and the overthrow of civil government, Britain remained as she had been since the eleventh century, an impregnable island fortress: it is not altogether surprising that in the years after the war Britain's spokesmen continued to regard their country as somehow still apart from Europe and, if truth be told, rather better than the rest of Europe. Likewise they came to feel that a 'special relationship' had been established with the United States, who from the date of her entry into the war on 7 December 1941 increasingly shared in its burdens. (There was, of course, not the same direct contact with Russia, converted into an ally by Hitler's invasion of 22 June 1941.) Alliance with these two mighty powers in the long run ensured Germany's defeat, but meantime British military operations in North Africa, successful against the Italians, went badly after the arrival of German forces under General Rommel, who in June 1942 captured the city of Tobruk and 33,000 British soldiers. Even worse defeats were the loss in the East of Hong Kong and Singapore to the Japanese. Then, in October 1942, General Montgomery's victory at El Alamein heralded the long, slow, painful three-year slog which was finally to lead to the defeat of Germany. First came the Anglo-American invasion of French West Africa, followed, in July 1943, by the invasion of Sicily. In Italy there were many set-backs, and, the problems of a sea-borne attack on well-defended positions being enormous, the Normandy landings did not begin till 6 June 1944. Germany's final unconditional surrender, upon which, with memories of the previous war in mind, the Allies insisted, did not come till May 1945. Throughout this period, a substantial proportion of Britain's resources were devoted to bombing raids on German cities, culminating in the destruction of Dresden in February 1945, a sad end to the noble scruples that had once troubled British governments asked to follow a policy of 'Frightfulness'.[6] Worse was to follow in this the most horrendous demonstration of the destructive powers of science that history had so far witnessed: on 6 and 8 August 1945 the Americans dropped atomic bombs on Hiroshima and Nagasaki.

In that it ushered in the age of nuclear weapons, the war was a loss to the whole of civilization; a new, implacable insecurity entered the everyday life of millions throughout the world. For Britain there was a further weakening in relative military power, since nuclear weapons and their delivery systems were extremely costly to produce. It soon became clear that only the United States, and, subsequently, Russia, had the resources to keep up with the speed at which new developments constantly rendered existing weapons obsolete. America and Russia had emerged from the war as super-powers: Britain, though unlike France, Germany and Italy she had not suffered the bitter blows of conquest and occupation, was too small and too lacking in natural wealth to be able to compete. She had in any case suffered some very serious direct losses: to finance the war effort overseas investments, the return on which had for three-quarters of a century helped to bridge the gap between Britain's imports and her exports, had been sold to the tune of £1,000 million; two-thirds of the small but vital gold reserve of 1939 was used up; domestic capital was run down (by about £3,000 million) while new external debts were run up (also by about £3,000 million); exports, upon which more than ever before Britain's future economic survival would depend, had dropped to one-third of the pre-war level, the great South American market being lost to the United States. Contemporary writings, both official and unofficial, are full of profound consciousness of Britain's economic plight; they show less awareness that now at last the sun was beginning to set on the British overseas Empire. True enough, what had been lost to the Japanese had been rewon; but if territorially the Empire was still intact, Japanese victories had given a tremendous stimulus to Asian nationalisms. India, in any case, was in the final stages of seething discontent: her military participation, reluctant for the most part, could lead only to independence. Yet the picture was not a simple one: parts of the Empire could no longer be held as dependencies, and must, graciously or ungraciously, be granted independence in the post-war years; but there were other areas where nationalist movements were still relatively undeveloped and where the British continued to rule. The war therefore involved a loss of territory for Britain, but not a total loss. In name and in fact Britain remained a world power to a degree which was not true of the other European powers, whose efforts to retain their remaining colonies in the post-war years were to prove disastrous. A world power, but, unhappily, a world power without the economic potential to sustain the role. It would be unhistorical to blame British statesmen in 1945 for not clearly perceiving this fact, still more unhistorical to expect them at one fell swoop to abandon a century-old position as the price for having just won a victory which cast all previous history into the shade. When General Smuts forecast in 1943 that Britain's post-war position would be 'one of enormous prestige and respect . . . but she will be poor',[7] contemporaries put as much weight on the first part of the prognostication as the latter. None the less the key features of British history after 1945, relentlessly impinging on social development, are a constant battle with an adverse balance of payments and a tardy and painful adjustment to the new realities of the world power situation.

Total war involved the same sort of disruptions in domestic social life as had the conflict of 1914–18, underscored by the heavy bombing raids and the use of the island as a base from which Britain's overseas Allies could participate in European military operations. Aerial bombardment and threat of aerial bombardment produced very marked movements in population. The original National Register compiled at the end of September 1939 indicated that $2\frac{1}{4}$ million people (5 per cent of the total population) had left their homes in Great Britain during the first month of war. Thereafter many millions of changes of address were notified under the

National Registration Act. Up to June 1942 nearly 20 million removals (often by the same people, however) from one area to another were recorded. In the early part of the war removals from one area to another were fairly steady at around $1\frac{1}{2}$ million per quarter (3 to $3\frac{1}{2}$ per cent of the population). In the latter half of 1940, when the Blitz was at its height, removals were at the rate of 6 per cent of the population per quarter, with a total of 3 million removals in the last quarter of 1940. If removals within each area, which were computed as running to about two-thirds of the total removals from area to area, are included, one is presented with a scene of enormous flux, like ants scurrying at a picnic: over the whole war, all changes of address totalled 60 million – more than the total population of the country. Two out of every seven houses were affected more or less seriously by bomb damage.[8] Throughout most of the war almost half a million foreign troops were stationed on British soil, rising to $1\frac{1}{2}$ millions at the time of the Normandy landings. Fathers were again called from home for armed service, mothers for work in the factories. An upsurge in illegitimate births, in the incidence of venereal disease and in juvenile delinquency[9] were inevitable consequences.

One disease within the judicial system which had seemed ready for final cure in 1939 now raged, temporarily, with a new virulence. The Cadogan Committee, reporting in 1938, had recommended the total abolition of corporal punishment as a judicial sentence passed on adults or juveniles: sentences carried out on males over sixteen fluctuated between 13 in 1935 and 17 in 1938; those inflicted on boys under sixteen had dropped steadily from 227 in 1935 to 65 in 1938. The war, however, prevented the Government from developing its abortive Criminal Justice Bill of 1938–39, and in 1940 sentences of corporal punishment on boys rose to 302, and to 531 in 1941, before falling away to 8 in 1947 and nil in 1948.[10] By a sad mischance, the day set for the long overdue raising of the school leaving age to 15 was the day war broke out: not only had this reform to be postponed but in the years that followed air-raids destroyed one-fifth of all the country's schools. With the interruption of normal schooling (especially when children were evacuated to safer localities) went interruption in school health and feeding facilities. Undoubtedly the destructive influence of war produced a massive negative total to be substracted from the social gains resulting from the military participation of the lower classes and from the test-dissolution-transformation process. The educational paradox was well summarized by a leading historian of education, G. A. N. Lowndes:

... although in the realm of ideas the effect of the war had been to advance by 15 years the popular demand for a public system of education genuinely capable of serving a classless democracy, in the realm of hard facts it had retarded by at least 20 years the possibility of the substantial realization of any such ideal.[11]

Housing progress similarly was disrupted: 200,000 houses were totally destroyed and a further 250,000 rendered unusable, while necessary maintenance and repairs were neglected on countless others. The total manpower of the building industry steadily declined as men were called away to other tasks: from 1 million in 1939 it fell to 337,000 in 1945. Over the same period only 200,000 houses were built.[12] While bombing raids were rendering even more chaotic the condition of British industrial civilization, the report of the Barlow Commission, appointed two years before the war to investigate the question of the distribution of the industrial population, necessarily had to be pushed aside, though as a vivid map of the new Britain that must be built on the waste land of the depression it could not be totally ignored. In fact, as had happened a generation earlier, the cumulative effect of all the destruction was to render imperative massive action to make good the ravages of war. Nowhere was this more apparent than in environmental planning. As age-old slums tottered to the ground there arose in unexpected places a firm determination to build something rather better in their place: 'bombs,' declared the journal of the Federation of British Industries, 'have made builders of us all.'[13]

2. TEST, DISSOLUTION, TRANSFORMATION

Bomb attacks were the most obvious physical manifestation of the test presented by war to domestic social institutions. Doing its homework in advance, the Government produced two schemes which in the long run resulted in a considerable transformation in British social attitudes and styles of social provision: these were the Evacuation Scheme for the country's mothers and children, and the Emergency Hospital Service for air-raid casualties. Sir John Anderson's report setting out possibilities and plans for moving civilians from 'evacuation' to 'reception' areas (those in 'neutral' areas being left alone) was drawn up in July 1938 and published the following October.[14] The Munich crisis gave the Government a push towards the practical implementation of some of the Anderson suggestions, but its policies had certain characteristic weaknesses. The whole burden of responsibility for evacuation was placed on the Local Authorities, resulting in some rather complicated financial provisions: education, for instance, was to be provided by the host locality but paid for by the authority in whose area the child normally resided. The scheme was to be entirely voluntary, with no one being evacuated without his own consent. Special local billeting officers were appointed in reception areas and were not always unsusceptible to pressure by influential local citizens anxious to evade their responsibilities. When war broke out, of 3 million declared eligible for the official evacuation scheme $1\frac{1}{2}$ million went, while a further 2 million made private arrangements. The official scheme was pretty chaotic:

... there was little evidence of the completion of the railway time-tables, and many teachers received their first suspicion of the scheme when they saw how the children were marched on to the platforms and put on any train until it was filled, with no organized attempt to control their destinations or even, in many cases, to preserve schools intact.[15]

Many mothers and children returned within days to their city homes; many more returned when, on 4 October, the Government misguidedly announced its intention of recovering part of the billeting allowance paid to those households in reception areas which gave hospitality to evacuees. Yet for all that it was a muddled failure, the first evacuation scheme took many middle-class families a further stage along the social exploration that had been a characteristic of the Thirties. If for genteel families in rural areas the invasion of slum children, some disgustingly lacking in the rudiments of toilet training, others pathetically unable to believe that they were actually to sleep in, and not under, their beds, accompanied by mothers who were often worse, could be hard to bear, it could also be a staggering revelation of the nature of the society in which they lived. A somewhat sentimental social worker who had been one of the first middle-class munitions girls of the First World War went so far as to subtitle her study of evacuation 'A Social Revolution':

... a London worker visiting the reception areas can only feel delight at the fit and happy children who surround her, alert with new interest and new vigour. Commenting on this to a West Countryman he answered me, 'Yes – I don't know what you Londoners do to them that they arrived looking the way they did.'

'I still ask myself,' she continued,

'in the new world that we have presently to build, is this evacuation experience to be one of the things that will force us to accept a levelling up of the income of the insecure section of the community, even though we shall inevitably experience a levelling down of our comparative middle-class ease?'[16]

By the end of 1939, 900,000 of the original evacuees had drifted home, and in February a new scheme was drawn up, which, though still voluntary, required parents to sign an undertaking that if they joined the scheme they would go through with it. This second scheme came into effect with the Blitz of 1940 while in Scotland the second official evacuation reached its peak during the bombing attacks of March and May 1941. There was a third wave of evacuation during the flying bomb attacks of July to September 1944, when a census showed there to be 1,012,700 evacuees in official billets, including 250,000 from the earlier movements. Side by side with the official schemes private individuals made their own arrangements. Evacuation to North America was largely a private matter,[17] government aid being provided for only 2,666 out of 8,862 children who crossed the Atlantic, before the sinking of a liner bound for Canada in October 1940 brought the experiment to a tragic close. It was the second evacuation scheme which had the most striking effect in stirring up a positive interest in the evil conditions in which many of the country's children were being reared. A key document was the report *Our Towns*, published by the Women's Group on Public Welfare, a 'window through which English town life was suddenly and vividly seen from a new angle'.[18] The *Economist* at this time went so far as to declare evacuation 'the most important subject in the social history of the war because it revealed to the whole people the black spots in its social life'.[19] Almost certainly the importance of evacuation has been exaggerated, but equally certainly it was an outstanding example of war testing and exposing existing social institutions.

The history of the Emergency Hospital Service began with the government survey conducted in 1938 of all available hospital accommodation – the politicians then being obsessed with the problem of civilian casualties, rather to the exclusion of any consideration of how to deal with damage to housing. The basis of the plan was that in all types of hospitals, voluntary and municipal, certain beds paid for by the Government were set aside for air-raid casualties. Thus a kind of *ad hoc* national organization, and an enforced co-operation between voluntary and local hospitals was brought into being. By March 1941 80 per cent of all hospitals were involved in the scheme, and a Ministry of Health report of that date well summarizes the expansion of the scheme by an almost natural process:

The scope of the Scheme has continually widened. At the outset it envisaged provision for air-raid casualties, and for all military sick and casualties for whom the Army could not find hospital beds. Provision on a much smaller scale was also made for Navy and Air Force sick and casualties. With time the term 'E.H.S. patient' has been extended to cover persons suffering from war service injuries (e.g. Civil Defence workers, members of the Women's Auxiliary Services, and Home Guards injured, not necessarily by enemy attack, while on duty); the 'transferred sick' (i.e. patients transferred from hospitals in urban areas because the accommodation is needed for casualties, or because it has or may be damaged by enemy action); evacuees (who may be un-accompanied children sent out under the Government Evacuation Scheme, or other persons billeted by the Government or by private arrangement); transferred war workers (i.e. whole-time Civil Defence Workers or workers in essential industries whose work has taken them away from their homes); and certain other classes of persons for whom no satisfactory facilities would otherwise exist. Treatment is free for air-raid casualties and for a great number of other E.H.S. patients.

A year later the ministry wisely recognized the likely long-term consequences of these developments:

In the last year or so the numerous organizations and authorities whose interests lie in the hospital world have been giving increasing thought to the future. All start from the accepted premise that there can be no return to the pre-war position of unrelated hospital units pursuing independent and often wastefully competitive courses ...[20]

On 9 October 1941 the Minister of Health did indeed make the first public political pronouncement pointing a faltering way towards a National Health Service.[21] One point frequently made in the various discussions of the problem is worthy of special note: the need to base any new hospital service on areas wider than those provided by existing local authorities.[22] If the inadequacies of the existing hospital system were now exposed, and the basis of a new national scheme laid, also revealed was the niggardly nature of the existing welfare provision for children, once again, at a time of mass slaughter, held in high esteem as the guardians of the future of the race. The emergency Milk and Meals Scheme of 1941 brought to an end the old class distinction whereby only 'necessitous' children were eligible, for in war there was no time for elaborate social distinctions, nor, in any case was it always true, as Boyd Orr had shown, that reasonable income levels necessarily connoted decent standards of nutrition. Concern for the future of the race was manifest in the appointment in March 1944 of a Royal Commission on Population, echoing the institution of the first population census during the French Wars in 1801. An all-party deputation of M.P.s on 16 June 1941 induced the Government to draw up a *Memorandum on Family Allowances* (May 1942), a review of the 'practical questions' rather than a statement of intent. Nor, when their needs were newly illumined by the flares of war, were adults neglected. Insurance coverage for 'black-coated workers' had been an obvious requirement in pre-war days: the dislocations of war brought recognition that it was imperative. A sudden rise in the cost of living brought extreme hardship to old-age pensioners, so, also in 1940, a new system of supplementary pensions was introduced, administered through the once-hated Unemployment Assistance Board, which now operated more simply and less offensively as the Assistance Board.

As in the previous war, the most striking readjustments in face of the challenge of war came in the separate but clearly inter-related areas of the extent and nature of government power and the economic ideology informing the use of that power. On the short term what was most obvious was the colossal power again assumed by the State; on the long term, though the State would never again give up all that it had taken unto itself, the structure of British politics still remained remarkably unchanged. The new economic policies were far more subtle than the blunt experiments of 1916–18; though they involved far less of a break with the past, they had far more enduring effects. While in the background there was always, if needed, the coercive authority of the Government, the new policies were as much a demonstration of the virtues of Keynesian managed capitalism as of State socialism. During the twilight of the Chamberlain régime moves were made hesitantly and fumblingly. Ten days before the war broke out an Emergency Powers (Defence) Act, the 1939 counterpart of D.O.R.A., was passed. By 1 September six new ministries had been established, Supply (Munitions), Economic Warfare (Blockade), Information, Food and Shipping all having ancestors in the First World War. Home Security having its paternity in the expectation of a bombing war. A Military Training Act of August, which for the first time instituted conscription in time of 'peace', was succeeded on 3 September by a National Service (Armed Forces) Act. Bank rate was put up by 1 per cent to 4 per cent on 1 September for no very good reason other than that it was felt to be the done thing in time of emergency. At the end of the month a National Register was compiled, raising not a trace of the controversy of 1915. For all the experience of the First World War and the preparation of the Thirties, there was no efficient stockpiling and no restraint was placed upon recruiting from the mines. Despite the continuance of unemployment, no direct effort was made to build up industrial production; only in aircraft construction was the position satisfactory, and here again developments were based on projects put into operation in pre-war years. Despite 1914–18 there was no haste to introduce domestic rationing, and this did not appear till 8 January 1940. Sections of the Press at first contributed to the 'business as usual' atmosphere. At the turn of the year the *Daily Mirror* thought the country had grounds for 'calm and grateful acceptance' though not for 'carefree jubilation'. In praising the decision to compile a National Register, the *Observer* had declared it would facilitate, 'when necessary',

the application of the old Socialist motto: 'From each according to his ability, to each according to his needs', and create 'a new nexus between the individual and the State'.

Eden, speaking as if to one of the major themes of this book, told the House of Commons on December 1939 that war 'exposed weaknesses ruthlessly' and required 'revolutionary changes in the economic and social life of the community'.[23] But during the invisible war it is difficult to discern any revolutionary changes in economic and social life or the 'new nexus between individual and State'. The Federation of British Industries had been very unhappy about the setting up of a Ministry of Supply but, aware of Britain's threatening balance of trade problems, on 5 December it placed before the Prime Minister a memorandum calling for the creation of a separate Ministry of Economic Affairs 'charged with the direction of our export trade'; Chamberlain would not hear of it.[24]

In the early months of the new year criticism of continued unemployment, insufficient control over the domestic front and, above all, the absence of any new initiatives at all either at home or abroad began to break into the open, though it was never as forceful as that which Asquith attracted in the latter half of 1916. Early in January personal frictions within the Government brought the resignation of the War Secretary, Hore-Belisha, who was widely believed to be a supporter of a more democratic Army. The *Daily Mirror* openly took his part. The *Manchester Guardian* declared that the resulting ministerial changes did not 'go far, and certainly not far enough'. Two days later it returned more strongly to the charge: 'There are still many,' it warned, '. . . who have not realized that . . . we must be prepared for revolutionary changes and for large sacrifices.'[25] Restored to more pensive frame on 1 April it mused upon that future time 'when it is the duty of the House of Commons in the interests of the country to remove the Government of the day'. By March the *Daily Mail* was openly rude about the Government: 'Creeping paralysis is dulling our movements, our resolution.' *The Times* was less direct, more discreet, but the message was there all right:

There is thought to be a slightly leisurely air about our methods. Are we hitting as hard as we can wherever we can?

The *Daily Telegraph* and the *Daily Express* remained loyal to Chamberlain, the latter's defence of present inactivity providing an interesting final flicker of the cinders which the First World War had cast over the domestic hearth during the inter-war years: 'We want no more Passchendaeles, no more Neuve Chapelles.'[26]

Four days before Hitler's invasion of Denmark and Norway, Chamberlain made the foolhardy remark which shadowed him thereafter: 'Hitler has missed the bus.' The appointment of Churchill to the post – more apparent than real – of chairman of the Military Co-ordination Committee, was noted with approval but did not completely silence criticism. Later in the month Sir John Simon's budget, after a few initial gasps of relief, ran into almost universal condemnation for being far too feeble in its grasp of the problems of war finance. Criticism on this score reached a peak on 1 May. Next day the bungled attempt to land British forces in Norway fizzled to its inglorious conclusion. The *Manchester Guardian* led the way in bitter condemnation, saying of Chamberlain that 'his capacity for self-delusion is a national danger'. The *Daily Mirror* was not less forthright in a leading article headed 'Missing the Bus'. In strict equity the Norway failure should have rested more heavily on the shoulders of the First Lord of the Admiralty, Churchill, than on the Prime Minister; but as the *Manchester Guardian* perspicaciously pointed out, Norway was only a 'symptom' of eight months' malaise.

If we look back over these eight months, with problem after problem mismanaged or neglected, with speech after speech revealing the same lack of grasp and imagination, we are driven to the conclusion that we are facing the greatest crisis in our history with a government weaker than any government that has made war since Addington faced Napoleon. A comparison of the Government's trivial handling of such questions as munitions, unemployment, taxation, nutrition, agriculture and evacuation with the scale of the tremendous task on our hands is enough to show that there is something fundamentally wrong with the Government's view of its duty. . . .

What is needed is a government that can organize the nation's strength, touch its imagination, command its spirit of self-sacrifice, impose burdens fearlessly on all classes, put the war before everything else, look ahead with cool and deliberate courage. Nobody can pretend that the Government answers to these needs.[27]

The following day a two-day debate on the Norwegian campaign began in the House of Commons. Among prominent Conservatives who were highly critical of the Government, the limelight was shared by Sir Roger Keyes, resplendent in the uniform of an Admiral of the Fleet, and Leopold Amery, who quoted Cromwell's magnificent words to the Long Parliament: 'Depart, I say, and let us have done with you. In the name of God, go!' Yet it was widely held not to be good tactics for Labour to attempt to force a division, since such action would be likely to force dissident Conservatives into the government lobby. Those who argued thus (practically the entire Press) were, as it proved, just too cynical in their appraisal of the value Conservatives placed on the call of patriotism. So inadequate was Chamberlain's own speech, and so appallingly worse that of Oliver Stanley, that Herbert Morrison announced during the second day's debate that Labour would in fact force a division, thereby incurring the contumely not only of *The Times,* but also of the *Manchester Guardian. The Times* leader, at this crucial moment in the country's history, was indeed a classic instance of all that was worst in the established British attitude towards vital public decisions:

A government, with the armoury of the Whip's office intact, is not un-horsed by frontal attack, and a General Election is out of the question. What happens – it has happened before and it will happen again – is that detached and public-spirited individuals rise above their normal loyalties, answer by instinct to the needs of the hour, take their soundings of public opinion in the lobbies, the constituencies and the news-papers, and find quieter means of assuring a Ministry that it no longer fulfils the aims or holds the confidence of Parliament and of the country.[28]

Not less pathetic was Chamberlain's own reply to the challenge:

I do not seek to evade criticism but I say this to my friends in the House – and I have friends in the House. . . . At least we shall see who is with us and who is against us, and I call on my friends to support us in the Lobby tonight.

It was left to Lloyd George, the man who had been out of office for most of the inter-war years, to make the apt rejoinder:

It is not a question of who are the Prime Minister's friends. . . . He has appealed for sacrifice. . . . I say solemnly that the Prime Minister should give an example of sacrifice, because there is nothing which can con-stitute more to victory in this war than that he should sacrifice the seals of office.

When the division came 41 ministerial M.P.s voted with the Opposition; a further 60 odd did not vote at all. A government whom the 'armoury of the Whip's office' could normally furnish with a majority of about 240 now had a majority of precisely 81.[29] Next day *The Times* was still griping about this unmannerly 'frontal attack', but the Press as a whole was in no doubt that Chamberlain's day was over.

Who would replace him? In high political circles in both major parties, the favoured candidate, strange as it may seem, was the somewhat nondescript Lord Halifax – Labour, it is true, had little cause to love Churchill. Through his own diffidence, and he had much to be diffident about, Halifax let the opportunity slip. That it was ever his in the first place says little for the top leadership of either party. All along, from the first sounds of criticism of Chamberlain's way of running the war, Churchill had been the popular candidate. At the time of the Hore-Belisha resignation, the *Daily Mirror* said of the government from which he had just departed:

Apart from Mr Chamberlain, that Ministry possessed two men whose names are not merely names to the people: Churchill and Hore-Belisha.

One of them has gone. Mr Churchill remains as the lone possessor of an imagination and therefore of a popular appeal.

On 10 May the *Daily Express,* which had supported Chamberlain unto the last, was clear that 'the public will now undoubtedly demand that Mr Churchill should be raised to the place which Mr Chamberlain vacates'.[30] Chamberlain did not vacate his place with alacrity: indeed, on 9 May, he invited Attlee and Greenwood to join him in a reconstructed government. From the two Labour leaders he received no encouragement, but a final decision was left to the Labour Party National Executive, which was then meeting at Bournemouth where the party's annual conference was about to begin. The next day's message from Bournemouth sent Chamberlain to the King with his resignation: after all the muddles of the Thirties, Labour had twice in three days acted with decisive effect. The King still hankered after Halifax, but Chamberlain made it clear that it must be Churchill. Next day no national newspaper carried Churchill's accession as the main news story: he had been chased from the headlines by Hitler's invasion of the Low Countries.

The advent of the Churchill government brought no immediate

revolution in the economic management of the war. It took a further series of external disasters to bring the country hard against the final choice: reorganize or perish. Churchill was not always himself well disposed towards the measures taken by his ministry, but his was the prestige and unchallenged power which enabled them to be successfully and smoothly implemented. By the end of May the rapid German advance had compelled the British Expeditionary Force to retreat upon Dunkirk, where it was completely hemmed in. This disaster was mitigated by the resourceful deployment of shipping of all sizes and descriptions to evacuate nearly 340,000 soldiers, of whom almost 140,000 were French. The British could withdraw to their island; the French could not: on 21 June France surrendered. Throughout the difficult days that followed, and for the entire period of the war, Churchill asserted a much firmer control over the British military effort than ever Lloyd George had done. Theoretically the source of his power, much stressed by historians, was that, in addition to being Prime Minister he also took the office of Minister of Defence; in reality it lay in his own exuberant strength of character, his ability to speak the same language as the service chiefs, his huge appetite for his task. Churchill made many mistakes, but during his lifetime (he died in 1965) he was, unlike Lloyd George, little criticized, perhaps because he had no responsibilities for immediate post-war policies. But however critically future historians examine his record, his position is secure.

Military reverse was accompanied by a severe crisis in Britain's overseas payments' position, and this forced the Government to control the foreign exchanges. As Treasury influence waned, direction of the domestic effort passed into the hands of a number of Cabinet committees: the Production Council and the Economic Policy Committee (both headed by Greenwood), the Food Policy Committee and the Home Policy Committee (both headed by Attlee) and the Lord President's Committee (headed by Chamberlain till ill-health precipitated his resignation on 3 October, when Sir John Anderson took over). The Economic Policy Committee had the services of an expanded Central Economic Information Committee.[31] This unsatisfactorily complex structure endured throughout 1940, during which time Sir Kingsley Wood's July Budget revealed the new Chancellor of the Exchequer as no great advance on his predecessor. The Government was digging its fingers into the cliff-face but had not yet found a secure hold. As so often in the past, J. M. Keynes was on hand to indicate to the politicians the error of their ways with the latest of a series of works combining seminal economic thought with immediate political relevance. In *How to Pay for the War* (1940) Keynes called for taxation to be based on total national income rather than on an unsatisfactory aggregation of individual incomes; between the yield of the latter and the potential of the former lay, he said, the 'inflation gap'. When fighting for survival Britain does not ignore her prophets. Keynes, for the first time since 1919, was brought back into the Government as adviser to the Treasury; Kingsley Wood served up a rehash of *How to Pay for the War* as the White Paper *The Sources of War Finance*, and his 1941 Budget was the first in the country's history to adopt the National Income approach.

At the same time unification of economic and domestic policy was steadily achieved by the rise to power of Sir John Anderson and his Lord President's Committee. The Economic Policy Committee disappeared, and the Central Economic Service split into two – the Central Statistical Office and the Economic Section, which in effect became Anderson's economic staff. The pattern of central administration was completed with the establishment in 1942 of a Ministry of Production. At the top were Churchill and the service ministers and chiefs of staff responsible for military matters and also for foreign policy and major domestic questions: Churchill's freedom of action was limited on the one side by the service chiefs, to whose opposition on specific points he had from time to time to give way, and on the other by the realities of the world situation, particularly when it became necessary to plan strategy in close association with the Americans. Secondly, to look after home and economic policy there was Sir John Anderson and his Lord President's Committee. Thirdly, the Minister of Production, along with the supply ministers and their joint staffs, handled the general issues of supply programmes, with the Defence (Supply) Committee coming in on major issues. There remained to the War Cabinet, whose members, unlike those of the Lloyd George Cabinet, all had specific tasks to perform (Attlee as Deputy Prime Minister chaired the Cabinet on Churchill's frequent absences), the discussion of foreign policy, major issues of military policy and any social economic and production questions which could not be dealt with by either the Lord President or the Minister of Production. Lloyd George was critical of what he called 'not a War Cabinet but a Churchill Cabinet'. The truth of the matter was that on military policy none of Churchill's colleagues felt that they were in a position to challenge his superior wisdom; on other matters they could, and did, assert their influence.[32] From April 1941 the British economy was controlled and managed on an even grander scale than had been true of the latter stages of the previous war. Agriculture was directed and prodded in much the same manner as it had been in 1917 and 1918, with the added advantage that the legislation of the 1930s had already begun the process of boosting British agricultural production. But although the railways were again run as a unified concern, newspaper advertisements familiarizing the British public with the phrase 'British Railways', it took a major coal crisis in 1942 to bring the establishment of the Ministry of Fuel and Power and control of the coal industry in June 1942. In contrast with the previous war, the Government did not undertake the direct ownership of munitions or other factories: given the elaborate framework of controls and planning and co-ordinating committees this was scarcely necessary. New capital issues at home were firmly regulated: after June 1940 there was strict import control; and the establishment of international exchange controls led to the development of the modern 'sterling area.'

Two points must be made about the economic innovations of the war period. By any obvious reckoning they were successful. While a war effort which involved the massive deployment of munitions and ancillary industries, the heavy use of resources in maintaining convoys, transporting troops and, finally, mounting sea-borne invasions was fully maintained, the domestic population was well and equitably fed. Production of aircraft rose from just under 8,000 in 1939 (2,800 in 1938) to 20,000 in 1941 and over

26,000 in 1943 and 1944. Between 1940 and 1942 production of tanks multiplied fourfold. Between 1939 and 1942 production of machine tools rose from 35,000 to 100,000. Despite the fact that there were well over 5 million men in the Armed Forces at the end of the war, the agricultural labour force was expanded by one-fifth and the number employed in the engineering and chemical industries by two-thirds.[33] The total acreage of land under cultivation rose from 12 million to 18 million. These successes were, as in the First World War, made a matter for much self-congratulation. Yet, to move on to the second point, though they were the product of a managed economy, that economy owed almost as much to the willing co-operation of a community faced with a struggle for survival as to the elaboration of any fully effective permanent system of national planning. Keynesian economists for the first time achieved positions of power. One of the economists' proudest achievements was the system of rationing by points which allowed the consumer a certain limited choice among various scarce commodities, a mixed economy writ small.

None the less the changes in economic thinking were real and lasting. The innovations in political control were less so. Churchill's pre-eminence may have taken the country a step further from Cabinet government towards prime ministerial, or even presidential government: but then Churchill was defeated in 1945. The small War Cabinet proved again to be a temporary expedient, though the greatly extended use of Cabinet committees did continue on into the peace. If the House of Commons was for the most part relegated to a deeper impotence than ever, it did have its one great moment of glory in May 1940, and almost had another in the debate over the Beveridge Report in February 1943: a time of total war, anyway, was scarcely the one in which to seek a new role for the private M.P. Much more worthy of attention is the case of local government and of the Civil Service. The judgement of a bombing war on some of Britain's institutions of local government was pretty clear:

It was more than bricks and mortar that collapsed in West Ham on the 7th and 8th of September 1940, it was a local order of society which was found hopelessly wanting, as weak and badly constructed as the single-brick walls which fell down at the blast.[34]

Too small, too poor, bogged down in pettifogging local pedantries, many authorities simply could not cope with the war emergency: it was necessary, with the Emergency Hospital Service, to cut across one of their functions; so, likewise, did the creation of a National Fire Service, rendered essential by the incendiary bomb, cut across another. The sight of Plymouth in flames moved Lady Astor to send the following indictment to the local Regional Commissioner:

Local authorities did not profit from each other's experience; neither regional headquarters nor Whitehall succeeded in conveying to them the need for a bigger, swifter, more efficient preventive organisation; small air-raids had the unfortunate effect of making many satisfied with inadequate civil defence: the peacetime system of slow committee rule, or red tape, of endless letter-writing between London, regional head-quarters and the periphery has shown itself an absolute danger to human life.[35]

From the start of the war there grew side by side with the old local councils a form of *de facto* regional government. Again this had its origins in the government plans of the late Thirties, when it was decided that to meet the problems of Civil Defence the skeleton regional organization, kept in being since the General Strike, could be put to use. In 1937 a sub-committee of the Committee of Imperial Defence (the Warren Fisher Committee) recommended the immediate institution of

a revised administrative organization which would include not only the existing headquarters of staff in London, but the formation of 13 areas outside London, each with its own headquarters staff. This change is necessary in peacetime for the purpose of the effective examination of local authority schemes, and in war a regional system of administration will be an essential element in the wartime organization.[36]

On 1 November 1937 a first regional office was opened at Leeds, and the next day a second was opened in Birmingham. By the summer of 1938 there were offices at Edinburgh, Liverpool,

Newcastle-on-Tyne, Nottingham, Reading, Bristol, Glasgow, Cambridge and Cardiff. The Munich crisis put urgency into the various plans and was followed immediately by the Fisher-Hankey proposals for a Ministry of Home Security and for a full regional organization. In July a list of Civil Commissioners, who in war would become Regional Commissioners, had been drawn up, and this was followed by 'Civil Defence Emergency Scheme "Y" ' – essential instructions for the Commissioners.

The Commissioners would act as the representatives of His Majesty's Government in their Regions with the responsibility of seeing that effect was given to the Government's 'measures for civilian defence'. Their powers would normally derive from the appointment to their Regions of representatives of central Departments invested with powers by their respective Ministers; and their function would thus be to act as chairmen of Regional Committees, with responsibility mainly for co-ordination. But circumstances might arise which would necessitate the Commissioners taking emergency action on the Government's behalf beyond the power entrusted to Departmental representatives, and without consultation with the Ministers concerned. They would then assume a personal executive responsibility and their action would subsequently be supported by the Government.

The most important of the Departmental representatives at Regions would be a Ministry of Health official, to be described as 'principal Official' and to bear responsibility for all matters within the Region concerning his Ministry. A Hospital and a Finance Officer from this Department, and representatives of the Ministry of Transport, Food (Defence Plans) Department of the Board of Trade, Office of Works and General Post Office were among others to be appointed.[37]

At first, in keeping with the general tone of National Government policy, the Regional Commissioners were required to establish their headquarters in secret, and these ranged from a small suburban villa to a prison. In Leeds the suspicions of the City Council became so aroused that they resolved to send a deputation to the Home Secretary. Only at the end of the last year of peace was the secrecy lifted, and only in April 1939 was a list of Commissioners (substantially different from that drawn up at the time of Munich) published. The offices of the Regional Commissioners, primarily concerned with the problems of Civil Defence, but inevitably of growing importance as co-ordinating authorities, throughout the war provided one form of regional administration.

But within the same areas there was a second focal point, the Regional Boards (called Area Boards when first set up in January 1940), responsible for problems of productivity. These consisted of six 'industrial members' and nine 'official members'. The employers and the workers each provided three industrial members, from whom were appointed a chairman and vice-chairman, one from the workers' side, one from the employers' side. The official members were: the Regional Officer of the Admiralty; the Regional Representative of the Ministry of Aircraft Production; the Regional Controller of the Ministry of Supply; the Regional Controller of the Ministry of Labour and National Service; the Regional Representative of the Board of Trade; the Regional Transport Commissioner; the Regional Raw Materials Officer of the Ministry of Supply; the Regional Representative of the Emergency Repair Department of the Ministry of Works and Buildings; the Chairman of the Machine Tool Regional Committee. The Regional Boards began life under the aegis of the Ministry of Supply, then, after shuttling about in a most unsatisfactory manner, settled down under the mighty Production Executive.[38]

Deficiencies revealed at West Ham, Stepney, Southampton and, later, at Plymouth created a strong sentiment in favour of increasing the powers of the Regional Commissioners at the expense of the old-established local authorities. During the winter of 1940-41 the Civil Defence Committee of the War Cabinet gave much attention to this issue, especially when the Regional Commissioner responsible for Southampton asked for 'definite authority . . . to co-ordinate and direct'. Any such formal concrete extension of the Commissioners' powers, however, foundered on the opposition of the Minister of Home Security, Herbert Morrison: himself a local government man, Morrison would not countenance anything that might discourage local responsibility and self-help.[39] None the less the official historian of Civil Defence has summed up the position in the true British manner:

The war had brought a revolutionary, if temporary, innovation to the relationship between central and local government and it was typically British that the innovations, the new rules of the game, were not codified on paper. The arrangements by which the Regional Commissioners functioned were not necessarily logical, but they had the great merit that they worked.[40]

That, too, was exactly the opinion of all concerned at the time. Inevitably the upheavals of war, the appearance of *de facto* regional government and a general interest in the future created a wealth of literature on local government reform, prepared by the Local Government Association and other interested bodies and individuals. Everybody was in favour of 'reform', but existing local authorities were not keen to see themselves legislated out of existence, and ardent reformers did not wish to see their reconstruction plans bogged down in the intricacies of administrative change. Anyway, the glorious British system had survived this, the greatest of all wars: why change it? As the White Paper on *Local Government during the Period of Reconstruction* put it:

The use throughout the Paper of such terms as 'machinery' and 'structure' must not be allowed to obscure the fact that local government in this country is a living organism capable of adaptation to meet new conditions. Both members and officers of local authorities have given proof of this under the stress and strain of two great wars. They have shown themselves capable of shouldering with marked success varied and novel responsibilities. For this they have earned the gratitude of the nation, and there is no reason to doubt that they will prove equally capable of dealing with the problems of post-war reconstruction.[41]

During the first half of 1945 all the Commissioners and their departments resigned. The various organs of Britain's vast central government have continued to need, and to have, their regional offices; but the opportunity to create out of the war experience an *elective* regional government was never seized.

The tale in regard to the Civil Service is very similar. The obscurantism of the typical Civil Service mind at the beginning of the war is superbly illustrated in the notes prepared by the

Ministry of Information in November 1940 to counteract the seduction of Hitler's 'New Order'; despite two decades of industrial depression and inglorious financial policy, these sought to extol the advantages of private enterprise and the Gold Standard.[42] Here too the searching light of war was switched on:

In peacetime the Civil Service is a target of frequent criticism; in wartime criticism is very largely increased. There is apprehension lest the Government machinery may not adapt itself to the urgencies of war; while the inevitable encroachments of Government control on personal liberty and private life are a source of new and daily irritations.[43]

In June 1941 the Foreign Secretary announced the Government's intention to reform the Foreign Service, long the peculiar preserve of a type Palmerston had defined for eternity as 'indolent aristocrats and time-servers playing in their offices like the fountains in Trafalgar Square from ten o'clock till four'. The Government's *Proposals for the Reform of the Foreign Service* included the astonishing discovery that

Economics and finance have become inextricably interwoven with politics; an understanding of social problems and labour movements is indispensable in forming a properly balanced judgement of world events. The modern diplomat should have a more intimate understanding of these special problems and greater opportunities to study them than he has usually possessed in the past. His training must be wider.

Another of several committees concerned with the problem listed the prevailing defects of the Civil Service:

Over-devotion to precedent; remoteness from the rest of the community, inaccessibility, and faulty handling of the general public; lack of initiative and imagination; ineffective organization and misuse of manpower; procrastination and unwillingness to take responsibility or to give decisions.[44]

These were fighting words. During the war, too, the personnel of the bureaucracy was affected by direct recruitment from industry and the professions. But in the end there was no great reform, partly because of the strength of internal resistances, partly because of the belief that the necessary adaptations had been carried through under the pressure of war and need not be carried further once the war was won, partly because any wholesale reform must depend on wholesale educational reform – and that too was not achieved.

In passing judgement upon the use made by Britain of the potenial of science the war raised two questions: was existing scientific knowledge being fully exploited, and were sufficient resources being devoted towards extending existing scientific knowledge? Inevitably it was easier to bring about a satisfactory answer to the former rather than to the latter question. Government expenditure through the M.R.C. and the D.S.I.R. greatly increased, but was mainly concerned 'with the object of supplying quick answers to practical questions as they arose'. The wartime report of the M.R.C. discussed the ultimate limitations of this approach:

This type of *ad hoc* investigation, however, can be based only on information and methods already available, and more complete answers often have to await the acquisition of greater fundamental knowledge. Thus, there comes a time when the research worker has to decide whether to confine his interests to giving limited answers or to delve deeper, and inevitably more slowly, and to obtain a fuller grasp of the principles involved. So it is that, although war acts at first as an internal stimulus to certain branches of medical research, in the long run it tends to lose its effects as an incentive to discovery. The late war was in this way beginning to lose much of its stimulating effect on medical research when it ended.

Nevertheless, the report continued, 'the harvest has been great':

and it will bring much benefit to mankind under conditions of peace, to which many of the results obtained have also a valid application.

The harvest was most golden in the field of nutrition, where intensive research made it possible to maintain a high dietary level for the whole population despite the worst scarcities of food, and in the control of infectious disease. In the main, however, it was less a question of new fundamental research than of the way in which the crises and emergencies of war have ... been found to have an important influence in shortening the customary time-lag between the acquisition of scientific knowledge by research and its executive application to practical problems of human welfare and efficiency.[45]

The defects in pre-war lower-class diets were well known, but it was only after the outbreak of war that the M.R.C. was able successfully to advocate the provision of extra milk, cod-liver oil, and other sources of fat-soluble vitamins to pregnant and nursing mothers, infants and children, and the addition of vitamins D and A to all makes of margarine, and of calcium to bread. Immunization with tetanus toxoid was known before the war, but its use was effectively proved during the war. Similarly the Swiss discovery of D.D.T. was first used on a large scale against louse-borne typhus. Progress in the treatment of malaria depended less upon the increase in fundamental knowledge during the war than upon improved methods of administering and ascertaining the optimum dosage of the drug 'atebrin', which had been developed in Germany in 1929 and was manufactured in Britain from 1940 as mepacrine. However, by the end of the war the I.C.I. Manchester laboratories had developed an entirely new antimalarial drug, paludrin. The most celebrated example of the process was Professor Howard Florey's development of Sir Alexander Fleming's neglected discovery of penicillin. But here the challenge of war merged with its destructive influence. While fighting for survival Britain simply could not afford the resources to exploit to the full the pioneer work of her own scientists: in 1941, therefore, Florey and his assistant Dr Heatley went to the United States, where penicillin was produced on a massive scale. The gains to mankind were enormous, but not least among the beneficiaries was the American pharmaceuticals industry. Meantime new sulphonamides were produced and

unique opportunities were provided by war conditions for large-scale field trials which accelerated the assessment of their true place in the therapeutic armamentarium especially in competition and in association with penicillin and other remedies.

Advances were also made in the development of blood transfusion services, skin grafting, plastic surgery, anaesthesia and the treatment of 'traumatic shock' (the 'shell-shock' of the former war).[46]

As with penicillin, so with nuclear physics: by 1942 the Rutherford group, greatly aided by the French scientists Halban and Kowarsky, had established a world lead in the preliminary development of atomic power, but again, for practical reasons, all further efforts were concentrated in North America. The threat of war as much as the advent of war fostered the development of the jet engine (patented by Frank Whittle in 1929) and radar (developed by R. H. Watson Watt), the two essential elements in contemporary air travel. The need to miniaturize gave a boost to researches in solid state physics, which yielded, for peacetime use, the transistor radio; and the application of the growing applied science of electronics to the problem of computing at speed the range and trajectories of rockets and shells yielded the sophisticated electronic computer. Of more immediate relevance to British social experience was the jump in production of radio valves from 12 million per annum in 1940 to over 35 million in 1944: sound radio had been launched by a similar development in the First World War; after 1945 the new industrial capacity was channelled into the expansion of television. Another agent of mass communication received a stimulus directly related to the war, though not in any way to science. Propaganda needs had nurtured the film in 1914–18; now the British Government began to make use of the representatives of Britain's nascent advertising industry, whose brighter brains conjured up, on behalf of the Minister of Food (Lord Woolton), such jingles as:

> Those who have the will to win
> Cook potatoes in their skin
> For they know the sight of peelings
> Deeply hurts Lord Woolton's feelings.

In its official account of such stirring contributions to the war effort, the Ministry of Information, naturally, could not avoid a note of self-congratulation on 'Britain's secret weapon', her sense of humour.[47]

As science produced the goods so the scientists gained in status, furthering the slow reorientation of British society in a scientific direction. Two official war historians have gone so far as to comment that:

When one compares the freedom and authority enjoyed by the civilian scientists and technicians both at headquarters and in the establishments, in the period 1943–45 with the isolation and subjection of the pre-war days, the change is among the most striking features of British war production.[48]

The belief that, after centuries of misrule by the politician and the businessman, the scientist is finally about to assume his proper role in the counsels of the nation, is very apparent at two wartime conferences organized by the British Association. In 1941 J. D. Bernal declared 'that science has got a far wider and more thorough-going application to governmental affairs than had previously been accepted or even imagined' and in 1944 Ernest Bevin, since 1940 Churchill's choice as Minister of Labour, told the scientists:

I think it is true to say that science has not merely a place in industry, but does in fact dominate it now.[49]

Such major crises of human conscience as the dropping of two atomic bombs and the strategic bombing raids, culminating in the attack on Dresden, raised in virulent form the problem of the correct relationship between science and politics. It could be pointed out that scientists were not necessarily always right about the possibilities of their own subject, let alone competent to handle political matters:[50] but it was also clear that ministers needed expert advice. Could that advice be integrated into ordinary parliamentary procedures? In October 1942 the Scientific Advisory Committee of the War Cabinet was appointed. Sitting at first under the chairmanship of Lord Cherwell, who was given the nominal office of Paymaster-General, the committee consisted of the President and two Secretaries of the Royal Society and the Secretaries of the D.S.I.R., the M.R.C. and the Agricultural Research Council. Access to the War Cabinet was through the proto-Minister of Science, the Lord President, who from December 1942 also took over the presidency of the committee. As the White Paper, *Scientific Research and Development*, concluded in some confusion:

... the Lord President of the Council has, as a matter of administrative convenience, come to be regarded as the member of the War Cabinet responsible for the general oversight of the Government scientific organization. This does not, however, in any way derogate from the individual responsibility of the other Ministers concerned for the organizations and establishments in their Departments.[51]

The problem, then, was tampered with, scarcely solved. At bottom it could only be solved on the basis of an educational system which created politically-minded scientists and scientifically-minded politicians, or better still an educational system which recognized no such apartheid.

Important segments of British industry, notably engineering, iron and steel, chemicals and agriculture, benefited greatly from the new emphasis on science, and indeed in general from the increased demand for their products. Aircraft, motor vehicles, machine-tools, drugs, plastics, electronic devices, these are the basic industrial items in twentieth-century civilization and ones upon which Britain's future as an exporter would depend: fortunately the whole thrust of this scientific war effort was towards their manufacture on a larger scale than ever before. Gains here more than offset the destructive effect of war on other industries. Where the economy benefited, so did society: the nation at war could not afford the scandal of the depressed areas, which now at last got some of the new industrial capacity they had been crying out for. Scotland, for once, profited. New developments included: at Hillington, just outside Glasgow, a new Rolls-Royce factory; at Motherwell, a Ministry of Supply clothing depot; at Falkirk, an aluminium rolling mill; at Bishopton, one of several royal ordnance factories; in Edinburgh, a Ferranti (electronics) factory; at Garelochhead, a Metal Industries Ltd depot. Subsequently Hillington became one of the first post-war industrial estates, and the Motherwell clothing depot was allocated to the engineering firm of Metropolitan-Vickers. Even the rural Highlands received attention, sometimes in connection with the building of a military airfield or training ground, sometimes because of the need to maximize food production. If there was spoliation, at least, for the first time since General Wade's 'pacification' programme after the Jacobite rebellions in the eighteenth century, an attack was made on the fundamental problem of poor communications. There were extensive road works in the Orkneys, the Shetlands and the Western Islands of Lewis, Benbecula and South Uist, the last two being linked together by the completion of the South Ford Viaduct. New pier works were carried out at various towns, including Wick, Thurso, Tarbert, and Ullapool, and a hospital for 640 patients was built at Raigmore, Inverness. The campaign to exploit all possible sources of food supply brought the Highland Counties benefits in the form both of Marginal Agricultural Production Scheme grants and hill sheep and hill cattle subsidies.[52]

3. MILITARY PARTICIPATION

The underprivileged groups in the community who benefited through being drawn into participation in the war effort were the same as those who underwent a similar history in the First World War: the working class, the female sex, and children and young people. The working class benefited because of their strong market position when labour power was again an essential ingredient to success in war; they benefited because the Government knew it was vital to secure their full support and co-operation; they benefited because the Government felt it necessary to recompense them for their sacrifice of life and limb in battle and of trade union privileges at home. The strong market position of labour is seen in the Ministry of Labour figures for average weekly earnings: standing at 53s. 3d. in October 1938 these rose 30 per cent (while the cost of living rose 26 per cent) to 69s. 2d. in July 1940 and 80 per cent to 96s. 1d. in July 1945 (when the cost of living was only 31 per cent above 1938). To a degree these figures in turn reflect full employment and more overtime – in 1943 15 millions out of a total population of working age of 15·9 millions were in employment, the balance being invalids and students. But the figures also reflect increases in wage rates and reductions in the standard working week. Wartime changes were ratified in 1946 when there were general reductions in the working week from 47–48 hours to 44 or 45.[53] Market power also showed itself in the growth in strength of the trade union movement from a membership of 6 millions in 1938 to 8 millions in 1944; this, in turn, made possible further gains for Labour. At the height of the war crisis in 1940 and 1941 there was a slight drop from the 1939 figures in the number of days lost due to strikes, but thereafter there was no shyness on the part of local Labour leaders over using their refound power to press their claims, and the number of days lost due to strikes steadily mounted throughout 1942, 1943 and 1944, dropping slightly in 1945, when it was still double what it had been in 1939.[54]

Politically, Labour drew from the war what might well be termed a 'double dividend'. From the time of the formation of the Churchill government Labour leaders shared in, and got the credit for, executive decisions; from the very beginning of the war, indeed, the industrial side of the movement was represented in the National Joint Advisory Council appointed to advise the Ministry of Labour. Yet at the same time the Labour Party continued to hold its annual conferences, passing resolutions critical of the Government and apparently offering itself as a party with a constructive alternative policy. It was as an 'in'-group that the General Council of the T.U.C. was able to initiate the process which led to the famous Beveridge Report. In 1940 the General Council, after referring to the inadequacies of national health insurance, 'came to the conclusion that what was necessary was the complete overhauling of the whole scheme and the related social services'. A deputation to the Minister of Health (Ernest Brown, a Conservative) in February 1941 stressed the 'necessity for the linking up of all the social service schemes into an adequate and properly coordinated scheme' and for drawing up 'a comprehensive plan ... for implementation immediately after the war'. In May the Government announced that a survey of the entire social services would be conducted under the auspices of one of Labour's representatives in the Government, Arthur Greenwood, Minister of Reconstruction: this survey became the Beveridge Report.[55] As an 'out'-group Labour was able to publish on its own account a series of policy documents which went well beyond anything officially sponsored by the Government and which, building upon Labour's theorizing of the 1920s, became the true blueprint of the Welfare State as it was constructed after 1945. It was able, too, to attract to itself a great deal of disgruntled middle-class opinion starkly struck by the contrast between working-class participation in the national survival and the continuance of traditional Conservative attitudes. One young officer who subsequently became a Labour M.P. wrote:

There was no excuse whatever for the Conservative government's apparent unconcern for the welfare of servicemen and their families. It made many people like myself feel that their toleration of mass unemployment had been due to similar heartlessness. Later, pay and allowances improved, but when they did so it appeared to be under pressure from the left.[56]

The use of 'Conservative' for what was formally a Coalition government including Labour is highly significant.

When in May 1940 the Government assumed totalitarian control over all employees, it recognized that it must at the same time safeguard the conditions of work of those who were being deprived of the right to leave an unsatisfactory employer. The movements of population, the influx of women and the building of new factories all contributed to an increased concern with welfare problems on the part of the Ministry of Labour and National Service, which was headed by the great trade union leader, Ernest Bevin. In June 1940 the administration of the Factory Acts was transferred from the Home Office to this ministry, where a Factory and Welfare Department was set up. From July 1940 the Chief Factory Inspector was given power to compel firms to establish canteens and other forms of industrial welfare. In March 1941 when the Essential Work Orders were introduced it was laid down that the Minister had to satisfy himself that the factories concerned had suitable welfare facilities. All over the country there was a great expansion in the use of personnel officers, very necessary at a time of high levels of output and extreme emotional strain.[57] This development in private industry had a parallel in local government where post-air-raid crises forced a new recognition of the value of the trained social worker. Ernest Bevin seized the occasion provided by war to attempt to improve from above the conditions of some of the worst-paid workers. Despite considerable Conservative opposition he insisted on the enactment of his Catering Wages Bill; and he also addressed himself to the problem of decasualizing dock labour, though twenty-five years later his efforts seem less successful than they did at the time. In 1941 the Determination of Needs Act turned aside one great source of working-class fury by converting the family Means Test into a personal Needs Test, in which family resources would not be taken into account. Ernest Bevin's exultation was justified if slightly premature:

The only thing now left of Queen Elizabeth was one toe striking out of the ground and that for the rest of the Poor Law was now buried.

The history of women's involvement in the war effort is similar to that of 1914–18: there was less song-and-dance, though the Government went the whole hog of the conscription of women, often believed to be imminent in the previous war but never actually carried through. However, as with most of the other Draconian-seeming legislation of this war, the Act in regard to women was administered with great respect for the preservation of civilian support and morale and in fact conscription played a very minor role in the changes in women's employment during the war. Married women not living apart from their husbands were wholly exempt, as were women with children (including illegitimate children) under fourteen years of age. Of those not thus exempt only women of the age-group 19–24 were in practice called up, where they had a choice between serving in the Auxiliary Services (where they would not be called upon to handle a lethal weapon unless they signified willingness to do so in writing), Civil Defence or certain specified forms of civilian employment. At

the end of the war there were rather fewer than half a million women enrolled in the WRNS, the ATS and the WAAF, and the
larger proportion of these were volunteers, not conscripts. Though
among men there were almost 60,000 Conscientious Objectors,
and doubtless many cases of injustice and unnecessary hardship,
the issue of Conscientious Objection did not have the same
political importance that it had held in the more obviously
'imperialist' or 'King and Country' war of 1914–18. Conscientious
Objection was of negligible incidence among women: there were
1,072 women C.O.s altogether, and 66 were imprisoned for failure
to comply with the National Service Acts.[58]

In 1939 there were 7,000 women employed in government ordnance factories; in October 1944 there were 260,000. In 1929,
partly as a consequence of the transformations of the previous war,
fully 25 per cent of the non-industrial Civil Service were women:
ten years later the proportion had edged up fractionally to a total of
95,000 women. In October 1944 there were 320,000 women Civil
Servants, 48 per cent of the total (the Civil Service as a whole had
expanded greatly from 375,000 in 1939 to 670,000 in 1944). Outside of the government service women's employment in 1939 was
still concentrated in certain specific trades such as hosiery, launder-
ing and dressmaking, it too; centred mainly in the pre-marriage
age-groups. On the other hand the new engineering, light metal
and electrical industries had already in the Thirties provided new
scope for industrial employment for women. The war greatly
accelerated this particular trend. The number of women employed
in engineering and vehicle building increased by 770,000, the
proportion of women employed rising from 9 per cent to 34 per
cent. As in the First World War there was also a marked expansion
of women's employment in commerce: comprising 33 per cent of
all employees in 1939, they totalled 62 per cent in 1944. Meantime
the number of women employed in the traditional areas of textiles
and clothing fell by 400,000: since these trades anyway were run
down as non-essential to the war effort, the actual proportion of
women employed did not change much. In agriculture much
greater use was made of women's labour than had been the case
in the previous war: altogether in June 1945 there were 204,000

women working on the land (including 65,000 in the Women's Land Army), compared with 93,000 in 1939 and they were doing 'all-round farm work hitherto performed almost entirely by men'. Thus it was a question of

not merely a net influx into industry but a migration from more familiar to less familiar fields of work and tackling on the grand scale of jobs normally performed by men.[59]

It had been expected that where women were substituted for men it would require three women to do the work of two men, but in fact a one to one substitution proved perfectly possible; this was partly because modern technology had rendered sheer strength less essential to industrial work. In a previous generation the symbol of female rights which had been gained at the end of a previous war was the vote; now, though there had been no organized movement comparable with the suffragists and suffragettes, the symbol was equal pay. In the last year of the war, when there was much intensive discussion of all aspects of the post-war world, a Royal Commission on Equal Pay was appointed. As is the way with such commissions, this one delivered itself of an orotund proposition very reminiscent of the statements on women's rights being made towards the end of the previous war:

We believe that conventions and prejudices ... have been crumbling fairly fast in recent years, and that, in spite of the exodus of women out of gainful employment after each of the two great wars, the record of what they were able to achieve in those wars has exerted and will continue to exert a lasting influence in breaking down whatever elements of the old-fashioned or irrational remains in the public's estimation of the capabilities of women.[60]

For all that, the commission was unable to recommend wholeheartedly in favour of equal pay, on the specious grounds that this would not be in women's own best interests since it would have adverse effects on the expansion of women's employment. Three women members of the commission, who probably had a clearer idea of women's own best interests, dissented.[61] But whatever shilly-shallying verdict the Royal Commission might give, the movement for equal pay had undoubtedly received an enormous accession of strength from the war experience. In the House of Commons a minor constitutional crisis was created when an amendment was carried against the Government calling for equal pay in the teaching profession. Where further positive gains were made was in overcoming the still persistent prejudice against the employment of married women.[62]

The Registration of Boys and Girls Order of 22 December 1941, though undoubtedly primarily motivated by a desire to see young people assist the national effort in some form or another, did result in stirring government interest in an age-group which, not covered by school welfare services, had hitherto been rather neglected. Avowedly the purpose of compelling all boys and girls over sixteen to register was to enable local education authorities to get in touch with them for the purpose of encouraging them to join a Boys' or Girls' Club, the Guides, the Scouts, one of the brigades, a Youth Centre, or one of the junior service organizations such as the Air Training Corps or the Sea and Army Cadets; the local authorities at the same time were to make clear the leisure-time opportunities which existed for helping the national effort. When the order was revoked in December 1945 the Ministry of Education asked the local authorities to continue to encourage boys and girls to join youth organizations. The wartime labour market favoured young people and many were able to secure good wages. At the same time there was anxiety over the nature of the employment many juveniles were taking up and, as a result of the deliberations of the Ince Committee, reporting in September 1945, the Central Juvenile Appointment Executive was set up in April 1946.[63] For school children and pre-school children the main gains of the war came in the form of welfare foods designed to preserve a high nutritional standard. Many of the deeper problems concerning young children would quite probably have been ignored had it not been for an almost Victorian scandal in 1944 concerning a local authority's treatment of a child entrusted to its care, and the protests of one or two individuals, notably Lady Allen of Hurtwood and Mrs Eirene White, which set going the course of events leading to the Children Act of 1948.[64]

4. MIXED EMOTIONS

'Dunkirk' is still a word of high emotional supercharge, springing lightly to the lips of every British politician worth his salt; it is everything that 'Appeasement' is not. Dunkirk, as Churchill made abundantly clear, was a defeat. It brought home in concrete terms that the war for survival had truly begun, that invasion might come at any time. But the successful evacuation showed also that by skilful improvisation, imagination and courage something could be done other than allow Hitler to dictate the course of the war. Dunkirk was a warning; but built into it was its own exhortation. The 'Dunkirk spirit' was the natural response of a people in danger, who yet saw a real means to salvation. There was an immediate response to the Government call for the suspension of all holidays; latecoming and absenteeism practically vanished; phenomenally long hours were worked; productivity soared.[65] The effects were only temporary: longer hours, as the First World War had amply demonstrated, do not over a period yield higher productivity; the zeal born of immediate danger could not endure indefinitely. It is as wrong-headed to write off the 'Dunkirk spirit' altogether, as it is muddle-headed to believe that a new quality of community spirit entered permanently into the soul of the British people. The Dunkirk spirit was real, but it was temporary.

In his volume of the official history of the war, Professor Titmuss wrote that 'Dunkirk, and all that the name evokes, was an important event in the wartime history of the social services'. Professors Hancock and Gowing write of an 'implied contract between government and people'.[66] It is true that the real beginnings of the wartime social reforms are to be found in the months following Dunkirk, but these arose not so much from one military incident as from the full impingement of the war on British society, of which Dunkirk is only the beginning. The psychological climate created by Dunkirk and its aftermath did serve to reinforce the processes of social change, whose other origins have already been examined. Almost a month after the Dunkirk evacuation *The Times* published its celebrated and much-quoted leading article promulgating the ethic of economic democracy, of, indeed, the Welfare State:

If we speak of democracy, we do not mean a democracy which maintains the right to vote but forgets the right to work and the right to live. If we speak of freedom, we do not mean a rugged individualism which excludes social organization and economic planning. If we speak of equality, we do not mean a political equality nullified by social and economic privilege. If we speak of economic reconstruction, we think less of maximum production (though this too will be required) than of equitable distribution.[67]

The Dunkirk experience was followed by one which for populace and publicists alike was even more dramatic: the German bombing raids. It is possible, especially in the smaller cities to the north, that public morale occasionally faltered slightly, but there can be no doubt that overall (as has been the case among other communities subject to bomber attacks – from Germany to North Vietnam) civilian morale was toughened by the direct involvement in war. Certainly there was no noticeable increase in psychoneuroses among civilians. At the height of the Blitz, a psychiatric social worker wrote to Dr R. D. Gillespie of Guy's Hospital, London, describing 'the spirit of the people' as 'simply amazing'. 'It is impossible,' he continued, 'to describe the bravery of the A.R.P. services – which really means to say the ordinary populalation.' 'Actually,' the writer concluded, 'there have been amazingly few psychiatric casualties.' Similar reports came in from other parts of the country. After the destruction of Marks and Spencer's store in the Coventry holocaust the shop-girls carried on in temporary premises without any abnormal absenteeism.[68] Just as shared danger in the trenches of the First World War had for a time created a spirit of social unity, now in this more total war that spirit was brought a stage further into the home front. 'It is hard,' Constantine FitzGibbon wrote, 'to persist in looking down upon, or resenting, a man who night after night is sharing the same dangers and doing exactly the same work as yourself.' Not every public shelter was the classless *mélange* of some popular accounts, and there is plenty of evidence of the rich continuing against every discouragement to lead their own segregated existences.[69] The first shelter census of November 1940 showed that, of the 40 per cent who resorted to shelters, 27 per cent used their own domestic shelters and only 9 per cent used public shelters, while 4 per cent imitated their parents in the First World War by flocking into the London Underground 'tubes'. None the less over a brief period of time substantial sections of British society were thrown into a gigantic cocktail shaker, even if shortly the snooty vermouth might insist on separating itself off from the humble gin.

. . . Certain impressions of these early days have been confirmed so frequently by all sorts of men and women that they seem to have a general validity.

People become extraordinarily friendly. City life in normal times is one long series of attempts to avoid unwanted contact, to preserve an element of privacy even amidst the jostling crowds at rush-hour. . . . This reticence went very quickly.[70]

In September the London correspondent of the *New York Herald Tribune* was reporting to his readers that 'Hitler is doing what centuries of English history have not accomplished – he is breaking down the class structure of England', and his report was approvingly quoted in the *Observer*.[71] The Federation of British Industries said of the Blitz that 'it has already linked London's east and west in a new sense of civic unity and responsibility'. In December 1940, Seebohm Rowntree wrote to some American friends of what he described as a 'growing spirit of friendliness between class and class'. In 1941, Lord Woolton, Minister of Food, reflected that

There had been – whether it was temporary or permanent who could tell – a moral as well as an economic revolution in our society.[72]

Woolton wrote with Conservative prescience: the 'moral revolution' for the time being furthered the other social changes of the period, but it was to prove less enduring than men of sentimental outlook believed and hoped. Left-wingers sensed this too: in February 1941 Sam Grafton shrewdly wrote in *Tribune*:

It was so obvious that the old England had been a bust, that only a new England could force the Nazi bullies down, that men of goodwill were seduced by their own logic into assuming the new England to be a fact.[73]

Something of the stirrings of the human spirit of the times can be traced in the condition of the arts. As early as December 1939, thanks to the private initiative of the Pilgrim Trust, a conference was held at the Board of Education between Lord De La Warr (President of the Board), Lord Macmillan (of the Pilgrim Trust) and Sir Walford Davies and Sir Kenneth Clark (representing music and art respectively), 'to discuss the problems of preserving and promoting cultural activities in wartime'. Out of this conference came the Council for the Encouragement of Music and the Arts–always known, in the military style of the day, as CEMA – supported by a grant of £25,000 from the Pilgrim Trust. In April CEMA was given official government recognition and a subsidy of £50,000.[74] Philistines were not slow to attack:

The Government gives £50,000 to help wartime culture. What sort of madness is this? There is no such thing as culture in wartime. Wartime is itself the enemy of culture. And cultural activities, which bring so much benefit to the people in peace, must now be set aside.[75]

A brief reflection on the experience of the previous war might have shown the *Daily Express* how wrong were both its diagnosis and its treatment. Whatever reservations British intellectuals might have had about the villainies attributed by official propaganda to the Kaiser, there could be no doubt that the present chief foe was an obscurantist barbarian, who had already driven from Germany the greatest upholders of her cultural traditions. The arts, as well as social welfare and economic democracy, came to symbolize the antithesis of Hitlerism. The quickening of life in wartime quickened also the demand for the serious arts. The work of CEMA went vigorously ahead. Guarantees against loss were given to the London Philharmonic Orchestra, the London Symphony Orchestra, the Halle Orchestra, the Northern Philharmonic and the Scottish National Orchestra, with additional grants for concerts given outside the usual geographical sphere of the orchestra concerned. During the crisis months of 1940 CEMA guaranteed two tours by the Old Vic – to Lancashire and Wales: at Burnley, the *Manchester Guardian* reported with enthusiasm, the company played

Goldsmith's *She Stoops to Conquer* and Sierra's *The World is Yours* thirteen times in one week to packed houses of adult and juvenile audiences.[76] Less ambitious concerts, theatrical performances and exhibitions were sponsored in villages and small communities throughout the country. Theatres, which had closed during the first two weeks of war, were from January 1941 given permission to open on Sundays. Strenuous efforts were made to ensure that the British cinema industry should not suffer the knock-out blow dealt it in 1914-18. Protection was maintained and film-makers encouraged to stay at work: if many of the feature films produced were mawkish in their patriotic message, for the first time a genuine British style with real roots in British experience was discernible. A new school of directors, including Sidney Gilliat, David Lean and Carol Reed, established itself, and such important films as *Brief Encounter* and *The Way Ahead* were produced.

Altogether the cultural gains of the war period were very real ones: the founding of CEMA (renamed the Arts Council at the end of the war) as an agent of State patronage to the arts, was an event of major significance in Britain's twentieth-century history. Writing in the *Music Review* in 1947, R. J. Manning declared that 'despite the blackout and general war-weariness, music has had in this country an extraordinary flowering'.[77] The wartime National Gallery concerts organized by Myra Hess were famous. Bomb damage in 1941 chased the Sadler's Wells Opera Company out of their London home, to the immense profit of the provinces, where the Company had to remain continuously on tour for four years. The reopening of the Sadler's Wells Theatre in the summer of 1945 was celebrated with a first performance of *Peter Grimes*, the very modern work of a relatively unknown British composer, Benjamin Britten. If, as well as being an act of remarkable imagination and vision, this was a patriotic gesture, it was patriotic in a very wide sense, for Britten had been a Conscientious Objector. Such an action would have been impossible in the very different climate of opinion of 1918. Again there was government sponsorship of official war artists, handled with the same liberality that surprisingly had characterized the earlier experiment. English painting, which (as distinct from Scottish painting) had always been rather derivative, now took a turn towards a kind of romanticism – especially apparent in the work of John Piper – which seemed genuinely English. However, to expect that a nation of philistines overnight would become a nation devoted to serious cultural pursuits would be to expect the absurd. There were many contingent reasons for the apparent cultural explosion: the dispersal of Civil Servants and other members of relatively high-income groups to unpromising parts of the country created a new local core of support for artistic ventures; the monotony of much of wartime life created a willingness to attend any entertainment offered, even a symphony concert; the educational programmes of the armed forces stirred new interests into life. It is instructive to consider the immense popularity of the Warsaw Concerto, Richard Addinsell's theme music for the film *Dangerous Moonlight*: as Mr Mackerness has suggested, the significance of the popularity of this piece

lies in the fact that it was received with rapturous applause by audiences who were convinced that in responding to it they were enjoying authentic 'classical' music.[78]

Yet to have the wish was part of the way to fathering the full achievement.

Across the endless plains of human thought the rifts and faults scored by the Great War shifted but an inch or two in the second holocaust. Reason and revealed religion had already been dethroned: they could fall no further. There was no school of disillusioned painters, poets or novelists. But at last a few hints of really fundamental change in the writing and teaching of history did break through. The cataclysmic discontinuity of the Second World War tore to shreds the 'seamless garment' of nineteenth-century historicism, with its emphasis on continuity and the idea that 'the nature of everything is entirely comprehended in its development'. The thirty years' crisis in historical studies was about to begin.[79]

5. OPINION AND POLITICS

Again we have examined the four modes through which total war affected British society; it is now time to examine the concrete results. First, we shall look at the various opinions on social reform and reconstruction being clearly expressed from 1941 onwards and at the sort of people who were voicing these opinions; then we shall turn to the Government's response to the pressures brought to bear on it – the great series of reconstruction White Papers (the 'White Paper chase', in Beveridge's witty phrase) and the major items of legislation enacted before the end of the war; finally, we shall consider the deeper changes which have taken place within society irrespective of conscious government action.

Acceptance for the idea that the war had rendered new initiatives in social planning urgently necessary was to be found among industrialists and right-wing politicians as well as among trade unionists and liberals and socialists. Speaking of the Londoner's defiance in face of the Blitz, *British Industry*, the Journal of the F.B.I., declared, 'So great a people deserve the best. We must build again.' Two years later (May 1942), in a report on reconstruction requested of it by the President of the Board of Trade, the Federation was clear that

we are on the threshold of a new world, and the theories and practices of the past cannot be taken for granted in the future. . . . The physical replanning of the country, which is intimately bound up with the question of what industries will have be contracted, the problem of the concentrated industries, and what are the most suitable locations for industry, will demand an ordered programme. . . . For the solution of all these problems a certain measure of regulation will be essential, probably for some years, until this country and the world settles down to its future shape.[80]

In the summer of 1941 the Conservative Post-War Problems Committee was founded by R. A. Butler, Churchill's choice as President of the Board of Education, a man who shared many of the characteristics of the soft-centre of the 1930s and lacked only the will to show disloyalty to the Conservative Party. David Maxwell Fyfe, a Scot whose Conservatism was of a moderate, common-sense type, was vice-chairman, and the members of the committee were typical upper-class Conservatives, Eugene Ramsden, Marjorie Maxse and Sir Robert Topping, with Miss Peggy Butler as secretary. The study of housing was delegated to John Watson, of education to Sir Geoffrey Faber, the publisher, and of legal aid to Cecil Havers. The preparation of a series of 'Signpost' articles was entrusted to Cecil Laver and Kenneth Pickthorn, a Cambridge historian. Among the authors in the series was one of the few men of working-class origins to rise high in the Conservative Party, and one of the still fewer to retain an essentially progressive political outlook, Aubrey Jones. His liberalism was well matched by the weird reactionarism of a fellow author, economist George Schwartz. All in all the committee was by no means representative of the most advanced wing of the Conservative Party; it shows instead an awareness from within the mainstream of Toryism of the need to give serious consideration to reconstruction problems.[81]

The most interesting social policy developments were to be found in the true political centre. This was partly because of the emergence of certain outstanding personalities who managed to command a popular attention denied to most professional politicians, and, more critically, because of the wider swing towards social involvement of the uncommitted middle classes – those, for instance, who were most affected by the evacuation revelation. Supreme among individual non-political figures stands William Temple, Archbishop of York till 1941, thereafter Archbishop of Canterbury and primate of England's established Church. As Temple's biographer has written:

From the day of his first broadcast after the outbreak of war, on 3 October 1939, Temple became a national leader who through the five years that followed spoke for the conscience of Britain.

Temple was responsible for calling an Anglican conference at Malvern in January 1941, at which he himself talked of a number of 'stumbling-blocks' to the advance of society in a truly Christian direction:

We believe that the maintenance of that part of the structure of our society, by which the ultimate ownership of the principal industrial resources of the community can be vested in the hands of private owners, may be such a stumbling-block.

Private ownership, the Archbishop argued, could be placed in 'the same category of potential social dangers as beer, tobacco, and sixpenny bridge'. A year later Temple's *Christianity and Social Order*, published as a 'Penguin Special', sold 139,000 copies.[82] The immense popularity of radio during the war, when so much time had to be passed in lonely vigil, and when every radio news broadcast was pregnant with matter of national and personal import, assisted the rise to a position of some influence of the novelist J. B. Priestley, who was given a regular commentary programme by the B.B.C. A similar popularity for the illustrated news magazine *Picture Post* loaned authority to its owner and founder, Edward Hulton. A fourth figure who was to prove most active of all in the movement of the intellectuals from the liberal centre to the liberal left was Sir Richard Acland, son of a distinguished Liberal M.P.

In studying the movements associated with these figures we are essentially studying a continuance of the very important centre movements of the 1930s, which, sand-blasted by war, began to take on a much harder political edge, eventually going into service on behalf of the Labour Party. In 1941 Acland, together with Priestley and Hulton, founded the 1941 Committee. Associated with them were Vernon Bartlett, Eva M. Hubback, Mary Stocks, Sir Stanley Unwin, the publisher, Ritchie Calder, pioneer of science journalism, and Francis Williams of the *Daily Herald* (all of whom had been active proponents of 'middle opinion' in the Thirties), and Victor Gollancz of the Left Book Club, Phyllis Bottome, the novelist, A. D. Lindsay, political scientist, educationist and Master of Balliol, C. E. M. Joad, and John Macmurray, both philosophers, C. H. Reilly and Elizabeth Denby, both town planners, Augustus John, the artist, David Low, the cartoonist, Thomas Balogh, an economist of radical Liberal sympathies, and Kingsley Martin, editor of the *New Statesman*. Meetings were usually held 'at Hulton's house over Hulton's food'. The committee's first leaflet, *We Must Win*, declared:

We must set out ideals and objectives in clear terms and we must so order our own mode of life and social system that men may know that we offer a happiness, freedom and prosperity which can never flourish under Hitler's military totalitarianism.[83]

A further leaflet, *On Siege Economics*, which argued that social inequalities were hindering the war effort, and therefore that the State should deliberately foster social egalitarianism, is a good practical exposition of my test and transformation theory of war. Later, when the committee coalesced into the political party Commonwealth, the vice-chairman of the new political movement, Tom Wintringham, published as a 'Penguin Special' a quintessential statement of the military participation theory, *People's War* (1942).

The 1941 Committee essentially spoke for managers, businessmen and technocrats. But the official spokesmen of organized labour, so reticent on social policy in the troubled Thirties, had now refound their voices. In 1942 the Labour Party, enjoying, as we have seen, the prestige of office and the freedom of opposition, stated its 'four essentials':

We have to provide full employment: we have to rebuild Britain to standards worthy of the men and women who have preserved it; we have to organize social services at a level which secures adequate health, nutrition and care in old age for all citizens; and we have to provide educational opportunities for all which ensure that our cultural heritage is denied to none.[84]

When, under pressure from the T.U.C., the Minister of Reconstruction appointed an inter-departmental committee of Civil Servants under the chairmanship of William Beveridge to 'undertake . . . a survey of the existing national schemes of social insurance and allied services . . . and to make recommendations', this was welcomed by the 1942 Labour Party Conference, which called for:

(a) One comprehensive scheme of social security.
(b) Adequate cash payments to provide security whatever the contingency.
(c) The provision of cash payments from national funds for all children through a scheme of Family Allowances.
(d) The right to all forms of medical attention and treatment through a National Health Service.

In developing this last point the Labour Party returned to the ideas it had canvassed in the 1920s. *National Service for Health* (1943) called for a 'fully salaried medical service' and, more vaguely, for 'public and voluntary hospitals alike' to be 'brought within a National Health Service on equitable terms'. Most important of all, the document insisted that the proposed Health Service must be based upon the reorganization of the country into new regional units of local government – described in detail in its sister document *The Future of Local Government*, to which all readers of *National Service for Health* were referred.[85]

Given the deep interest to be found everywhere in the future of social reform it is not surprising that the deliberations (private, of course) of the Beveridge Committee aroused considerable speculation. This was heightened by the line taken by the Government: Churchill was himself opposed to the diversion of energies away from the war effort to the discussion of social policy: to avoid entering into any such discussion ministers adopted the expedient of declaring that Parliament (and public) must await the findings of the Beveridge Report. Thus expectation was heightened, though the actual terms of reference of the committee, clothed in the hodden grey of standard government prose, scarcely gave grounds for much excitement. Beveridge, however, was a man of powerful character (as well as a somewhat conceited one), and due to what might well be termed his *sacro egoismo* the nature of the report was transformed. The survey was brief, the recommendations detailed and controversial. Because of its controversial nature it was decided that the Civil Servants should not put their names to the report, which would go out over Beveridge's signature alone.[86]

Before that point was reached it was clear that Churchill was not alone in his opposition to any extensive plan of social reform. Whatever vague gestures leading industrialists might make towards 'planning' and 'social harmony' they clearly feared the possible implications of the Beveridge Report. Addressing the Leeds branch of the F.B.I., the President of the Federation, Lord Dudley Gordon, made an oblique but unequivocal reference to the deliberations of the Beveridge Committee:

Today many schemes are being proposed and much discussion is taking place as to the shape of things to come. We are all agreed that we are fighting for freedom and to save the world from being dominated by force. Once that primary goal is reached everyone wishes the world to be a better and happier place to live in than it was before the conflict started. We must be careful to avoid suggesting change for its own sake. I say this because there is undoubtedly a tendency to feel that because a thing was done in a certain way before the war it should be done differently afterwards. It is vitally necessary too that we should avoid debasing our desire for a better world into a mere wish for less work and more pay.[87]

The *Daily Telegraph*, in what purported to be an interview with Beveridge, introduced the phrase 'half-way along the road to Moscow'. Veiled attacks on Beveridge were linked with more open attacks on Archbishop Temple, who was specially singled out by the *Sunday Times* on 15 November. All of this was too much for one Labour M.P. (and former active member of the I.L.P.), C. G. Ammon: in a speech at Swindon he declared:

Utterances such as that lately given by Lord Croft [another critic of the Beveridge committee] and the strong criticisms called forth by the utterances of the Archbishop of Canterbury are calculated to raise doubts as to the genuineness in some quarters for a new world when the danger is past.[88]

The following day the *Daily Mirror*, which in its own pungent, popular fashion had been in the van of the reconstruction discussion, remarked:

There are few people who by now have not heard of the 'Beveridge Report'. And yet not a single word of this famous document has been published! No one, except the authors, knows precisely what it contains, which makes it singular that in certain quarters there has already developed a distinct note of hostility towards it. Can it be that certain interests, having received 'intelligent forecasts' of the proposals, think it well to prepare the ground for attack? Are they people who *fear* the report and have therefore adopted the sinister practice of damning it in advance? ... It seems that while others have been merely talking about reconstruction, Sir William Beveridge and his colleagues have tabulated a series of definite proposals. . . .

Meanwhile we suggest to the gentry who display so ardent a desire to criticize a report they have not seen that they should restrain their suspicious activities. Whatever this report may prove to contain, it is on a subject which the mass of the people recognize as of vital interest to the welfare of the country as a whole. Vested, sectional or personal interests cannot be allowed to intervene. And so we say, 'Hands off the Beveridge Report'.[89]

This controversy prior to publication helps to explain why, when finally published on 1 December 1942, the Beveridge Report, which, despite Beveridge's own improvement upon the terms of reference, is no miracle of revolutionary social theory, had such a colossal impact. Practically the whole of the report is taken up with highly detailed and rather technical proposals for improved social security – only one of the four major pillars of the modern Welfare State – the 'social insurance and allied services' of the terms of reference. The major innovations were that the scheme should cover all classes in society, that it should cover all possible contingencies, and that it should provide uniform benefits which would guarantee a minimum subsistence. The scheme was to be as respectably grounded in insurance as ever Lloyd George's 1911 scheme had been, though, in recommending the abolition of all restrictions upon the length of time for which unemployment insurance could be claimed, it did offer a bold defiance of existing administrative beliefs. As a safety net for those who failed to qualify for insurance benefits, there would be national assistance, claimable on the basis of need, and administered by the same Ministry of Social Security as would be responsible for social insurance. On the advice of J. M. Keynes, Beveridge recommended that the upgrading of old-age pensions to the new uniform rate should be postponed for twenty years in order to maintain the strict financial viability of the scheme.[90] Beveridge saw his scheme as providing only a basic minimum, though it was to be a *subsistence* minimum: as a good Liberal he believed it should be left to the individual to make additional provision through private insurance. But two extra features transformed this document: in striking rhetoric

Beveridge made it clear that he realized that social security was only one of several problems that must be tackled simultaneously; and he set out certain 'assumptions' which he declared to be essential to the implementation of his report.

Organization of social insurance should be treated as one part only of a comprehensive policy of social progress. Social insurance fully developed may provide income security: it is an attack upon Want. But Want is one only of five giants of the road of reconstruction and in some ways the easiest to attack. The others are Disease, Ignorance, Squalor and Idleness.

By this slightly Victorian terminology Beveridge meant ill-health, inadequate education, bad housing and environmental conditions, and unemployment. He further declared that:

No satisfactory scheme of social security can be devised except on the following assumptions:
(a) Children's allowances for children up to the age of 15 or if in full-time education up to the age of 16;
(b) Comprehensive health and rehabilitation services for prevention and cure of disease and restoration of capacity for work, available to all members of the community;
(c) Maintenance of employment, that is to say avoidance of mass unemployment.[91]

Thus Beveridge succeeded in introducing into his report clear proposals for a National Health Service, the 'avoidance of mass unemployment' (a more modest proposal than that subsequently adopted, 'full employment'), and family allowances (a reflection of the discovery made by the various surveys of the Thirties that large families were a frequent source of poverty); and implied proposals for an improved educational system and a national housing and town planning programme. It was the assumptions and the implications which gave the Beveridge Report its breadth of appeal and enabled it to become the symbol of the aspirations of large sections of the British people for a better society. It was given tremendous assistance towards becoming just such a symbol by the efforts of the Ministry of Information, which believed that the report could be made into a powerful propaganda weapon. On the day of publication broadcasts on it were delivered in twenty-two languages, and various editions and summaries were prepared for foreign consumption. In his own broadcast of 2 December Beveridge said of his plan, 'It's the first step, though it is one step only, to turning the Atlantic Charter from words into deeds' – a curious remark, since the Atlantic Charter (the statement of common aims subscribed to by Churchill and President Roosevelt in August 1941, four months before the American entry into the war) contained only one bare reference to social welfare, and that inserted hastily on the insistence of the Labour members of the Churchill Cabinet. A special summary prepared by the Ministry of Information was, because of Churchill's hostility, suppressed by the War Office: and that, together with the renewed controversy in the British Press, probably gave the report its final push towards best-sellerdom.[92]

The bulk of the British Press, certainly, gave the report an enthusiastic welcome. *The Times* saw it as presenting

an opportunity for marking this decisive epoch with a great social measure which will go far towards restoring the faith of ordinary men and women throughout the world in the power of democracy.

The association between Beveridge and war objectives was stressed by both the *Daily Express* and the *Manchester Guardian*, the former talking of 'a far-reaching project to achieve in Britain that Freedom from Want which is one of the basic aims of the United Nations' and the latter, in a strange pre-echo of Beveridge's own broadcast, of 'the redemption, on a large section of the home front, of the promises of the Atlantic Charter'. The *Economist* called the report 'one of the most remarkable State documents ever drafted', and the *Daily Mirror* gave it the full front-page heavily-leaded treatment, listing 'cradle to grave benefits' among which it gave priority to 'free medical, dental, eyesight and hospital treatment'. No major paper offered outright condemnation. But after a few words of faint praise, the *Daily Telegraph* proceeded to the following warnings:

If the Beveridge plan had been in existence 100 or 150 years ago it is certain that the British race would not have spread itself so adventurously and beneficially over the far corners of the globe. ... Let us pursue security by all means, but let us also beware of its excesses.[93]

British Industry maintained a masterful silence, preferring in its December issue to reprint from the Economic League's 'Notes and Comments' an article extolling the virtues of private enterprise! The Conservative Party newsheet, *Onlooker*, presented a bland mixture of praise and evident hostility. While journals feared to tread the path of total condemnation representatives of various vested interests felt less need to hold back. There was a vigorous attack from Mr Percy Rockcliffe, secretary of the Joint Committee of Approved Societies and National Union of Friendly Societies, who probably feared that their business would disappear under the terms of Beveridge's comprehensive social insurance scheme (though Beveridge himself favoured an, on the face of it, unworkable compromise which would have retained *bona fide* Friendly Societies as agents of the scheme).

The author of this report is an economist turned spendthrift; having himself exchanged frugality for thriftlessness, he has no further use for either friendly or approved societies. He would push compulsorily – not a section of the community – but the whole nation back into the days of a glorified Poor Law system, destroying in the process every vestige of self-reliance and self-help which during the past century or more has permeated and strengthened the British character. After 1944, if this scheme were to come to pass, truly might Ribbentrop allege that the Anglo-Saxon race was decadent. ... Under the Beveridge plan, industry will become a veritable post-war Tom Tiddler's ground.

Another spokesman for the great insurance interests, Sir Edward Mountain, saw the plan as a threat to Britain's balance of payments:

A principal contribution to 'services rendered' has been our magnificent insurance business, which has been the admiration of the world, and any infringement on that would have very serious repercussions.[94]

By the end of December the insurance companies had opened a concerted attack on the Beveridge proposals. Doctors, too, were quick to express hostility to Beveridge's assumption *(b)*. It is a commonplace today that the Beveridge Report stands at the head of an all-party tradition of social improvement, and that it contained nothing that was really new or startling. It is worth stressing therefore the powerful opposition that it did in fact arouse. Its liberal and non-revolutionary character is indisputable: for all that it had the whole-hearted support of the British Communist Party. More important it had, as far as such a fact is ascertainable, the support of the majority of the British people. From the moment of publication widespread support was reported both at home and among the troops. Two weeks after publication a national opinion poll found that 95 per cent of those interviewed showed some knowledge of the report; 88 per cent approved of the idea of doctor and hospital services for all (again showing how an 'assumption' achieved centrality); 53 per cent believed the Government would put the plan into operation, while 18 per cent doubted this.[95] A year later it was reported that 256,000 copies of the full report had been sold and 369,000 copies of an abridged version (a further 40,000 copies were sold in the United States). The *Daily Mirror*, the newspaper which during the war had its finger most firmly on the pulse of the biggest section of the British people, provided a remarkably shrewd assessment of the stature of this astonishing best-seller:

Too much has been made of the Beveridge Report. It is no revolutionary document. Mainly it is a co-ordination of existing services with certain modest additions thereto. It is a beginning, not an end, and it must not be confused with reconstruction in the larger sense.

Three days later the same newspaper added a perfect summing-up when it referred to 'the depth of feeling in the country which has made the Beveridge Report, in itself of no paramount importance, into a symbol of the new Britain.'[96]

The most critical opposition to the Beveridge Report was that to be found in high places: Churchill, we have seen, was not enthusiastic. The report was published just as Parliament was about to debate the problems of reconstruction: the debate accordingly was postponed and no parliamentary discussion of the Beveridge proposals took place till 16 February 1943, when a three-day debate was initiated by Arthur Greenwood who was himself no longer a member of the Government. Much depended on the actual tone of the 'welcome' extended by government spokesmen: in fact Sir Kingsley Wood and Sir Oliver Lyttelton (both Conservatives) were so feeble and hesitant in their advocacy that they aroused the justifiable suspicion that the Government had no serious intention of implementing the report. Four Conservative back-benchers, headed by a leading businessman, Sir Patrick Hannon, who had planned an amendment calling for the postponement of any legislation based on the Beveridge Report, felt they now had no need to proceed with it. Members of the Parliamentary Labour Party, on the other hand, were outraged, and resolved, despite the fact that their own leaders were in the Government, to table an amendment calling for early legislation based on the Beveridge recommendations. The amendment was introduced by James Griffiths. Not only Labour members spoke to the amendment, but also some younger Conservatives, including Quintin Hogg and Lord Hinchingbrooke, and several Liberals. At the end of the debate 97 Labour members (all but two of their members who did not hold office) and 22 Conservatives and Liberals voted against the Government. The debate marks the real beginning of the formation of a nucleus of younger Conservatives – the Tory Reform Group – genuinely committed to some of the ideals of the modern welfare state. It also shows the great symbolic strength of the report itself in that no spokesman of the Right went far in open denunciation of it, though Sir Herbert Williams, stressing the burden on taxation the Beveridge proposals would involve, called it 'a very bad report'.[97] Finally Labour's valuable double dividend, as at once Opposition and Government, is again illustrated.

So strong was the resentment aroused by the Government's handling of the debate that Churchill devoted a broadcast of 21 March to a 'Four Year Plan': actually, though he spoke of his own part in the national insurance scheme of 1911, expressed approval for 'putting milk into babies', and support for compulsory insurance 'for all classes for all purposes from the cradle to the grave', the qualifications and warnings which Churchill issued were far stronger than the constructive proposals.[98] As the *Daily Express* put it, 'Mr Churchill gives the public sound advice ... beating Germany is the first task'; the *Telegraph*, however, produced the curious verdict that 'the Four Year Plan, as the Prime Minister unfolded it, goes far beyond the scope of the Beveridge proposals'. *The Times,* still keeping up its remarkable leadership for the cause of social reform, was less impressed:

It will be a grave disappointment to the people of this country if no foretaste of the forthcoming reforms can be offered even while the war lasts.

The *Manchester Guardian* summarized neatly: 'Eager reformers are asked to pipe down and trust the government.'[99]

Two other issues which came up at around the same time as the Beveridge Report illustrate the divide over social reform which existed among Britain's rulers, and the manner in which the various pressures engendered or strengthened by the war gave at least a qualified victory to the reformers. The first issue was that of town and country planning, brought up first by the publication in 1940 of the Report of the Barlow Commission, then more forcibly by the destruction wrought by bomb attacks. As a sequel to the Barlow Report two further committees were appointed to investigate specific aspects of planning: a committee under Mr Justice Uthwatt on 'payment of compensation and recovery of betterment in respect to public control of the use of the land', and one under Lord Justice Scott on 'land utilization in rural areas'. Reporting in 1942, the Uthwatt Committee, while dismissing land nationalization as impractical, recommended that the State, on payment of fair compensation, should be vested with the development rights in all lands outside built-up areas, and that local planning authorities should have the power of compulsory purchase over properties in built-up areas needing redevelopment. The most important single contribution of the Scott Report, issued in August 1942, was its adoption and definition of an idea originated by Sir Raymond Unwin and developed experimentally in the 1930s, the 'Green

Belt', a ring of open land for agricultural and recreational use to be preserved around the major conurbations.[100] Again resentment was aroused when the Government seemed even less enthusiastic about these reports than it had been about Beveridge: in November 1943 there was almost another revolt by Labour back-benchers together with members of the Tory Reform Group. Open revolt did come on the other big social issue of 1942; Ernest Bevin's plan to reform the wages structure of the catering industry – only this time the revolt came from the Right. On 12 November and 17 December 1942 individual Conservative M.P.s issued threats of large-scale disaffection if the War Cabinet let Bevin have his way. But Bevin was a strong man, and, as the leading representative of organized labour, a valuable one: his proposals were duly presented to the House of Commons on 9 February 1943, when 116 Conservatives voted against them.[101]

In the months that followed the demands of Press, publicists and Labour Party conferences mounted. In the autumn of 1943 Sir Richard Acland founded the Commonwealth Party, which, combining the aspirations of middle-class social reformers with the solid voting power of the Labour rank-and-file, succeeded in winning a number of by-elections from the Government. As the world scene lightened, it was inevitable that the Government should show some response.

6. THE WHITE PAPER CHASE

During 1943 the period of discussion and controversy gave place to a period of concrete government proposals, served up in the form of White Papers. After all the delays and arguments over the Beveridge Report, the White Papers on social insurance (part I dealing with the main part of the scheme, part II with industrial injuries, formerly treated separately as workmen's compensation but now to be integrated with the main scheme) followed Beveridge remarkably closely, though without, of course, the 'giants' and the 'assumptions'. Other differences, too, were significant of the reassertion of the bureaucratic mind: it would not be possible to pay benefits at subsistence level, nor to pay them for indefinite periods of time; the administration of national assistance must be clearly divorced from that of social insurance; the Friendly Societies would definitely have to go. But the fundamental purpose remained: a unified national insurance scheme (based on Beveridge's principles of flat-rate contributions and flat-rate benefits) which every adult member of the community must join. Shortly after the publication of the report the Government introduced a Bill to establish a new Ministry of Social Insurance (Beveridge had called for a Ministry of Social Security); in the committee stage a Conservative amendment was carried changing the title to Ministry of National Insurance. Although Greenwood and the main non-government Labour spokesmen opposed the amendment, which seemed to aim at narrowing the scope of the ministry, Aneurin Bevan, the leading left-wing critic of government policy throughout the war, for some perverse reason of his own, supported it.[102] By the time the war ended the Ministry of National Insurance, which in the first instance took over the insurance functions of the Ministry of Labour and National Service, had been established. One special aspect of social security which Beveridge had stressed was also legislated for before the war ended: family allowances, payable to the mother in respect of a second and all subsequent children. The Wages Act for which Bevin worked so hard became law in June 1943, and another Act designed to protect the normal income of the lowest-paid workers, the Wages Council Act, passed into law in March 1945.

Beveridge had hoped that he would be invited by the Government to formulate proposals for the implementation of his assumption (c), which must form the basis of the whole edifice of social security – the avoidance of mass unemployment. But the earlier controversy had left too acrid a memory and when Beveridge went ahead on his own account with the report published as *Full Employment in a Free Society* he was denied access to official sources, while the Government produced its own White Paper, *Employment Policy*. The latter, though a declaration of intention only, was really the most revolutionary document of the whole war period. Since the middle of the nineteenth century British Treasury policy had been governed by the conscious assumption that the strength of the pound sterling must be maintained – if this involved mass unemployment that was unfortunate, but first things must come first. Now the Government, representing all political parties, was committing itself, through the maintenance of the necessary level of total national expenditure, public works and controls, to the preservation of 'a high and stable level of employment'.[103] A conflict with the older Treasury aim was not foreseen, but in fact it proved in the future to be the case that whatever plight the pound might get into, no government would seek escape by allowing a return to mass unemployment. Beveridge's study and the government Paper were extremely similar in content, both drawing their inspiration from the theories of J. M. Keynes, but Beveridge expressed some strong criticisms of the official report, which beat him hands down in the race to publication. His charges were that the White Paper

understates the seriousness of the disease, that is to say the extent of the past failure of the unplanned market economy. And its practical proposals are inadequate, not only through deficient diagnosis, but even more because action is inhibited by a sense of values that is wrong in two respects: of treating private enterprise as sacrosanct – a sovereign power independent of the State, and of treating maintenance of budgetary equilibrium as of equal importance with full employment.[104]

It is important always to bear in mind that the policy documents of the war period were those of a Coalition government in which the Conservatives predominated, and of a Civil Service essentially traditionalist in composition and outlook. When after the war a Labour government swung the country sharply in the direction of a peacetime mixed economy it followed Beveridge rather than the White Paper.

Within the medical profession and its professional organizations there had for many years been considerable support for the extension of the country's medical services, so that when the White Paper *A National Health Service* appeared in 1944 it could expect, and did get, a warm reception from inside and outside the profession. The paper announced the principle of a free, comprehensive medical service, but it was purposefully vague on all the major

contentious issues: the question of a salaried service; the future of
the voluntary hospitals; and the continuance of a private sector.
Older traditionalists, of course, would not be appeased; and as the
reality of change came closer other members of the profession, too,
began to become alarmed. Pressure therefore was brought to bear
on the Minister of Health, Henry Willink (a Conservative), who
gave the doctors assurances that there would be no question of
forcing them into a National Health Service against their will,
and that there would be no salaried service.[105]

In educational policy there was greater continuity between the
earlier and later stages of the war than in the other areas of social
policy we have examined. In part this may have been because from
the outset there was, in R. A. Butler, a Minister at the Board of
Education who was both a reformer and a Conservative, in part
because already from the Thirties there was a substantial body of
educational proposals still waiting to be put into practice; but
mainly it was because the challenge of war is particularly marked in
education. The Federation of British Industries might ignore the
Beveridge Report, and indeed all other aspects of purely social (as
distinct from general planning) policy, but it did not ignore
education. Echoing its own pronouncements of a generation earlier
the Board of Education declared:

In the youth of the nation we have our greatest national asset. Even on
the basis of mere expediency, we cannot afford not to develop this asset
to the greatest advantage.[106]

From the outset, in other words, vested interests prepared to frustrate other social reforms, accepted the need for educational reform.
Thus a major Education Act came sooner than any other important
piece of Welfare State legislation – it was indeed the only really
basic Act to be passed before the war ended. But it was also,
being conceived by and acceptable to the Right, much less sweeping than those measures which were forced on the Right by the Left.
Education in England was still bedevilled by religious influences,
and much energy which in a better world would have been spent
in a more constructive way had to be devoted to evolving elaborate

formulae to meet the problem of State support for schools providing denominational education. From June 1941, when the Board of Education published its 'Green Book', it was clear that on the positive side the objective was the implementation of policies which had been advocated by leading educationists in the 1920s; unhappily the Labour Party had no constructive alternative to offer, still being stuck on its own outmoded 'Secondary Education for All' policy. Labour's Chuter Ede acted as a valuable second-in-command to Butler, but does not seem to have tried to push policy beyond the general consensus. The White Paper of 1943, *Educational Reconstruction*, announced the three basic principles on which reform would proceed: the essentially Whiggish one that 'the new educational opportunities must not . . . be of a single pattern' for 'it is just as important to achieve diversity as it is to ensure equality of educational opportunity'; second, the great discovery of the 1920s, that 'education is a continuous process conducted in successive stages' – primary, secondary and further; third, the egalitarian one that 'after 11 secondary education, of diversified types but of equal standing, will be provided for all children'. These principles were duly embodied in the English Education Act of 1944 which, when a comparison is made between the utterly deplorable state of English education prior to 1939 and its condition after 1945, is a great Act, but which, when thought is given to the continuing inadequacies of English education since 1945, seems a bungled opportunity. Secondary education (of a sort) for all did become a reality; in going after 'diversity' the Act signally failed to achieve equality. Free education was available in various types of 'county' schools – local authority schools subsidized by the central government. But both fee-paying direct grant schools and the exclusive public schools were left untouched. A left-wing Labour amendment on the committee stage of the Bill, seeking to abolish fees in all schools, would with one blow have provided for the rebuilding of the system on a fresh basis: the amendment was not successful, though the idea had been canvassed in the Liberal as well as the Leftist Press.[107] The idea of diversity among the county schools was based on the educational psychology of twenty years previously, and was reinforced by an unwillingness for change on the part of well-established local authority grammar schools. As the new system worked in practice, therefore, children took an examination at 'eleven-plus' to determine whether they should go to a grammar school or to a 'modern' school; it had been the intention of the framers of the Act that there should also be 'technical' schools, but very few of these in fact materialized; it had also been the intention that the various types of school should be of 'equal standing', a deluded hope. A similar Education Act for Scotland was passed in 1945: in Scotland's longer tradition of secondary education the change-over from primary education had customarily come at 'twelve-plus', and this situation was retained. Because of the greater number of grammar school places proportional to demand the 'qualifying' exam in Scotland did not become the scandal that the English 'eleven-plus' did. On the other hand grammar school education in the major cities was dominated by old-established and highly-respected fee-paying day schools which retained their status as direct grant schools: the would-be grammar school pupil, therefore, had the choice between paying fees (often relatively modest) or going to what were thought to be inferior schools.[108]

Despite the Government's apparent indifference to the Barlow, Scott and Uthwatt reports, interest in town and country planning was maintained at a high peak. First J. H. Forshaw and Sir Patrick Abercromby produced for the London County Council their County of London Plan; then, at the request of the Minister of Works and Buildings, Sir Patrick Abercromby drew up his epoch-making *Greater London Plan* (1944). Meantime the Government did implement the Barlow recommendation that there should be a central planning agency by establishing a Ministry of Town and Country Planning (1943). It was to the new minister that Abercromby presented his plan, which among other things recommended the creation of 'New Towns' as a solution to London's constant population overspill. In 1943 the Town and Country Planning (Interim Development) Act was passed. As the law (which was concerned solely with land not yet developed) stood under the 1932 Act, areas for which the local authority had resolved to prepare a planning scheme were subject to interim development control, which meant that while the scheme was in preparation would-be developers would be forced to seek permission for their own projects since otherwise these could be removed by the local authority without payment of compensation. The 1943 Act extended interim development control to areas where as yet no planning schemes were in preparation. It also greatly extended national control of town and country planning by giving the newly-created Minister the power to revoke local authority decisions and to decide on development permission in the light of national policy. The Town and Country Planning Act of 1944 introduced a new positive element in that it provided for planning powers in respect of areas which were already developed provided either that they were areas of 'extensive war damage' or of 'bad lay-out and obsolete development'. Exchequer grants were to be made available in the case of the former, though not the latter.[109]

Setting before itself a first objective of a 'separate dwelling for every family which desires to have one' the wartime government estimated that on that score 750,000 new homes would be needed. A second objective was the rapid completion of pre-war slum clearance and overcrowding programmes, requiring a further 500,000 new houses. To meet the immediate post-war situation it was decided to embark upon a two-year emergency programme, involving normal and special releases from the forces and training schemes to provide a work force of 800,000 by the end of the first year, the use of new methods of construction, prefabrication and 'Duplex' flats, and conversion of existing structures. The target was 300,000 houses by the end of the second year. To further this programme the Housing (Temporary Accommodation) Act of 1944 authorized the spending of £150 million on temporary houses. The programme in fact was seriously disrupted, first by a shortage of pressed steel from which it had been proposed to construct the temporary houses (wood, concrete and asbestos cement had to be substituted), then by the flying bomb attacks of the summer of 1944. After August 1944, however, the scheme did begin to gather momentum: in operation it involved a complicated feat of co-ordination between the local authorities, private industry and various central ministries (principally the Ministry of Works and the Ministry of Health, but the Ministry of Town and

Country Planning, the Ministry of Labour and National Service and the Ministry of Reconstruction were also involved).[110] It was the sort of balancing act that could just about be carried through in a war emergency, but did not augur well for the future. However, more permanent plans were also being prepared. In one of its many wartime policy documents the Labour Party, repeating what it had said in 1920, advocated the financing of public housing by low interest State loans.[111] However official opinion, fully aware of the fact that in the aftermath of war housing costs would be grossly inflated, preferred to adhere to the Addison policy of direct annual subsidies, a policy which has the defect that the local authority must in the first place borrow the initial capital cost of the house so that much of the subsidy is taken up with servicing the loan. It was the policy of the Churchill government that subsidies would be provided for houses built both by local authorities and private enterprise. Aware of what had gone wrong with the Addison scheme, the Government also planned to maintain control over the price of building materials and to control building contracts. Housing was the social issue over which most people felt strongest, as a public opinion poll during the 1945 election revealed.[112] The upheavals of war, as well as greatly aggravating the problem, had given a new emphasis to housing and town planning. But the exact lines along which development should take place, as with many of the other social issues here discussed, were not made clear until the first post-war government had come into power.

But the lines of government policy were not alone, or perhaps even principally, important. Whatever the State might do, irreversible changes had taken place within society. Qualitatively the big shake-up in the old class structure had come during the previous war; short of a total revolution and the achievement of a 'classless society' there was less scope for major change this time. None the less, within a framework which, once things had settled down, was recognizably the same as that of the inter-war years, important developments had taken place. Heavy taxation, rationing, a positive nutrition policy and high wartime wages had produced a levelling of standards (up as well as down) over a period of six years – long enough to seem more than just a temporary aberration. Education in the forces and self-education in the air-raid shelters had assisted the developing consciousness of the inarticulate. Mr A. J. P. Taylor concluded his *English History 1914–1915* by remarking that 'in the Second World War the British people came of age'. Apart from the specific context in which he used the phrase, this was true also in the sense that at the end of the war the majority had a clearer idea than ever before of what it was they expected of a modern civilized industrial society: decent living standards, income and health security, a taste of the modest luxuries of life: once the idea was defined it became in itself an agent of further change. In addition to this the war hastened the scientific, technological and economic processes which in themselves were transforming (and left to themselves would over a longer period doubtless have gone on transforming) society. The 'wireless' had become a national property during the war in a way in which it had never been in the Thirties; mass television was on the way. A National Health Service with new drugs at its disposal would be twice as effective in stamping out the diseases that had been a special affliction of the lower classes. The rapid expansion of the light industries provided the economic base for a working class rather different from that which had worked and suffered in the traditional heavy industries.

J. B. Priestley undoubtedly had his own political axes to grind: yet his immense popularity during the war as broadcaster and novelist does lend weight to his words. In his short novel *Three Men in New Suits* (1945), which discusses the appearance and attitudes of three young men from very different social backgrounds newly demobbed at the end of the war, he writes: 'There was a distinct likeness between them, as if all three had come from the same place, and had been doing the same things there.' One of them declares their credo:

We don't want the same kind of men looking after our affairs. We act as if we've learnt something. We don't keep shouting 'That's mine – clear off!' We don't try to make our little corner safe –and to hell with anybody else! We don't talk about liberty when what we really mean is a chance to fleece the public. We don't go back on all we said when the country was in danger. We stop trying for some easy money. We do an honest job of work for the community for what the community thinks we're worth. We stop being lazy, stupid and callous. . . . Instead of guessing and grabbing, we plan. Instead of competing, we co-operate. We come out of the nursery – and begin to grow up!

NOTES TO CHAPTER SIX

1. Evelyn Waugh, *Sword of Honour*, 1952–62, 1964 edn, p. 266.
2. *Observer*, 10, 17 September 1939.
3. *Ibid.*
4. *Manchester Guardian*, 2 May 1940.
5. *House of Commons Debates*, 18 June 1940. The speech was repeated in a radio broadcast the same evening.
6. Cp. P.R.O., CAB 23/3, 154(3), 5 June 1917.
7. N. Mansergh (ed.), *British Commonwealth Documents, 1931–1952*, vol. I, 1959, p. 570.
8. *Report of Committee on Electoral Machinery*, P.P., 1942–43, IV, Cmd. 6408, pp. 3–5 S. Ferguson and H. Fitzgerald, *Studies in the Social Services*, 1954, p. 4. R. Titmuss, *Problems of Social Policy*, 1950, p. 330.
9. *House of Lords Debates*, 8 December, *House of Commons Debates*, 15 December 1942. Ferguson and Fitzgerald, p. 21. *Report of Committee on Children and Young Persons*, P.P., 1959–60. IX, Cmd. 1191, p. 3.
10. *Report of Advisory Council on Treatment of Offenders*, P.P., 1960–61, XIII, Cmnd. 1213, p. 31.
11. G. A. N. Lowndes, *The British Educational System*, 1955, pp. 5, 26.
12. *Housing*, P.P., 1944–45, X, Cmd. 6609, p. 2.
13. *British Industries*, October 1940.
14. P.P., 1938, XI, Cmd. 5837.
15. W. Boyd (ed.), *Evacuation in Scotland*, 1942, p. 38. See also W. Padley and M. Cole, *Evacuation Survey*, 1943, and Titmuss, *Problems of Social Policy*, pp. 122 ff., 174 ff., 437, 516.
16. M. Cosens, *Evacuation : A Social Revolution*, January 1940.
17. Boyd, pp. 33 ff., Titmuss, pp. 120 ff. P.P., 1945–46, XII, Cmd. 6710, p. 46.
18. Women's Group on Public Welfare, *Our Towns*, 1943, p. xi.
19. *Economist*, 1 May 1943.
20. *Summary Report of Ministry of Health for 1939 to 1941*, P.P., 1941–42, IV, Cmd. 6340, p. 23. *Ibid. 1941 to 1942*, pp. 24–25. In general see Titmuss, pp. 502–3.
21. *House of Commons Debates*, 9 October 1941.
22. In addition to the Parliamentary Papers cited above, note also P.P., 1942–43, IV, Cmd. 6427, pp. 8–9.
23. *Daily Mirror*, 1 January 1940. *Observer*, 24 September 1939. *House of Commons Debates*, 6 December 1939.

24. *British Industries*, August 1939, p. 205, January 1940, p. 49.

25. *Daily Mirror*, 6 January 1940, *Manchester Guardian*, 6, 8 January 1940.

26. *Manchester Guardian*, 1 April 1940, *Daily Mail, The Times*, 18 March 1940, *Daily Express*, 19 March 1940.

27. *Manchester Guardian*, 4, 6 May 1940, *Daily Mirror*, 4 May 1940.

28. *Manchester Guardian, The Times*, 9 May 1940.

29. *House of Commons Debates*, 7, 8 May 1940.

30. *Daily Mirror*, 8 January 1940, *Daily Express*, 10 May 1940.

31. W. K. Hancock and M. M. Gowing, *The British War Economy*, 1940, pp. 88 ff.

32. *Ibid.*, pp. 219 ff.

33. Pollard, *Developments of British Economy*, p. 312.

34. Introduction by M. Cole and H. J. Blackham to D. Idle, *War Over West Ham*, 1942, pp. 6–7.

35. Quoted by Titmuss, p. 318.

36. T. H. O'Brien, *Civil Defence*, 1955, pp. 65–66.

37. *Ibid.*, pp. 154–5.

38. *Report of Committee on Regional Boards*, P.P., 1941–42, IV, Cmd. 6360.

39. Titmuss, p. 317.

40. O'Brien, p. 615.

41. P.P., 1944–45, X, Cmd, 6579, p. 1.

42. Harrod, *Life of Keynes*, p. 503.

43. P.P., 1943–44, III, Cmd. 6325, p. 9.

44. *Ibid.*, p. 10. P.P., 1942–43, Cmd. 6420, p. 2.

45. *Medical Research in War. Report of the Medical Research Council for Years 1939–45*, P.P., 1946–48, XIII, Cmd. 7335.

46. *Ibid.*, pp. 17–24. See also W. Sargant, *The Unquiet Mind*, 1967.

47. Ministry of Information, *Modern Publicity and War*, 1941.

48. J. D. Scott and R. Hughes, *The Administration of War Production*, 1955, p. 288.

49. *The Advancement of Science*, new series, vol. II, 1941, pp. 294 ff., vol. III, 1944–46, pp. 107–8.

50. A careful perusal of the pages of *The Advancement of Science* reveals some completely wrong forecasts as to the future possibilities of scientific progress: at the end of the First World War scientists were stressing the great virtues of the airship over the aeroplane; at the beginning of the Second World War they were doubting the possibility of supersonic flight. cp. *British Industries*, November 1941, p. 18.

51. *Scientific Research and Development*, P.P., 1963–64, VIII, Cmd. 6514, p. 12.

52. *Industry and Employment in Scotland*, P.P., 1946–47, XIX, Cmd. 7125, pp. 5–9, 17.

53. *Ministry of Labour and National Service Report for 1939–1946*, P.P., 1946–47, XII, Cmd. 7225, pp. 4, 304–7.

54. *Ibid.*, pp. 307–8.

55. *Report of 73rd Annual Trades Union Congress*, 1941, p. 114. *The T.U.C. in Wartime*, 1962.

56. R. Blackburn, *I am an Alcoholic*, 1959, p. 46.

57. Cmd. 7225, pp. 112–15.

58. *Ibid.*, p. 25, 30–34. For detail on Conscientious Objection see D. Hayes, *Challenge of Conscience*, 1949.

59. *Report of Royal Commission on Equal Pay 1944–46*, P.P., 1945–46, XI, Cmd. 6937, pp. 7–46.

69. *Ibid.*, pp. 112–16.

61. *Ibid.*, pp. 164–5, 187 ff.

62. *Marriage Ban in the Civil Service*, P.P., 1945–46, X, Cmd. 6886, pp. 5 ff.

63. Cmd. 7225, pp. 249–53.

64. M. P. Hall, *The Social Services of Modern England*, 1963 edn, pp. 231 ff.

65. Mass Observation, *People in Production*, 1941, pp. 23 ff.

66. Titmuss, p. 508. Hancock and Gowing, p. 541.

67. *The Times*, 1 July 1940.

68. R. O. Gillespie, *Psychological Effects of War on Citizens and Soldiers*, New York, 1942, pp. 100–102. I. L. Janis, *Air War and Emotional Stress*, New York, 1951, pp. 74–75.

69. For a breathtaking example of upper-middle-class nonchalance in face of adversity see Anthony Weymouth, *Journal of the War Years*, 1948. See also H. Nicolson, *Diaries*, vol. II, 1967.

70. C. Fitzgibbon, *The Blitz*, 1957, p. 118, 135, 113.

71. *New York Herald Tribune*, 21 September 1940. *Observer*, 22 September 1940.

72. *British Industries*, October 1940, p. 1. A. Briggs, *Social Thought and Social Action: A Study of the Work of Seebohm Rowntree, 1871–1954*, 1961, p. 304. Lord Woolton, *Memoirs*, 1959, pp. 422–3.

73. *Tribune*, 28 February 1941. I am indebted to Mr Angus Calder for this reference.

74. *Manchester Guardian*, 30 September 1940.

75. *Daily Express*, 13 April 1940.

76. *Manchester Guardian*, 30 September 1940.

77. Quoted by E. Mackerness, *Social History of English Music*, p. 220.

78. *Ibid.*, p. 347.

79. G. Barraclough, *History in a Changing World*, Oxford, 1955, p. 8. For the 'Crisis in History' see 'New Ways in History', *Times Literary Supplement*, 7 April, 28 July, 8 September, 1966.

80. *British Industry*, 29 October 1940, p. 1.

81. Viscount Kilmuir, *Political Adventure*, 1964, pp. 63 ff.

82. Iremonger, *Temple*, pp. 431, 540.

83. *The 1941 Committee*, 1941. *We must Win*, 1941. Again I am indebted to Mr Angus Calder for allowing me to consult his own work in progress on the 1941 Committee.

84. Labour Party, *The Old World and the New Society*, 1942, p. 11.

85. Labour Party, *Annual Conference Report, 1942*, p. 132. *National Service for Health*, 1943, pp. 15, 21.

86. *Social Insurance and Allied Services* (The Beveridge Report), P.P., 1942–43, VI, Cmd. 6404, p. 19.

87. *British Industries*, June 1942, p. 136.

88. *The Times*, 2 November 1942.

89. *Daily Mirror*, 2 November 1942.

90. Harrod, *Keynes*, p. 535.
91. Cmd. 6404, p. 6. Cp. p. 170.
92. W. Beveridge, *Power and Influence*, 1953, pp. 282–323.
93. *The Times, Daily Express, Manchester Guardian, Daily Mirror, Daily Telegraph*, 2 December 1942. *Economist*, 5 December 1942.
94. *The Times*, 3 December 1942. For a series of hostile essays see J. W. Nisbet *et al.*, *Beveridge and his Plan*, 1943.
95. *Daily Mirror*, 3 December 1942. British Institute of Public Opinion, *The Beveridge Report and the Public*, 1943, pp. 5–11.
96. *Daily Mirror*, 16, 19 February 1943.
97. *House of Commons Debates*, 16, 17, 18 February 1943. W. S. Churchill, *The Second World War : The Hinge of Fate*, 1950, pp. 959–60. *Forward From the Right : A Statement by the Tory Reform Committee*, 1943. Viscount Hinchingbrooke, *Full Speed Ahead : Essays in Tory Reform*, 1944.
98. The broadcast is printed in *War Speeches* (ed. C. Eade), vol. II, pp. 424 ff.
99. *Daily Express, Daily Telegraph, The Times, Manchester Guardian*, 22 March 1943.
100. P.P., 1941–42, IV, Cmd. 6378, 6386.
101. *House of Commons Debates*, 12 November, 17 December 1942, 9 February 1943. *Manchester Guardian*, 24 October 1942.
102. *House of Commons Debates*, 10 November (col. 1842).
103. *Employment Policy*, P.P., 1943–44, VIII, Cmd. 6527.
104. W. Beveridge, *Full Employment in a Free Society*, 1944, p. 150.
105. See H. Eckstein, *The English National Health Service*, 1958, pp. 139 ff., 155 ff.
106. *Educational Reconstruction*, P.P., 1942–43, XI, Cmd. 6458, pp. 3 ff.
107. *House of Commons Debates*, 28 March 1944. *Manchester Guardian*, 11 November 1942.
108. See H. C. Dent, *The Education Act, 1944*, 1944, G. A. N. Lowndes, *The British Education System*, and G. S. Osborne, *Scottish and English Schools*, 1966.
109. P. Abercromby, *Greater London Plan*, 1944. *Town and Country Planning Bill 1947 : Explanatory Memorandum*, P.P., 1946–47, XIX, Cmd. 7006. p. 4. W. Ashworth, *Genesis of Modern British Town Planning*, 1954, pp. 227 ff.
110. *Housing*, P.P., 1944–45, X, Cmd. 6609, pp. 2–8.
111. Labour Party, *Housing and Planning After the War*, n.d., p. 8.
112. Cited by R. B. McCallum and A. Readman, *The British General Election of 1945*, 1947, p. 237.

CHAPTER SEVEN

Building the Post-War Britain, 1945-50

1. ECONOMIC AND POLITICAL SCAFFOLDING

The development of British society in the five years after the Second World War was primarily determined by the cost, economic and political, of victory, by the immense range of internal influences and cross-currents set off by the war, and by the advent to power of a political party committed by origin to the interests of the working classes and by philosophy to a belief in the power of the State to guide and control social and economic forces. That Labour politicians were both in office *and* possessed of the self-confidence to attempt to put their policies into practice was largely due to the war. It is conceivable that had war not intervened Labour might have won a general election in 1940, though given the marked failure in recent British history of the mystical 'pendulum' to swing in the absence of any serious discontinuity (such as war), this seems unlikely, a view which is borne out by a study of by-election results in the 1930s: as David Butler, the leading authority on British electoral behaviour, concludes:

Once the electorate had recovered from the shock of 1931 there appears to have been a very sharp swing in favour of the Labour Party, but from 1933 onwards their support seems, if anything, to have declined. The reason for the belief that the Labour Party was gaining ground presumably lies in the fact that between 1935 and 1939 it won twelve seats from the Conservatives in by-elections. But a study of the votes cast does not suggest any trend in its favour. It might be said to have won by-elections only because it had fared so ill in the General Election.[1]

Even had the Labour Party managed to achieve office in 1940, the hesitant, defensive and sometimes confused nature of its pronouncements – which contrast so sharply with the bold policy statements of the early Forties – suggest that its hold on the reins of government might not have been much firmer than in 1924 or 1931.

In the General Election held on 5 July 1945 Labour won 393

seats, the Conservatives 213, the Liberals 12, the I.L.P. 3, the Communists 2; there were 14 Independents. Of the total votes cast Labour secured 47·8 per cent, the Conservatives 39·8 per cent, the Liberals 9 per cent, and the others 3·4 per cent. The discrepancy between Labour's landslide majority in Parliament and its slightly less impressive majority in the country was partly due to the workings of the single-member constituency system, and partly due to the fact that the Conservatives put up more candidates than did Labour (618 to 599): Labour's average percentage vote per candidate was 50·4, that of the Conservatives 40·1.[2] Labour won because of the colossal mood for change engendered by the war, not just among working-class voters, but, much more critically, among middle-class voters, one-third of whom, it has been estimated, voted Labour, thus providing the real key to Labour's triumph.[3] Labour won because by conviction and composition it was the party most likely to respond in full to that mood, and because the limelight of office had banished the lingering shadows of doubt about its fitness to rule. Mass communications, particularly radio, played a bigger part in this election than in any previous one. It was not so much that Labour exploited this device more effectively than the Conservatives, but that the political broadcasts brought out more clearly than the printed word could ever have done that Labour had clearly thought-out plans, while the Conservatives could rely only on the appeal of Churchill and national victory. Churchill himself seemed able to rely only on rhetoric, and when he said of the party headed by Attlee and Morrison, two of the most inoffensive-looking little men ever to have led a political party, that 'they would have to fall back on some sort of Gestapo', he reduced to absurdity the essential difference between the parties; the point was driven home by Attlee's calm and constructive speech of the following evening.

Labour's victory in 1945 was a culminating triumph for the organized working-class movement, though Labour in power was actually a coalition of representatives of that movement along with a large number of upholders of the middle- and upper-class liberal tradition. Many of the new boys of 1945 were recent converts from impeccable social backgrounds; many of them, being livelier and better educated than the majority of trade unionists, achieved office pretty quickly. In a Cabinet of twenty, only six ministers sat for trade union-sponsored seats; there were only six other trade-union-sponsored senior ministers and thirteen junior ministers.[4] Attlee as Prime Minister had the qualities of a first-rate chairman, tolerant, shrewd and much tougher than his appearance or Churchill's jibes ('an empty taxi drew up and Mr Attlee got out' and 'a sheep in sheep's clothing' are two of the best) would suggest; at the same time he had a colossal respect for the traditions of British government; having been born into the same kind of upper-middle-class family as had most senior Civil Servants, he was not the sort of man to invite a direct confrontation with them. Later Attlee penned a somewhat fulsome tribute to the Civil Servants who had co-operated loyally with the Labour government;[5] sometimes one has the impression that it was rather the Government which co-operated loyally with the Civil Servants. Morrison was Deputy Prime Minister, Lord President of the Council and Leader of the House of Commons: he was a man of little political daring, who already visualized socialism as involving little more than the establishment of public corporations like his beloved London Passenger Transport Board, or the B.B.C.; it was unfortunate that he had to be given the general oversight of domestic legislation. Ernest Bevin, unrepentantly and above all else a trade unionist, became Foreign Secretary: Bevin detested Morrison, though politically he too was to the Right of the party – or perhaps the nature of foreign relations after 1945 made him seem more so than he really was. Hugh Dalton, one of the younger generation of upper-middle-class liberals who entered Labour politics at the end of the First World War, became Chancellor of the Exchequer: he made it a special mission to encourage the younger talents in the party, particularly those of non-working-class backgrounds. Greenwood, as Lord Privy Seal, continued his decline into oblivion. Sir Stafford Cripps, the earlier turbulence now firmly concealed behind a mask of religious asceticism, was President of the Board of Trade, and, the one major surprise, Aneurin Bevan, ex-miner and left-wing trouble-shooter, Minister of Health. Bevan was to prove the most controversial of the post-war generation of

Labour leaders. Without doubt he was the most imaginative of them, but he was somewhat lacking in the ability to handle administrative detail. He launched Labour's greatest achievement, the National Health Service, but he was not altogether successful in piloting it past the first rocks it encountered. Blasting his way through a natural stutter he became a fine orator, and he had a bitter wit. He was hated by his opponents (a later description of Conservatives as 'lower than vermin' was long remembered against him) and some claimed (usually with a good measure of British hypocrisy) to be offended by his patrician tastes.

The strength of the official working-class trade union influence on the Government, embodied in the person of Ernest Bevin, is brought out by the speed with which it passed a new Trade Union Act restoring the state of trade union law to what it had been before the passage of the hated Trades Disputes Act of 1927. The influence of democratic reformism is brought out by the enactment of the sixth and (so far) last Reform Act (more correctly – Representation of the People Act), which by abolishing the second vote held by owners of business premises and by university graduates completed the progress towards 'one man one vote', and by removing the last remaining property qualification still obtaining in local elections, brought complete formal democracy to local government. Middle-class radicalism and official trade unionism were much stronger influences than left-wing socialism. However much the Government might concede to Civil Servants and to outside vested interets, it conceded little to the left-wing core of about 30 within its own ranks; only in the case of peacetime conscription, where opposition went beyond the socialist idealogues, did the Government give way to the extent of reducing the length of the proposed period of conscription: even so it had to face a hostile vote of 73 from within its own ranks. In such situations the Government had the support of the Conservative opposition; but on controversial domestic issues the Conservatives were simply in no position to influence policy. They did in fact take their defeat in 1945 rather badly. A superb passage in the memoirs of Sir David Maxwell Fyfe, describing the descent of the Labour M.P.s upon Parliament, unwittingly lays bare the Tory soul:

Many spilled over on to the Opposition benches, from where they gleefully heckled the Conservative leaders – including Churchill – to the latter's undisguised consternation. Most of these disagreeable manifestations of triumph were due purely to ignorance of the customs and traditions of the House, and were quickly abandoned, but there was an obnoxious type of new Labour M.P. who seemed to attend the House solely for the pleasure of jeering at his opponents, and subjecting them to a stream of derisive interruptions and mocking laughter in debate.

He also flatly quotes one old Tory M.P. as describing the Labour M.P.s as 'just like a crowd of damned constituents'.[6] Conservative opposition in the first years of Labour government was factious and bitter but rather ineffectual, Churchill setting the tone with a variation on the fat-headed warnings he had issued during the election:

I believe profoundly that the attempt to turn Great Britain into a Socialist State will, as it develops, produce widespread political strife, misery and ruin at home . . .[7]

Other powerful voices outside Parliament were less easy to ignore. Short of establishing a dictatorship, the Government in its social policies would require the co-operation of doctors, social workers and teachers, and in its economic policies the support of industrialists as well as trade unionists. As the Government moved ahead quickly with its proposals for the nationalization of major sections of industry, the Federation of British Industries issued a statement which, after making the routine invocation of the spirit of Dunkirk,

rejected completely the conception that the nationalization of industry was in the interest of employment, of production, or of the consumer, and emphasized that the speed with which the Government's policy was being implemented and the uncertainty which surrounded their intentions were having gravely unsettling effects.[8]

However, in its day-by-day policies the federation preferred to eschew open attacks and aim rather at securing amendments in the proposed legislation, till the question of iron and steel nationalization again made open confrontation seem a potentially fruitful policy.[9]

The economic situation which faced the incoming Labour government was a bleak one: domestic capital run down by something like £3,000 million, overseas investments by £1,000 million; net debts of £3,000 million, exports reduced by two-thirds. It was made suddenly worse when the end of the war against Japan forced the American government to implement a previous resolution of Congress and bring to an end the Lend-Lease agreements which throughout the war had enabled Britain to lay hands on the supplies which she needed to keep the war effort going. Keynes was dispatched to Washington, where he found an incipient chilliness on the part of American officials, who were already beginning to see Britain, who after all was less badly off than the shattered countries of continental Europe, as a potential trade rival. Eventually, however, Keynes was able to secure the offer of credits to the extent of $3,750 million: interest would be 2 per cent, and repayments would be spread over fifty years from 1951. Canada added a further $1,250 million. In granting the loan the American government – concerned to resist the economic nationalism which had been rampant in the Thirties – insisted that the pound sterling should be restored to full convertibility and that Britain should work towards the abolition of her imperial preferences. When in the autumn of 1947 convertibility was restored there was an immediate flight from the pound as holders of sterling rushed to seize the opportunity to convert their holdings into scarce dollars. The crisis was severe and convertibility had again to be suspended. It was clear that the glorious age of the pound had gone for good: clear too that the Government had become a little complacent. Meantime the original loan was being used up too rapidly: however, from 1948 the British economy was able to draw a valuable transfusion from a new American plan to speed the reconstruction of Europe; between the end of 1948 and the beginning of 1951 Britain received a total of £2,400 million in 'Marshall Aid'. It was easy to suggest that Britain was living on the charity of the United States, charity which an incompetent socialist government did its best to squander. In fact American aid, a piece of enlightened self-interest as far as the Americans were concerned, did no more than enable Britain to touch bottom in the swampy economic pit she had dug for herself by her exertions in the common cause against Nazi Germany. As the *Economist* put it, patriotically, but not unfairly:

Our present needs are the direct consequences of the fact that we fought earliest, that we fought longest, and that we fought hardest. In moral terms we are creditors.

Britain's difficulties were aggravated by a number of world-wide economic trends. Throughout the world in the post-war years there was a persistent upward movement in prices, which, as a natural consequence of the disruptions of war and the return everywhere to civilian production, was particularly marked in the primary materials which Britain had to import. Because of the destruction of capital during the war and need to rebuild industry after the war, and because of the movement everywhere towards new technologies requiring high levels of investment, there was a world-wide shortage of capital. Against this Britain did stand to profit from the expansion in world trade which took place in the post-war years: in 1939 world trade in manufactures was little higher than it had been in 1913; by 1950 it was already 50 per cent higher. Britain, with much of her 'invisible income' of pre-war days gone, must, to make her way in the post-war world, not only regain her lost export markets, but increase exports to 75 per cent above their pre-war figure. In a serious situation some comfort could be derived from the fact that for the first time the country had attained a reasonable level of production of modern machine tools (though still far below that of the Americans), was possessed of rapidly growing chemicals, electronics and aircraft industries, and was beginning to develop synthetic fibres to replace the cotton industry to which the war had practically given the *coup de grâce*. Unhappily industry is only as good as its power supply. Coal had been a long time a-dying as a central element in the world economy and as a basic British export, but Britain's power supplies, whether in the form of electricity, gas or solid fuel, still depended overwhelmingly upon it. The new strains imposed on the industry by the Second World War, after the appalling neglect of the inter-war years, almost brought the whole antique fabric to the ground: in 1945 coal production was at the very low level of 175 million tons. Not even prompt nationalization, the workers' battle-cry in the 1920s, could win over miners who had been left to rot in the inter-war years, and output per man shift remained low, matching the pre-war level only in 1950. In the meantime there came the big fuel crisis of February and March 1947. To the British their erratic climate is a source of never-ending humour: behind the humour is self-congratulation, the assumption that, though it may not be good for picnics, or even cricket, it is, in keeping with the British character, essentially temperate. Severe floods or extreme cold are regarded as something utterly exceptional, like political violence: something against which no permanent safeguards are necessary. The winter of 1946–47, without doubt, was extremely cold: the enfeebled coal industry simply could not meet the extra demand; massive cuts in power supplies spread a wave of temporary unemployment throughout British industry which reached a peak of 800,000.[10]

In the 1945 election manifesto, *Let Us Face the Future*, the Labour Party stated its ultimate purpose at home as

the establishment of a Socialist Commonwealth of Great Britain – free, democratic, efficient, progressive, public-spirited, its material resources organized in the service of the British people.

Although the Government went through many of the motions which might be associated with the establishment of a Socialist Commonwealth, its first justification for its various economic policies was always that they were necessary to further the export drive and to increase efficiency and production, rather than that they were essential to the transformation of the economic basis of society or to the development of social equality. The form of the nationalization programme, though the details varied from industry to industry, was primarily shaped by Morrison's faith in the public corporation and by the Government's strange innocence of the realities of the managerial revolution: ownership changed, management, and therefore control, remained largely the same. Several of the nationalization measures were mere routine: Cable and Wireless Ltd became a public corporation; British European Airways and British South American Airways joined with B.O.A.C. in running British civil aviation; the formal nationalization of the Bank of England proved of much less consequence than the beginnings of Exchange Control in 1932. For the two major public utilities two separate Acts, with a year's interval in between, were passed, establishing an Electricity Board and a Gas Board, with an infra-structure of Area Boards: no attempt was made to create a single co-ordinated public service. Nationalization of the ailing coal industry was scarcely to be avoided, though it was attacked by the Conservatives, who would presumably have resorted to a policy of subsidy and 'rationalization'. More genuinely controversial was the granting to the former coal-owners of compensation totalling £164,600,000. This was a heavy financial burden for the new régime to shoulder, especially when on their past record the owners did not really deserve a penny. However, having set itself on the course of democracy and non-confiscation, it would have been practically impossible for the Government to act with the ruthlessness of strict equity and logic. The miners were not enchanted by the thought that some of the product of their labour was continuing to go to the pockets of the former owners; still less by the fact that as in other industries most of the old management was left unchanged. By setting up a central British Transport Commission, the Transport Act was theoretically supposed to clear the way for an integrated inland transport system: but separate Boards administered rail and road transport, so that the main outcome was simply that the expense of maintaining railways which were no longer economic (and which had long since ceased to be in competition), plus substantial compensation, was thrown on to the public, while the compensating advantage of a curb on the chaos which was already developing on British roads was not in sight when the Labour government fell from office. Because of doubts and reservations among some Cabinet ministers the Government delayed so long over its Bill for the nationalization of iron and steel that it was unable to put this into effect before 1950, when the law demanded that it resubmit itself to the electorate.[11]

This somewhat haphazard nationalization programme was supposed, by giving the Government control of the 'commanding heights', to play a part in the planning of the economy as a whole. Actually planning by the Government was more apparent than real: partly this was because ministers accepted that the techniques which had been successful in war, when a principal problem had been the allocation of scarce resources, would be adequate in peace; partly because, in a fashion which repeated itself over and over again during this government's period of office, ministers constantly mistook the wish for the fulfilment. Ministers spoke so often of their faith in planning that eventually the word became a stick with which Conservatives could beat the Government. Because of its faith in British traditions, above all its supreme belief in the adaptations of British traditions that had carried the country through the war, and, no doubt, because of resistance from within the administrative system, the Labour government proposed no constitutional changes to facilitate the overall planning of the economy. At the top of such 'system' as there was stood the Cabinet, with its various committees, of which the most important was the Lord President's Committee, chaired by Herbert Morrison. It was Morrison who first announced the Government's specific rejection of the idea put forward by Keynes in the Twenties and taken up by 'middle opinion' in the Thirties, that there should be an Economic General Staff responsible for planning policy.[12] The economic section of the Cabinet Office and the Central Statistical Office were strictly ancillary to the Cabinet and its committees, which could themselves aim at no more than 'co-ordination' of economic activities. Without the constitutional and administrative machinery for direct planning, the natural frictions of human nature took over. As Patrick Gordon Walker, a junior minister in the Labour government of 1945, later put it:

Ministers conceive a deep distaste for embarking upon projects that will entail more and larger meetings with their colleagues. This means that even Socialist Ministers are selective about the sector of the national life that they can attempt to plan.[13]

That sad memorial to non-planning, the coal crisis of 1946–47, provoked the Government to move half a step forward from 'co-ordination through Cabinet committees': a new Central Economic Planning Staff of higher Civil Servants and economists was formed under the direction of a chief planning officer, Sir Edwin Plowden, who, typically of the Government's dependence on the leaders of private industry, was a director of British Aluminium and of two other companies. The convertibility crisis, which was accompanied by a spell when Morrison was thrown out of action by illness, led to the creation of a Ministry of Economic Affairs under Sir Stafford Cripps, to which this new planning staff was transferred, and the abolition of the Lord President's Committee, which was replaced by an Economic Policy Committee. In a word which was coming to have the same hollow ring as planning itself, Attlee explained that Cripps's position was 'one of co-ordination'. A month later Dalton was forced to resign as Chancellor of the Exchequer, because, with the hearty lack of discretion which characterized him, he let a pressman in on one of the secrets of his special November budget. Cripps thereupon became Chancellor, taking with him all the apparatus of his short-lived ministry. Division of economic responsibilities between a Treasury concerned above all to hold down expenditure and a separate ministry charged with long-term planning and expansion was not really a very good idea, as a repetition of the experiment by a more recent Labour government seventeen years later was to show. Under the post-1947 régime the economy was subjected to much firmer direction than before, though this probably owed more to Cripps's own determination and strength of character than to any great inherent virtue in the final shape which the administration of central planning assumed as the result of the last of many reshuffles.[14]

The remainder of the system had the same unsatisfactory *ad hoc* quality about it, being shaped partly by the legacy of war, partly by immediate needs as they arose, and above all by an abiding belief in the abilities and goodwill of existing leaders of industry. Of the various advisory bodies of which use was made, the National Joint Advisory Council had been founded in 1939, and the National

Production Advisory Council on Industry in 1941: as constituted under the Labour government the former consisted of twelve employers' and seventeen T.U.C. representatives plus representatives of the nationalized industries; the latter consisted of seven representatives each of employers and T.U.C., two representatives of nationalized industry, various senior Civil Servants and chairmen of regional boards of industry. The Economic Planning Board and the Dollar Export Board were not established until 1947 and 1949 respectively. The maze of boards, councils and committees established during the war for liaison between government and industry was kept in being by the Labour government, which also continued to act through the established employers' trade associations. For most of the period the principal adviser to the Board of Trade was Sir William Palmer, chairman of the British Rayon Federation, and most of the advisers to the Ministry of Food were recruited from the business world. Many of the devices of planning control which so irked private industry were in practice remarkably toothless: the Government, putting undue faith in its ability to control the commanding heights of the economy through nationalizing 20 per cent of all industry, devoted little thought to the problems of overall planning for the 80 per cent left in private hands. New investment, theoretically, was controlled by the Capital Issues Committee (composed, naturally, of bankers, stockbrokers and industrialists) but since it took cognizance only of issues of over £50,000 much private development which was not necessarily in keeping with the Government's major economic aims got through this hole in the net; such development could also be financed by bank advances which, beyond issuing memoranda on lending policy, the Government did not control. Successful exporters were encouraged through being given higher raw material quotas, but for all the stress the Government placed on its 'export drive' there was no positive direction of exports. Foreign exchange control was maintained from the war period, but there were leakages, particularly through outlying parts of the sterling area, legally defined as the 'scheduled territories' in the 1947 Exchange Control Act. While the Government persisted in basing its policies on the recognition of established economic interests, British financiers did not hesitate in 1949 to speculate against the pound, helping to make devaluation inevitable.[15]

The best statement of the Government's intentions when the flush of high aspiration still glowed on its cheeks is the *Economic Survey for 1947*, for which Attlee wrote a special preface: the Labour government believes in planning, but it believes also in democracy.[16] This was the basic dilemma: the inherent conflict between central planning and full individual liberty as traditionally conceived in Britain was one the Labour government was unable to resolve. It is easy to see now where the Government's economic policies failed: it can also be seen that in the end Attlee, Morrison and even Aneurin Bevan had that same ingrained democratic sensibility which had bedevilled the policies of MacDonald and Baldwin. In 1945 the Labour government had a unique psychological opportunity to be bold: but bounded as they were by the empiricist traditions of British politics they were not able to seize it – though they did have a clearer vision of the needs of the hour than their political opponents. The first and second *Economic Surveys* did no more than set targets for the succeeding twelve months; there was no breath of anything so scandalous as long-term planning on the style of the Russian Five Year Plans. A loss of confidence in even these modest objectives was apparent after 1949 and subsequent *Surveys* provided 'estimates' rather than 'targets'.[17] Loss of confidence in overall planning was projected into the 'bonfire of controls' of November 1948 ignited by Harold Wilson, who had taken Cripps's place as President of the Board of Trade: there was a second bonfire in March 1949.

Hugh Dalton's most distinctive contribution to policy was his insistence upon 'cheap money' – a Bank Rate of 2 per cent. Arguably, in what proved to be a time of full employment and inflationary pressure, this was exactly the wrong policy. However the belief when the Labour government took office was that, once the post-war boom had passed, an unemployment level of $8\frac{1}{2}$ per cent might be expected. Furthermore it was necessary that capital should be made as readily available as possible for the basic social reconstruction that had to be undertaken. The Government was not successful in restraining inflation (a world-wide phenomenon):

Cripps came nearest to success when for a brief period he secured trade union co-operation in a voluntary 'wage freeze'. The one solid achievement was the raising of exports, in 1950, to the target level of 75 per cent above the pre-war level. But many of the major structural weaknesses of British industry remained untouched: productivity was high in the newer industries, very low in the old ones. There could be no change as long as the Government went no further than exhortation and continued to work through existing trade associations and trade unions. A series of White Papers show that the Government had a grasp of what was essentially wrong with the economy, but none at all of what was to be done about it. The 1947 *Statement on the Economic Conditions Affecting Relations between Employers and Workers* was aware that 'increased output ... is the thing which is needed more than anything else'. But the answer to the question 'How is this increase of production to be obtained?' is less than impressive:

By ensuring that those industries which provide essential supplies are fully manned up; by maintaining full employment so that we can make use of all the manpower we can muster; and while costs and prices are held steady, by raising the level of output per head without prejudice to earnings.[18]

The 1947 *Statement on Personal Income, Cost and Prices* made a perceptive point:

The last hundred years have seen the growth of certain traditional or customary relationships between personal incomes – including wages and salaries – in different occupations. Those have no necessary relevance to modern conditions. The relation which different personal incomes bear to one another must no longer be determined by this historical development of the past, but by the urgent needs of the present.[19]

However, an equally long liberal-democratic tradition of the right way of doing things must not be infringed:

It is not desirable for the Government to interfere directly with the income of individuals otherwise than by taxation. To go further would mean that the Government would be forced itself to assess and regulate all personal incomes according to some scale which would have to be determined. This would be an incursion by the Government, into what has hitherto been regarded as a field of free contract between individuals and organizations.[20]

The achievements and the failings of the motor-car industry are instructive. By 1947 the industry had almost recovered the 1947 peak output of well over half a million vehicles. By 1950 production had reached 903,000 vehicles, 52 per cent of the total European output. But in some respects the British industry had it easy: European countries had not yet had time fully to rebuild their own productive capacity; in the meantime they had no wish to spend dollars on American cars. In this situation the British manufacturers carried on in the old tradition, producing too wide a range of different models, generally built with British rather than foreign needs in mind, and failing to give adequate attention to the problem of providing after-sales service and spare parts.[21] The wartime golden age of science dimmed, as it had dimmed after the First World War. A spirit of dejection took over in, for instance, Medical Research Council (M.R.C.) reports, where reference is made to 'conditions often of frustrating difficulty' and to 'grave shortages of accommodation, of equipment and also of trained men'.[22] The Development of Inventions Act of 1948 led to the establishment in 1949 of the National Research Development Corporation, one of whose major tasks was to be the provision of 'financial and other support' for the development of electronic computers, a sphere in which Britain, though far behind the United States, has to the present maintained a long lead over other West European countries.[23]

The pound remained weak, and some devaluation was probably inevitable in 1949; it seems, however, that in reducing the pound from $4·03 to $2·80 Sir Stafford Cripps rather overdid things – Sir Roy Harrod has suggested that $3·64 would have been a more appropriate figure, though Cripps may have hoped by a drastic 'once for all' devaluation to end speculation against sterling. The upshot in any event was that while exports, by being rendered cheaper to overseas buyers, did receive a temporary boost, the cost of British imports rose, thus, in value terms, offsetting the gains.[24]

2. THE WALLS OF THE WELFARE STATE

A 'welfare State' is one which accepts a responsibility to ensure the social well-being of all its citizens: the commanding heights, so to speak, of social well-being are income security (which ideally, as well as insurance or assistance to cover interruption of earnings, includes an economic policy directed towards the maintenance of a high level of employment), health, housing and environment, and education. Beyond the commanding heights a sophisticated welfare State may try to extend its domain to the romantic mist-capped peaks of culture, entertainment, morals and the manifold lesser problems of social relations and social welfare. The phrase was first coined to point a punning contrast to Germany's 'warfare state': it was first used descriptively of the Britain of the Labour government 1945-50, though a welfare State in all but name already existed in New Zealand on the eve of the war. Similar social legislation to that passed in Britain after 1945 was enacted at roughly the same time in other European countries, where the military participation factor derived a special potency and urgency from the actions of the resistance movements who claimed their social rewards at the end of the war.[25] In the minds of some historians, therefore, the phrase

is now a socio-political category deemed generally descriptive of the states of our time.[26]

This surprising definition in fact arises from a confusion between *welfare* as the conscious pursuit of State or community and *affluence*, springing from technological change and economic growth, assisted at most by a few Keynesian nudges. It presupposes that the principles of the Welfare State are not a matter of political controversy in the 'states of our time'. Conceivably, though doubtfully, the American 'Great Society' of the 1960s can be termed a welfare

State; earlier than this the term is certainly not applicable. If one returns to the period 1945–50, when aspects of the Welfare State were matters of sharp controversy within Britain, and generally mistrusted in the United States, the British social legislation of the period may be seen as worthy of a little more attention than it has now become fashionable to warrant it, even if it will no longer support the extravagant claims once made on its behalf.

The primary characteristic of the Labour government's welfare legislation was its universality; and this, almost certainly, is where Conservative legislation would have been different. On the principle of universality free medical treatment, family allowances, pensions, insurance benefits and, to some extent, subsidized housing were to be available to rich and poor alike. Thus, it was hoped, the poor would feel no stigma about making use of the social services, and so a mighty blow would be struck at class distinctions; furthermore, on a more realistic plan, it was clear that only when the rich shared the services with the poor would the poor get the best available. The concept of universality was attacked from the Right at the time and later. Disillusioned left-wing intellectuals were also to fear that in the blissful dawn of 1945 they greatly overrated it: in 1960 Professor Richard Titmuss remarked:

Most of us must now admit that we put too much faith in the 1940s in the concept of universality as applied to social security. Mistakenly, it was linked with economic egalitarianism.[27]

Yet looked at in the context of 1945 the insistence on universality can be seen as one of the few aspects of Labour policy that do show a genuine social revolutionary intention, in the sense of aiming at a substantial modification of the class basis of British society. If the services were to be universal, they were also supposed, in the manner indicated by Beveridge when he overstepped his terms of reference, to be unified into one integrated welfare state. The metaphor, first used by R. A. Butler and enthusiastically taken up by Labour spokesmen and publicists, was of the 'mosaic' of the social services. But no Byzantine ikon was ever created by the work of several hands over several months, each artist tinting his glass and adding his pieces according to his own theories and his own taste. As separate ministries established the separate enactments of the Welfare State, unification and integration remained no more than pious aspiration: the mosaic became a crazy paving. Even within each major area of welfare there was a lack of integration: the items of social security, especially, were separately parcelled, and administrative division was perpetuated between the Ministry of Pensions and National Insurance and the National Assistance Board.

In legislating for universal social security, the Labour government accepted the inevitability of insurance. In this it was simply following the best expert opinion as embodied in the Beveridge Report, just as Ramsay MacDonald, in face of a majority of the party, had accepted expert opinion in 1911: while opposition to the contributory principle had been a steady theme in Labour attitudes to welfare policy, it had become overlaid by an even deeper hostility to any sort of 'dole' to which prior entitlement had not been secured. Around the noble trees of national insurance there must inevitably be a thick undergrowth of qualification and requalification conditions and limits upon the length of time for which benefits would be paid; the Beveridge Report and the government White Paper on Social Insurance had devoted many pages to fine actuarial calculations, though in these heady days the Labour Party had sided with Beveridge in rejecting the notion of a time limit upon the payment of benefits.[28]

In the House of Commons debate on the 1946 National Insurance Bill, a group of Labour back-benchers attempted to strike from it the restrictions upon the right to claim benefit imposed in order to maintain the actuarial respectability of the scheme: they failed.[29] To administer the complicated clauses of the Bill as enacted a vast army of bureaucrats was required. The Minister of National Insurance was a former Welsh miner, a master of emotional rhetoric, James Griffiths: the Bill, he said, marked the beginning of the establishment of the 'principle of a National Minimum Standard':[30] such an objective was in keeping both with a Labour Party tradition going back to before the First World War, and with the ideas of William Beveridge. But a minimum in the Beveridge sense implied that the individual should be able privately to make additional provision for himself. Up until the recent past Labour spokesmen had favoured the idea of the nationalization of all insurance, though it was never made clear whether this implied the total supercession of private insurance by national insurance, or whether it meant that additional individual policies could be taken out with nationally-owned companies. During the election campaign, however, the close connection between Labour interests and the Friendly Societies led to promises being given that within the framework of national insurance a place would, as Beveridge had intended, be reserved for the Friendly Societies to continue to operate as 'Approved Societies'.[31] Wisely, these promises were repudiated: all 'approved societies' were abolished, and national insurance became genuinely national. But for additional individual cover private companies remained, and they were not interfered with in any way save that an effective curb was placed on 'industrial insurance' – the touting among working-class households of funeral policies, paid for at exorbitant rates. The national minimum did not materialize: the basic flat-rate benefit (from which in practice there were a number of variations) of 42s. per week soon fell far behind rising living costs; but Griffiths assured the House of Commons that it was administratively impossible to tie benefits to the cost of living, a statement which should be construed as meaning that administrators thought it undesirable that benefits should be tied to the cost of living.[32] The Government's position was that they were not going to let the cost of living rise anyway.

The object of the National Insurance Act as defined in the preamble was 'to establish an extended system of national insurance providing pecuniary benefits by way of unemployment benefit, sickness benefit, maternity benefit, retirement pension, widows' benefit, guardians' allowance and death grant'. Clause 1 required that

every person who on or after the appointed day, being over school leaving age and under pensionable age, is in Great Britain, and fulfils such conditions as may be prescribed as to residence in Great Britain, shall become insured under this Act and thereafter continue throughout his life to be so insured.

The only exceptions were married women and the self-employed earning less than £104 per annum. The insured were divided into three classes: employed persons, who would be eligible for all benefits; self-employed persons who would be eligible for everything save unemployment benefit; and non-employed persons who would not be eligible for sickness or unemployment benefit. Clause 12 of the Act stated the qualification and requalification conditions, basically that any claimant must have paid a minimum number of contributions since his entry into the scheme, and that a specified number of contributions must have been made in the year prior to the claim. It was this clause which was most heavily attacked by the Labour left, led by Sydney Silverman, who declared that it conflicted with the party's long commitment to 'work or maintenance', and Barbara Castle, with the support of Campbell Stephen of the I.L.P. and many others. Silverman's amendment calling for the deletion of Clause 12 had the support of 44 Labour and Liberal members: it was defeated by 246 Labour loyalists, while the Conservatives abstained.[33] While sickness benefit could be claimed for an indefinite period if a minimum number of 156 contributions had been paid (otherwise it would be limited to 312 days), unemployment benefit was normally limited to 180 days, which could, if the insurance record of the applicant was good, be extended up to a maximum of 492 days. The Act, Griffiths explained in defence of these limitations, was not intended to deal with the problem of long-term unemployment: however clause 62, which was to remain in force for the five years during which exceptional post-war disruptions might be expected, provided for 'extended unemployment benefit' which could be granted on the recommendation of the local insurance tribunal. This at once raised the spectre of the old Means Test: while the I.L.P. M.P.s tried to secure the deletion of the instruction that local tribunals should consider 'the particular circumstances of the applicant', Sydney Silverman was successful in having a form of words spelled out which specifically outlawed any form of Means

Test and this made an incomprehensible shambles of the entire clause. Although the main pressure for broadening the scope of the National Insurance Act came from the Labour Left, some Conservatives did take up the interests of the self-employed (mainly small shopkeepers), claiming that Labour had a bias against this class. Actually Beveridge had planned that the self-employed should wait 13 weeks before becoming eligible for sickness benefits and the Government had reduced this 'waiting period' to 24 days: Conservative and leftist pressure secured its total abolition.[34]

In its provision for old-age pensions the Act departed from the Beveridge Report in making these payable from the start at the full rate of 26s. and 42s. Common justice and humanity required nothing less than this, but the Conservatives did, with reason, raise the matter of the additional cost this would involve. The government actuary expected old-age pensions to account for half of the total expenditure on national insurance; in fact, between July 1948 and March 1950 they accounted for two-thirds of the total expenditure. On the principle established in 1940, pensions were payable to men at 65 and women at 60, though inducements were built into the scheme to persuade people to continue working beyond minimum retirement age; the principle itself was founded in social rather than biological fact, the objective being that wives, who were often a few years younger than their spouses, should be able to retire at the same time as their husbands. In the major Conservative speech on the Bill, Butler warned of the dangers of too much speed, making the very sensible point that it was unwise to approve this major piece of social security legislation before the Government had revealed the content of its health policy; more vaguely he spoke of the need for encouragement of private thrift; he was critical of the brevity of the Bill, which he argued meant that too many important matters were left for administrative decision; and he was unhappy about the extended unemployment provision, a matter he thought better left to national assistance. The dropping of the Friendly Societies caused a good deal of controversy, Clement Davies, leader of the Parliamentary Liberal Party, arguing strongly for their retention. However, the only total denunciation of the Bill came from the ultra-Conservative, Sir

Waldron Smithers, who found only one supporter in his attempt to resist the Bill's second reading.[35]

Prior to the passing of the major National Insurance Act the National Insurance (Industrial Injuries) Act had ended the old separate treatment of industrial injuries as a matter for workmen's compensation, and had brought them within the main national insurance framework. Again the enactment of this measure provided an instance of a minor left-wing inroad upon the original actuarial basis: according to the Bill as first published no benefit would be paid for the first 3 days of incapacity unless the total incapacity lasted 28 days; after a back-bench revolt at the committee stage this was reduced to 12 days. Family allowances had already been legislated for when the Labour government took office. There now remained the problem of those who, though in need, did not meet all the qualification conditions of national insurance, or whose insurance benefits were insufficient to meet their needs. In insisting upon the maintenance of the insurance principle, Beveridge had recognized the need for a separate 'national assistance'; but he had also stressed the need for a single Ministry of Social Security which would administer both national insurance and national assistance, so that recipients of the latter would not be made to feel that they were somehow in an inferior category. Partly the Labour government was a prisoner of the circumstance that no Ministry of Social Security had ever been created; it again showed itself less than bold in attacking received administrative dogma when it decided that the ill-famed Unemployment Assistance Board of 1934, which from 1940 had taken on a gentler hue as the Assistance Board, should be given a new lease of life as the National Assistance Board, which would remain an autonomous organization though its annual reports would be presented to the Minister of National Insurance. Save in cases of emergency, national assistance would only be given after a personal Needs Test; thus an element of the old much-hated Means Test remained, and indeed the 1948 principle did not differ at all from that of 1941 when the family Means Test had been replaced. The basic rates of national assistance were determined by the central government, but considerable discretionary powers rested with the board's officials in 376 area offices and 11 regional offices. It was later to be shown that many persons whose indigent circumstances were just of the sort with which national assistance was supposed to cope were deterred from applying because of the sense of stigma which still attached to this residuary of the Poor Law tradition. (The Poor Law, legally, was abolished by the 1948 National Assistance Act.)[36]

The debate on the second reading of the National Health Service Bill took place at the end of February 1946; the proposed service came into operation in July 1948. It was to be open to all, and, save in the case of certain specified extra services, it was to be totally free. It failed to be completely comprehensive in only two respects: children's health services, despite a recommendation to the contrary of the Coalition White Paper, *A National Health Service*, remained the responsibility of the Ministry of Education, and responsibility for the health of the factory worker, despite frequent Labour Party references to the need for an industrial health service, continued to fall within the scope of the Factory Acts. In presenting his Bill, the Minister of Health, Aneurin Bevan, was hampered by the irrational hostility which had seized a substantial section of the medical profession, particularly its older members, in the later stages of war, and by the concessions which his predecessor had unwisely made. The Bill, therefore, specifically permitted medical practitioners who entered the service to continue at the same time to practise privately. The question of whether remuneration within the service should be by salary (the official Labour policy) or not was left an open question. On one vexed issue, however, Bevan did show greater boldness than had previous Labour policy: cutting through all the controversies over the respective rights of local authority hospitals and voluntary hospitals, he decided to nationalize the lot. On the other hand neither Bevan nor the Government paid heed to the party's earlier judgement that a national health service could only successfully operate on the basis of wholesale local government reform. In the absence of the elective regional units it had once been Labour policy to establish, an *ad hoc* regional organization had to be created, consisting in England and Wales of fourteen regional hospital boards, each centred on the medical faculty of a university, and appointed by the Minister of Health. Management committees for the 388 hospitals within the system were to be appointed by the regional boards, but the thirty-six teaching hospitals achieved a special position of relative independence in that their boards of governors were to be appointed directly by the minister. In Scotland, as laid down in a separate National Health Service (Scotland) Act, there were to be five regional hospital boards, four based on universities, the fifth based on Inverness where there was no university, and eighty-four hospital boards of management. No separate provision was made for the administration of teaching hospitals, save that medical education committees, appointed in part by the universities, in part by the regional boards, and in part by the Secretary of State for Scotland, were constituted to advise the regional boards on teaching and research matters.[37]

While one new administrative structure was created for hospital, specialized and ancillary services, yet another was created for family practitioner services, essentially in order to mollify the demands of the medical profession. In England and Wales there were to be 138 executive councils (in all but eight cases responsible for areas coterminous with counties or county boroughs), on which local professional interests were to be strongly represented (twelve members out of twenty-five): the remaining members would be appointed by the minister and by the local authorities. In Scotland, where the county councils and large burgh councils are smaller and poorer than in England, the twenty-five executive councils generally covered areas larger than that of any existing local authority. The cumbersome tripartite structure of the new service was completed by leaving certain 'local health services' to the larger local authorities (counties and county boroughs in England, counties and large burghs in Scotland – the smaller authorities were deprived of their health functions): these services were maternity and child welfare, domiciliary midwifery, health visiting, home nursing, domestic help, vaccination and immunization, prevention of illness, care and after-care, local mental health services, ambulance transport and the provision of health centres (in Scotland the last two were the responsibility of the Secretary of State for Scotland).

Whereas the hospital and general practitioner services were to draw directly on central funds, the net cost of local authority services were to be shared equally by the authority and the central Exchequer.[38]

In introducing his Bill, Bevan's main points were: that money should not stand in the way of health; that neither the self-employed nor the dependent families of the employed were being catered for; that doctors were not being supported with specialist services; that the location of hospitals was haphazard; that the community's needs in regard to teeth, spectacles, deafness and mental illness were not being met. The Conservatives, though anxious to make the most of the doctors' fears, found it difficult to mount an effective opposition. But after a fumbling opening speech by Richard Law (son of Bonar Law) an amendment was introduced in the name of Churchill and Willink supporting the idea of a comprehensive health service, but opposing the Bill on the ground that it would prejudice the patient's right to an individual family doctor, retard the development of the hospital services by destroying local ownership, menace all charitable foundations and weaken the responsibility of local authorities.[39] In the committee stage Labour back-benchers united with Conservatives in an attempt to preserve the health functions of the smaller local authorities (illustrating the internal resistance facing a Labour government bent on any local government reform); the Conservatives attacked the authority which the executive councils would have to exclude general practitioners from areas which were already adequately provided for (such as those South Coast towns to which the rich resorted in old age), and they opposed the Government's proposed ban on the sale of practices.[40] None of these amendments was successful; none the less Bevan's biggest struggle still lay ahead. Between the passing of the Act and the 'appointed day', opposition from within the medical profession was vociferous. Bevan took the constittutionally impeccable stand that it was not open to him as representative of a sovereign parliament to negotiate with the doctors, though he was happy to listen to their representations. Professional opposition reached a peak with a plebiscite conducted by the British Medical Association in February 1948 which indicated that about 90 per cent of the medical profession were hostile to the Act. But the opposition began to crumble when Bevan stated explicitly that there would be no salaried service: a second B.M.A. plebiscite in April 1948 showed that outright opposition had dropped to 65 per cent.[41] No health service could exist without the co-operation of the doctors; equally, in the absence of any developed private insurance system, few doctors could survive on private fees alone once the old 'panel' payments had come to an end. That the bulk of the profession did in fact swing behind the scheme (88 per cent in 1950) was entirely in keeping with an approach that throughout had shown little consistency and less dignity: as long as a national health service was merely a vague idea, the profession had favoured it; when the idea was set down in bold print the profession reacted hysterically against it; when faced with the cold decision of joining or not joining, the profession joined.

It was hard for some members of the Socialist Medical Association to conceal their disappointment over what they saw as 'unnecessary and unwise compromises' forced on Bevan by 'the vested interests'. Dr Stark Murray later reckoned that Bevan made these compromises because his character 'combined strength and weaknesses as do all men'. He also suggested that Bevan, not expecting Labour to be out of office after three years, did not appreciate how permanent his concessions would prove to be.[42] Dr Somerville Hastings, whose advocacy of a national health service in the Thirties had evoked little response in Labour circles, left a fair assessment based on his experience as a member of the parliamentary committee on the Bill:

After I had advocated unsuccessfully a full-time salaried service, and felt very sore about it, I spoke to Nye [Bevan] privately and told him that many of us who were members of the S.M.A. had given some of the best years of our lives to preparing the way for his Bill. He replied that he fully realized this and agreed with us, but knew that most of the doctors would never accept a full-time service.

Hastings also took issue with Bevan over the tripartite structure of the Bill, and the undemocratic character of the administration of the hospital and of the general practitioner services:

I again appealed to Nye, who assured me that most of the doctors would refuse to serve under a popularly elected local authority. To have produced a National Health Service that takes account of the prejudices of an individualist but indispensable profession and at the sametime delivers the goods is no mean achievement.[43]

On the other side, it should be said that a committee of investigation, appointed by the Conservatives in the 1950s, concluded that since none of the divisions of the service would be prepared to subserve the others no alteration was desirable in the tripartite structure, which, the committee declared in classic British style, bears 'the imprint of the historical circumstances from which it sprang'.[44]

The new service had to function very much on old resources. On the appointed day there were in England and Wales 1,143 voluntary hospitals with 90,000 beds, and 1,545 municipal hospitals with 390,000 beds, of which 190,000 were in mental hospitals and nearly 66,000 were still administered under the Poor Law. In Scotland there were 191 voluntary hospitals with about 27,000 beds, and 226 municipal hospitals with about 37,000 beds. A special task of the local authorities in England and Wales, and of the Scottish Health Department in Scotland, was to have been the construction of health centres, which, ever since the 1920s, informed opinion had seen as central to any effective health service. In fact few health centres were built: to the general post-war shortage of material resources was added the unenthusiasm of local authorities and the hostility of G.P.s, who had no wish to see a rival to the traditional domestic practice. Again there were very good reasons for Bevan's failure to implement the full Labour Party policy, but it is arguable that he was less than dedicated in endeavouring to persuade his Cabinet colleagues of the centrality of health centres to any really effective service.

In addition to the launching of the National Health Service, Bevan, as Minister of Health, retained responsibility for housing policy in England and Wales, despite the fact that the Labour election manifesto of 1945 had promised the establishment of a separate housing ministry: that no such division of responsibility materialized was a grave error on the part of the Government, as its poor record in actual house construction demonstrated. Formally the Housing (Miscellaneous and Financial Provisions) Bill of 1946, which Bevan introduced into the Commons on 17 October 1945, made no radical departures: it was an extension and amendment of the Act of 1936, which had preserved the 1918 principle of direct State subsidies, though only for slum clearance, over-crowding and such special cases as flats in high-cost areas and general housing in agricultural and very poor urban areas. Bevan, however, declared that despite the eleventh schedule of the 1936 Act defining the 'working class' which alone was to benefit from housing legislation, he would impose no such limitation. In place of class-bound housing estates he wished to recreate, he said, in an imaginative but entirely misguided excursion into history, the villages of the seventeenth and eighteenth centuries.[45] Bevan, furthermore, was insistent that subsidized housing should not be of an inferior quality: from the former standard size of 800 square feet, local authority houses were raised to an average of 1,000 square feet, and were provided in full measure with the amenities of modern living. Fully reflecting the lack of any real innovation in the financial provisions of the Bill, the debate on the second reading, particularly the exchanges between Bevan and the principal Conservative spokesman, Captain Crookshank, was conducted with great urbanity. Houses would be built by local authorities, county and non-county, who would raise the money by borrowing. Repayment of the loan would be financed in three parts: by an annual grant per house from the central government, payable for sixty years (formerly such grants had been paid for only forty years); by a contribution which the local authority was empowered to make from its own rates; and by the rent paid by the tenant. Conservative criticism mainly concentrated on the absence of any provision for private builders, on what was claimed to be an inadequate stimulus to housing in agricultural areas (what the Conservatives really objected to was the Bill's implied attack on 'tied houses' – houses which by being part and parcel of the job put the farm labourer in a position of undue subservience to the farm owner), on the failure to make subsidies available for conversions, and on the Government's arithmetic. Bevan was assuming net rents of 12s. 6d. in London, 7s. 6d. in country districts, with 10s. as an average. Such rents would only have been attainable if the cost of houses could be kept down to £960 (in 1939 a local authority house cost £380). In 1947 the average cost of a local authority house proved to be £1,242, so rents rose to an average of around 20s. per week. A separate Scottish Act repeated most of the main features of the English one. Housing conditions in Scotland were rather worse than in England and Wales; in the interwar years relatively fewer houses over all had been built in Scotland, though a relatively large proportion of them had been State-subsidized local authority houses; in Scotland, too, there was less mobility among middle-class householders. The Scottish Act, therefore, offered higher State subsidies which varied with the size of the house. Again in introducing the Bill, the Secretary of State for Scotland, Joseph Westwood, stressed that although the phrase 'for the working classes' must be retained as laid down in the principal act of 1925, this was to mean 'all sections of the working population'. The strongest attacks on the two Housing Bills came from left-wing Labour M.P.s and from the one Communist in the House, Willie Gallacher: they called for the nationalization of all house-building, with the entire cost from the outset being met by the central government. J. Kinley, the former I.L.P. Member of Parliament declared of the English Bill:

It is as much a capitalist Bill as any yet, and my regret is that we have not, with a Socialist Government, adopted a Socialist basis and changed entirely the whole of the financial contribution.[46]

A further Act of 1949 did take socialist theory a stage further by expressly dropping the phrase about 'the working classes' from housing legislation; it also met Conservative criticisms by making subsidies available for conversions and renovations. Labour's main housing legislation was completed by two Acts which sought, by maintaining the existence of rent tribunals and rent control, to protect the interests of the tenant of the private landlord in a time of rapid inflation: the Furnished Houses (Rent Control) Act of 1946 and the Landlord and Tenant (Rent Control) Act of 1949.

In meeting the problem of converting Acts of Parliament on paper into houses in bricks and mortar, the Government could and did point, as in other areas of social policy, to the grave material shortages of the time. In only one year were more than 200,000 houses built. Side by side with the high quality housing which Bevan insisted on, the Government also put into the fields the temporary prefabricated housing which had been planned for at the close of the war: altogether between 1945 and 1950 157,000 of these 'prefabs' were constructed; in the same period 806,000 permanent homes and 333,000 conversions were completed.

In many ways the wider environmental planning of the period was more ambitious and more successful. The Town and Country Planning Act of 1947, in keeping with a trend shown by most other legislation of the period, removed all planning functions from the small local authorities, and placed them firmly in the hands of the large ones, creating an obligation (instead of, as formerly, a discretionary power) to survey their areas and present plans relating not just to bombed areas and areas of 'obsolete development', but to the areas as a whole; to further their comprehensive planning, the authorities were given greatly extended powers of compulsory purchase, and – another complete novelty – they were to be assisted by grants from the central government. Among the powers now possessed by the planning authorities, which were to have quite an important effect in mitigating the worst uglinesses of modern civilization, were control of advertisements and power to preserve historic buildings. The most controversial innovation was actually an implementation of one of the conclusions of the wartime Uthwatt Report: through the medium of a central land board the State would levy a development charge on any increase in land values brought about by development or projected development. Legislative provision for another great vision of the war period was made in the new Towns Act of 1946, which established a number of development corporations responsible for building, on publicly-owned land, new towns near London, in the North of England and in Scotland. Again a programme initiated by the Labour government fell to be developed by the Conservatives. In relieving population pressure in slum areas, raising the quality of living, and diversifying industry, it was highly successful: whether any government could successfully have created the classless communities Labour idealists envisioned is a very moot point. In 1949, years behind individualist America, Britain, through the National Park and Access to the Countryside Act, made a first attempt to reverse the industrial spoliation of two centuries and set aside areas for national recreation.

Where Labour seemed to make no effort at all to strive towards a classless objective was in education, the area most central to the whole problem of class distinctions. To some extent its hands were tied by the fact that a major Education Act had just been put on the statute book, so that it was scarcely feasible to bring in still another one. Yet if ever there was a good psychological moment for dealing with the snobbism built into the system, it was in the aftermath of the 1945 election victory. The major public schools were then at low ebb, and certainly expected little mercy at the hands of a Labour government. In fact the Government, while scrupulous in ensuring that the 1944 Act did become a reality (which certainly puts it ahead of its predecessors of 1918), seemed content to accept the principle of 'variety' embodied in that Act, and to allow the local authorities to institute the eleven-plus exam implicit (though not actually mentioned) in the Act. More adventurous policies were followed in regard to university education, with a wider and more positive role being allocated to the University Grants Committee, whose terms of reference as amplified in July 1946 were:

to inquire into the financial needs of University education in Great Britain; to advise the Government as to the application of any grants made by Parliament towards meeting them; to collect, examine and make available information on matters relating to University education at home and abroad, and to assist, in consultation with the Universities and other bodies concerned, the preparation and execution of such plans for the development of the Universities as may from time to time be required in order to ensure that they are fully adequate to national needs.[47]

If a Labour government, some of whose members were products

of public schools, and more of whose members were happy to send their sons to public schools, failed to meet the challenge of educational reform, it did (perhaps for the same reasons) make the effort to build walls against not only poverty and ill-health, but also against philistinism. The wartime CEMA, renamed the Arts Council, was continued as the Government's official agent for support of the arts. The Local Government Act of 1948 empowered local authorities to raise a penny rate purely for the support of the arts. Not many did, but one important theatrical company at least was to profit thereby, the Bristol Old Vic: the famous Bristol Theatre Royal had been rescued from threatened extinction by local enthusiasts at the height of the wartime reconstruction period in 1943, and in 1946 the company was created as an arm of the London Old Vic. Other minor items in this period of hectic legislative activity, easily forgotten, are worth mentioning as showing the breadth of vision, whatever the blindspots, of this government: the Children's Act of 1948, which firmly defined the responsibilities of local authorities towards homeless children: the Employment and Training Act of 1948, creating the first comprehensive and efficient youth employment service throughout the country; the Criminal Justice Act of 1948, abolishing corporal punishment; and the Legal Aid and Advice Act of 1949, making possible legal aid to those too poor to pay for it.

3. THE PEOPLE INSIDE

As the major items of Welfare State legislation did not take effect till 1948, life under the Labour government was in large measure determined by wartime rather than post-war legislative developments. By 1950, however, some of the combined effects were beginning to show. In the last of his three social surveys of York, Seebohm Rowntree discovered that post-war children in all sections of the community were taller and heavier than in 1936.[48] In 1950 infant mortality fell below 30 per 1,000 for the first time in British history, though rates continued to be higher among low-income than among high-income groups. Even the birthrate began to show an upward movement, to the ultimate confusion of many careful calculations of future demand for school places, etc. World-wide food shortages, the ending of Lend-Lease and post-war economic tribulations meant that in some respects food supplies were even more restricted than they had been during the war. Yet even in the crisis year of 1947, when complaints were loudest, the ration was in most respects much better than the average pre-war diet: though total calories declined from 3,000 to 2,880 per day fats falling from 130 to 106 grams per day, protein and vitamin content substantially increased.[49] The fiscal decisions dictated by the needs of war had involved a considerable redistribution of income. The Labour government, it is often said, simply maintained the momentum of the redistribution: this is true, but it was still something of a break with the past to continue in peace the tax levels of war. Between 1938 and 1949 there was a fourfold increase in taxation: in 1938 7,000 persons had had net incomes of over £6,000 per annum: in 1947–48 there were only 70 such incomes. Even within the limits imposed by scarcities and controls, the redistribution of income, the introduction of welfare schemes and the various wartime dislocations produced discernible changes in spending patterns, so that by 1950 the Board of Trade had concluded that a complete reappraisal of the basis upon which it assessed the 'cost of living' was overdue.[50]

Vital statistics looked good: so also did certain events on the cultural front. By taking over the Henry Wood Promenade Concerts the B.B.C. ensured not only their continuance, but their extension to a wider public than ever before. By setting up (in 1946) a new Third Programme the corporation ensured that there would be a definite and guaranteed place in British broadcasting for serious discussion and serious music. After the Sadler's Wells production of *Peter Grimes*, Benjamin Britten went on from strength to strength, while in ballet Margot Fonteyn established a world reputation. In 1947 the Van Gogh exhibition attracted 12,000 visitors per day to the Tate Gallery. Art sales (as in 1914–18) had done well during the war, and continued to boom. English painting persevered with its emancipation from continental modes, while at the same time remaining apart from the Abstract Expressionist movement of contemporary America. The Glyndebourne Festival

Opera (founded in 1934 by John Christie) had gone into suspension because of the war: however, discussions between the opera's general manager, Rudolf Bing, Harvey Wood, director of the British Council in Scotland and Sir John Falconer, Lord Provost of Edinburgh, resulted in plans for the launching in 1947 of the most ambitious of the post-war ventures, the Edinburgh International Festival of Music and Drama.

But for the nation as a whole these were like coloured lights strung high across the muddy waters of ordinary life and perceived but dimly through an enveloping mist of scarcities and austerity. Rationing for main food items lasted for the whole period under review; clothes rationing was only relaxed towards the very end; wartime 'utility' schemes were maintained to the discouragement of the production of high-quality durable goods. In neither world war, though the whole gamut of adulteration was run in 1918, had it proved necessary to institute bread rationing; but in 1946 the Minister of Food John Strachey introduced this ultimate symbol of belt-tightening. The big freeze-up associated with the fuel policies of Emmanuel Shinwell brought forth the Tory witticism, 'Shiver with Shinwell and Starve with Strachey.' Already-modest rations had to be further reduced in the aftermath of the convertibility crisis of 1947, and there was at no time great public enthusiasm for the various delicacies offered by the Ministry of Food such as whale meat, and the mysterious but aptly-named canned fish, snoek. Inevitably a flourishing black market came into being: seen through the eyes of the popular anti-Labour Press there was little to choose between the 'spivs' and their ministerial adversaries the 'snoopers'. The worst deprivations of all for sizeable sections of the community resulted from the Government's inability to build, or even to seem likely to build, desperately needed houses.

Refuge from austerity, from constant exhortations to increase productivity and, often, from grim conditions of overcrowding, was sought by the majority of British people not at Promenade Concerts or the Edinburgh Festival, but in the cinema, which reached a peak of 1,635 million attendances in 1946; to the inestimable gain of the British cinema industry, if not necessarily to the gratification of war-weary audiences, austerity imposed severe restrictions upon Hollywood importations. Central Office of Information inquiries conducted in March and October 1946 revealed that 32 per cent of the adult civilian population went to the cinema at least once a week, that 13 per cent went more than once, and that only 24 per cent did not go at all. Among children of school age 65 per cent went to the cinema once a week or more, and only 5 per cent did not go at all. On balance women were more frequent attenders than men, and, as was to be expected, young people went more often than old people. While the cinema attracted its audience from all economic groups, the higher-paid sections of the working class went more frequently than others. Relatively high proportions of factory workers and of clerical and distributive workers (about 40 per cent) went to the cinema once a week or more, whereas a high proportion of professional and managerial workers went less frequently, and about half of retired or unoccupied persons did not go at all. Housewives, the survey reported, went with 'average frequency'. Working-class children were more frequent attenders than middle- and upper-class children. 'Compared with newspapers,' the survey concluded,

the cinema as a medium of publicity is likely to reach relatively high proportions of young people, particularly those aged under twenty, and of women and housewives and the more prosperous sections of the working class.[51]

None the less the British were undoubtedly a nation of newspaper readers. Between 1937 and 1947 the total circulation of national and provincial daily newspapers increased by 50 per cent; by 1948 three people out of four were reading one national morning newspaper and one in four were reading at least two. The desire, and indeed need, to read, stimulated by the war, had clearly been maintained. But again satisfactions were only partial: though circulations had increased, the size of newspapers had been drastically curtailed since the beginning of the war, and in 1948 total consumption of newsprint, 18 pounds per head, was less than a third of what it had been in pre-war days. In the reading of books, fostered by the blackout and by the tedium of army life (and, incidentally, a good measure of the intellectual and imaginative qualities of a nation), Britain, as an international Gallup Poll conducted in 1950 revealed, stood well in advance of any other country in the world: 55 per cent of the British sample claimed at the time of the poll to be reading a book, against 43 per cent in Norway, 40 per cent in Canada, 35 per cent in Australia, 33 per cent in Sweden, and 21 per cent in the United States.[52] Books, naturally, were still being published in their war-economy format.

There is, in the period 1945-50, nothing at all akin to the cynical betrayal of promises and bitter disillusionment that followed upon the First World War. On many of the counts that matter, the British had good reason to be a relatively contented people. Possibly there was too much contentment: in the striking phrase of Ernest Bevin – who had more right to pronounce such judgements than most – the British suffered from a 'poverty of desire'. Relative contentment with things as they were is at any rate suggested by the continued rise in the popular vote accruing to the Labour Party in the General Elections of 1950 and 1951. Even the middle classes, over whose alleged sufferings so much crocodile ink was lavished, were in fact the ones who profited most from the extension upwards of the social services: above all it was middle-class children who benefited from the new educational opportunities. However there were undoubtedly some hard-felt grievances, particularly in the upper sections of the middle classes and in the upper classes. High taxation was no more acceptable because it had been in existence since the beginning of the war. In the case of members of the higher professions who had once been able to set aside enough from their normal earnings to secure a separate investment income which would enable them either to live a life of leisure or go into public life, taxation enforced a real change of living habits, though it can be noted that David Maxwell Fyfe continued an active career as a leading Opposition politician while earning an average of £25,000 per annum as a barrister. The other blow to upper-class ease came from the culmination of a process initiated in the First World War but delayed by the depression, the flight from domestic service into more remunerative and more dignified occupations.[53]

There were therefore many and growing centres of discontent with public policies in the period after 1945. This did not so much lead to an effective consolidated opposition to the Government as to an uneasiness over the values which in 1945 members of the Labour Party had taken for granted: the uneasiness affected ministers as much as anyone else. In preaching egalitarianism, without taking even the most obvious steps to develop egalitarianism, the Government in fact provoked and nurtured a form of snobbism. This was particularly apparent in the columns of the *Daily Express*. It was also seen more curiously in the number of grammar schools which switched from Association Football, held, erroneously (it was played at Eton and Winchester), to have exclusively proletarian connotations, to Rugby football, the game of the aspiring middle classes.[54] As the sphere of public education widened slightly there was a rush among those who could possibly afford it towards the fee-paying schools. No gratitude, naturally, was felt to the Government for being so free with escape routes from Utopia. A further irritant was the great American society, whose diffuse image of plentiful consumer goods, good living, and the virtues of individualism could no longer be ignored when, with the beginning of the Cold War, 30,000 American airmen, most of whom brought their own way of life with them, were based in Britain. A new twist, therefore, was given to the historic, and in some respects antiquated, collectivist versus individualist controversy, especially as the proponents of the latter gathered encouragement from the more spectacular failures of the Labour government. Thomas Wilson, an Oxford economist, entered cautiously upon what proved to be a powerful and persuasive advocacy of private capitalism as the best defence of individual liberties:

A book in defence of capitalism by a teacher of economics will be deemed eccentric by those who believe that all economists are Socialists nowadays.[55]

Professor John Jewkes of Manchester University spoke more brusquely of *Ordeal by Planning*. Churchill had raised no more than a delicious shiver with his pre-election warning that a Labour government would have to employ 'some form of Gestapo'; the thunderous success of George Orwell's black political satire of totalitarianism, *1984*, written in 1948, suggested that the shiver had become a chronic ague. In 1950 a committee on broadcasting showed itself less sure of the virtues of a State monopoly than had its counterpart a quarter of a century previously, though there was only one small voice, that of Mr Selwyn Lloyd, in favour of commercial television.[56] The socialist intellectual's avowed commitment to the cultural aspects of Welfare State policies could be indicted as leading to no more than a pompous and patronizing B.C.C., with a Third Programme which, though magnificent in content, was openly presented as designed only to appeal to a minority audience. In its own hesitations over the nationalization of steel, and over the scope of the economic surveys, the Labour Party showed the extent to which it was succumbing to doubts as to the exact role which should be given to the State in a modern society.

But whatever the hesitations of Labour policy-makers, whatever the discontents stirring in various sections of the population, the Conservatives could have no hope of profiting from them unless they came to terms with the undoubted successes of Labour policy – such as the National Health Service, which by 1950 was being used by 95 per cent of the population. In 1945 the Conservatives had appeared as the party which had been lukewarm on the Beveridge Report, was likely to yield to the importunities of the medical profession, and was more eager to stress the virtues of private enterprise than the need for constructive social reform. In November 1945 Churchill appointed Butler to the headship of a revived Research Department and to the chairmanship of the party's Committee on Policy and Political Education. Working under him in the Research Department Butler had some of the brightest of the new generation of Conservatives, including Reginald Maudling, Iain Macleod and Enoch Powell. None the less for two years the Conservatives remained in a state of defensive confusion: cries for a more positive policy at the 1946 Party Conference led to the appointment of the Industrial Policy Committee, consisting of Butler, Macmillan, Oliver Stanley, Oliver Lyttelton and Maxwell Fyfe from the Shadow Cabinet, and David Eccles,

Heathcoat Amory, Sir Peter Bennett and J. R. H. Hutchison from the back benches, with David Clarke as secretary. The report, subsequently published as the Conservative *Industrial Charter*, was completed within a year and, with some show of reluctance in certain quarters, given the support of the Party Conference. Through adoption of the *Industrial Charter* the Conservative Party was in effect making its peace with the major part of both the Welfare State and the managed economy, accepting above all the levels of taxation implied in the former. In part this was a reflection of the constant Conservative will to power, in part it was a re-assertion of a Conservative tradition of Tory democracy, in part it represented a Conservative inheritance of that part of upper-class liberalism which had not fallen to the Labour Party. In calling upon the Party Conference to endorse the new programme Eden made a noble statement of political principle:

We are not a Party of unbridled, brutal capitalism, and never have been. Although we believe in personal responsibility and personal initiative in business, we are not the political children of the *laissez-faire* school. We opposed them decade after decade.

Where did the Tories stand when the greed and squalor of the industrial revolution were darkening the land? I am content with Keir Hardie's testimony: 'As a matter of hard dry fact, from which there can be no getting away, there is more labour legislation standing to the credit account of the Conservative Party on the statute-book than there is to that of their opponents.'[57]

As important in broadening the appeal of the Conservative Party were certain changes made in party organization, above all the abolition of the old restrictive tradition whereby Conservative candidates were expected to finance their own election campaigns. As older reform Conservatives merged into the leadership, younger ones, free of the ghosts of the Thirties, or indeed of 1945, rose to take their places: first came the 'One Nation' group of 1950, followed by the still younger Bow Group, both centres of radical Conservative opinion.[58]

By removing the fear that if returned to power they would dismantle the constructive legislation of the Labour government the Conservatives put themselves in a strong position to canalize the various discontents generated by Labour rule. Politics, in the narrowest sense, were again of importance. A skilful Labour leadership would retain the initiative by exploiting the better side of Labour's record. Even a middling Labour leadership might survive. As it turned out a middling Labour leadership was exposed by yet another war – the limited conflict waged in Korea. Having carried through their own reforms, the Conservatives were able to seize their opportunity. Slowly they gave rein to the resentments which had built up under Labour rule, and which were to colour much of British life in the later Fifties.

NOTES TO CHAPTER SEVEN

1. Butler, *Electoral System in Britain*, p. 184.
2. *Ibid.*, p. 177. In general see McCallum and Readman, *British General Election of 1945*.
3. R. Bonham, *The Middle Class Vote*, 1954, p. 163.
4. W. L. Guttsman, *British Political Élite*, pp. 241 ff.
5. C. R. Attlee, 'Civil Servants, Ministers, Parliament and the Public' in W. A. Robson (ed.), *The Civil Service in Britain and France*, 1956.
6. Lord Kilmuir, *Political Adventure*, p. 138.
7. W. S. Churchill, *The Sinews of Peace* (Post-war Speeches), 1948, p. 60.
8. Federation of British Industries, *Statement of Policy*, 20 February 1946.
9. Federation of British Industries, *30th Annual Report, 1946, 31st Annual Report, 1947, 32nd Annual Report, 1948*, p. 14.
10. P.P., 1958–59, XVII, Cmnd. 827 ('Radcliffe Report') pp. 8–18. A. J. Youngson, *The British Economy Since 1920*, 1960, pp. 163–72. *Economist*, 8 December, 1945.
11. A. A. Rogow, *The Labour Government and British Industry 1945–1951*, 1955, pp. 167 ff., 186 ff.
12. *House of Commons Debates*, 28 February 1946.
13. P. Gordon Walker, 'On Being a Cabinet Minister', *Encounter*, April 1956.
14. Rogow, pp. 13–25.
15. Harrod, *British Economy*, p. 25.
16. *Economic Survey for 1947*, P.P., 1946–47, XIX, Cmd. 7046, p. 1.
17. Cp. Youngson, p. 264.
18. P.P., 1946–47, XIX, Cmd. 7018, p. 7.
19. P.P., 1947–48, XXII, Cmd. 7321, p. 2.
20. *Ibid.*, p. 3.
21. Pollard, *Development of the British Economy*, p. 381.
22. *M.R.C. Report, 1945–1948*, P.P., 1948–49, XVIII, Cmd. 7846, p. 13.
23. See J. D. Bernal, *Britain's Part in the New Scientific Industrial Revolution*, 1964.

24. Harrod, *British Economy*, p. 25.

25. See A. Briggs, 'The Welfare State in European Perspective', *Archives Européennes de Sociologie*, vol. II, no. 2, 1961, C. L. Mowat, 'The Approach to the Welfare State in Great Britain', *American Historical Review*, vol. 58, 1953, D. Wedderburn, 'Facts and Theories of the Welfare State', *Socialist Register*, 1965.

26. L. Krieger, 'The Idea of the Welfare State in Europe and the United States', *Journal of the History of Ideas*, XXIV, 1963, p. 556.

27. R. Titmuss, *The Irresponsible Society*, 1960.

28. Labour Party, *Preliminary Observations on the Government White Papers on Social Insurance, Workman's Compensation and National Health Service*, 1944.

29. *House of Commons Debates*, 22 May 1946.

30. *Ibid.*, 6 February 1946.

31. R. Brady, *Crisis in Britain*, 1950, p. 329.

32. *House of Commons Debates*, 6 February 1946.

33. *Ibid.*, vol. 419, cols. 619–70.

34. *Ibid.*, vol. 423, cols. 350 ff.

35. *Ibid.*, vol. 418, cols. 1733–842, 1894–2004; vol. 419, cols. 44 ff., 105.

36. For a good survey see M. P. Hall, *Social Services of Modern Britain*, pp. 19–48.

37. P.P., 1955–56, XX, Cmd. 9663, pp. 51 ff.

38. *Ibid.*

39. *House of Commons Debates*, vol. 422, cols. 43 ff.

40. *Ibid.*, vol. 425, cols. 1734–74, 1917, 1947–70.

41. Eckstein, *English National Health Service*, pp. 161–2.

42. Socialist Medical Association, *Aneurin Bevan: An Appreciation of His Services to the Health of the People*, 1961, p. 8.

43. *Ibid.*, p. 1.

44. Cmd. 9663, pp. 62–63.

45. *House of Commons Debates*, 17 October 1945.

46. *Ibid.*

47. *Ibid.*, 30 July 1946.

48. B. S. Rowntree and J. Lavers, *Poverty and the Welfare State*, 1951, p. 10.

49. J. Burnett, *Plenty and Want*, p. 269.

50. *Interim Report of Cost of Living Advisory Committee*, P.P., 1950–51, XI, Cmd. 8328, p. 3.

51. C.O.I., *The Cinema and the Public*, 1946.

52. British Institute of Public Opinion, *The Reading Public*, 1950.

53. R. Harrod, *British Economy*, pp. 63–64. Kilmuir, *Political Adventure*, p. 149.

54. M. Marples, *A History of Football*, 1954, p. 225.

55. T. Wilson, *Modern Capitalism and Economic Progress*, 1950, p. v.

56. P.P., 1950–51, IX, Cmd. 8116, esp. pp. 79–84, 201–10.

57. Conservative Party, *Report of Annual Conference 1947*, pp. 35–54, *Industrial Charter*, 1947.

58. Cp. Conservative Political Centre, *One Nation*, 1950. In general see J. D. Hoffman, *The Conservative Party in Opposition*, 1964, and S. H. Beer, *Modern British Politics*, 1965, pp. 302–17.

CHAPTER EIGHT
Britain in Midstream, 1950-55

1. SOCIETY AND A LIMITED WAR

In a fifty-year survey of British history such as this it is not possible to study every phase and every topic in the detail that a complete understanding of the many facets of British social behaviour would require: the fire of detailed research has been mainly directed upon the times of stress during the two total wars; but it could be argued that for an understanding of the British, based on a limited period of time studied in intense detail, there could be no more rewarding period than the first half of the middle decade of the twentieth century. In two exciting elections in 1950 and 1951 the Labour Party continued to increase its total popular vote, yet, by virtue of winning more seats in the latter election, the Conservatives returned, for the first time since 1940, to sole control of the reins of office; in a less exciting election in 1955 the Conservatives increased their majority and, for the first time since 1935, won a clear majority of the popular poll. With an overall majority of only 9 the fourth Labour government, in its nineteen months of office, seemed to lose all the heroic self-confidence of 1945 and showed instead that same propensity for taking nervous glances over its shoulder which had characterized the first two Labour governments. Ruling with a majority of 20, the Conservatives for four years gave a text-book demonstration of Tory adaptability, accepting and absorbing the major changes wrought by its predecessors. Much of the greyness of life, much of the traditional 'poverty of desire', perforce, continued. On the other hand in 1950 the prospect looked brighter than it had at any time since 1945, and brighter in a completely different sense: 'reconstruction' was over, peace could be enjoyed. It was in this spirit that the Labour government planned a Festival of Britain to be held on the centenary of the Great Exhibition of 1851. Already Mr Harold Wilson had played a successful Guy Fawkes to controls which had been in force for nearly ten years.

Then, as the prospect brightened, a single cloud plunged it into gloom again. Towards the end of June conflict broke out between North Korea, which was in the Russian and Chinese sphere of influence, and South Korea, which was in the American. On the night of Sunday 25 June, the Security Council of the United Nations (Russia not being present at the time) passed a resolution condemning North Korea for aggression against South Korea and calling upon members to support the United States, whose troops were already involved. On Wednesday 28 June, Attlee announced to the House of Commons that Britain would fulfil the obligation thus incurred under the charter of the United Nations, by taking an active part in the war. In the two major wars of the twentieth century Britain had entered early and was joined late by the United States: now, in what was obviously the new fashion of a new age, Britain followed in behind the United States. In October, General McArthur took the United Nations forces north of the 38th parallel (dividing North and South Korea), which had the immediate effect of bringing Communist China into the war. After a series of Chinese successes, President Truman on 30 September made a Press statement which seemed to imply that the atom bomb might be used. A few days later, after an anxious debate in the House of Commons, Attlee flew to Washington on what may have been the most important mission ever undertaken by a British Prime Minister: the atom bomb was not used. American casualties, 60,000 after one year, continued to mount. For Britain, whatever reservations there might be about McArthur as military leader (he was dismissed in April 1951) and President Syngman Rhee as a ruler of South Korea, it became increasingly difficult to pull out: to do so would be to rupture relations with America.[1]

A small far-off war, the Korean conflict produced some of the negative effects on British society associated with total war: it had few of the positive effects. On the profit and loss account, it was a dead loss to Britain. Vast new arms programmes were proposed in August 1950 and revised upwards in January 1951, when an expenditure of £4,700 million over three years was announced, with an immediate rise from £830 million in 1950–51 to £1,300 million in 1951–52. Just when industry seemed to be securing the necessary peacetime export targets, resources had to be diverted from the battle of the dollar gap to battle in Korea. Britain's import bill soared, and once again there was a sterling crisis, with a total gold and dollar loss between July and December 1951 of $1,600 million. A minor compensation was that the Treasury, caught on the hop once again, was forced to improve its methods of gathering economic information. In other respects the challenge of this little war brought dissolution rather than transformation: in particular all the weaknesses of Labour in office were brought to the surface. The Left, whose uneasiness over Bevin's foreign policy had to some extent been submerged in enthusiasm for the whirl of domestic social policy, became restive over the rather muted programme offered for the 1950 General Election, especially since there was a good deal of talk about the need to impose a ceiling on the mounting cost of the health service. The Korean War brought a 'guns versus butter' controversy into sharp focus. At the same time Labour's lack of an able second generation of political leadership was exposed; though it was rather bad luck that in the space of a few months (October 1950 to March 1951) Cripps, Bevin and Attlee should be stricken by illness, the first two fatally. Hugh Gaitskell, a 44-year-old former public school boy and Oxford economist of belligerent honesty, but, arguably, little political sagacity, became Chancellor of the Exchequer; Morrison became Foreign Secretary, and, shortly after, took on Attlee's role as chairman of Cabinet meetings: his talents were not well suited to the foreign secretary-ship (the Government's reaction to the Persian nationalization of the Anglo-Iranian Oil Company was neither noble nor strong), and neither he nor anyone else could rival Attlee's genius for chairman-ship. It fell to Gaitskell to make the formal announcement in favour of 'guns' – represented in a miserable economy of £13 million to be secured through charges on spectacles and dentures. Aneurin Bevan, recently shifted to the Ministry of Labour, had already publicly announced his hostility to any infringement of the principle of a free health service, but his speech of resignation included both the argument that 'the defence programme must always be consistent with the maintenance of the standard of life of the British people and the maintenance of the social services' and the severely practical point that the programme envisaged was actually beyond possibility of fulfilment and would create 'irreparable damage to the economy'.[2] Harold Wilson, President of the Board of Trade, and John Freeman, Parliamentary Secretary to the Ministry of Supply, also resigned, Wilson speaking of a 'rearmament programme which I do not believe to be physically practicable with the raw materials available to us'. Wilson remarked that Gaitskell's budget involved

the first cutting-in to our social services, which we have built up over these past years, and which represent a system in which all of us rightly take great pride. It is a minor cut I agree, but I cannot believe it to be necessary.[3]

Faced with so many difficulties, external and internal, the Labour government seemed to lose all will to go on governing. Harold Wilson, fourteen years later, was to show that by making events and monopolizing the headlines a government could govern successfully despite a minuscule majority – and less evidence of popular support than Labour had in 1950 – though he had, it is true, resources of televisual communication that were denied to Attlee. Attlee in any event, having proved himself an effective Prime Minister in a traditional British mould, was showing all the old hyper-respect for 'the rights of democracy', and even perhaps something of the notion that now it was time to give the other fellow a chance. Although conditions were undoubtedly uncomfortable for government supporters there was no utterly compelling reason for Attlee's decision to ask for a dissolution and an election in October 1951. As the country's natural rulers, the Conservatives, back in office after this election, were less inhibited by their minority position in the country and their parliamentary majority of only 20 than Labour would have been, but they too proceeded with extreme caution. The new Prime Minister, Winston Churchill, scion of the great Marlborough family, was 77; of his entire ministry of 65, only 8 had not attended public school.[4] However, if this was a ministry of the old ruling *élite*, some of its members appeared as strong upholders of the upper-class reform tradition: R. A. Butler in particular, the new Chancellor of the Exchequer, carried with him the aura both of the Education Act of 1944 and of the recent reorientation of Conservative social policies. Both the Foreign Secretary, Anthony Eden, and the Minister of Housing and Local Government, Harold Macmillan, trailed from the Thirties a reputation for opposition to the unhappy Conservative policies of these days. One feature which marked off the Conservative Party all through the Fifties both from Labour and from its own counterpart in the Thirties was its steady appeal to the brighter well-educated young men, an appeal which Labour had possessed in full measure in the later stages of the war but had lost as it became a somewhat stodgy governing party. Changes in voting preferences among the electorate are so slight that they are only of importance over an extended period: of much more immediate importance is the kind of people who are being recruited into the political *élite* and the political allegiance which they choose within that *élite*. Behind the Conservative leadership were the able men who had organized the radical 'One Nation' group, Enoch Powell, Iain Macleod and Edward Heath, and behind them the still younger men who were shortly to organize the Bow Group.

The Korean War helped to destroy the Labour government and it diverted scarce resources away from much-needed social investment. There was no compensating constructive effect resulting from the military participation mode coming into play. Indeed, the whole programme of peacetime National Service was socially disruptive in its effects on youths from lower-class homes, who as a matter of course left school at the age of 15. An attempt by the Ministry of Labour and National Service to argue to the contrary was demolished by two independent surveys, one carried out by the King George's Jubilee Trust, the other by the Economic Research Council. The former concluded that the gap between school leaving and National Service

has profoundly affected the outlook of the boy who leaves school at 15 years of age. ... For him it is more than a breakaway from education; it cuts his life into two almost unrelated parts – before and after National

Service; it creates an artificial interlude in which the high hurdle still ahead of him obscures the need to plan and work for his future. Often the years of the gap are a time of 'wait and see', a time in which irresponsibility can become a fixed habit of mind, a time even of deterioration, in which some boys forget so much of what they knew when they left school that those who receive them into National Service are discomfited to find that some of these new recruits are barely literate.

During the gap, the report also pointed out:

Many of these boys tend to take the most highly paid temporary jobs in order to ensure the acquisition of those pleasures which are likely to be unobtainable or, at any rate, hard to come by as soon as the services claim them. It is the anticipation of unaccustomed discipline and a comparative shortage of money which are factors in determining this policy of 'eat, drink and be merry'. This is not an unnatural attitude, since many boys have no reason to suppose that they will not have changed their minds about the nature of the career for which they might think they are best suited by the time they are demobilized.[5]

The Korean War ended in 1953. National Service continued.

Conservative policy was well described in the neat word coined by the *Economist*, 'Butskellism', which implied a continuity of economic policy between two Chancellors of the Exchequer, Gaitskell and Butler. It was not very difficult to halt the nationalization of iron and steel (over which the Labour leadership had been by no means unanimous) and sell the industry back to the private owners: the Conservatives recognized the need for 'an adequate measure of public supervision' and set up the Iron and Steel Board to assert this. Large parts of the road transport industry were returned to private ownership – a step which would have seemed more unfortunate if the previous government had shown more signs of using nationalization as the basis for a unified transport policy rather than as an end in itself. While the Korean War, and its attendant economic dislocations, continued, controls were retained and, in some cases, strengthened. On the other hand a favourable swing in the terms of trade, downwards for the primary products Britain imported, upwards for the manufactured goods she exported, brought the international account into balance in 1953, for the first time since the war, and allowed for the steady abolition of rationing, fully achieved a year later.

2. SOCIAL POLICY IN A MIXED ECONOMY

The term 'Butskellism' could be applied to social as well as economic policy. Butler had been a leader in securing Conservative acceptance for the financial commitments of the Welfare State, Gaitskell had been the Labour minister responsible for introducing charges into the National Health Service. The period 1950-55 is the first in which the Welfare State can be examined in working order, with the facts, as distinct from the woolly optimism of socialists and the prejudiced denunciations of Conservatives, being fully presented in three important official studies: the *Government Actuary's First Quinquennial Review of the Working of the 1946 National Insurance Act, The Report of the Committee on the Economic and Financial Problems of the Provision for Old Age,* and the Guillebaud Committee's *Inquiry into the Cost of the National Health Service.*[6]

As matters stood at the beginning of the Fifties the national insurance scheme was running up larger balances than expected, largely because the original actuarial calculations had been made on the basis of an $8\frac{1}{2}$ per cent unemployment rate: full employment meant that while disbursements were low, contribution income from the employed class was high. Furthermore, although there were more retirement pensioners than originally estimated, claims for sickness benefit were below expectation by 15 to 20 per cent. Increases in contribution rates of 2d. a week for both employed persons and their employers, and of 4d. a week for self-employed persons, came into effect automatically under the terms of the 1946 Act in October 1951. At the same time the Labour government, without any further increase, in a modest attempt to mitigate some of the effects of a rising cost of living, raised the pensions of those *over* 70 (65 for women) from 26s. to 30s.; as a transitional measure the increase was granted to younger pensioners who had reached 65 (60 for women) before 1 October 1951. The actuarial assumption behind the scheme was now of a 4 per cent unemployment rate and a 3 per cent interest rate. A further Act of 1952 (after the Conservatives came to power) increased rates of benefit and restored the principle of a common basic weekly rate for pensions and other benefits: both contributions and Exchequer supplements were increased. The National Insurance Act of 1953, without increasing contributions, reorganized and slightly enlarged the system of maternity benefits, and an Act of 1954 (effective in 1955) increased benefits all round.[7]

At 31 December 1953 the estimated number of people over minimum pensionable age was 6,934,000. Of these 4,310,000, or about two-thirds, were receiving national insurance retirement pensions. The full rate was now 32s. 6d. for a single person and 54s. for a married couple, payable in respect of an average of at least fifty contributions a year, lower rates being paid for lower averages; if the average was below thirteen contributions no pension would be paid. Yet the insurance principle of a claim established as of right was violated by an earnings rule applied to the first five years of retirement: 1s. was deducted for every shilling earned over 40s. a week, so that someone earning 72s. 6d. a week received no pension, whatever his insurance standing. There were still 345,000 recipients of the old non-contributory old-age pension, administered by the National Assistance Board, subject to a Means Test, and worth only, at the maximum, 26s. for a single person, 42s. for a couple. Since the National Assistance Board recognized a minimum subsistence income of 35s. for a single person or 59s. for a couple, exclusive of rent, it is scarcely surprising that a large number of pensioners of both types had to apply to the board for additional assistance. Altogether national assistance payments were being made to about 1,800,000 people, of whom all but around 400,000 were over the age of retirement; in addition assistance was being given to those who could not afford the new health service charges. Roughly 300,000 claims for assistance were rejected each year, but doubtless a proportion of the 400,000 who did pass the scrutiny of the national assistance officer were work-shy and ne'er-do-well; some were the victims of particular misfortunes; many were victims of the peculiarities and inadequacies

of the national insurance structure. Of the 80,000 drawing unemployment insurance in 1954, 30,000 also required national
assistance to supplement their benefits.[8] None of these figures in
themselves provide a clear statement of the extent of continuing
poverty in Britain at mid-century, but there was one other feature
of the welfare edifice left by the Labour government which created
a good deal of avoidable hardship; this was the Wage Stop
principle introduced by the National Assistance Board, which
insisted that no one could receive more in national assistance than
he normally received in full employment, a Smilesian regulation
which meant that if a man normally received a wage below the
board's own definition of a subsistence he must be kept there, lest
he be tempted to give up work altogether. It does seem that, within the limitations placed upon them, the local offices of the
National Assistance Board made a genuine attempt to carry through
their tasks in a humane and efficient fashion: administrative expenses took up just under 5 per cent of the board's annual expenditure. None the less the cumbersomeness of a double scheme
of insurance and assistance is brought out by the board's own
lament over the difficulties involved in implementing the increase
in national assistance levels to 37s. 6d. and 63s. operative from 2
February 1955, when increases in national insurance benefits were
also shortly due to take effect:

Most of the assistance allowances are paid by order-books with a
currency of three or six months and, because there is no 'standard'
amount of payment, as, for example, there is for the retirement pension,
the amount of the individual recipient's allowance has to be entered on
each weekly order by hand. The revision of over one-and-three-quarter
million individual allowances to give effect to new Regulations is therefore a considerable undertaking. Moreover, on this occasion the increases
in assistance were to be followed later (in April and May, 1955) by the
increases, under the National Insurance Act, 1954, in insurance pensions
and other benefits. . . . More than two-thirds of the assistance allowances
were being paid to persons receiving such benefits; and in all these cases
the allowance had to be further adjusted to take account of the subsequent benefit increase. The complications caused by this double adjustment should have been avoided only by increasing assistance and

benefits on the same date, which would have meant deferring the assistance increases for a further three months. [9]

From within two years of its inception, official thinking about the National Health Service was dominated by apprehension over the speed with which costs outran the original estimates. The Conservative assertion of their special dedication to the extirpation of waste is very clear in the terms of reference set for the Committee of Inquiry appointed in May 1953 under the chairmanship of Professor Guillebaud, a professional economist:

To review the present and prospective cost of the National Health Service; to suggest means, by modifications on organization or otherwise, of ensuring the most effective control and efficient use of such Exchequer funds as may be made available; to advise how, in view of the burdens upon the Exchequer, a rising charge upon it can be avoided while providing for the maintenance of an adequate Service; and to make recommendations. [10]

The entire first part of the Ministry of Health Report for 1954 is pervaded by the idea of cost. [11] Yet the findings of the Guillebaud Committee were the exact opposite of what the Government had clearly expected in appointing it. In England and Wales, the committee reported, the current net cost of the National Health Service in productive resources had been £371½ million in the period to 1950; thereafter it rose by roughly £15 million each year, reaching £430½ million in 1953–54. This rise of £59 million over the last four years was the combined result of a larger rise in gross costs, offset by a saving of £18 millions resulting from new and increased charges. Expressed as a proportion of the gross national product the current net cost of the health service actually fell from 3¾ per cent in 1949–50 to 3¼ in 1953–54. Taking into account the price rise between 1948 and 1956, along with the 2 per cent rise in, and changes in the age-structure of, the population, 'the cost *per head* at constant prices was almost exactly the same in 1953–54 as in 1949–50'. Increases in expenditure had been greatest in the hospital services (£71 million). Expenditure on local authority services had increased by £11 million, while expenditure on general practitioner services had fallen by £24 million. The committee also noted that demands upon the health service were already falling before charges were introduced, as the accumulated arrears of needs had by then been largely dealt with. Some of the gravest weaknesses in the National Health Service as it existed in the early Fifties were due to the low level of capital expenditure on the service, which, with regard to fixed assets, ran at a fairly steady rate of about £12 million a year; given the rise in prices this in fact meant a progressive decline in capital expenditure in real terms. Thus the rate of fixed capital expenditure on hospitals since the founding of the National Health Service averaged about one-third of the pre-war rate in real terms, leading to a rather shocking situation in which 45 per cent of all hospitals in use in England and Wales had been built prior to 1891, many of them 'regarded by expert opinion as seriously in need of replacement or radical reconstruction'.[12]

Before it left office the Labour Government began a process of divesting the Ministry of Health (where Hilary Marquand had filled the place left by Bevan's move to the Ministry of Labour) of all functions other than the administration of the National Health Service; these would be transferred to the former Ministry of Town and Country Planning, henceforward to be known as the Ministry of Local Government and Planning. On coming to office the Conservatives changed the title to Ministry of Housing and Local Government, stressing the bid the party was making as the people who would get the much-needed houses built and the manner in which an open stress on 'planning' was going out of fashion. Reducing somewhat the ambitious standards which Bevan had set and encouraging increased use of 'new tradition' (formerly known as 'non-traditional') methods of construction, the ministry, under the energetic leadership of Harold Macmillan, did in 1953 reach the target of 300,000 new houses completed in Great Britain. Practical recognition was given to the hard fact of rising building and interest rates in the Housing Act of 1952 which increased annual standard subsidies (in England and Wales) from £22 to £35 with proportionate alterations in the other rates of subsidy. Under the Labour ministry the emphasis had been almost exclusively on the building of subsidized local authority housing.

In 1950 and 1951 local authorities who issued licences for private house-building could issue them only up to the ratio of one house to every four built by the local authority. From 1 January 1952 they were given discretion to license house-building up to the same number of houses as they were building themselves, and, a year later, to license smaller houses without question, and large ones on their merits. Under the Small Dwellings' Acquisition Acts and the 1949 Housing Act, local authorities had the power to make advances to prospective house purchasers or builders: the Conservatives set out positively to extend these facilities. This modest encouragement of private enterprise showed through clearly in 1954 when 28·5 per cent of houses completed were constructed by private builders. In November 1954 the Minister of Works revoked the wartime Defence Regulation 56A thus releasing private enterprise house-building from licensing control. There were other more substantial moves towards 'freedom' in the housing market. At the end of 1952 section 1 of the Local Authorities Loans Act of 1945 was allowed to lapse, pushing the local councils in the direction of seeking loans on the open market rather than through the Treasury-supported Public Works Loans Board; thus in 1953–54 the proportion of new loans raised through this body fell to 54 per cent, compared with 79 per cent over the preceding seven years. The Town and Country Planning Acts of 1953 and 1954 abolished the Development Charge, and in effect, if not necessarily in intention, paved the way for a costly free-for-all in the land market in the later part of the decade. During this first five years of mid-century Conservative rule the twelve New Towns designated by the Labour government made substantial progress, though no new ones were designated. The Town Development Act of 1952 marked a slight step away from the New Town ideal in that it was designed to facilitate the expansion of existing small towns willing to take overspill population. Another Act of the same year allowed the brewery interests into the New Towns in place of the State-managed public houses of Labour philosophy.[13]

In education the period 1945 to 1950 had been one of struggle to implement by any possible means the 1944 provisions, despite the desperate shortages of accommodation and of teachers. The years

1950 to 1955 are the first in which the gains of the Act can be seen operating in a state of equilibrium. Throughout the Ministry of Education *Report for 1954* there is a ringing note of optimism: no longer just a question of keeping pace with growing demand, there was now the prospect of further advance, though the same report noted that (in England and Wales) there were still 212,000 pupils in all-age schools – over one-quarter of them in rural areas. By January 1955 the number of pupils throughout the kingdom remaining at school to the age of seventeen and beyond was twice what it had been in pre-war years, although, expressed as a percentage of the total age-group, the figures were still distinctly unimpressive: 7·9 per cent in England and Wales and 9·1 per cent in Scotland. While Labour ruled many local authorities had instituted the eleven-plus examination; now, under the Conservatives, most of whom favoured the separation between grammar and modern schools, the first three specially-designed comprehensive schools were opened by the Labour-controlled London County Council: such were the ironies of 'Social Butskellism'. In 1948–49 the university population, swollen by the inflow of ex-servicemen, had reached a peak of 85,421. Following a low-point of 80,602 in 1953–54, when ex-service demand had fallen off, there was a steady expansion to 89,886 in 1956–57. The proportion of students drawn from 'the lower occupational categories' was higher than in 1947–48, when education reform had had little time to take effect: but the odds were still heavily weighted against a university education for a working-class child. Less change had taken place in the traditional pattern of student interests than might have been expected: a slight expansion of the percentages studying science and technology was largely balanced by a drop in the percentages studying medicine (this was mainly a consequence of the disastrous report of the government committee headed by the same Henry Willink who had given way to professional opinion in 1945, and who now compounded his earlier failure by proposing, because doctors feared over-recruitment to their profession, a 10 per cent cut in the intake into the country's medical schools); the proportion of students studying arts, 44·7 per cent in 1938–39, 43·6 in 1949–50, and 43·1 in 1956–57, remained remarkably constant.

NUMBER OF FULL-TIME STUDENTS BY FACULTIES

	1938–39		1949–50		1953–54		1956–57	
	No.	%	No.	%	No.	%	No.	%
Arts	22,374	44·7	37,243	43·6	34,673	43·0	38,714	43·1
Pure Science	7,661	15·3	16,917	19·8	16,971	21·1	19,899	22·2
Medicine	11,883	23·8	14,147	16·6	13,239	16·4	12,937	14·4
Dentistry	1,488	3·0	2,724	3·2	2,564	3·2	2,733	3·0
Technology	5,288	10·6	10,933	12·8	10,036	12·4	12,496	13·9
Agriculture and Forestry	1,043	2·1	2,773	3·2	2,066	2·6	1,914	2·1
Veterinary Science	265	0·5	684	0·8	1,053	1·3	1,140	1·3
TOTAL	50,002	100·0	85,421	100·0	80,602	100·0	89,833	100·0

Increased central grants to the universities were announced in 1952 and, following further increases in costs, supplementary recurrent grants were made available in 1954–55. A situation in which the great bulk of university income came straight from the Government and was becoming firmly established: in 1951–52 Parliament footed the bill to the extent of 66·5 per cent of the universities' income; by 1956–57 the proportion had risen slightly to 69·9 per cent. Over the same period the total university expenditure rose from £26.35 million to £41·78 million. Since full university status was granted to the colleges at Southampton (1952), Hull (1954), Exeter (1955) and Leicester (1957), there were now twenty-one universities and one university college (North Staffordshire).[14]

3. SOCIAL STRUCTURE OF MID-CENTURY BRITAIN

The social and geographical statistics of the 1950s when compared with those of the Edwardian period, both express the great transformations associated with the two world wars, and the unchanging elements in Britain's modern history. A few observers argued that the famous British weather had clearly embarked upon a long spell of change for the worse: however against a few very severe winters (such as that of 1946–47) and the East Coast flood disaster of January 1953 (when 307 lives were lost and 32,000 rendered homeless), could be placed the summer of 1959 which matched that of 1911 for continuous sunshine, and which instead of inflaming syndicalist tempers ushered in yet another Conservative election victory. A new atmospheric hazard was that of 'smog', product of the reaction between natural climatic conditions, the smoke borne aloft by age-old methods of burning solid fuel, and the exhaust-fumes thrown promiscuously into the atmosphere by the lengthening lines of petrol- or diesel-engined vehicles. The London smog of 4 to 10 December 1952 was responsible for 4,000 deaths. However, the Clean Air Act of 1956 subsequently did much to mitigate the problem. By 1961 the population had reached 51,298,245, representing a density of 573 per square mile, a figure exceeded only by Japan, Belgium and the Netherlands. 80 per cent of the population lived in towns; nearly 40 per cent in Greater London and the six provincial conurbations (West Midlands, South-East Lancashire, Merseyside, West Riding, Tyneside and Clydeside).[15]

Social and economic change, despite the spate of activity during the Second World War, had still failed to overcome the basic geographic differentiation of the Highlands of Scotland from the rest of Britian. The government *Review of Highland Policy* noted:

Their natural features endow the Highlands with great scenic beauty which, with their historical and cultural associations, will always exert a powerful attraction. But the combination of a sparse population and geographical disadvantages presents a formidable administrative and economic problem if the development of the Highlands is to keep pace with the progress that is being made elsewhere in the United Kingdom.[16]

The seven crofter counties of Argyll, Caithness, Inverness, Orkney, Ross and Cromarty, Sutherland and Zetland covered 9 million acres, one-sixth of the area of Great Britain or about 47 per cent of the area of Scotland: but they supported a population of only 277,000 – 5 per cent of the Scottish total. The decline in Highland population had been rapid at the beginning of the century, had been halted during the wars and to a lesser degree at the height of the industrial depression, and was resumed in full flood in the Fifties. Only in Caithness, where the remote Dounreay had been chosen for an atomic energy site, was there a recent increase in population; Dumfriesshire, in the southern uplands, likewise gained from the atomic station at Chapelcross. In Wales the towns of the Rhondda Valley had, relative to other working-class areas, been doing well in 1911; between 1931 and 1951 they suffered a more severe loss of population than any other group; but the 1961 figures suggested that the tide had been stemmed, and that the Rhondda was once again entering the central stream of British industrial life. Tyneside, which had been in such desperate plight in the Thirties, was refloated on the industrial and military needs of war and continued a remarkable revival in the 1950s, the population in 1961 being 2 per cent up on 1951. The South-East Lancashire and Merseyside conurbations had shown no increase in population for thirty years, and the woollen towns of West Yorkshire declined slightly over the Fifties: but none of these regions assumed the configuration of depressed areas. The most remarkable expansion took place in the Midlands: in 1951 the West Midland conurbation had a population 7·6 per cent above that of 1939, and by 1961 it had expanded by a further 4·8 per cent; there was at the same time a steady growth in the population of the East Midlands,[17] scene of Alan Sillitoe's important novel (and film), *Saturday Night and Sunday Morning*. Concealed within these regional variations was a much more vital change, not readily detectable from the statistics: the problem of urban living was giving way to the problem of suburban living. The migration from city centres to the suburbs was first apparent in London, where between 1921 and 1951 the central population declined by a quarter of a million; but it was now evident in all the major conurbations. In 1955 central London had a population of only 225,000, though during business hours it housed 1,252,000 workers:[18] a minor irritant in 1914, commuting from suburbs to city was now a lusty, brawling, unmanageable problem.

London in the 1950s still maintained that exceptional position which, in modern society, accrues automatically to a historic metropolis: and London was still an international trading and financial centre to an extent which Paris no longer was, and a political centre to a degree which New York had never been. Burgeoning mass communications first helped to spread London-born ideas to the provinces, then later began to be used to foster something of a provincial revolt: yet ready access to, if not residence in, London remained a desirable commodity. 'The Top' in John Braine's post-war novel of social mobility, *Room at the Top*, is a purely local top in a Yorkshire town, but high jinks in London are a noteworthy feature of Braine's later *Life at the Top*, as also of Kingsley Amis's *Take a Girl Like You*: in this work the hero's hero is a laird-like figure with, apparently, London society at his finger-tips and the latest London slang on his lips. Amis's first novel *Lucky Jim* (1956) was a brilliant exposure of the fatuities of provincial university life from which Lucky Jim finally escaped to London. C. P. Snow's novels of 'the corridors of power' chart, in the biography of Lewis Eliot, a progress from provincial worthiness to the great metropolitan centre of business and Civil Service power. William Cooper, who is sometimes credited with begetting the post-war provincial novel, followed his *Scenes from Provincial Life* with *Scenes from Married Life*, set firmly and proudly in London, the protagonist now a Civil Servant instead of a provincial schoolmaster. Even those polemicists who denounced most forcibly the poverty of British provincial life preferred themselves to remain within the warm embrace of London.

Carr-Saunders and Caradog Jones, now assisted by C. A. Moser, had again, in 1958, changed their standpoint on the nature of social class – though there was no return to the self-confident dismissal of the 1920s:

Social class is a most elusive concept and one that has long interested sociologists, both as a subject in its own right and as a method of classification to be used when investigating social conditions, behaviour and attitudes. The difficulty of the concept lies, not in deciding whether social classes have reality, in the sense that social class attitudes have a share in everyday behaviour and thought, but rather in defining appropriate class boundaries for statistical purposes.[19]

The writers, therefore, were now prepared to suggest a division into 'upper middle', 'lower middle' and 'working class', still showing the traditional reluctance to speak nakedly of an 'upper' or 'ruling' class: the implication is that in the mid-twentieth century the country's rulers are simply the more successful members of the middle class, still closely bound to that class. Actually a survey of British management conducted by the Acton Society in 1955 brought out the sharp distinction which existed between top management and other management.[20] The confusion has been confounded by the feeling that 'it is no longer meaningful to talk of a landed aristocracy'.[21] Yet landed aristocrats still existed in the 1950s, and, if they no longer dominated a ruling class, they formed a component of it. The continued existence of such a class is clearly brought out in W. L. Guttsman's brilliant study of the British *élite*: after examining in detail the biographical data of politicians, members of royal commissions, research councils and such bodies as the B.B.C. and the Arts Council, as well as of top managers, he concluded:

There exists today in Britain a 'ruling class', if we mean by it a group which provides the majority of those who occupy positions of power, and who, in their turn, can materially assist their sons to reach similar positions.[22]

The notion of an 'upper middle' and a 'lower middle' conflicts also with the most obvious single feature of the class structure, upon which all commentators were agreed, the extension *downwards* of the sense of middle-classness, a consequence primarily of the manner in which technological developments were making unskilled manual work increasingly redundant. As wage rates and material standards rose towards the end of the decade, some commentators detected an *embourgeoisement* of the working class,[23] though a careful study by J. H. Goldthorpe and David Lockwood suggested that this was more myth than reality.[24] Certainly many of the environmental conditions which had characterized Edwardian working-class life still existed. At the Census of 1951 one-third of the houses in England and Wales had no bath. Over a million houses had no water closet. It was difficult even to attempt a middle-class way of life in such surroundings.

The two most important points to be made about the social structure of mid-century Britain are, then, that an identifiable three-fold division of social classes still existed, but that, secondly, since 1939 further developments, without fundamentally altering the core of each class, had affected the relationship between class and class, the mobility from one class to another and the proportions of the population who could be allocated to one class or another. Quantitatively the most significant fact was that the middle class, using the term in a sense that would not have been unrecognizable to the Edwardians, had continued to swell, or perhaps more accurately, the working class had continued to shrink. John Bonham, writing in 1954, suggested that the middle class now formed 30·4 per cent of the population.[25] Within the working class, and, effectively, out of it, the movement since 1931, accelerated during the war for reasons we have studied, was from traditional working-class occupations to the newer metal industries, and from manual to clerical work. In 1931 mining and quarrying occupied 5·1 per cent of the country's employed population of all descriptions and classes: in 1951 only 2·9 per cent; over the same period the proportion employed in textile manufacture dropped from 5 per cent to 3 per cent, while the proportion employed in metal manufacture and engineering increased from 9 per cent to 12 per cent. Remarking on the increased percentage (7 per cent in 1931 to 10½ per cent in 1951) employed as clerks, Carr-Saunders, Caradog Jones and Moser concluded:

The clear impression is that relatively fewer people are concerned directly in producing things, and relatively more in professional, technical and clerical tasks. We are indeed increasingly becoming a nation of clerks.

The proportion of those employed in professional and technical occupations had in fact risen from 4·2 per cent to 6·1 per cent, and was especially marked in the scientific professions, which in 1931 comprised only 11,000 men and 2,000 women, but in 1951 numbered 64,000 men and 19,000 women.[26]

The high taxation of the war period, and its continuance by the post-war Labour government had wiped out some of the grosser income inequalities of pre-war years. The effects were most obvious at the top: whatever the middle-income groups may have felt they lost was, in the opinion of many observers, more than compensated for through the new social services which these groups made extensive use of.[27] At the top, there were methods of softening the blows of income tax: between 1945 and 1951 Britain's shareholders and financial institutions made £2,000 millions in tax-free capital gains,[28] the British system in this respect being far behind the American. There was little reduction in the inequality of property distribution as between the Thirties and the Fifties.[29]

Extended educational opportunity did inject an added element of mobility into the social structure. In one sense educational provision was not ungenerous: State subsidies to direct-grant schools and to universities meant that even those who paid fees were receiving cut-price education; by 1955–56, in any case, over three-quarters of all students in England were receiving public grants (the proportions were higher in Scotland and in Wales). But even leaving aside the continued existence of the private sector (2 per cent of children at the age of 13 in direct grant schools, 7·5 per cent in independent schools), the public education system was coming more and more to resemble a lottery in which those who did well could carry off desirable prizes in the form of free or cheap education, but in which the chances were still stacked against the child of lower-class background.

4. THE INCREDIBLE SHRINKING SOCIAL REVOLUTION

During both world wars hopes were high in many quarters that the end of war would usher in a magnificent new society. The First World War was followed, therefore, by a deep sense of disillusionment. There was no similar disillusionment in the decade following upon the Second World War, though arguments steadily developed over exactly what had happened in Britain since 1945. First of all there was what practically amounted to a collusive agreement among the older politicians of both major parties that a 'social revolution' had indeed taken place: this, naturally, was a matter of pride for Labour leaders, and, as the Fifties moved on, a means of excusing continued electoral failure – the successful, once-for-all social revolution had taken the ground away from beneath the feet of the party of protest and progress; Conservative leaders were especially happy with the 'once-for-all' notion, and keen to pose as the pragmatic party which had contributed to the wartime reconstruction plans and which would now not only accept what Labour (excellent chaps in many ways, but a bit careless with money) had done, but administer it more efficiently; Conservatives, finally, were drawn from those upper classes which felt high taxation and the absence of domestic servants most heavily, and therefore were most conscious of 'revolution'. In the words of the Tory radical turned Tory elder statesman, Robert Boothby:

Britain has undergone one of the greatest social revolutions in her history. The strength of the Tory Party in Britain and its continuance as a major force in British politics lie in its empirical approach to current problems and its readiness to accept facts, not as we should like them to be, but as they are. We accepted the revolution of 1832 and governed England for a considerable part of the nineteenth century in consequence. I am glad to tell you that we have accepted the revolution of 1945 and are looking forward to governing England again for a good part of the rest of this century.[30]

Many historians were prepared to accept, what might be called the traditional political view, that something which could meaningfully be termed a social revolution had taken place in Britain since the Second World War. E. Watkins spoke of a 'cautious revolution' and the most recent historian of the Labour Party has again talked of Labour carrying through a 'social revolution more profound than many political revolutions'; I must myself confess to having used the phrase.[31]

Given the nature of the social structure as described in the previous chapter it is not surprising that very soon a good deal of scorn was poured on the whole idea, particularly from leftist intellectuals who had themselves had high hopes during the war period, and who now, in the early Fifties, felt that these hopes had been dashed. The note of optimism which characterized Richard Titmuss's volume in the official history of the war, *Problems of Social Policy*, is completely replaced by an angry scepticism in his later writings. In *New Fabian Essays*, R. H. S. Crossman declared that 'the post-war Labour government marked the end of a century of social reform and not, as its socialist supporters had hoped, the beginning of a new epoch'. A very much younger commentator from the Left put it still more forcefully: 'The overwhelming Labour victory of 1945 brought about the greatest restoration of traditional social values since 1660.'[32] A compromise view put forward by Professor Thomas Marshall was that up to 1951 the lines were being laid for social revolution, but had been pulled up again with the return of the Conservatives. But the younger radical Right (or 'new liberals', as I shall call them to distinguish them from a rather different group in the U.S.A.) had a version of their own, not widely expressed till the late Fifties and early Sixties, but which reinforced the views of Titmuss and Crossman, even although different political conclusions were intended: politicians such as Enoch Powell and economists such as A. T. Peacock and John Jewkes argued that the welfare legislation of the Labour government had essentially been the inevitable response to a phase of temporary difficulties in the capitalist system, prior to the onset of affluence; with affluence, they argued, much of the legislation could be dismantled. To them, accordingly, no social revolution had taken place, only the steady evolution of modern capitalism. Some academic historians agreed, so historigraphically as well as historically the notion of a social revolution in Britain since 1945 has certainly been a shrinking one. The phrase did have some validity in so far as it was the conscious aim of the Labour government to achieve 'classlessness' through asserting the principle of universality in the social services, though in practice the achievement fell dismally short of the aim.

Whatever meaning may be given to the word 'revolution', and it is a word which is best used as infrequently as possible, it is clear that the nature of British society in the middle of the century was a grave disappointment to leftists and liberals who less than ten years before had hoped for much better things; as material conditions began to get markedly better in the later Fifties, this seemed obviously due to the processes of economic growth rather than to any guided political action. The coming of affluence (which will be the main subject matter of the next chapter), these same commentators felt, was accompanied by grave fundamental weaknesses, political, social, moral and, indeed, economic. The reasons for the failure of change to materialize to the extent predicted are to be found in matters we have already discussed: the compromises; the traditionalism; the gap between the paper Welfare State and the real Welfare State, basically attributable to the economic losses of war, but widened by a continued adherence to the policy of the 'imperfect machine'; and the unyielding character of the political structure, which had never been exposed to the full transforming blast of war. But for the future of social progress in Britain there were even more serious implications. Boothby's parallel between 1832 and 1945 was by no means a farfetched one. In 1832 the middle classes had secured the political rights for which they had long been agitating; thereafter they were quite happy to go on being ruled by the landed aristocracy. In 1945 the working classes got the basic economic and social rights for which they had been long agitating; they too, it seemed, were happy thereafter to go on being ruled by their social superiors.

With the building of the Welfare State the organized working class, with its liberal middle- and upper-class allies, assisted by the constructive effects of war, had succeeded in removing the most obvious disabilities suffered by the working class *as a class*. To the extent that they were successful, the working class and its allies lost potency as agents of further social change. So Britain moved into an era of 'group politics', in which now one interest gained, now another, but in which there was no concerted pressure for fundamental redistribution of power, wealth or status. The Conservatives, certainly, had learned the lesson of 1945 when the working class really had chucked its weight around, and henceforth they would avoid a direct confrontation with specifically working-class interests: electoral considerations, indeed, had played a primary part in the adoption of Butskellite Conservative policies.[33] Continued economic and technological advance, also accelerated by the war, helped to ameliorate some of the evils still existing after 1950. Others called for definite political action: the problem was to find a socio-economic or ideological base from which to launch the necessary reforms.

5. A WEAK CONSTITUTION?

Pioneers in the arts of self-government, the British by the later nineteenth century had created a system of representative government that was the admiration of liberals throughout the world, and provided refuge for foreign radicals and agitators of all shades of opinion. By the mid-twentieth century that system had by no means lost its distinctive virtues, but, since the basic construction dated from an undemocratic age, it was inevitably ill-suited to dealing with some of the problems of twentieth-century social democracy.

In the Fifties and Sixties the British constitution was still orchestrated upon the same five themes which stand out in the constitutional history of the previous 150 years. Britain was still a monarchy – oddly enough the feature least under attack from radicals and critics of any political persuasion; or not so odd if one agrees that there must attach to the Head of State what Bagehot so rightly described as the *dignified* part of government. A sense of history, a love of pageantry, an essential conservatism lies deep in the heart of many British people. For such a people the Crown is doubtless a sensible institution; in 1957 court presentation parties of 'debutantes' were ended, though the Crown continued to be surrounded by a good deal of the vulgar snobbism deeply rooted in the British class system, as well as by excessive protocol. Politically, the Crown retains the legal power of granting or refusing a dissolution of Parliament, and of inviting a particular politician to attempt to form a government. Of little importance during the normal working of party government, these powers give the Crown a valuable mediating position in time of political crisis.

It is upon the second theme, the development, in concert and in conflict, of Prime Minister and Cabinet, that much recent controversy among historians and political scientists has concentrated. Has the 'Cabinet government' of the nineteenth century become, in the mid-twentieth century, 'prime ministerial government' or even 'presidential government'? My own answer is a qualified 'no'. Certainly a relatively simple series of political relationships in the nineteenth century has become an immensely more complicated one in the twentieth century: but a glance at the charismatic powers of such great nineteenth-century Prime Ministers as Gladstone and Disraeli suggests that the simpler relationships of the nineteenth century could not be totally subsumed under the heading 'Cabinet government'. A vast new range of interests and pressures have created a bigger *opportunity* for the Prime Minister to emerge as a single super-force. But over a hundred years the particles of change are subtle and do not all flow in one direction. Because of the creation of many new offices of State to deal with the expanding areas of government concern, the total size of a government is not now coterminous with that of the Cabinet. The simultaneous growth of the bureaucracy and of special administrative procedures has made the individual Cabinet minister (or other minister for that matter) less than a giant in his own sphere. Extended use of Cabinet committees has derogated from the Cabinet itself as general policy-maker (though the fact that they are still *Cabinet* committees is significant). The expansion of the electorate by the Reform Acts of 1918 and 1928, together with the rise of the mass media, have made easier, and perhaps more desirable, the projection of the Prime Minister (present or future) as the embodiment of his party and his government; yet again one cannot help detecting a common human refrain in the charges levelled at Sir Robert Walpole in the eighteenth century that he had made himself *Prime Minister*, in Queen Victoria's disgust over Gladstone's 'appeal to the people' in his famous Midlothian campaign, and in the present somewhat hostile admiration for Mr Harold Wilson's manipulation of the mass media; it is to be remembered, too, that Conservatives have always placed great stress on the leadership principle. Finally, the great crises of war have exposed the cumbersomeness of government by Cabinet, and made necessary a greater concentration of executive power; but, as stressed throughout this book, the political innovations of war have always proved the least enduring ones.

Earl Attlee, it is true, remarked that the most important quality for a Prime Minister was a willingness to fire incompetent Cabinet ministers: Lord Salisbury, fifty years before, had not thought a Prime Minister possessed quite so much authority over his colleagues. The Suez venture seems to have been very much the personal policy of the Prime Minister, Sir Anthony Eden. Mr Harold Macmillan, on a famous occasion, sacked half of his Cabinet[34] ('the wrong half, as it happened', in Mr Wilson's famous witticism of 1964) and survived. On the other hand, Mr Wilson has recently shown a marked reluctance to rid himself of Cabinet incompetents. The important sanction which the Prime Minister has over his colleagues is his exclusive right to recommend a dissolution of Parliament to the Monarch and thus place not only the offices, but the parliamentary seats of recalcitrant colleagues in jeopardy, though conceivably the Monarch could in fact refuse to grant a dissolution for the furtherance of a personal vendetta by the Prime Minister against his colleagues. Formally the Cabinet is still the co-ordinating body of government policy for which, in consti-tutional theory, it shares collective responsibility; this pre-supposes a right to protest against certain policies, with the sanction in this case being a threat of resignation. Undoubtedly the clear reserve of power, if he has the character to exploit it, does lie with the Prime Minister since Cabinet ministers have a natural reluctance to push opposition the length of resignation.[35] Only with the creation of the Cabinet secretariat and the Prime Minister's office during the First World War did the two major executive offices take administrative shape. Only with the Chequers Estate Act of 1917 was the dangerously newfangled office of Prime Minister actually mentioned in an Act of Parliament; no legal definition of the Cabinet was attempted until the Ministers of the Crown Act of 1937.

The last real battle between Commons and Lords was settled in 1911, though in its belated efforts to push through iron and steel nationalization against the two-year delaying power that still remained to the Lords, the Labour government, by the Parliament Act of 1949, reduced the delaying power to one year: the Commons has not since had occasion to demonstrate its reinforced supremacy.

Meantime the composition of the House of Lords has been altered slightly: the Life Peerages Act of 1958 made it easier for good men (and women) to be got into the Lords, while the Peerage Act of 1963 made it easier for good men, who felt the lure of an active career in the House of Commons, to get out of it. Clearly a House of peers, most still hereditary, is in the mid-twentieth century an unsatisfactory institution: the trouble is that no great crisis of war or peace has forced anyone to put forward a rational alternative. As Professor Bernard Crick has summed up:

The 'Second Chamber' endures because the work it does is extremely useful to the House of Commons. The 'House of Lords' endures because the Conservative Party has a political interest in retaining a connection between the order of Peerage and the membership of the House of Lords, and because the Labour Party has no better idea of how to find enough people to do the work.[36]

Tightening party discipline and the growing power of the executive greatly reduced the independence and status of the individual member of the House of Commons, so that he was often despised as mere lobby fodder, voting at the dictates of the party whips; not, some critics added, that there was now really much difference between the two main political parties in any case. Edward Hyams's political satire, *Gentian Violet* (1953), describes how plain Jim Blundell is elected to Parliament as a Socialist and also, having risen through a distinguished war career into circles where he is known as James Stewart-Blundell, as a Conservative. In this sad latter-day House of Commons there was no danger of exposure:

Nobody noticed anybody else. . . . A member might be on his feet talking away yet boring nobody, as nobody was obliged to listen . . . it reduced the most ambitious and domineering public men to the status of mere prefects, with certain privileges, like putting their feet on the table. . . . If democracy was to be found anywhere, Jim felt, it was here in the House of Commons.

And Jim soon began to be very proud of being two members of it.[37]

The argument usually advanced in defence of House of Commons debates, the results of which were a foregone conclusion, was that they served as a vital public forum for the airing of matters of great public importance, a dubious line of reasoning when few newspapers took the trouble to report parliamentary proceedings in any detail. In matters of State of the highest importance the control over public money and public policy which was supposed to reside in Parliament was almost totally illusory. Nowhere was this more true than in that area always euphemistically delineated as 'defence'; despite the fact that since 1945 defence consistently consumed between one-quarter and one-third of all central government expenditures, only 4 or 5 per cent of all the available time of the House of Commons was allocated to debating these expenditures.[38] It is not surprising if, in the eyes of many critics, Parliament with its medieval flummery and ponderous ritual (all set down in the venerable pages of Erskine May) appeared as one gigantic sham. There could be no going back to the 'golden age of the private M.P.' of the mid-nineteenth century, but it did seem that the considerable talent mustered within the walls of Parliament might be set to more useful tasks than the enactment of a nineteenth-century charade. In the United States congressmen had long been fruitfully involved in the processes of law-making through service on congressional committees. Since 1964 greater use has been made in Britain of parliamentary committees, though any fundamental reappraisal of British parliamentary institutions still seems as far off as ever.

The British notion that 'His Majesty requires an Opposition as well as a Government'[39] relates both to Parliament and to the electorate. In Parliament there should be a strong and coherent body of politicians, headed by a Leader of the Opposition and his 'shadow Cabinet', who will carefully check, scrutinize and expose the follies and inadequacies of the Government. In the country the elector should be presented with two clear choices, the governing party and the opposition party: the choice is narrow, but at least he can see what he is voting for, can see whether or not this is carried out, and can give clear notice to quit if he does not like what he sees. Statutory recognition of the position of Leader of the Opposition (and entitlement to an extra salary) did not come till the 1937 Ministers of the Crown Act, passed, curiously, at a time when recent events had suggested that the whole Government-Opposition diarchy was in collapse. The period since 1945 has seen the return to effective working of what is on the whole a desirable feature of the British system, though thirteen years of Conservative rule between 1951 and 1964 made it abundantly plain that the 'swing of the pendulum' theory was as dead as Gladstone and Disraeli. In recent years the two major political parties (to turn to the fifth theme) have undoubtedly come to resemble each other more and more, both in composition and in basic political outlook. Yet there remain very fundamental distinctions, social as well as ideological. The kind of person who joins a political club for purposes of social prestige rather than any commitment to political activism, will join the Conservative Party, never the Labour Party. Though as long ago as 1929 a German observer remarked approvingly upon the fraternization at Westminster between Conservative and Labour M.P.s, which he thought would be impossible in the Reichstag,[40] there is still within the House of Commons today a very sharp, and very real polarization between gin-and-tonic-drinking Tories in the plushy members' lounge, and tea-drinking Socialists in the cafeteria.[41]

Upon this system of Monarch, Prime Minister and Cabinet, Parliament, Opposition and Party has been grafted democracy, both formal and social. Formal democracy arrived in principle with the Acts of 1918 and 1928 and was completed by the abolition of plural voting in 1948. Freedom of speech, freedom of assembly, freedom of the Press were not seriously in doubt, though the tendency to monopoly in newspaper ownership discernible in the Fifties and Sixties could well have anti-democratic implications. The judiciary remained securely apart from political control, though not, we shall see, immune from criticism on other scores. Educational levels had not been pushed much above the basic minimum required for an effective political and social democracy. Political democracy had been a main objective for upper-class liberals; in the quest for social democracy, involving collectivist and Welfare State legislation, they were joined by the organized working-class movement. Before long there emerged the central paradox of the modern democratic State: that the very expansion in the scope of State action required to secure economic and social democracy may menace the individual rights which lie at the base of formal political democracy. Already the powers of the individual member of Parliament, theoretically the protector of his constituents, had been impaired. The major threat seemed to come from the central bureaucracy, expanding, in size and power, at the expense of Parliament, the localities and the individual. Because of the increasing pressure of government business, because, also, slight changes in economic or other circumstances might frustrate the spirit of a law which was spelled out too explicitly, there was a steady growth of delegated legislation – legislative details filled in by the Civil Service under the blanket of a general Act passed by Parliament. One of the main Conservative criticisms of Labour's National Insurance Act of 1946 was that it was *too short* – too much was being left to the bureaucrats.[42] Actually there exists, in the form of the Committee on Statutory Instruments (another name for delegated legislation) first appointed in 1944, a parliamentary check on all delegated legislation; presumably it would be still better if M.P.s had a more constructive part to play in drafting this kind of legislation.

Much of the conflict between central and local authorities arose from the unsatisfactory condition of British local government. The story of the non-reform of local government between 1945 and 1967 is certainly among the funniest and the saddest in Britain's recent history. The documents are so eloquent, and so redolent of the graces of the British way of doing things (more correctly, of not doing things) that I propose to let them speak for themselves. For what it is worth, I can assure the reader who justly baulks at so much small print, of more laughs than he will get from the rest of this book taken together. In 1945, it will be recalled, for all the ferment over the possibilities of reform of local government, there was little real intention actually to do anything, partly because of the complacent feeling that the system had proved itself in war, partly because of the hostility of vested local interests, partly because the Government (and, above all, the responsible minister, Aneurin Bevan) was more interested in immediate welfare policy than long-term administrative reform. The Government's one gesture in the direction of reform was the appointment of the Local Government Boundary Commission which was charged with the task of upgrading, downgrading, or altering the boundaries of, existing local authorities; charged, that is to say, with the task of tinkering with the problem. At the end of 1947 the commission produced a long and thorough report. Now read on:

... We may be asked why the Commission after two years of existence have made no single Order altering the status or boundaries of any local authority. ...

... We have definitely reached the conclusion that in many areas – and these cover the great bulk of the population – our present powers and instructions do not permit the formation of local government units as effective and convenient as in our opinion they should be.

Much of this Report will be occupied by drawing attention to defects in the present system and to our proposals for its improvement. ...

... The allocation of function to different types of authorities has been unsystematic and the process has gone on without much reference to local government as a balanced organism. Much of this legislation was passed in the pressure of wars or the aftermath of wars. Piecemeal decisions had to be taken in the course of Parliamentary debates and often as the outcome of Parliamentary bargaining; and the fact that each new arrangement has emerged after a struggle between the various types of local authorities has not conduced to fruitful co-operation between them. Another result has been to create a mass of joint boards, joint committees and other combinations for particular purposes.[43]

The commission's proposals went by no means as far as those of the most advanced reformers of the time, and the magic word 'region' was avoided; basically they aimed at enlarging the units of local government, creating a unified administration for the conurbations, and breaking down the artificial distinction between urban and rural areas. The conurbations would have become new one-tier counties, the smaller non-county boroughs together with urban and rural districts would have been melded as county districts within the two-tier counties.[44] The silence from the Government was deafening, so much so that a year later the commission wrote to Bevan asking for his reactions. Four months after that came Bevan's formal reply referring the commission to the following question and answer in the House of Commons on 25 March 1949:

Q. – To ask the Minister of Health, whether he is yet in a position to make a statement with regard to legislation on local government in the light of the recommendations made in the reports of the Local Government Boundary Commission for 1946 and 1947.
A. – This question has been under consideration by the Government, who have decided that it will not be practicable to introduce comprehensive legislation on local government reconstruction in the near future.[45]

A few years later the Ministry of Housing and Local Government, after remarking on the 'far-reaching' changes proposed by the commission, proceeded in superb flat Civil Service prose to pronounce its epitaph on the whole episode:

However, the Government did not adopt these proposals; and in 1949 they dissolved the commission and reinstated, with minor amendments, the previous procedure for effecting changes in local government areas.[46]

'Previous procedure' usually meant non-county boroughs making so much stink that either the Government was prevailed upon to turn them into county boroughs, or else the surrounding county made so much counter-stink that the Government was prevailed upon to leave the non-county boroughs as they were. Between 1949 and 1953 three boroughs, Ealing, Ilford and Luton, were unsuccessful in their bids for the coveted county-borough status. In February 1954 the County Councils Association, the Rural District Councils Association, the Urban District Councils Association and the National Association of Parish Councils submitted to the Minister of Housing and Local Government, Harold Macmillan, agreed proposals for the reorganization of local government. The Association of Municipal Corporations, however, submitted a series of exactly contrary proposals.[47] Under pressure once more from Ilford and Luton, now joined by Poole, Macmillan parried in masterly style:

This is the last time that I hope either I or my successor will ask the House to refuse approval to a Bill giving county borough status to a local authority solely on the ground that a new prospect is just around the corner. . . . Before such Bills as this are due to be brought forward next session, the Government will either have informed the House that they cannot introduce the Measure that will take the place of such Bills as this, or they will have announced in broad outline what their proposals are.[48]

When, shortly, the 'broad outline' appeared it had a familiar shape:

The test of any system of local government in this country should be whether it provides a stable structure, capable of discharging efficiently the functions entrusted to it, while at the same time maintaining its local democratic character.

Since the present system of local government was established there have been far-reaching alterations in the distribution of population and industry, the scope and cost of services, the speed of communications, and the relationship between central and local government. But it does not necessarily follow that radical changes in organization are needed. A fundamental alteration of the existing structure could be justified only if it had shown itself to be incapable of maintaining present-day needs. That is not the situation. The present system has, over many years, stood up to the severest tests. It responded well to the abnormal demands made on it during the war and, despite certain weaknesses, has on the whole shown itself capable of adaptation to changing conditions. Moreover, the present system is firmly established and the local loyalties and civic pride which have grown up around it are a source of strength to local government which should not be underestimated.

There is, therefore, no convincing case for radically reshaping the existing form of local government in England and Wales. What is needed is to overhaul it and make such improvements as are necessary to bring it up to date.[49]

The tone of this paper will immediately recall that of 1944.[50] For the historically-minded it may even recall the arguments of the Tory opponents of the Reform Bill of 1832. All that happened was that two more local government commissions, one for England, one for Wales, were appointed. However, during the Fifties local government reform developed as a possible political issue: the Liberals made the running, then the Labour Party followed. So in November 1957 the Government appointed a royal commission on local government in London, and by the Local Government Act of 1958 established a series of commissions to look at specific localities and, above all, at the problems of the major English conurbations, the West Midlands, South-East Lancashire, Merseyside, the West Riding, and Tyneside. By 1961 the London Royal Commission and three of the local commissions had presented reports. Before it fell from office the Conservative government had succeeded in carrying through the major recommendation of the former, the establishment of a Greater London Council in place of the old London County Council, though as a concession to local Labour sentiment it kept in being an Inner London Education Authority analogous to the old L.C.C. Education Authority. It failed, in face of intense local feeling, to carry through the East Midlands Commission's recommendation that the tiny county of Rutland should be merged in neighbouring Leicestershire. Since coming into office in 1964 the Labour government, apart from getting into a tangle with one of the local commissions, has appointed two royal commissions to look at the whole problem in England and in Scotland respectively: sweeping change will be believed when seen.

It is not surprising, in the light of the foregoing, that the central bureaucracy has frequently simply by-passed existing local authorities. But there has been less justification for contemptuous treatment of individuals, the most notorious case of which concerned the mandarins of the Ministry of Agriculture, which in 1949 had assumed responsibility for 725 acres of land at Crichel Down in Dorset, originally purchased by the Air Ministry in 1937. Reporting in June 1954, a public inquiry accused civil servants at the ministry of having shown 'a most regrettable attitude of hostility' to Commander Marten, heir of one of the previous owners, who had been trying to repurchase the property. The report noted that:

In present times the interests of the private citizen are affected to a great extent by the actions of Civil Servants. It is the more necessary that the

Civil Servants should bear constantly in mind that the citizen has the right to expect, not only that his affairs will be dealt with effectively and expeditiously, but also that his personal feelings, no less than his rights as an individual, will be sympathetically and fairly considered.[51]

Between 1931 and 1955 the total size of the Civil Service expanded from 340,000 to 720,000. Undoubtedly there were important changes in recruitment and structure, and, through the development of the specialist grades, an attempt was made to destroy the jaded image of amateurism.[52] For uncorruptibility and relative objectivity the record of the British Civil Service still stood very high indeed in the world, but none the less, as much because of the education system as because of bad recruiting methods, the top echelons of the service remained too narrow in base adequately to serve the needs of a twentieth-century social democracy.[53]

Of all major British social institutions, the established churches very definitely not excluded, the legal systems of England and Scotland were the least touched by two total wars: short of the total collapse of the whole of society war simply does not touch the law, save in instigating profitable new litigation over property rights, war losses, etc. To an even greater degree than is the case with the principles of government, the law emanates from the mists of antiquity: just as there is no one document identifiable as 'the British Constitution', so there is no single code of law for England and Wales, nor for Scotland (whose system many authorities regard as superior to that of England and Wales). Both systems make a distinction between criminal law (wrongs against the community) and civil law (issues arising between individual members of the community); but despite the continuing expansion of governmental activity there is no administrative law, so in the same way that *ad hoc* regional organizations have grown up side by side with the historic local authorities, so an *ad hoc* structure of administrative tribunals exercising judicial or quasi-judicial functions has grown up outside the ordinary hierarchy of the courts. At the bottom of the hierarchy of English criminal law stand the Magistrates' Courts, which try the less serious offences or, in the case of more serious offences, decide whether there is sufficient evidence to justify committal of the defendant for trial in a higher court before a jury. In Scotland there is no equivalent of this public preliminary hearing, which has been attacked by critics of the law as both a waste of time and gravely prejudicial to the defendant. Magistrates are holders of the ancient office of Justice of the Peace, appointed on behalf of the Crown by the Lord Chancellor (himself a member of the Cabinet) on the advice, in the counties, of the Lord Lieutenant (a sixteenth-century office) assisted by a local advisory committee, or, in the boroughs, of separate advisory committees. It is possible by deliberate political fiat to ensure that property-owners alone are not represented on the benches of magistrates, but it cannot be said that the system as it evolved was specially intended to serve the needs of a modern democracy. The higher courts are the Quarter Sessions, which, for reasons now buried in history, vary slightly in style and form from county to borough and from one area to another, and the Courts of Assize, of which the most famous is the Central Criminal Court at the Old Bailey in London. Lesser civil cases are heard in the county courts (about 400 in all), important ones in the High Court of Justice, which forms part of the Supreme Court of Judicature, and hears appeals as well as cases at first instance. The High Court is divided, on a basis which only a lawyer could attempt to explain, into the Chancery Division, the Probate, Divorce and Admiralty Division, and the Queen's Bench Division: most of the work is done by sixty-two puisne judges. The higher branch of the Supreme Court of Judicature is the Court of Appeal, which has a criminal as well as a civil division, and contains such dignatories as the Lord Chief Justice, the Master of the Rolls and eleven Lord Justices of Appeal. The highest appeal court is the 'House of Lords', that is, the Lords of Appeal in Ordinary sitting under the presidency of the Lord Chancellor. Appointments to all the high positions (Lords of Appeal in Ordinary, President of the Probate, Divorce and Admiralty Division, etc.) are made on the recommendation of the Prime Minister; the puisne judges, the County Court judges, the chairmen of Quarter Sessions, the recorders of boroughs and the various stipendiary magistrates are made on the recommendation of the Lord Chancellor (the Chancellor of the Duchy of Lancaster still has rights of appointment for county judges and Justices of the Peace in the county of Lancashire). Appointments (apart from Justices of the Peace) are made from among men well versed in, and well qualified in, the traditions of the legal profession. Effectively they last for life, or till statutory retirement age. There can be no question that the highly-valued principle of the theorists of the eighteenth century (when it was more principle than practice) that the judiciary should be independent of political influence has been well maintained in twentieth-century Britain. Though statute law takes precedence over all other forms of law, it is still open to the courts, in interpreting statute law, to use case law and common law to frustrate the intentions of parliamentary legislators. Like English law, Scots law has been remarkably unravaged by the passing of time. The lowest civil courts are the Burgh (or police) Courts presided over by local councillors serving as magistrates, or, in the counties, Justice of the Peace Courts. The Sheriff Courts have both civil (corresponding in this respect to County Courts in England and Wales) and criminal jurisdiction. At the top of the criminal system is the High Court of Justiciary, and at the top of the civil system the Court of Session. In Scotland, unlike England, criminal proceedings may not be instituted by the police: the decision rests with the appropriate Public Prosecutor – the Lord Advocate (at highest level), the Procurators Fiscal (at Sheriff Court level), or the Justices of the Peace Fiscal or Burgh Prosecutors. Sudden or unusual death in England and Wales is followed by a special public inquiry conducted by the local holder of the venerable common law office of coroner; in Scotland such inquiries are made in private by the Procurator Fiscal. Arguments over the relative merits of the two systems suggest that both have considerable defects: coroners' law is at present being reviewed by a Departmental Committee.[54] Permanent, as well as *ad hoc*, commissions for legal reform are in constant existence, but the law is like a well-fortified and well-provisioned medieval keep, unaffected by the passing cannon-fire of the occasional war, triumphant in the face of protracted siege, and amenable only to direct frontal assault.

NOTES TO CHAPTER EIGHT

1. For this and the following paragraphs see: J. Mitchell, *Crisis in Britain 1951*, 1963, esp. pp. 15–23, 54–55, 84–85, 111, 144, 168–83, 287.
2. *House of Commons Debates*, 22 April 1951.
3. *Ibid.*, 23 April 1951.
4. Guttsman, *The British Political Élite*, p. 312.
5. King George's Jubilee Trust, *Citizens of Tomorrow*, 1955. Economic Research Council, *Social Problems of Post-war Youth*, 1956. Ministry of Labour and National Service. *Report of Enquiry into Effects of National Service on Education and Employment of Young Men*, 1955.
6. P.P., 1954–55, VI, (1); Cmd. 9333; P.P., 1955–56, XX, Cmd. 9663.
7. P.P., 1954–55, VI, (1). pp. 4–29.
8. Cmd. 9333, pp. 3–10. *Report of National Assistance Board for 1954*, P.P., 1955–56, XI, Cmd. 9530, pp. 4–6.
9. *Ibid.*, p. 8.
10. Cmd. 9663, p. 1.
11. P.P., 1955–56, XX, Cmd. 9566.
12. Cmd. 9663, pp. 46–50.
13. *Report of Ministry of Housing and Local Government for 1950 to 1954*, P.P., 1955–56, XXI, Cmd. 9559.
14. *Education in 1954, Education in 1955*, P.P., 1955–56, XIV, Cmd. 9521 and 9785. P.E.P., *Planning*, 8 November 1954. *University Development 1952–1957*, P.P., 1957–58, XVIII, Cmd. 534.
15. J. B. Mitchell (ed.). *Great Britain: Geographical Essays*, 1962, pp. 33–34.
16. P.P., 1958–59, XXV, Cmnd. 785.
17. Mitchell, pp. 45–49.
18. A. Carr-Saunders, D. Caradog Jones and C. A. Moser, *Social Conditions in England and Wales*, 1957, p. 54.
19. *Ibid.*, p. 115.
20. Acton Society Trust, *Management Succession*, 1956.
21. Guttsman, *The British Political Élite*, p. 137.
22. *Ibid.*, p. 356.
23. See esp. F. Zweig, *The Worker in an Affluent Society*, 1961.
24. J. H. Goldthorpe and D. Lockwood, 'Affluence and the British Class Structure' in *Sociological Review*, n.s. vol. XI, 1963.
25. J. Bonham, *Middle Class Vote*, p. 113.
26. Carr-Saunders, Jones and Moser, pp. 105–6.
27. See esp. J. Vaizey, *The Cost of Education*, 1958, p. 84.
28. Rogow, *Labour Government and British Industry*, pp. 124 ff.
29. Carr-Saunders, Jones and Moser, pp. 176–7.
30. Quoted by A. Havighurst, *Twentieth-Century Britain*, 1966 edn., pp. 423–4.
31. E. Watkins, *The Cautious Revolution*, 1950. C. F. Brand, *The British Labour Party, A Short History*, 1965, p. 266. A. Marwick, *The Explosion of British Society, 1914–62*. 1963, p. 113.
32. R. H. S. Crossman (ed.), *New Fabian Essays*, 1952, pp. 5–6. A. Howard in M. Sissons and P. French (eds.), *The Age of Austerity*, 1963, p. 31.
33. See Beer, *Modern British Politics*, p. 309.

34. See below, p. 424.
35. J. Mackintosh, *The British Cabinet*, 1960, pp. 384-95.
36. B. Crick, *The Reform of Parliament*, 1964, Garden City, N.Y., edn., 1965, p. 104.
37. E. Hyams, *Gentian Violet*, 1953, p. 175.
38. W. P. Snyder, *Politics of British Defence Policy*, 1966, p. 46.
39. Jennings, *Cabinet Government*, p. 16.
40. E. Wertheimer, *Portrait of the Labour Party*, 1929, p. 81.
41. Private information.
42. See above, p. 347.
43. P.P., 1947-48, XIII (86), pp. 2, 3, 6.
44. *Ibid.*, p. 20.
45. *Report of Local Government Boundary Commission for 1948;* P.P., 1948-49, XVII (150), p. 4. *House of Commons Debates*, 25 March 1949.
46. Cmd. 9831, p. 4.
47. *Ibid.*, Cmd. 9559, p. 26.
48. *House of Commons Debates*, 18 March 1954.
49. Cmd. 9831, p. 5.
50. See above p. 281.
51. *Report Arising Out of Crichel Down*, P.P., 1953-54, X, Cmd. 9220. See also *House of Commons Debates*, 15 June 1954 and 20 July 1954.
52. See esp. R. K. Kelsall, *Higher Civil Service in Great Britain*, 1955. Anthony Sampson, *Anatomy of Britain*, 1962, p. 226.
53. B. Chapman, *British Government Observed*, 1963. *Report of Royal Commission on the Civil Service*, P.P., 1955-56, XI, Cmd. 9613, esp. p. 10.
54. For the law see R. M. Jackson, *The Machinery of Justice in England*, 4th edn., 1964. P. Archer, *The Queen's Courts*, 1963. T. B. Smith, *Scotland: The Development of Its Laws and Constitution*. B. Abel-Smith and R. Stevens, *Lawyers and the Courts*, 1966. A. Harding, *Social History of English Law*, 1966.

CHAPTER NINE

All For Affluence (or, The World Well Lost), 1955-64

I. WINDS OF CHANGE

In the early Fifties the British were still living in the first age of the universal Welfare State, still affected by a war-imposed austerity, and by that 'poverty of desire' of older vintage, and still governed by a philosophy which was part twentieth-century collectivist, part nineteenth-century moralist, and which involved social as well as economic controls. They were still basking in the glory of having been the one unconquered European power, of being an imperial power which had graciously condescended to grant independence to a number of her imperial possessions, of being again presided over by a world statesman who would tolerate no 'socialist scuttles'. By the late Fifties the British were living in an era of unprecedented material prosperity and were in process of being relieved of much of the remaining apparatus of social control dating from Victorian times. They were also being forced painfully to face up to the changed power situation bequeathed by the war, though for a time concealed in the disturbances and excitements of the immediate post-war period. The two major themes of the later Fifties and the Sixties, then, are economic affluence and its attendant freedoms, and abrupt (and unsatisfactory) reaction to the realities of the wider world. Conductors for this strange symphony were, once Churchill had stepped off the platform, two men of high reputation dating from the Thirties and the war years, Anthony Eden (Prime Minister from April 1955 to January 1957) and Harold Macmillan (Prime Minister from January 1957 to October 1963).

The war ushered in the age of the two super-powers, America and Russia; for a time Britain could derive some consolation from ranking herself first among the remaining powers, and a good way ahead of any of them. Such a ranking was constantly menaced by Britain's own balance of payments problem and the prohibitive cost of her remaining world commitments, and it rapidly disappeared with the economic recovery of the European countries in the early Fifties and the beginnings of various forms of European co-operation. The war also ushered in the age of nuclear weaponry, soon shown not to be, as at first hopefully believed, an American monopoly. 1954 was the critical year in which Britain's rulers, with the shuddering awareness of an obsolete aircraft landing on the pock-marked tarmacadam of a badly-defended air strip in a rebellious colony, began in various ways (some of them contradictory) to respond to the world situation. Churchill put it magisterially:

I have not held my mind closed to the tremendous changes which have taken place in the whole strategic position in the world which makes the thoughts which were well-founded and well-knit together a year ago obsolete – absolutely obsolete – and which have changed the opinions of every competent soldier I have been able to meet.[1]

One obvious consequence of new thoughts was the decision to withdraw by 1956 80,000 British troops from the Suez canal zone, a decision which provoked the opposition of Captain Waterhouse, Julian Amery, Lord Hinchingbrooke and Angus Maude. Crusty Tories all, these men were scarcely the representatives of any large section of the British people; yet Waterhouse's words were to find worrying echoes – at one brief point amounting to a deadly roar – for another decade: he talked of Britain 'becoming weary of our responsibilities ... our burdens are becoming too irksome for us and we are really losing our will to rule'.[2]

In 1951 the European Coal and Steel Community had been founded, the first of the organizations which led eventually to the establishment of the European Common Market. Britain refused to join, partly because of a xenophobia which characterized all classes in Britain, more specifically because an outgoing Labour government did not wish to risk Britain's experiment in social democracy, and an incoming Conservative government did not wish to risk Britain's traditions of independence and her imperial connections. The British knew 'in their bones', Sir Anthony Eden said in January 1952, that they could never join a European federation.[3] However, military involvement in Europe, arising from the first post-war defence arrangements, particularly the establishment of the North Atlantic Treaty Organization, could not be avoided, and it was in 1954 that Britain took what has been called the 'final and critical step' in her military entry into Europe, when she agreed to maintain in Europe for fifty years a force of four divisions and a supporting tactical air force element.[4] Also in 1954 was announced the decision to create a Strategic Nuclear Force, which was supposed to serve as a 'deterrent' and lead to manpower reductions. From 1954 there was indeed a trend towards reduction in defence expenditure from the peak years of the Korean War, followed by a period of holding expenditure at a constant proportion of about 7·5 per cent of the gross national product. In 1957 it was announced that conscription would be ended in 1960; numbering 875,000 men in 1952, the British Armed Forces had been reduced to 425,000 men in 1962. At the same time, in pursuit of the 'independent nuclear deterrent' vast sums of money were spent: again and again the stewards of Britain's precarious finances were brought up against the astronomical costs of nuclear weapons, made even more frightening by the rapidity with which obsolescence set in. Of Britain's first two missile projects, Blue Steel suffered from the fatal defect that it would have had to be carried to within a hundred miles of its target by Vulcan, Victor or Valiant bombers, and Blue Streak, a ballistic missile to be launched from underground, simply proved too costly: £100 million had already been spent, with further expenditures still to come, when in 1960 the project was cancelled. Instead it was planned that Skybolt, a missile similar in principle to Blue Steel but much superior in range, would be purchased from the United States on the understanding that Britain would supply her own nuclear warheads. Thus in pursuit of the independent deterrent, Britain in fact became still more dependent on the United States, a process already apparent in the development of supporting systems, such as the Ballistic Missile Early Warning System. The irony of dependence was brought out when in December 1962 the Americans cancelled their Skybolt project. There followed the Nassau conference between President Kennedy and Harold Macmillan at which it was agreed that the U.S. would make available to the U.K. both the latest nuclear wonder, the Polaris missile, and technical data relating to the nuclear-powered submarine from which the missile would be fired. The Macmillan government thereupon decided to build five submarines, at roughly £100 million a time.[5]

The great unhappy event which symbolized Britain's painful readjustment to a changed world, and the powerful psychological reactions to this readjustment, was the Suez war of 1956 when Britain, in consort with the French and the Israelis (who since the British withdrawal from the canal zone earlier in the year had been at constant risk of Egyptian aggression), and in flagrant violation of her obligations under the United Nations Charter, attacked the Egyptian Republic. Up till this point Sir Anthony Eden had shown considerable statesmanship in striving to act as a counterpoise to the belligerence of the American Secretary of State John Foster Dulles, but now, in a tragic example of how not to read the lessons of history, he saw the Egyptian President, Colonel Nasser, as another Hitler who must be stopped even in advance of his Rhineland: not appeasement, but the facile denunciations of appeasement were now coming home to roost. The 'armed conflict' (as Eden called his war) lasted for a week, long enough to demonstrate that Britain no longer had the logistic power to mount an efficient seaborne operation in the Middle East, and for Britain to be branded by the United Nations as an aggressor, before American opposition, Russian threats, and the inevitable run on the pound brought an ignoble venture to a humiliating conclusion.[6]

Leaving Suez aside for the moment, the main lines of British defence policy seem, as far as one can determine from public opinion polls, to have had the support of a majority of the British people, though there was usually a sizeable number of dissenters. In January 1949 57 per cent of those interviewed agreed that conscription should be continued in peacetime, while 33 per cent wished it to be discontinued; in November of the same year the percentages were 53 and 38 respectively. In September 1950, before the official announcement of the increase in length of service from eighteen months to two years, 55 per cent gave advance endorsement of this move, while 33 per cent disapproved. Two and a half years later 45 per cent of those polled favoured continuing the two-year term, 45 per cent favoured a reduction to eighteen months. A year later (May 1954) when Churchill's name was introduced into the pollster's question as a believer in the necessity of Britain's retaining two-year conscription, 49 per cent agreed with Churchill, 35 per cent disagreed. But after the Government had announced in October 1955 that it proposed to cut national service the majority of those polled echoed the change in policy: 47 per cent favoured cutting the two-year period, 34 per cent thought such a cut would be unwise. In September 1956 44 per cent were in favour of abolishing national service, 38 per cent were against such abolition.[7] These figures, Professor Snyder has concluded,

suggest that public attitudes on conscription were transient and sensitive to pronouncements by national political leaders. In the period 1949–54 a majority or near majority approved peacetime conscription; public support, in short, was anchored in the firm commitment of both Government and Opposition to national service. By 1956, one year before the Government announced its plan to end conscription, public support had fallen somewhat, much as the support for national service had declined among political leaders. The Labour Party persistently questioned the need for conscription and the length of the period of service, and their criticism was especially sharp in 1955 and 1956. Despite Labour's criticism and somewhat equivocal support of the Government – the Tories also wanted to end national service but there seemed no easy way to meet military manpower needs without maintaining the period of service at two years – the mass public only mildly disapproved of what was thought to be an intensely unpopular policy.[8]

The reaction to the question of the level of total defence expenditure was very similar: majority support (58 per cent in February 1952) for the steady increase in defence expenditure to 1953; a slightly less decisive majority support for cutting defence expenditure after 1956. With the testing of the first British hydrogen bomb in 1955, the question of the independent nuclear deterrent became an issue of much greater popular concern than that of the total level of defence expenditure with which the Bevanites were so pre-occupied. Throughout the second half of the Fifties opinion polls suggested that between one-quarter and one-third of the British public favoured Britain's unilaterally renouncing nuclear weapons, an issue which was dramatized by the most important of public pressure groups of the time, the Campaign for Nuclear Disarmament, which was founded in 1958. The campaign reached a peak in 1960 when the annual Labour Party conference adopted a resolution in favour of Britain's unilateral nuclear disarmament. Thereafter, however, the campaign seemed to lose impetus, and a similar resolution was rejected by the following year's conference (a somewhat arbitrary matter, in fact, given Labour's block-vote system of 'democracy') and polls suggested a decline in public support. However, after the death in January 1963 of Hugh Gaitskell, a belligerent non-disarmer, and the succession to the Labour Party leadership of the former associate of Bevan's, Harold Wilson, official Labour policy was announced as the abandonment of the independent deterrent and a renegotiation of the Nassau agreements.[9]

The storm over Suez was intense, but it passed away quickly, and the issue was little mentioned in the general election campaign of 1959, which in any event was won by the Conservatives led by Harold Macmillan, a determined supporter of Eden's policy. At the time the division of opinion followed party lines very closely. Opinion polls gave little support to the widely-held contention that a substantial section of Labour supporters found their patriotic senses agreeably titillated by this venture in gun-boat diplomacy. The one Labour M.P. to support the Government, Stanley Evans, was shortly forced to resign by his constituency party. On the other side those Conservatives who could not support their government were treated with similar roughness by their local organizations. That Labour voters in the main opposed the Suez venture does not, of course, close the door to the likelihood that substantial sections of the working class, who might in any event be Conservative voters, approved of it. Equally many of the most influential organs of Conservative opinion came down in opposition to Eden.[10]

The Suez crisis came right in the middle of a period in which the whole nature of the Commonwealth was undergoing rapid change. In 1948 India, Pakistan and Ceylon had become the first non-white self-governing states to join with Britain and the four former white dominions (the Union of South Africa was a white dominion in the sense that only whites had full civic rights). Ghana in 1957 became the first self-governing African country in the Commonwealth, and before 1964 was followed by eight others. While over Suez the Prime Minister of Australia gave the Eden government unqualified support and the Canadian government strove sorrowfully but manfully to bail it out, Prime Minister Nehru of India was forthright in his denunciation of 'naked aggression' and what he called the 'predatory method of the eighteenth and nineteenth centuries'. The Commonwealth, for many Conservatives, was beginning to lose its charms.[11]

That, and various economic considerations, turned Britain's rulers back towards the Europe they earlier had scorned. Within the British political leadership only the Liberals had favoured British participation in the movement which culminated in the European Economic Community ('The Common Market') established by the Treaties of Rome, March 1957. As the economic potential of the Common Market became more clearly apparent, and ties with the Commonwealth came to seem less clearly advantageous, the British Government took the initiative in the moves leading to the Stockholm Convention of January 1960, which set up a European Free Trade Area of Norway, Sweden, Denmark, Portugal, Austria, Switzerland and Britain. In July 1961 the Macmillan government decided to embark upon negotiations for entry into the Common Market, arousing the hostility of certain Conservatives (mainly on the Right) who still put faith in Britain's old imperial connections and her world role, and from a majority of Labour Party spokesmen (concentrated most strongly on the Left) who expressed faith in the moral force of the multiracial Commonwealth and denounced the Common Market as an inward-looking 'rich man's club', dominated by the arch-reactionaries President de Gaulle of France and Chancellor Adenauer of Germany. None the less, while Britain suffered recurrent balance of payments crises, the Germany of Adenauer had its 'economic miracle' and the France of de Gaulle seemed on the way to establishing an independent and influential voice in world affairs. It was at any rate the voice of de Gaulle which in January 1963 pronounced a negative to the British attempt, which

had been conducted with skill and vigour by one of the 'One Nation'
generation of Conservative leaders, Mr Edward Heath. Whether
one wanted to join or not, it was not pleasant to feel that the
decision rested in other hands.[12] Events seemed to be conspiring
to show that the nation which in two world wars had striven hard
and honourably to influence the course of world history now
counted for little or nothing: in October 1962 the Cuban missile
crisis brought the world near the brink of nuclear disaster, and the
only men who mattered in rescuing civilization from the brink were
the leaders of the two super-powers, Russia (who, in the first place,
attempted to install nuclear launching sites in Cuba) and the United
States (who persuaded the Russians to withdraw). One month
earlier a former American Secretary of State, Dean Acheson, in a
speech at the U.S. Military Academy at West Point which was
much quoted, cruelly delineated the position of the one-time world
power:

Great Britain has lost an empire and has not yet found a role. The
attempt to play a separate power role – that is, a role apart from Europe,
a role based on a 'special relationship' with the United States, a role
based on being head of a 'commonwealth' which has no political structure
or unity, or strength, and enjoys a fragile and precarious economic
relationship by means of the sterling area and preferences in the British
market – this role is about played out. Great Britain, in attempting to
work alone and to be a broker between the United States and Russia, has
seemed to conduct policy as weak as its military power. H.M.G. is now
attempting – wisely in my opinion – to re-enter Europe, from which it
was banished at the time of the Plantagenets, and the battle seems about
as hard-fought as were those of an earlier day.[13]

Harold Macmillan's response was bold:

In so far as he appeared to denigrate the resolution and will of Britain
and the British people, Mr Acheson has fallen into an error which has
been made by quite a lot of people in the course of the last 400 years.

But Macmillan had already made a less bold, but far better and
justly more famous speech when addressing a joint session of the

South African Houses of Parliament on 3 February 1960, when he referred to the growing strength of 'African consciousness':

In different places it may take different forms, But it is happening everywhere. The wind of change is blowing through this continent.[14]

The British withdrawal from Empire was not glorious, it was not even, by the mid-Sixties, total. But, if comparisons are made with the Dutch experience in the Congo, or the French experience in Indo-China, it was not entirely lacking in grace.

2. THE 'AFFLUENT SOCIETY'

The much-used, and much-abused, phrase which heads this section was coined by Professor J. K. Galbraith, in a classic denunciation of the major features of American society in the late 1950s; he pointed in particular to the existence side-by-side of private affluence and public squalor.[15] In Britain the dichotomy was less sharp: if, traditionally, *étatiste* traditions were weaker than on the European continent, they were a good deal stronger than in the U.S.A., and in the 1940s the flag of public power had been carried deep into hitherto inviolate territories; private wealth, on the other hand, was considerably less than in the United States. 'Affluence' – the wide diffusion of high living standards – primarily was a function of economic and technological growth, rather than the direct consequence of political action stemming from progressive or labour agitation. The question, therefore, was raised as to whether the objectives once set by socialist and liberal reformers had not now been overtaken by history: were the affluent society and the Welfare State complementary, or had the advent of the former rendered the latter unnecessary? What in any case were the essential preconditions of affluence? If it depended primarily on internal economic and technological factors, should not external government action be cut to a minimum? Conservatives had been restive under Labour's collectivist policies of 1945–50, but had not, in the first half of the Fifties, drastically reversed them; radicals in the party, emboldened by the example of the consumer boom in America or the 'economic miracle' in Germany, preached the virtues of rejuvenated capitalism. These were the matters of debate in the Fifties, muted in the ruling Conservative Party, rather more raucous in the Labour Party, where moderates argued for an acceptance of a role for private capitalism in the spread of affluence.[16] They produced the new economic liberalism which called for less government intervention in economic matters (one of our topics in this section) and called in question many of the fundamentals of the Welfare State as conceived by the post-war generation of Labour leaders (our topic for the next section). But, while much of the argument was academic, the impelling realities were clear: there was affluence; but the British economy as a whole, seemingly well set for recovery in 1950, and again in 1954 after the Korean interlude, began openly to reveal signs of serious weakness. The third reality, seized upon by the upholders of the Galbraith analysis, was that, while living standards for the many rose, conditions for the substantial minority, by-passed for one reason or another by affluence, got sharply worse.

First, a few of the facts of affluence. Average weekly earnings of male manual workers over twenty-one, £3 10s. 11d. in 1938, £6 2s. 8d. in 1946, £8 8s. 6d. in 1951 and £11 7s. 10d. in 1955, reached £13 16s. 6d. in 1959 and £18 8s. 10d. in 1964. Average wages in real terms rose by 20 per cent between 1951 and 1958, and by another 30 per cent by 1964. The consequent swelling in consumers' expenditure can be seen in the aggregate figures. Total expenditure, standing at £10,154 million in 1951 and £13,019 million in 1955, had risen to £16,833 million in 1959 and £20,915 million in 1964. Expenditures on food remained remarkably stable, suggesting that wartime and Welfare State policies had by 1951 created a plateau of reasonable nutrition: £4,008 million in that year, food expenditure had only risen to £4,995 million thirteen years later. Most striking was the rise in expenditure on cars and motor cycles: £90 million in 1951, £354 million in 1955, £522 million in 1959, £910 million in 1964. At the same dates expenditures on furniture, electrical and other durable goods were £526 million, £664 million, £888 million and £975 million. Expenditure on alcohol and tobacco showed a steady but scarcely a staggering rise, from £843 million and £898 million respectively in 1951 to £1,195 million and £1,055 million in 1964. In 1962 three houses out of four had a vacuum cleaner, four out of five a television set, one in three a refrigerator and one in five a washing-machine; there were over 6 million cars on the roads (only 2½ millions in 1951). High incomes were only one part of the base upon which the pile of consumer purchases was raised: the other was hire purchase. The total hire-purchase debt outstanding in 1951 was £208 million, in 1955 £461 million, in 1959 £849 million and in 1964 £1,115 million.[17] By 1959 30 per cent of the people owned, or were buying, their own homes. The Co-operative Permanent Building Society reported in 1960 that 37·7 per cent of mortgage purchasers of new houses were wage-earners.[18] Higher up the social scale affluence was still more in evidence: wherever one looked, new shop frontages, office blocks and various forms of extravagant private buildings were to be seen.

The first draughts of Conservative 'freedom' in the early Fifties had set the Stock Market swinging: between June 1952 and July 1955 the *Financial Times* index of industrial ordinary shares rose from 103 to 224; a second bout of ebullience came between 1958 and May 1961, when the *Financial Times* index rose from 154 to 366. The total market value of all securities, including Government bonds as well as industrial shares, was not, at £26,900 million in 1961, significantly higher than it had been five years earlier; but by April 1964 it had reached a figure of £59,841 million. In the intervening thirteen years gross dividends and interest amounted to £18,536 million.[19] The gains, naturally, went mainly to those who were already wealthy: Nicholas Davenport, an expert and experienced commentator, reckoned that in thirteen years the average rich man more than doubled his capital; if shrewd, he trebled it.[20] After 1957, when the system of control allied with Development Charges was completely dismantled, there were high profits to be made in the property market. But attempts were not lacking to spread some of the new wealth to the masses. In 1958 certain Conservatives launched a 'Wider Share Ownership' campaign, mainly to be achieved through the expansion of unit trust plans; and invested funds in unit trusts did, it is true, rise from £60 million in 1958 to £400 million in 1964. In 1961 there came the first trade union participation in a specially-formed unit trust. On the whole, however, the new fashion seems to have been predominantly a middle-class rather than a working-class one. If the slogan (taken from a speech by Harold Macmillan) which many Conservatives were happy to bandy about in the election campaign of 1959, 'You've Never Had It So Good', lacked something in dignity, it was not noticeably further from the ascertainable facts than most political pronouncements of this sort. Three years later the *Daily Express* chipped in with a happy phrase of its own, characterizing affluence and the plenitude of consumer goods as 'the rollicking revolution of merry England'.[21]

But all was far from well with Merry England, or indeed with marginally less merry Scotland and Wales (Northern Ireland, part of the United Kingdom but not of Britain, and therefore excluded from this book, was, it may be remarked, scarcely merry at all). Absolutely and relatively the British economy was not doing well. The 1956 *Report of the Ministry of Labour and National Service* contained an ominous sentence:

The post-war expansion in industrial production as a whole and in output per man was halted in 1956, the rates remaining approximately at the 1955 level.[22]

The middle years of the Fifties did indeed seem to mark a point of change for, in this respect, the worse. From 1948 to 1955 the average annual increase in the gross domestic product at constant prices was 3·5 per cent; between 1955 and 1961 it was only 2·2 per cent. In 1954 Britain provided 20 per cent of the world's manufactured exports; by the early Sixties she was providing only 15 per cent. Meantime Germany's share had gone up from 15 per cent to over 19 per cent, and Japan's from 5 per cent to nearly 7·5 per cent; France was increasing her exports three times as fast, Germany and Italy six times as fast, as Britain. Taking 1950 as 100, British productivity per man in 1960 stood at 125; the German and French figures for 1960 were 159 and 177 respectively.[23] The halt in industrial expansion meant a decline in unfilled vacancies and an increase in unemployment to, in 1957, an average level over the year of 313,000: at the end of the year unemployment in the hardest-hit communities, Wales and Scotland, were 3 per cent and 2·9 per cent respectively, still very low figures by pre-war standards. In 1958 and early 1959 there was a definite recession and unemployment rose to 621,000, the highest figure since the fuel crisis of 1947: Wales, Scotland, and the older industrial areas of England stood out as centres of high concentration of unemployment.[24] Productivity was lost not only through unemployment, but also through strikes. Well organized and self-conscious as they were, British trade unionists had not hesitated to strike in war or in time of Labour government, and, just as other groups within the community used whatever means came most readily to hand to secure their own ends, it was natural that labour should do so too. But in 1957 more days were lost through industrial disputes than at any time since the year of the General Strike (1926): 80 per cent of the total of 8,412,000 days lost resulted from national strikes among the shipbuilders, the engineers and the busmen. In 1959 days lost totalled the still high figure of $5\frac{1}{4}$ millions, $3\frac{1}{2}$ millions of them due to a national printing strike.[25] Many strikes seemed to be over somewhat trivial matters, demarcation disputes between different trades, the timing of a tea-break: the popular Press introduced the pejorative American phrase 'wild-cat strikes'. Overstated as it undoubtedly was, Arthur Koestler's diagnosis published in the *Observer* in February 1963 was none the less shrewd in its perception of a wider malaise in British industrial relations:

In no other country has the national output been crippled on such frivolous and irresponsible grounds. In this oldest of all democracies class relations have become more bitter, trade union politics more undemocratic than in de Gaulle's France and Adenauer's Germany. The motivation behind it is neither communism, socialism, nor enlightened self-interest, but a mood of disenchantment and cussedness.[26]

Where, then, did the faults lie? The Conservative governments of Sir Anthony Eden, Harold Macmillan and Sir Alec Douglas-Home (October 1963 to October 1964) were no better than most

other British governments in the twentieth century; they were
certainly not significantly worse. If they deserve little credit for
the higher material standards brought by economic progress, they
cannot be condemned out of hand for the failings of the British
economy. In social composition, it is true, despite the readjustments of the late Forties, the Conservative Party had changed little.
As W. L. Guttsman concludes:

It is clear that the 'silent social revolution' of the past half-century has
largely by-passed the leadership of the Conservative Party. Its leading
strata have remained firmly fixed in the upper levels of our stratified
society. Admittedly wealth rather than birth has become significant and
professional men are not prominent in the hierarchy of the Conservative
Party organization.[27]

The business connections of Conservative M.P.s were not quite as
strong as in pre-war years. In 1938 Conservative M.P.s between
them mustered a total of 775 directorships, some in very large
businesses: in 1958 their counterparts, on an approximate assessment, held 379 directorships, in 1961 490 directorships. The
switch in commercial interests was towards finance and the service
industries, towards investment trusts, insurance companies,
property development corporations, advertising and public relations
firms, entertainment and the mass media. The incidence of great
wealth was less now among Conservative M.P.s than had been the
case before the war, a consequence in part of the removal of the
burden of electoral expenses from the candidate to the party.[28]

More noticed by contemporaries than the obvious business
affiliations of the ruling party was the reassertion of the aristocratic
'grouse-moor' image. Under Harold Macmillan, whose wife was a
daughter of the Duke of Devonshire, government by class seemed
to revert to government by Whig cousinage; in 1958 seven out of
nineteen Cabinet ministers were related to the Prime Minister by
marriage.[29] In an age when the holders of ancient titles and elegant
country seats were exploiting for monetary reward the enduring
snobbishness of wide sections of the British people by parading
the former before, and opening the latter to, the public, Mac-

millan appeared to invite satire by assuming the pose of a slightly eccentric but completely unflappable Edwardian. The image was fixed by the undergraduate review which became a West End success, *Beyond the Fringe*, by Papas, cartoonist of the *Guardian*, who drew him as a happy-go-lucky tramp, and, most cuttingly, by Malcolm Muggeridge, one-time editor of *Punch*:

He exuded a flavour of moth-balls. His decomposing visage and somehow seedy attire conveyed the impression of an ageing and eccentric clergyman . . . induced to play the part of a Prime Minister in a dramatized version of a Snow novel put on by a village amateur dramatic society.[30]

Doubtless Macmillan was consciously echoing Stanley Baldwin when he reported to his old school in 1959:

Mr Attlee had three Old Etonians in his Cabinet. I have six. Things are twice as good under the Conservatives.[31]

The memoirs of certain Conservative statesmen of the time read in parts like parodies of a bad Edwardian novel. In the space of three pages Oliver Lyttelton, ennobled as Lord Chandos, manages references to 'Bobbety' Cranborne, 'Billy' Brown, and 'Crinks' Harcourt Johnstone (the inverted commas are his).[32] Lord Salisbury remained an *éminence grise* in modern Conservative politics, playing an important part in the episode which, on the retirement of Eden, resulted in Macmillan rather than Butler being invited by the Queen to assume the prime ministership. Ill health brought Macmillan's resignation in October 1963. Still taking care to avoid any procedure which might, in the ordinary sense of the term, suggest democracy, the party 'evolved' a new leader, and therefore Prime Minister, the fourteenth Earl of Home, who had been Macmillan's aristocratic choice for Foreign Secretary; Butler, who had some claim to be regarded as being a reformer, less to being possessed of any political courage, was strongly disliked by an influential section within the party: he clinched the issue by refusing to make any show of fight. It was obviously unfair that anyone who had the misfortune to inherit a peerage should automatically be barred from the highest political office in the land, and earlier a young Labour M.P. (and, in the words of the Press, 'reluctant peer'), Anthony Wedgwood Benn, had waged a long but ultimately successful fight to make it possible for him to renounce the title inherited from his father, the first-generation Labour peer Lord Stansgate. What made Home less than perfect as Britain's Prime Minister at this stage in her history was not the fact that he was a peer (going through the same procedure as Benn, he soon re-emerged as humble Sir Alec Douglas-Home), but that as a peer of old lineage, deriving his substantial income from ownership of land, he was by education, upbringing and the whole tenor of his adult life even more cut off from the mainstream of British life than the rest of the older generation of Conservative leaders. Sir Alec Douglas-Home's twelve-month tenure of the prime ministerial office is really the culmination of that long failure of the British political structure, even during the upheavals of war, to change in anything like the same degree as social institutions.

The economic policy associated with Conservative rule was characterized as one of 'Stop-Go-Stop', obviously an unsatisfactory policy compared with the ideal of steady, planned growth; however it has to be borne in mind that in 1968, in the aftermath of the biggest 'Stop' ever, Britain still seems very far from attaining this ideal. In 1953 Butler had been praised in some quarters for taking the overtly Keynesian action of pumping more money into a slightly deflated economy.[33] The process, however, was allowed to continue rather far, and very strong inflationary pressures were apparent by 1955; none the less, presumably because a general election was due in May, the April budget actually reduced income tax. The election was won, and a second budget, imposing increased taxation, was introduced in the autumn: there was also a very sharp cut-back in public expenditure, as can be seen from the following directive issued by Butler, Duncan Sandys (Minister of Housing and Local Government) and James Stuart (Secretary of State for Scotland):

We are writing to you, and to all other local authorities on behalf of the Government to ask you to undertake an immediate review of your capital expenditure for the period from now to 31st March 1957. We also ask you to review your current expenditure in order to secure economies wherever possible and to refrain, save in cases of exceptional need, from undertaking new services which will involve additional expenditure either from Government grants or from the rates. . . .

The aims of your review should be to ensure first, that your authority's total capital expenditure [excluding housing in the case of county district councils] in the year 1956–57 does not exceed that of 1954–55, and secondly, that no new works, even those already authorized, are undertaken unless your authority are satisfied that those works are urgently necessary to meet the needs of the area. . . .

We appreciate that to give effect to the request in this message may result in the postponement of improvements which local authorities would like to make in the standards of their services. But the essential condition for all future progress is to ensure the nation's internal and external economic stability. Failure to take the necessary action for this purpose would involve later a much more serious setback to employment and the standard of living.[34]

Butler was then replaced at the Treasury by Macmillan, and the 'Stop' intensified by raising the Bank Rate to $5\frac{1}{2}$ per cent (January 1956), suspending investment allowances, imposing restrictions on hire purchase, and cutting public investment. When, after the Suez venture, Macmillan became Prime Minister, he appointed as his Chancellor of the Exchequer Peter Thorneycroft, who, at a time when Britain's gun-boat aspirations were collapsing in waves of ridicule, was determined that the pound at least should be strong. A 'soft' budget in April 1957 was followed by some speculation against sterling, to which Thorneycroft overreacted, bumping the Bank Rate up to 7 per cent in September 1957. The result was the recession of 1958 and early 1959. Thorneycroft, therefore, was fired, Macmillan having no desire either to see a return to the Depression conditions against which he had led the Tory rebels in the Thirties, or to lose the next general election. The new Chancellor of the Exchequer, Heathcoat Amory, one of the reform Conservatives of the Butler Research Group days, soon returned to 'Go', or, as the *Economic Survey* for 1959 put it with magnificent circumspection: 'The year 1958 saw a considerable change of emphasis in economic policy.'[35] In other words, in good time for the 1959 general election, a new boom in consumer spending was launched: the Bank Rate by the end of 1958 was back to 4 per cent; the Budget of April 1959 cut taxes, restored investment allowances and released post-war credits. With the Conservatives safely back in office for the third successive time, against a Labour Party still racked by internal dissensions, the inevitable 'Stop' came in the 1960 Budget: higher taxes, and, in June, the Bank Rate up to 6 per cent.

Amory was succeeded by Selwyn Lloyd, a quiet unassuming man, inarticulate almost to the point of incoherence, who had served Macmillan loyally as his first Foreign Secretary (once when Macmillan entered the House of Commons during an attack on Lloyd, Bevan issued the glad cry, 'Why attack the monkey when the organ grinder's here?'). The consumer boom of 1959 was followed by a deficit in the balance of payments for 1960 of £258 million, followed in turn by a flight from the pound. To save sterling heavy borrowings had to be made from the International Monetary Fund, and a severe deflation imposed at home. Out came the stock remedy, a 7 per cent Bank Rate; but Lloyd, on the advice apparently of the chief Treasury official, Sir Frank Lee, also essayed something which had not been attempted since the days of Sir Stafford Cripps: what he called a 'wages pause'. There was good sense in this, in so far as one of Britain's problems was the wage inflation born of a full employment economy. Unhappily Lloyd acted in a high-handed and arbitrary fashion, crashing in on such long-established income-determining bodies as the Burnham Committee for teachers' salaries, and various wages councils. In practice the 'wages pause' was observed only in the relatively small sector of the community over whose incomes the Government had direct control, and scarcely at all in private industry, so that it proved not only unfair, but ineffective.[36] Selwyn Lloyd was the principal victim in one of the most ruthless political purges of modern British history when, in July 1962, Macmillan got rid of one-third of his Cabinet – and himself survived: a magnificent testament to the deep will to power and reserves of strength held by the Conservative Party. Actually Selwyn Lloyd, for all his political ineptitude and dedication to the principles of private enterprise, had pointed the road which the future management of the economy must take. Inflation could only be combated by a wages policy, and a wages policy could only be achieved within a frame of national planning: the National Economic Development Council (N.E.D.C. or 'Neddy') which he appointed in 1961, a modest body indeed, was none the less the nearest any government had yet got to the 'Economic General Staff' advocated by Keynesian Liberals in the 1920s and the proponents of political agreement in the 1930s. An important sign of a desire to remedy the structural weaknesses of a major public service was the appointment of a leading industrialist, Dr Richard Beeching, as chairman of the British Transport Commission, with a mandate to produce a programme for rationalizing the railway system. Yet for all that Macmillan announced himself reconverted to the belief in economic planning which he had professed in the Thirties, for all that the N.E.D.C. was joined by a National Incomes Commission, and for all that the new Chancellor, Reginald Maudling, was a man of first-class ability, the economic picture did not basically alter. Once again 'Stop', which culminated briefly early in 1963 with a total of 800,000 unemployed, was succeeded by 'Go', as Macmillan's successor, Douglas-Home, prepared for the General Election of 1964. When the election was over, and Labour returned to office with a tiny majority, it became clear that, as always, the latest consumer boom had produced an enormous deficit in the balance of payments, which in turn meant the usual sterling crisis.

A qualified programme of economic liberalism somewhat promiscuously applied had not, then, proved more successful – it was probably in fact rather less successful – than the qualified programme of socialist planning, somewhat erratically applied, followed by an earlier Labour government. When handled by some of the Government's younger members, however, the programme had its courageous aspects: the 1956 Restrictive Practices Act aimed a first blow at one feature of British industry which perennially hampered growth, and in 1964 Edward Heath took matters further when, despite much Conservative opposition, he pushed ahead with his attack on Re-sale Price Maintenance, the means by which British manufacturers kept up prices by prohibiting price-cutting among retailers.[37]

Britain's economic problems went deeper than the clumsy administration of a 'Stop–Go–Stop' policy. Essentially they derived from the complicated legacy of the war, and the continued failure of politicians to face up to the implications of that legacy. Put more simply, in the rush to escape from the austerity and restrictions associated with post-war reconstruction, British economic policies, in parallel with the Suez venture, betrayed an unjustified arrogance and complacency. As the committee appointed by the Treasury in May 1957 to investigate the working of the monetary and credit system (the Radcliffe Committee) pointed out, the war had yielded a certain bonus:

Whereas it had been necessary between the two wars to reverse many of the changes in the industrial pattern resulting from the First World War and the boom that followed it, the industrial pattern that took shape in the Second World War and in the early post-war years was well adapted to the trends in demand over the succeeding decade.[38]

Hence full employment and, ultimately, affluence. But in conditions of full employment the tendency was for wages to outstrip productivity, engendering inflation and a weakening in the value of the pound. If industrial productivity was the prime concern, as with other West European countries, then the pound could be allowed to weaken, and indeed be devalued if necessary; but if Britain was to continue with what remained of her world financial role, still furnishing one of the world's reserve currencies, then the pound must remain strong – as Thorneycroft had insisted. The dilemma had been apparent in the inter-war years, especially in August 1931 – now, because of the further economic losses of the Second World War, it was much more starkly posed. Yet, refusing to make any fundamental reappraisal of Britain's position – and there was no evidence of the Labour Party being prepared to do this either – the Government necessarily fell back on an oscillation between industrial expansion and the deflation required to restore the pound to strength. The Radcliffe Committee itself clearly, if cautiously, favoured the tough policy which Thorneycroft had tried to implement:

The public undoubtedly now expects the maintenance of a level of employment that would have been thought Utopian a generation ago, and the pressure of demand implicit in this extremely high level of employment is believed by an important body of expert opinion to have substantially compromised government efforts to maintain the external and internal value of the pound.[39]

A special problem for Britain was her poverty in useful natural resources, masked in the days of imperial and trading supremacy before 1914, and of low consumption after 1918, but now fully exposed. Rising material standards at home inevitably meant an increase in imports; even increased exports depended to some extent upon increased imports of the necessary raw materials upon which British manufacturing industry was based. Where there was a failure at government level in the Fifties was in the too ready abandonment, in the name of 'Conservative freedom', of the artificial restraints on imports which hitherto had been maintained. As Sir Roy Harrod has commented:

the United Kingdom began to adopt too complacent an attitude during the course of the 1950s. It was not sufficiently appreciated that such success as had been achieved was partly due to the effect, or after-effect, of import restrictions. Thus the authorities appeared to have ceased to think of balance of payments difficulties as essentially arising from the financial losses of the war. The structural readjustment required in consequence of these was not one which the ordinary process of monetary and fiscal policies could be relied on to achieve.[40]

Within industry the problem was one of plant, ideas and practices which, having had no real stimulus to change, belonged to the world of the 1930s or earlier. Whatever might be said about trade union restrictive practices, wild-cat strikes and so on, it was pretty apparent that the major fault lay with management, a theory borne out by the wide variations in levels of productivity in different sectors of industry.[41] This in turn had its roots in an inefficiently rigid class structure, and in an ineffably bad educational system where, even at the most expensive levels, there was a disregard for scientific, technological and managerial education. The gap between British achievement in the realm of scientific discovery and the industrial application of such discoveries is a continuing theme. At best, British technology, as in the aero-engine or computer industries, was well in advance of the continent of Europe. At government level British expenditure on scientific research and development compared favourably with that of the United States: in 1955 the British figure corresponded to 1·6 per cent of the gross national product, while the American expenditure in 1953 had been 1·5 per cent of the American gross national product. In private industry, however, British expenditure was only about 0·8 per cent of total industrial output, whereas in the United States in 1953 it had been 1·9 per cent of industrial output, and was steadily rising. A final problem in Britain was the low level of industrial investment compared with European countries, something which again clearly reflected on the quality of British management.[42]

3. WITHERING AWAY OF THE WELFARE STATE?

Ideology apart, there were sound economic reasons for advocating a retrenchment in the universalist provisions of the original Welfare State: a substantial section of the populace now seemed to be pretty well off, while the central Government was in constant difficulties over the balance of payments and the associated sterling crises; since the universal level of benefits was low, those who were genuinely in need were assisted less effectively than they might have been if all available resources had been concentrated entirely on the really poor. In practice, however, the main divide on welfare policy tended to fall between the upholders of the theory that a social revolution had taken place after 1945, the older generation of Conservative leaders along with the majority of the Labour Party, on the one side, and the Bow Group Conservatives and Radical Liberals, who saw the Welfare State as a temporary expedient necessary to see the community through a transitional phase in the development of modern capitalism, on the other: as Marxists visualized the ultimate withering away of the State, so the radicals visualized the withering away of the Welfare State. A Bow Group pamphlet, *Reform of the Social Services*, published in 1961, quoted with approval a famous dictum of the nineteenth-century economist Alfred Marshall, that

a service should contain in itself the seed of its own disappearance . . . which would make it shrivel up, as the causes of poverty itself shrivelled up.[43]

From the mid-Fifties onwards, therefore, the Bow Group Conservatives and the radical Liberals (mainly University intellectuals, like Alan Peacock, Professor of Economics at the University of Edinburgh, and subsequently Dean of Social Sciences at the new University of York) mounted an attack of increasing intensity on the basic doctrines of the Welfare State. Economic arguments were inextricably bound with ideological ones. Remarking that he had been nurtured on the doctrine that 'our civilization . . . is built up on private property', one Bow Group member stated the objective as

to restore the freedom of each individual to spend his income as he thinks best or to save it in order to create more wealth or to provide for some future emergency.[44]

The idea that the social services were here to stay, another declared, was 'not ennobling but degrading'. Peter Goldman, widely acclaimed as the Conservative Party's leading young back-room intellectual, stated that

there is both a need and an opportunity for a major shift in the nature, direction and emphasis of social spending – away from the crude services which working people ought increasingly to be able to provide for themselves.[45]

The idea of welfare policy as a means towards removing class distinctions was explicitly disavowed: 'what disfigures our modern society is not class, but squalor';[46] benefits should be diverted, not towards a theoretical egalitarianism, but towards removing squalor.

The aim of these 'new liberals', then, was nothing short of the total dismantling of the post-Beveridge social security structure. For those really in need, as assessed on the basis of income tax coding, benefits would be payable by the State, but the essence of the new scheme would be compulsory subsistence insurance contracted through private companies, and yielding benefits strictly related to contributions. For the bad risks, the eternal stumbling-block to plans of this sort, the State would devise and 'if necessary run itself' a special scheme. Thus:

People who are at present obliged by the compulsory insurance scheme to 'take in each other's washing' must be allowed, and indeed encouraged, to do their own. All this will involve a deliberate reversal of certain aspects of Conservative policy as it has been applied in recent years.[47]

The other aspect of contemporary social security orthodoxy most attacked by the new liberals was the universal payment of family allowances, arguably too small to be much help to the poor, and used by the rich for the purchase of toys or other extras (though allowances were subject to income tax). In 1956 the Conservative government introduced the principle of graduation: 3s. per week for the second child, 10s. for a third and subsequent children. With regard to the National Health Service the objective of the new liberals was that people should be encouraged to contract out of it,[48] a process which, by giving a new leverage to the doctors, and diminishing the income of the service, would certainly seem well calculated to speed the process of 'withering away'. Education, whose weaknesses seemed to lie near the heart of many of Britain's social and economic failings, stimulated some of the most interesting ideas. Alan Peacock and others argued that instead of providing free education the State should supply parents with vouchers, which could be used to send children to private fee-paying schools; wealthy parents who insisted on sending their children to State schools would be required to pay something:

We would have taken a decisive step towards enlarging the responsibility of parents for the education of their children. There is, of course, a corresponding risk that some children, whose talent the nation needs to develop, would thus be deprived of educational opportunity – because these parents underrated its value. But with rising standards all round the traditional enthusiasm of the middle classes for educating their children at least in part at their own expense is certain to spread. There is moreover a substantial minority of angry parents, who see their children of moderate ability (having 'failed' the eleven-plus) deprived of any opportunity of a grammar school education. There is good reason for believing that many such children would achieve more in grammar schools than the theoretically more able children from poorer homes.[49]

The radical demand for a 'Self-help' rather than a Welfare State had not had any great practical success before the Labour Party, with its deeper organic commitment to the original concept of the 1940s, returned to office in 1964, though under Conservative government the advent of affluence was undoubtedly accepted as lessening the need for further development of the Welfare State. While the community got richer, there was no proportionate increase in social service expenditures: the Health Service, for example, claiming 4·1 per cent of the gross national product in 1950, received only 3·7 per cent in 1958 and 3·9 per cent in 1960. The shortages of men, materials and facilities, as well as the various legislative anomalies bequeathed from the time of the founding of the Welfare State, therefore became more pronounced. Having itself been responsible for the distinction between national insurance and national assistance, the Labour Party began in the Fifties to argue for a unification of the two schemes. More than this, one of its liveliest spokesmen, Richard Crossman, whose breathtaking switches in tactics had frequently astonished friend and foe alike, put forward a scheme in which retirement pensions would, as in many European countries, be linked to previous earnings instead of adhering to the original Beveridge-era flat-rate principle. In reply the Conservative government, worried by the mounting cost of old-age pensions, in 1961 introduced its own 'graduated scheme' in which higher contributions, graduated by income, would yield higher retirement pensions; while those whose employers ran private schemes furnishing pensions at least as substantial as the new graduated pensions, could contract out of the graduated part of the scheme (by 1964 about $4\frac{1}{2}$ millions were thus 'contracting out'). Socialist critics were now pointing out that the great private insurance companies, whose very existence had seemed in jeopardy with the immense Labour victory of 1945, had not only survived but, now strengthened by deliberate government action, were in the position of being the biggest source of capital on the British money market.[50]

More important, however, than matters of political and social ideology was the very real plight of the country's 'hidden poor' discovered by various social investigators in the late Fifties and early Sixties[51] (it was very much to the credit of the new liberals that their concern was with the material realities of poverty). One fundamental reason for the continuance of poverty was the absence, despite the fact that this had been central to all the advanced social policies put forward by the I.L.P. in the 1920s, of any complete minimum wage policy: in 1964 about a quarter of a million families had less than the £8 10s. 6d. per week plus rent which the National Assistance Board reckoned as necessary for subsistence. Another cause of poverty for some families with low income was high rental or mortgage payments. The other major reason was the failure of social security to provide the basic coverage that it was supposed to provide; while national insurance benefits fell further and further behind the rising cost of living, many persons in need (including half a million unemployed) had never managed to fulfil the conditions qualifying them for benefits. In theory national assistance existed as a final resort for both classes: in fact in 1964 $1\frac{1}{2}$ million retired people were dependent for subsistence on the income provided by national assistance; a further half million, though entitled to claim by virtue of their poverty, were not doing so, and therefore were living below the subsistence minimum as defined by the National Assistance Board.[52]

There were other forms of personal deprivation, exaggerated by material change, which were too deep for remedy through mere Beveridge-style welfare. In the first period of affluence attention had been focused by Alan Sillitoe's novel, *Saturday Night and*

Sunday Morning (1956), upon the alienation of a prosperous factory hand, Arthur Seaton, from the values of contemporary society; but there could be no question as to the enjoyment Seaton derived from life. In the Sixties attention began to swing to that section of the populace left behind by a society in which advancing technology and automation had rendered unskilled manual labour less and less in demand, and where an educational system based on an inequitable competitiveness created an iniquitous segregation between those children designed to acquire useful knowledge and skills, and those who would be cast aside at the age of 15. Sid Chaplin described the lot of these 'sardines' of society:

Dead-end is right. Everybody down there, heaving coal, running errands, carrying meat, watching a machine, walking about or sitting on his backside, matterless what, is either dead or dying. Don't be killed by the odd one or two exceptions that kick the slats out of a foreman or grin and bear it, because they're just the same underneath: rejects, found wanting, defeated before they even made a start. Education is a sieve as well as a lift.[53]

Later Edward Bond's outstanding play *Saved* (1965), performed at the Royal Court Theatre, explored the condition of the 'rejects', their sense of alienation, and predisposition to senseless violence. Conceivably the very existence of national assistance, allowing the able-bodied man at odds with society to live a life of useless indolence, was a valuable check on the kind of violence already endemic in the United States. Sean Hignett in *A Picture to Hang on the Wall* (1966) drew a deft portrait of a frustrated art student living on national assistance: saddest of all was the human wreckage cast up by the great Depression of the Thirties and stranded ever since, the permanent clients of the National Assistance Board:

... the old men who'd been there so long they got narked if someone went to sleep on their bit of the hall-long bench, opened their eyes slightly, swallowed their forbidden spit and went into their comas again. They'd heard it all before sitting there since the Cotton Exchange had collapsed in the Thirties, leaving the bosses with only their holdings in Cunard and the old men with a lot of useless hooks that the kids used to tear the furniture apart with until the war brought the brief, unimaginable, steady job, gave them a taste of a new suit and a new Alsatian or cherry-eating youth over the fanlight window, almost got them into the affluent society, but not quite, they hadn't been brought up to expect work, it was beyond them. The long wooden bench became a habit and a strictly enforced hierarchy had grown up, not one of them along that wall would dare show his face if he started making a serious attempt at a job, he'd lose his well-polished place, the only company he knew in the winter mornings, before a pint over by St George' Hall, and a summer's afternoon kip with the pigeons in St John's Gardens.[54]

Some social problems, however, needed nothing so much as an expenditure of public money. In 1962 the Conservative government announced a ten-year hospital building programme, following upon a survey of the previous year which had referred to 'hospitals which should have been blown up, slum property, appalling fire risks, overcrowding, barrack-like buildings and degrading conditions for patients and staff'. Each year since 1945 less hospital construction had been undertaken than in each year in the decade before the Second World War; two-thirds of the hospitals still in use had been built in the nineteenth century. At the same time as half a million people awaited hospital places, over 10,000 beds lay empty due to shortage of staff. While shortages in accommodation and staff were the main signs of crisis in the Health Service, there was evidence that the apparently modest charges imposed at the beginning of the Fifties were deterring people from making use of facilities which, on grounds of health alone, they ought to have been using.[55] Where a change of emphasis in social policy was most marked was in housing. Should housing be considered as a social service at all? Or should the State stand aside and allow rising living standards to create a 'property-owning democracy'? It was in housing that the paradoxes of the Galbraithian affluent society showed up most vividly. Private home ownership was on the increase; but whatever the correct ideological solution, there could be no doubt as to the continued existence of housing conditions which would disgrace any civilized community. Out of a total of just over 16 million houses (in 1963) more than 5½ million were survivors from the nineteenth century, about 4 million having no baths, and a proportion of these no hot water systems at all and in some cases no inside lavatory facilities. Rent control had undoubtedly created anomalies and for some private landlords even hardships, but the Rent Act of 1957, which released from control all houses of annual rateable value of over £40 in London and Scotland and £30 elsewhere, and introduced 'creeping de-control' for all other tenancies as they fell vacant, failed to reveal the expected 'hidden accommodation', while creating evictions and hardship. The word 'Rachmanism' was coined to describe the particularly nefarious activities associated with the London slum landlord, Peter Rachman. Early in 1967 a report on housing conditions in Scotland brought out that matters were far worse than somewhat over-optimistic local authority accounts had suggested: 2 million Scots – one family in three – were living in 'scandalous' conditions; half a million houses required to be wiped out at once; Glasgow's slums were 'appalling' and 'atrocious'.[56] It might well be that in an ideal modern society housing ought to be a matter for individual choice, with the structure of public authority housing withering away in face of rising living standards: quite certainly Britain, in the mid-Sixties, had yet to reach this happy condition.

While there were slight modifications in the Beveridge-era conception of the Welfare State, there were much more substantial modifications in the forms of social control of much older vintage. It had been the Conservative government of Victorian-minded Stanley Baldwin which, throwing up its hands in horror over the excesses of American commercial radio, had instituted the paternalistic B.B.C. Although the authority of the B.B.C. stood high at the end of the war, its position was weakened by the rise of the new radical liberalism, extolling the virtues of private enterprise and the free market, by the general reaction against the grandmotherliness associated with the 1945–51 Labour governments, by the decline in the popularity of sound broadcasting which actually antedated the post-war rise of television,[57] and by the agitation of vested interests who, with considerable business acumen, saw the money-making possibilities of commercial television. It is probable that in the early Fifties a majority of the older leaders of the Conservative Party were strongly opposed to such a sharp break with tradition as would be involved in the institution of commercial television. None the less, through one of the most skilful pieces of political lobbying in Britain's modern history, a tightly-knit group of ideologically and commercially-motivated men succeeded, against strong opposition, in bringing about the Television Act of 1954, which provided for the commencement of commercial television in September 1955.[58] Though marking a revolutionary change in British social policy this was, characteristically, a very restrained revolution, as the announcement of the Government's 'three objectives' suggest:

the first is to introduce an element of competition into television and enable private enterprise to play a fuller part in the development of this important and growing factor in our lives; the second is to reduce to a minimum the financial commitments of the State; and the third is to proceed with caution into this new field and to safeguard this medium of information and entertainment from the risk of abuse or lowering of standards.[59]

A second public corporation, the Independent Television Authority, was established with the responsibility of allocating contracts for the provision of television programmes in different areas of the country. Once a particular company had received a contract either for all broadcasting, or for all broadcasting on certain days, in a particular part of the country, it would in its allotted area and on its allotted days have a complete monopoly of commercial broadcasting. The company would seek its profit through the sale of advertising time, which must come only in 'natural breaks' between programmes; there would be no sponsorship of programmes by advertisers. To the Independent Television Authority would remain the right and duty to lay down general conditions, to supervise the quality of programmes, and to provide regular bulletins of Independent Television News. First Director General of the I.T.A. was Sir Robert Fraser, former head of the Government's Central Office of Information. Both I.T.A. and B.B.C. would be governed by the Postmaster General's continued ruling – designed to prevent television from becoming too pernicious an influence on everyday life – that television broadcasts should not cover more than fifty hours a week (in 1957 a prohibition on week-day broadcasting between the hours of six and seven in the evening was lifted). Originally it had been planned that the commercial companies would share in the use of B.B.C. transmitters, but this proved technically impossible.

Several years elapsed before all independent television contracts were allocated and all commercial channels went into operation, while it was only in the same period that television finally asserted its supremacy over sound radio: the year of change was 1956–57, when for the first time the number of combined television and radio licences equalled the number of sound only licences[60] (even after the institution of commercial television it remained the law that all possessors of receiving sets must pay the B.B.C. licence fee, even if they had no wish to watch B.B.C. programmes). Wherever B.B.C. and commercial programmes were in competition it was soon apparent that the latter were much more popular. By 1960 a clear picture had emerged of between 60 and 70 per cent of viewing time going to commercial broadcasting and between 30 and 40 per cent to the B.B.C.[61] After initial losses, the commercial companies began to show very handsome profits, as gross advertising revenue mounted from £13 million in 1956 to £93 million in 1961. The Independent Television Authority had been empowered to borrow up to £2 million from the Government: in fact it had to borrow only £555,000, which it had repaid by 30 July 1959; thereafter, as was the original intention, it was fully self-financing.[62] Faced with competition and a loss of audiences, the B.B.C. boldly proclaimed that it would remain true 'to its traditional purpose and its mission to serve the cause of education and the arts' and to its 'obligations to the public'.[63] In practice it frequently succumbed to the temptation of trying to beat independent television on its own home-ground of trivial mass entertainment, as indeed was admitted in the B.B.C.'s comment that

Experience has ... shown that, in broadcasting, competition, whatever its other virtues may be, does not tend towards diversity of choice but rather towards choice between different programmes of the same kind.[64]

By the end of the Fifties much adverse criticism of the standard of television programmes, particularly of those offered on the commercial channels, was in circulation: denunciation of 'American-made telefilms' containing 'scenes of crude violence' was especially loud, and the Nuffield Foundation Report, *Television and the Child*, published in December 1958, drew attention to the special problem of the effects on children of certain television programmes. So in July 1960 the Postmaster General announced that a committee would shortly be appointed to investigate the various problems relating to broadcasting: the Pilkington Committee was duly announced in September, and it presented its report in June 1962. The situation was not a simple one. Obviously it was desirable that the viewer should have a choice of programmes; competition had certainly stimulated advances in production techniques; above all, commercial television had produced a second programme at no cost to the Government or to the viewer. The Television Act of 1954 had been cautious in intent and careful in expression: the fault seemed to lie with the Independent Television Authority which, carried away by the financial and popular success of the new system, had failed adequately to use its rights of control and supervision. But if the I.T.A. had served the nation badly, the Pilkington Committee also rendered poor service by producing such a one-sided denunciation of commercial television that it was made easier for the Government to by-pass some of its recommendations: in the judgement of the committee, 'the B.B.C. know good broadcasting; by and large they are providing it': whereas 'we conclude that the dissatisfaction with television can largely be ascribed to the independent television service'.[65] However, although the Pilkington recommendations that the I.T.A. itself should take over the provision of television programmes, and that in no contracting company should a newspaper interest predominate, were ignored, the strictures of the committee did help to ensure that when a third channel was inaugurated in 1964 it would be allocated to the B.B.C. ('B.B.C. Two'); control of the I.T.A. over programme contractors was at the same time strengthened. Whether the introduction of some form of commercial television in the modern age of high consumer spending could have been completely avoided is dubious: its place in the development of a mass culture with strong transatlantic overtones is very apparent, though it is not to be denied that the B.B.C., too, has relied heavily on material which was American in origin. At the same time the great expansion in television has created greater opportunities than ever before for British writers, actors and musicians.

Concern over recent trends in television was echoed in concern over the condition of the British Press. The second royal commission since the war, sitting throughout 1961 and 1962 under the chairmanship of Sir Hartley Shawcross, pointed to the disquieting concentration of Press ownership which had taken place since the previous commission reported in 1949: by 1961 the Daily Mirror Group, Associated Newspapers and Beaverbrook Newspapers together owned 67 per cent of all daily newspapers. As the newspaper industry approximated more and more to the pure conditions of monopoly capitalism, so the remaining traces of civic purpose which once had informed parts at least of the Press faded from the scene. While the Press was failing to provide the variety of opinions and the cultural and educational stimulus vital to a liberal democracy, it was at the same time exhibiting in exaggerated degree some of the worst features of British industrial inefficiency. While the earnings of printing workers were the highest of any manual workers, the industry lacked any high degree of co-operation between labour and management, being, indeed, characterized by an excessive use of labour, and by a reluctance to exploit new techniques.[66] While inefficiency and restrictive practices could be borne by the vast monopolistic combines, they were a constant danger to quality newspapers such as the *Guardian*, which had done much to keep alive the best traditions of British journalism.

Next to the Television Act in marking the change that came over British society in the later Fifties rank the institution of Premium Savings Bonds in 1956 and the Betting and Gaming Act of 1960. Public lotteries had been a feature of rumbustious, hard-living, hard-gaming eighteenth-century British society (the building of the British Museum was partially financed by one), but had been abandoned in the era of evangelical piety. Harold Macmillan's 1956 public lottery gave investors in this type of National Savings the chance every month (after an initial three months) of winning in lieu of interest prizes ranging from £25 to £5,000. Prior to 1960 the very strict and somewhat arbitrary legislation governing betting and gaming (also largely a product of Victorian evangelicalism) had resulted in widespread evasion of the law, especially in the form of off-the-course street betting on horse racing. The main purpose of the 1960 Act was the sound Conservative one of restoring respect and credibility to the law by openly legalizing certain forms of gambling: street betting-shops, gaming houses, and bingo followed. Within a couple of years it was clear that the Government had blundered: the gaming houses which theoretically were to be easy for the police to control became in many cases centres of organized racketeering as well as being an unfortunate temptation to the inveterate gambler. Again it was made clear that however desirable complete freedom of choice and absolute self-government might be as ideals, the first age of affluence was scarcely the best moment to choose for the relaxation of social controls, whatever undesirable pedigrees of piety, Victorianism, or socialism might attach to them.

In fact the particular stage in economic and social development, of which rising material standards for many was one facet, was bringing with it a whole host of new, or aggravated, social problems. The Committee on Children and Young Persons, appointed in October 1956 and reporting in October 1960, brought out how during the very period in which it was deliberating the whole scene had changed for the worse. By 1958 a great increase in crime in the population at large was apparent, but it was most significant in the 17–21 and 14–17 age-groups, where crime rates reached the highest ever known; among the 8–14 group, too, there was a rise from 924 criminal offences per 100,000 in 1955 to 1,176 per 100,000 in 1958.[67] The committee recognized the importance of the up-heavals of war, in both their immediate and delayed consequences, but they argued cogently that an equally potent factor in the recent increases in juvenile crime was the process of unguided economic change:

During the past fifty years there has been a tremendous material, social and moral revolution in addition to the upheaval of two wars. While life has in many ways become easier and more secure, the whole future of mankind may seem frighteningly uncertain. Everyday life may be less of a struggle, boredom and lack of challenge more of a danger, but the fundamental insecurity remains with little that the individual can do about it. The material revolution is plain to see. At one and the same time it has provided more desirable objects, greater opportunity for acquiring them illegally, and considerable chances of immunity from the undesirable consequences of so doing. It is not always so clearly recognized what a complete change there has been in social and personal relationships (between classes, between the sexes and between individuals) and also in the basic assumptions which regulate behaviour. These major changes in the cultural background may well have replaced the disturbances of war as factors which contribute in themselves to instability within the family.[68]

Within the same time-span the Christian Economic and Social Research Foundation detected a sharp increase in drunkenness among under-21s. Insobriety in all age-groups in the late Fifties was about 40 per cent above the average for the 1930s, which represented a relapse to the worst conditions of the mid-1920s. To concentrate on juvenile drunkenness alone, the foundation commented, was to receive ominous overtones of Edwardian or Victorian times.[69]

From the late Fifties reports on public health lay increasing stress on four new features: the marked rise in the incidence of venereal diseases; the increased number of road accidents; the importance of cancer in claiming one out of every five deaths; and the 'inward balance of migration'.[70] The first three are related in various obvious ways to a free-wheeling, free-living, heavy-smoking, car-owning society. The rising numbers of immigrants, mainly from the West Indies, partly also from India and Pakistan, was in minor degree related to the first experience of life in Britain which many members of the Commonwealth had had during the Second World War; in major degree it was due to changes in American immigration laws in the early Fifties which had turned the West Indians from the United States towards Britain; it also owed something to the tempting picture of attractive living conditions which Britain was now beginning to present. Total net immigration for the three years 1960–62 amounted to 388,000, about three-quarters from the

Commonwealth and almost half from the West Indies. By the mid-Sixties there were approximately 1 million coloured immigrants (about 2 per cent of the total population) living in Britain. From the time of the race riots in Notting Hill – a slum area of West London – it was apparent that a *laissez-faire* policy was inadequate. By providing much-needed manpower in industries and trades where white labour was in short supply, the immigrants made an invaluable contribution to the economy; but since housing was the weakest point in the social edifice they also created severe social strains. When the Government finally took action in 1962, it was action of the simplest and bluntest sort: the Commonwealth Immigrants' Act laid it down that all immigrants must either have a job waiting for them, or be possessed of certain special qualifications and skills; the Act also provided for a ceiling on the total number of immigrants admitted. But the easy way out was no way out at all. By taking only negative action the Government seemed to be giving official endorsement to what a wealth of evidence was already making all too plain: racial discrimination was already firmly established in the British Isles.[71]

It is when we set down the new strains, the new hazards, the new moral obliquity of affluent living, side-by-side with the old problems of undue conservatism, class-consciousness and economic weakness, that we see some of the essential difficulties of contemporary Britain. Prodded by certain identifiable agents of change, galvanized by two world wars, Britain had achieved much thus far in the century of total war; she had also lost much. Who now would do the prodding, whence would come the new electric shocks? Presented with the gratuitous offering of Sir Alec Douglas-Home on the other side, Harold Wilson's Labour Party offered itself to the electorate in 1964 as the party of modernization, the party of technology. Would such claims be vindicated? Would they be enough? The test would certainly prove real, because again and again after 1964 elements of the British paradox, recurrent items in the course of this book, broke through to dominate the flow of events.

NOTES TO CHAPTER NINE

1. Quoted by T. Robertson, *Crisis: The Inside Story of the Suez Conspiracy*, 1962, p. 5.
2. *House of Commons Debates*, 29 July 1954.
3. Quoted by L. Epstein, *Britain, Uneasy Ally*, 1954, p. 52. In general see M. Camps, *Britain and the European Community 1955–63*, 1964.
4. W. P. Snyder, *Politics of British Defence Policy*, p. 19.
5. *Ibid.*, pp. 19, 32.
6. See T. Robertson, *Crisis*. A. J. Barker, *Suez: The Seven Day War*, 1965. D. C. Watt (ed.), *Documents on the Suez Crisis*, 1957. J. Eayrs, *The Commonwealth and Suez: A Documentary Survey*, 1964. H. Thomas, *The Suez Affair*, 1967.
7. The findings of the British Institute of Public Opinion (Gallup) Polls are summarized by Snyder, pp. 54–55.
8. Snyder, p. 55.
9. *Ibid.*, pp. 56–61. C. Driver, *The Disarmers*, 1964.
10. L. Epstein, *British Politics in the Suez Crisis*, 1964, pp. 147 ff., citing British Institute of Public Opinion Polls.
11. N. Mansergh, in W. B. Hamilton, K. Robinson, C. D. W. Goodwin (eds.), *A Decade of Commonwealth, 1955–1964*, Durham, N.C., 1966, pp. 5 ff. Eayrs, pp. 194, 256.
12. See Camps, *Britain and the European Community 1955–63*.
13. D. Acheson, *Vital Speeches*, XXIX, no. 6, 1963, pp. 163–4.
14. *Decade of Commonwealth*, p. 9. Havighurst, *Twentieth Century Britain*, p. 491.
15. J. K. Galbraith, *The Affluent Society*, 1958, esp. pp. 195 ff.
16. For the two points of view in the Labour Party see e.g. C. A. R. Crosland, *The Future of Socialism*, 1956, and R. Miliband, *Parliamentary Socialism*, 1961. (Despite the titles the former is to the Right, the latter on the Left.)
17. Statistics from London and Cambridge Economic Service, *The British Economy: Key Statistics 1900–1964*, Tables C and D. J. Burnett, *Plenty and Want*, pp. 267–8.
18. D. E. Butler and R. Rose, *The British General Election of 1959*, 1960, pp. 11–13. H. Hopkins, *The New Look*, 1963, p. 348.
19. N. Davenport, *The Split Society*, 1954, pp. 66–67.
20. *Ibid.*, p. 67.
21. *Ibid.*, pp. 69–70. *Daily Express*, 19 December 1962.
22. P.P., 1956–57, Cmnd. 242.
23. R. Harrod, *British Economy*, p. 20. G. D. N. Worswick and P. H. Ady, *The British Economy in the Nineteen-Fifties*, 1962, esp. pp. 114–30.
24. *Ministry of Labour Report for 1957*, P.P., 1957–58, XV, Cmnd. 468, pp. 30 ff.: *Report for 1959*, P.P., 1959–60, XVII, Cmnd. 1059, pp. vii, 23.
25. Cmnd. 468, p. 90. Cmnd. 1059, p. viii.
26. *Observer*, 10 February 1963.
27. Guttsman, *British Political Élite*, pp. 294–5.
28. *Ibid.*, pp. 296–7.
29. *Ibid.*, p. 221.

30. M. Muggeridge in A. Koestler (ed.), *Suicide of a Nation?*, 1963, p. 29.
31. Quoted, A. Sampson, *Anatomy of Britain*, 1962, p. 175.
32. Viscount Chandos, *Memoirs*, 1965, pp. 195–7.
33. *House of Commons Debates*, 24 March 1953.
34. P.P., 1955–56, XXXVI, Cmd. 9607.
35. P.P., 1958–59, XXV, Cmnd. 708. In general see Worswick and Ady, *The British Economy in the Nineteen-Fifties*, esp. pp. 231–324, and J. C. R. Dow, *The Management of the British Economy 1945–60*, 1964, esp. pp. 66–111.
36. See Davenport, *The Split Society*, pp. 80–81.
37. See Harrod, *British Economy*, pp. 82–83.
38. P.P., 1958–59, XVII, Cmnd. 827, p. 9.
39. *Ibid.*, p. 18.
40. Harrod, *British Economy*, p. 32.
41. R. Malik, *What's Wrong with British Industry?*, 1964, p. 11. Sampson, *Anatomy*, p. 174.
42. P.P., 1956–57, XV (107), pp. 1–3. Beckerman, *British Economy in 1975*, p. 27.
43. G. Howe, *Reform of the Social Services*, Bow Group Principles into Practice, 1961, p. 59.
44. *Ibid.*, p. 60.
45. A. Seldon, *Choice in Welfare*, 1963. P. Goldman, *Future of the Welfare State*, 1964.
46. *Ibid.*
47. Howe, p. 61.
48. *Ibid.*, p. 70.
49. *Ibid.*, p. 82, See also A. T. Peacock and T. Wiseman, *Education for Democrats: A Study of the Financing of Education in a Free Society*, 1964.
50. R. M. Titmuss, *The Irresponsible Society*, 1960.
51. e.g. P. Townsend, *The Family Life of Old People: An Inquiry in East London*, 1957. D. Cole and J. Utting, *The Economic Circumstances of Old People*, 1962. D. Wedderburn, 'Poverty in Britain Today—the Evidence', *Sociological Review*, N.S., X, 1962. P. Townsend, 'The Meaning of Poverty', *British Journal of Sociology*, XIII, 1962. Cp. P.E.P., 'Poverty: Ten Years after Beveridge', *Planning*, XIX, 1952.
52. Wedderburn, 'Poverty in Britain Today'. Townsend, 'The Meaning of Poverty'.
53. S. Chaplin, *The Day of the Sardine*, 1961, Panther paperback edn, p. 27.
54. S. Hignett, *A Picture to Hang on the Wall*, 1966, New York edn, pp. 150–1.
55. Wedderburn, *loc. cit.* Townsend, *loc. cit.*
56. H.M.S.O., *Scotland's Older Houses*, 1967.
57. B.B.C. *Annual Report for 1956–57*, P.P., 1956–57, IX, Cmnd. 267, p. 5.
58. H. H. Wilson, *Pressure Groups: the Campaign for Commercial Television*, 1961.
59. *Television Policy*, P.P., 1953–54, XXVI, Cmd. 9005.
60. Cmnd. 267, p. 5.
61. B.B.C. *Annual Report for 1959–60*, P.P., 1959–60, IX, Cmnd. 1174, p. 9. I.T.A. *Annual Report 1958–59*, P.P., 1959–60, IX (2), p. 1.
62. *Ibid.*, p. 2. *Report of Committee on Broadcasting 1960* (Pilkington Report), P.P., 1961–62, IX, Cmnd. 1839, p. 68.

63. *B.B.C. Report 1955–56*, P.P., XI, 1955–56, Cmd. 9803, p. 7. Cmnd. 267, p. 7.
64. Cmd. 9803, p. 8.
65. Cmnd. 1839, pp. 46, 65.
66. *Report of Royal Commission on the Press 1961–62*, P.P., 1961–62, XXI, Cmnd. 1811, pp. 9–15, 29–31, 34–35, 208.
67. P.P., 1959–60, IX, Cmnd. 1191, pp. 3–4.
68. *Ibid.*, p. 7.
69. Christian Economic and Social Research Foundation, *6th Annual Report on Drunkenness Among Persons under 21 in England and Wales 1950–1958*, 1959, p. 5.
70. *Report of Ministry of Health for 1959*, Part II, P.P., 1960–61, XVII, Cmnd. 1207, pp. 1–2, 7. *Report for 1961*, Part II, P.P., 1961–62, XVII, Cmnd. 1550, pp. 1–2, 18.
71. P. Foot, *Race in British Politics*, 1964. P.E.P., *Racial Discrimination*, 1967.

CHAPTER TEN

Contemporary Britain: Coda and Recapitulation[1]

There are no beginnings and no endings, though there are sharp and significant discontinuities. The real starting-point of this study was August 1914. The earlier material (one item dating back as far as 1320) was provided in order to identify the main forces making for change irrespective of the incidence of total war, to pinpoint the built-in tendency to 'gradualism' (that is to say the resistance to change) within British society as it has evolved historically, and to clarify the workings of the four modes through which war affects society: *destruction* (which, as with an earthquake, or other natural disaster, *may* result in a rapid reconstruction going far beyond the limits of what was originally destroyed); *test – dissolution – transformation* (as, in Britain, the neglect of the internal combustion engine in Edwardian times issued, after 1918, in the creation of one of the world's foremost automobile industries, and, after 1945, in epoch-making developments in civil aviation); the *military participation* of new groups and classes (leading to the political emancipation of women, better material conditions for the working classes, and the surmounting of what Ernest Bevin called 'the inferiority complex amongst our people';[2] and the intense *emotional impact* of war, affecting the arts, religion, philosophy, and, above all, reinforcing the other modes of changes.

With the glasses polished, the stools in place and the beer pressure adjusted, there is no difficulty in knowing when it is time to open up shop. But the external logic which determines the moment at which the publican shall cry 'Time, gentlemen, please!' scarcely applies to the historian. My purpose would have been partially fulfilled had I concluded at a point when the major effects of the Second World War could be conveniently summarized: that point occurred in 1950, immediately before the outbreak of the Korean War. But the Korean War provided a good opportunity for a further development of my general theory, and showed that in a *limited* war the negative social effects far outweigh the positive ones, which indeed scarcely come into play at all. More important, that 'pressure generated by the unguided activities of individuals and groups mightily assisted by the great resources of science and technology ... [making for] a greater share for the many of economic and material well-being', to which I referred in Chapter One,[3] began to produce striking results (described, in the fashionable short-hand of our time, as 'affluence') in the years following the Korean War. In the late Fifties and early Sixties old arguments were given a new twist, issues which formerly had been half-obscured in the soft lighting of national complacency were illumined by the harsh light of imperial reverse and economic failure. Chapter Nine – the last substantial chapter of this book – ended with the election campaign of October 1964: not with a bang, but with a question-mark. Contemporary history, I believe, must lose half its virtue if the attempt, however unsatisfactory, is not made to relate its 'message' (the historian who says he has no message is either a fool or a liar) to the here-and-now. It is always possible, by a series of frantic gear-changes up through the proofs, to present an appearance of with-it, up-to-the-minute history. The impulse is almost irresistible, and is in similar case to that of the enthusiastic motorist, whose passengers find that having failed to persuade him to stop for lunch at noon, they will be lucky if they get a couple of sandwiches before the afternoon is over. The reader, I hope, will settle for lunch at two.

Having been concerned in the main body of this book with the mechanics of change, I want now, very briefly, to look at what might well be called the mechanics of non-change. Hopes were high in 1964 that a Labour victory would lead on to the major reforms Britain so manifestly needed; up to March 1966 it was possible to excuse the Labour government's inertia on the grounds of its minuscule majority in the House of Commons; by late 1967 all excuses had worn threadbare and everywhere there was evidence of disenchantment. This concluding chapter does no more than mention one or two of the more important incidents in this process, relating them to the overall themes of the book.

In the General Election of October 1964, Labour (led by Harold Wilson since the sudden illness and death of Hugh Gaitskell in

January 1963) secured an overall majority of only four seats, winning 317 to 304 for the Conservatives and 9 for the Liberals. The total poll for Labour was actually 11,000 less than in 1959, and their share of the poll was up by only 0·3 per cent. This was no landslide towards Labour, but rather a landslip away from the Conservatives, whose share of the poll dropped by 6 per cent, recalling for them the débâcle of 1945. The Liberals easily accomplished the objective they had set themselves, 3 million popular votes, and seemed, at first glance, to hold a strong balancing position in the House of Commons, though in face of the political skill of Harold Wilson this proved somewhat illusory. Patrick Gordon Walker, Wilson's shadow Foreign Secretary, was defeated at Smethwick (near Birmingham) where for several years coloured immigration had been a live issue and one on which the Conservative candidate did not hesitate to capitalize. Top politics being, as always, given priority over any sensitivities on the part of the electorate, a 'safe constituency' was shortly cleared for Gordon Walker at Leyton, where the sitting Labour member was 'kicked upstairs' to the House of Lords; unfortunately Gordon Walker, meantime made Foreign Secretary anyway, lost the by-election. Yet, despite this apparently grim setback, the Government survived without too much difficulty, Wilson consistently outplaying and outshining Sir Alec Douglas-Home. In July 1965 the Conservatives dropped their flagging leader and, making use for the first time of a formal system of balloting among Conservative M.P.s, they elevated in his place the radical and relatively youthful Edward Heath (he was 49, the same age as Wilson).[4] As a demonstration of the sanity of British politics, the good sense of the Conservative Party and its wish to come to terms with the 1960s, the choice of Heath was sound. Both Wilson and Heath were at pains to project the image of the bustling up-to-the-minute technocrat: unhappily for the Conservatives, it was Heath who tended to appear like the pale imitation. To many observers the new Conservative leader conjured a remarkable resemblance to the Hugh Gaitskell of the election campaign of 1959, very earnest, fantastically honest, slightly dull and occasionally not too adroit, while Wilson seemed to be taking well to the empty shoes of the master political tactician, Harold

Macmillan. Both during Wilson's promised 'hundred days of dynamic government' and after, there was a great flurry of activity, most of it merely on paper, some of it real. In the General Election of 31 March 1966, the party was strikingly successful in converting the scarcely visible majority on which it had ruled for seventeen months into the very satisfactory one of 97. The results were: Labour 363, Conservatives 253, Liberals 12; the two remaining seats were held by the Speaker, Dr Horace King, the first Labour M.P. in history to be raised to this historic post, and by a 'Republican Labour' member from Belfast West in Northern Ireland. With 47·9 per cent of all votes cast, to 41·9 per cent for the Conservatives, Labour now held the greatest percentage margin of any victorious party since their own triumph in 1945, though they were still short of a complete popular majority. Compared to 1964 their total vote had increased by three-quarters of a million, while that of the Conservatives had fallen by over half a million. Throughout the country the swing to Labour (3·5 per cent on average) was remarkably uniform, and both Smethwick and Leyton were regained.[5]

Concluding their study of the General Election of 1964, David Butler and Anthony King wrote:

The years before October 15th, 1964, were years of shifting political allegiances; never before had the electorate been so volatile. The election of 1959 had appeared as in some way the logical culmination of a period of British history. But the election of 1964 seemed less a confirmation of long-maturing trends than a break, a moment of change – a portent, perhaps, of greater changes to come.[6]

By 1966 and 1967 the notion of a break was receding into the mists of thick economic crisis; if one could find a moment of change it would have to be earlier in the decade, somewhere between 1961 and 1963, when the mood of deep, but vocal, introspection which for some years had increasingly characterized British publicists of all political persuasions reached full flood. But introspective radicalism proved less than a match for the unchanging verities of Britain's post-1945 predicament. The last Conservative 'Go' in 1964 presented the incoming Labour government with a huge deficit (around £700 million) in the balance of payments, which led to the inevitable run on sterling, probably made worse by a lack of foreign confidence in this precariously-positioned and perhaps even socialistically-inclined Government. Denying itself the possible remedy of an immediate devaluation of the pound (which apart from damaging London's position as an international financial centre would almost certainly have damaged Labour's position in a subsequent election), the Government resorted to deflation and a high Bank Rate. At the same time a determined attack was made on one of the country's long-term economic problems through the attempt to establish a workable incomes policy. Furthermore, on 16 September 1965 George Brown, Minister for Economic Affairs, published the country's first ever National Plan, which postulated an annual growth rate of 3·8 per cent per annum over the six years to 1970 and a total increase in the gross national product of 25 per cent. The National Economic Development Council, of Conservative ancestry, was supplemented by a task force of regional economic development councils. But in July 1966 the Government, in a fashion which in some respects recalled the disastrous over-confidence which the Attlee government had shown in 1947, found itself swamped in a new financial crisis. The response was a 'Stop' which went far beyond the wildest nightmares of the 1950s. The most apposite historical comment on the crisis and the Government's reactions was that of a reader of the *New Statesman*, who wrote that 'the ghost of Ramsay MacDonald must be laughing his bloody head off'.[7] For a time the *New Statesman* itself affected to believe that in enforcing its wage freeze (in a manner which the Attlee government in 1948 had believed to be impossible in a democratic society) the Government had inadvertently stumbled into the necessary programme of socialist planning.[8] As unemployment rose and long-term programmes (including the much-heralded National Plan) were revised or shelved this theory began to wear thin. No more than any other government had this one discovered how to balance the needs of economic expansion against the desire to maintain a strong pound and sufficient reserves to carry on a world-wide financial practice against, in turn, the heavy costs of a would-be world military role. No more than any other practising politicians were the leaders of the Labour government willing openly to disavow one or more of the terrible trio, economic growth, a strong pound, and heavy defence commitments – so by massive borrowings the pound was maintained, defence was whittled a little, and economic growth suffered.

From May 1965 onwards the newly-elected régime of Ian Smith in Rhodesia (formerly Southern Rhodesia), one of Britain's few remaining colonial dependencies, was pressing hard for the formal independence which had been conceded to other Commonwealth countries. Unhappily political power in Rhodesia was concentrated in the hands of the white minority: the position of the Wilson government, as indeed of preceding Conservative governments, was that independence could not be granted without guarantees of unimpeded progress to majority (i.e. African) rule. The stand on the principle of multi-racialism (much strengthened since South Africa's withdrawal from the Commonwealth in 1961) was a noble one; unfortunately, whatever Britain's legal rights and moral obligations in the matter, the fact was that ever since 1923 the substance of political, police and military power had been in the hands of the Rhodesian Government itself. On 11 November 1965 the Smith government made a Unilateral Declaration of Independence, thus technically placing itself in a position of open rebellion against the British Government, and, more seriously, placing at permanent risk the future development of the native peoples in Rhodesia. Had Britain still been a great world power, a short sharp military engagement would have been not only legally, but morally, the best way of dealing with the issue. But, for all the continuing burden of arms expenditure, such a venture in such a cause was beyond the nation's strength. Instead, a policy of economic sanctions was resorted to. Britain's second-rate international standing together with her dependence on American support for the pound was further exposed by the major world issue of the time, the Vietnam War: despite rising criticism of the American Government both on the continent of Europe and within the United States itself, the Wilson government, whether from conviction or discretion, maintained a loyal support of American policy. The one new initiative in Britain's international policy, the decision taken at the beginning of May 1967 to reapply for membership of the European Common Market, was scarcely a break in policy, since it merely repeated the Conservative attempt of five years previously; the only change was that now a majority in both main political parties favoured the move.

This swing in opinion could in part be regarded as a success for one of the main arguments of the introspective radicals. In some respects reminiscent of the 'commitment' of the Thirties, still more of the passionate self-analysis of 1916 and 1940–42, the mood of 1961–63 had a more sweeping and more fundamental character of its own; shared by new Liberals, Tory radicals, and Revisionist Socialists, it is not to be confused with the elemental protest which was the natural and permanent function of the political Left. In 1916 the emphasis had been on the need to reorganize the national effort in order to ensure victory against the Germans; in the 1930s the emphasis had been on detailed investigation and exposure of the plight of the poor; in the early Forties the concern was with the better world that must emerge from the holocaust of war. In each case eventual victory and ultimate remedy was pre-supposed; in each case, too, because of the categorical imperatives posed by the great discontinuities of war or of economic and political crisis, something concrete did emerge. In the first years of the Sixties the entire position of the nation, its relation to other nations and to history, was under examination: no one talked of victory or of obvious remedy. But serious as Britain's position undoubtedly was, there was no categorical imperative; the notes of crisis were too diffuse: nothing very concrete emerged.

Much of the sound and fury, indeed, was really concerned with men rather than measures, particularly during the period when the Macmillan régime was collapsing amid a spluttering of security leaks and scandal. The conviction in October 1962 of an Admiralty clerk, William Vassall, on charges of passing secrets to the Russians, led to a general investigation of security matters by a tribunal headed by Lord Radcliffe. For refusing to divulge sources of information, two journalists were imprisoned. Henceforth Harold Macmillan was to find, even in the right-wing Press, a hostility not usually manifested towards a Conservative Prime Minister. If historical events are measured by the amount of anguish, the amount of debate, the reams of paper and the decibels of speech lavished on them, then the great event of the Fifties was Suez; in long-term domestic consequences it proved in many respects to be something of a non-event. The equivalent in the Sixties – and the contrast between the sublime folly of 1956 and the ridiculous scandal of 1963, it could be argued, was a measure of what was going wrong in Britain – was the Profumo affair.[9] John Profumo, a not very competent Secretary of State for War who had already roused the deep political distrust of Labour's Colonel George Wigg, M.P., had consorted with Christine Keeler, member of an expensive call-girl circle (itself possibly an indirect consequence of the success of an earlier Conservative measure in pushing prostitution off the streets) with which Captain Ivanov, formerly of the Russian Embassy, and Stephen Ward, a society osteopath, were also associated. The golden rule for politicians, as, for that matter, for anyone else, is 'don't get caught'; because, in a time of general sensitivity over security matters, there was a genuine fear that the Ivanov connection involved a security risk, because of the skilled detective work of Colonel Wigg, and because of the withdrawal of Press tolerance from the Macmillan government, Profumo was caught. The obvious and sensible thing would have been for him to fade from the scene, temporarily at least. Macmillan's willingness to accept Profumo's public denial of allegations made against him did great credit to the Prime Minister's heart, but not to his head. Meantime Stephen Ward, who was eventually charged with living on immoral earnings, attempted to divert police attention from himself by, in effect, confirming the charges against Profumo, who therefore, on 4 June, resigned from the Government, admitting that previously he had lied to the House of Commons. Later in the year, in the final stages of a trial which did no credit whatsoever to the canons of English justice, Stephen Ward committed suicide. The Profumo affair undoubtedly weakened the position as Prime Minister of Harold Macmillan, though as a matter of actual fact his resignation, when it eventually came in October, was based purely on ill health. It also provided a magnificent peg upon which to hang denunciations of Britain's moral decadence, thus in appearance intensifying the storm of radical protest; in practice *The Times* pronouncement (11 June), 'It *is* a moral issue', scarcely formed the ideal banner behind which to march towards the new Britain. Whether the affair revealed more about British immorality or about British hypocrisy (and neither sanctimoniousness nor salaciousness were British monopolies, for the Profumo story had readers and listeners around the world) depends on the point of view of the beholder.

However the real concern of the radicals lay with the inter-connected problems of Britain's poor economic showing and her relationship to the rest of the world. On the former there was general agreement that in some way or another Britain had gone 'soft', on the latter there was disagreement between those who accused Britain of maintaining delusions of world grandeur, and those who attacked her for, in John Mander's brilliant phrase, taking a 'holiday from history'.[10] Typical studies of the economy were Michael Shanks's *The Stagnant Society* (1961), Eric Wigham's *What's Wrong with the Unions?* (1961) and Rex Malik's *What's Wrong with British Industry?* (1964) – all published in paperback by Penguin Books. A wider front was covered by Anthony Sampson's *Anatomy of Britain* (1962), Bryan Magee's *The New Radicalism* (1962) and the collection of essays edited by Arthur Koestler, *Suicide of a Nation* (1963). Politically these writers stood in the centre (Wigham was industrial correspondent for *The Times*): while the revisionist Labour M.P. Anthony Crosland spoke of *The Conservative Enemy* (1962), 'new liberals' within the Conservative Party joined the attack in Timothy Raison's *Why Conservative?* (1964) and in the collection of essays *Rebirth of Britain* (1964), edited by the Bow Group member, Arthur Seldon.

To a degree there was response from both the Macmillan and Douglas-Home governments. The much-maligned Selwyn Lloyd was the first to lay one hand on the prickly problem of a wages policy, and to stretch out the other towards the ideal of long-term economic planning. It was during 1961 that the Robbins Committee on Higher Education and the Newsom Committee on Secondary Education were appointed; it was Sir Alec Douglas-Home who announced acceptance of the Robbins proposals for the expansion of higher education, and his government that appointed the Franks Commission to investigate the part to be played in that expansion by the University of Oxford; it was in this same period that a whole new clutch of universities at Sussex (Brighton), York, East Anglia (Norwich), Lancaster, and Essex (Colchester), followed in 1965 by Kent (Canterbury) and Warwick (Coventry), were opened: and it was, it might be added, during the retrenchment imposed by the Labour government that the impetus was taken out of the Robbins expansion, though plans went ahead with the launching of Stirling University (October 1967) and the conferring of University status on various leading colleges of technology. Other reports emanating from the autumn of Macmillan's rule were those of the Trend Committee on the organization of the Civil Service and the Buchanan Committee on traffic and roads. Though the Labour government dispensed with the services of Dr Beeching, it did subsequently, under the aegis of its energetic Minister of Transport Mrs Barbara Castle, begin to move in the direction of trying to establish an integrated transport system. The Wilson government took some modest shots at the reform of parliament (morning sessions and greater use of committees) and appointed a Parliamentary Commissioner (or Ombudsman) to investigate grievances suffered by the individual at the hands of the State – both points strongly urged by the more administratively-minded radicals.[11] Where change was most noticeable after 1964 was in social policy, though much that was originally planned had to be postponed in face of economic stringency. Many of the basic principles of the Beveridge Report were now in rather low repute: it became fashionable, even among Labour politicians, to stress the need for 'selectivity' rather than 'universality' in the social services;[12] and in January 1966 a Bill was published which was intended to replace flat-rate benefits by earnings-related benefits. Yet only in August 1966 was there created the unified Ministry of Social Security which Beveridge had called for a generation earlier: national assistance (renamed supplementary benefit) was to be administered from within the ministry by a new Supplementary Benefits Commission; it is hard, however, to believe that in practice the change amounted to much since, for one thing, the commission kept in being the National Assistance Board's policy of the Wage Stop.

There was, indeed, no lack of evidence of the continuing inadequacy of British social provision. In 1967 the *Report on Scotland's Older Houses* stripped away the comfortable belief that, bad as Scotland's slums had been in the past, the problem was now well on the way to being solved – revealing instead that conditions were still truly scandalous. The Ministry of Housing and Local Government itself admitted that, compared with countries such as Italy, Sweden, and West Germany, Britain was simply devoting too small a proportion of her gross national product to house-building: in the early Sixties these countries had been in the habit of spending 6·1 per cent, 5·3 per cent and 5·3 per cent respectively, compared with 3·1 per cent in the United Kingdom.[13] The National Health Service, magnificent in conception – and Labour restored the original immaculate conception by abolishing prescription charges, while the Conservatives and the new Liberals grumbled that the· money would be better spent on much-needed hospitals – was still burdened with its crazy administrative structure, which made the much-needed rationalization of costs extremely difficult to carry through.[14] In opposition to the eleven-plus examination and the principle of selection, the policy of the Minister of Education, Anthony Crosland (and that of his successor Patrick Gordon Walker), was to encourage, though not compel, the development of comprehensive schools. Close observers, however, noted that at a still earlier stage in a child's career his path was crossed by an even worse monster than the eleven-plus, 'streaming', which could involve the same kind of arbitrary selection and condemnation to inferior schooling as was involved in the eleven-plus.[15] The problems of social policy are like the problems of writing a book: no sooner have you disposed of one issue (you think) than another pops up for attention. More than ever it was clear that ideological enthusiasm was of little value without facts and professional expertise. Nowhere was this more true than in the case of one social issue which in 1966 for the first time figured prominently in the election campaign: crime. Here the emotional response, despite the overwhelming weight of professional opinion to the contrary, showed itself in the call for stiffer punishments, preferably corporal. It was very apparent that, linked very closely with one particular aspect of the upsurge in crime, was the manner in which earlier Conservative policy had converted Britain into a gamblers' paradise. But it was equally apparent that to return to the gamblers' hell created by the nineteenth-century evangelicals would take more political courage than any government could be expected to possess.

From whence could the energy and initiative come to put right all these British wrongs? To some observers the British had already sunk so far in slothful decadence that no hope of recovery was likely: an American journalist wrote in *Life* Magazine of the 'Shrinking Pains of Mini-England'[16] – 'mini', following upon the fashion for the mini-skirt, being the modish prefix, almost the *sine qua non* of witty conversation, in 1966. Other transatlantic observers took a different view. Concluding his excellent study of *Twentieth Century Britain*, Professor Alfred Havighurst, writing in 1965, declared:

This little island with few resources but favored by geography and by nature and with the energy and ingenuity of the British people has become a state, a nation and a civilization. The writer, now leaving the role of historian, may venture the hope that it will still endure.[17]

The sentiments were echoed by Professor W. L. Arnstein, ruminating on the death of Sir Winston Churchill in 1965:

But the end of a man and an era does not denote the end of a nation. The history of the England which Churchill preserved and led to victory in World War II has been filled with many brilliant chapters, medieval, Elizabethan, Augustan, Victorian and Churchillian, and one may feel confident that many more chapters remain to be written.[18]

Most fulsome of all was the tribute of a provincial Republican newspaper:

How can such a little nation weigh so much?
What's left of the British Empire is an island no larger than the state of Illinois. Its population is only about one-fourth our own.
Yet Britain continues to lead the world in so many ways.

No longer can the British claim to rule the seas or the skies or the corners of the earth. Yet pick up a copy of almost any American newspaper and you'll see a dozen British datelines.

On almost any American telecast, the British influence is obvious, for better or worse, on politics, music and fashions. . . .

On the books, Britain is bankrupt – yet the bankers of the world predicate plans on the British pound sterling.

Britain has no entry in the space race, no billions for nuclear research – yet British scientists command the attention of the world's scientific fraternity.

It is an amazing phenomenon, the manner in which Britain has recently been dictating miniskirts and mod music to the whole world.[19]

To argue, from the international successes of British pop music and British mod fashion, that there was still within British society a reserve of energy and imagination would be unwise, though even the crustiest square might be tempted to smile over the thought that after tolerating the products of American mass culture for so long, Britain was now repaying the debt with interest. The plain truth was that in both words and music the celebrated Liverpool group, the Beatles, did, in such numbers as 'Eleanor Rigby', set standards beyond those usually associated with pop music, and that the fashion wave released by Mary Quant showed both flair and imagination. Perspective is restored if it is recalled that alongside these went the artistic (and often commercial) successes of the Royal Ballet, the Royal Opera House, the National Theatre, the Royal Shakespeare Theatre, a growing number of bold provincial theatre ventures, and British films, from *Room at the Top*, *I'm All Right Jack* and *The Entertainer*, to *Morgan* and *The Caretaker*.[20] More significant were the less-heralded successes of British technology. In some areas Britain lost through being too soon, rather than too slow, with new advances. The first turbo-jets to go into civilian operation in the later Forties were British; the first pure jet to go into scheduled civilian air service was the de Havilland Comet (May 1952). The Comet crashes of January and May 1954 which resulted in the planes being withdrawn from service showed that the cost of pioneering could be high: the upshot, however, was the discovery of the hitherto unknown phenomenon of metal fatigue. Working together, the British Aircraft Corporation and Aviation Sud in France aim to put the world's first supersonic civilian transport, the Concorde, into flight in 1971 (the prototype is due to fly in 1968). An outstanding international success in the mid-Sixties was the B.A.C. One-Eleven, the world's first economical short-haul jet. Hovercraft was a British invention and Britain continued to lead in its production.[21] The world's first nuclear power station was that opened at Calder Hall in October 1956. However backward British industry might be in exploiting new developments, it could hardly be said that the British were less inventive in the 1950s and 1960s than they had been two hundred or one hundred years before. Here and there within the patchy map of social policy and social experimentation, certain areas, even within the parched valleys of education, attracted the admiring attention of knowledgeable visitors: such 'third generation' new towns as Livingstone in Central Scotland and Washington in the North–East seemed likely to outshine the considerable fame already attaching to their predecessors.

The purpose of this little chauvinistic flourish is not to demonstrate that all is essentially well with the Britain of today, but to suggest that what is lacking is the mechanism for harnessing the energies of her people. Much of the old Collectivist versus Individualist controversy may well be out of date, but it is clear that many problems, the deteriorating race situation for example, still call for positive State action, even if that action no longer always coincides with the obvious interests of the organized working-class movement. Asked what could be done to improve the slum-ridden muddle which history and industry together had made of early twentieth-century Leeds, George Bernard Shaw advised dropping a bomb on it: to see the force of a drastic remedy is not necessarily to recommend it as a practical expedient. 'We must start a revolution', declared Harold Wilson in 1964. 'We want a revolution', read a Liberal slogan in 1966. 'Britain needs a revolution,' said Edward Heath in September 1967.[22] Neither in 1914 nor in 1939 was there so clear a consensus among politicians in favour of 'revolution': yet revolutions took place all the same, for total war in this century has, amid all the confusing legacy of destruction and loss, had the effect of bringing about social change on a major scale. Economic crisis can have some of the same effects, but what is then lacking, as the history of commitment in the Thirties and introspective radicalism in the Sixties makes clear, is the vital element of participation. Beyond that, in time of peace the dead weight of 'gradualism', so important in British history before 1900, so unfortunate since, takes full effect. What is required is the Jamesian 'moral equivalent of war':[23] even as a joke,[24] we dare not now conjure up the vision of another war. A big one would finish us all; a little one would have only negative results because it would not bring fully into play those military participation, psychological, and test-dissolution-transformation factors which are at the centre of the relationship between war and social change.

NOTES TO CHAPTER TEN

1. For a list of books on contemporary Britain see Bibliography, pp. 480–483.
2. Bullock, *Bevin*, vol. II, p. 381.
3. See above, p. 16.
4. D. E. Butler and A. King, *The British General Election of 1964*, 1965, pp. 289 ff., *The British General Election of 1966*, 1966, pp. 8–43, 48–53. See also A. Howard and R. West, *The Making of the Prime Minister*, 1965.
5. Butler and King, *General Election of 1966*, pp. 259–61.
6. *General Election of 1964*, p. 300.
7. *New Statesman*, 29 July 1966.
8. *Ibid.*, 16 September, 21 October 1966.
9. The best account is C. Irving *et al.*, *Scandal '63 : A Study of the Profumo Affair*, 1963.
10. J. Mander, *Great Britain or Little England?*, 1963.
11. B. Crick, *The Reform of Parliament*, 1964, B. Chapman, *British Government Observed*. 1963. A Hill and A. Whichelow, *What's Wrong with Parliament?* 1964.
12. See D. Houghton, *Paying for the Social Services*, 1967; H. Sewill, *Auntie*, 1967 and B. Rhys-Williams, *New Social Contrast*, 1967 (the latter two being publications of the Conservative Political Centre). For the case against selectivity see R. M. Titmuss, *Commitment to Welfare*, 1968.
13. *Housing Policy 1965 to 1970*, Cmnd. 2838, 1966.
14. See esp. R. Stevens, *Medical Practice in Modern England*, 1966.
15. See B. Jackson, *Streaming, An Education System in Miniature*, 1964.
16. *Life*, 16 December 1966.
17. A. Havighurst, *Twentieth Century Britain*, 2nd edn, 1966, p. 533.

18. W. L. Arnstein, *Britain Yesterday and Today*, Boston 1966.
19. *Buffalo Evening News*, 19 January 1967.
20. For a critical appraisal of the structure of the British film industry see T. Kelly *et al.*, *A Competitive Cinema*, 1966.
21. See A. J. Youngson, *British Economy*, p. 208. Central Office of Information, *Britain, An Official Handbook*, 1967, pp. 295–6.
22. Quoted in the *Guardian*, 16 September 1967. Mr Heath's remarks were published in the Conservative Party *Weekly News*, 15 September 1967.
23. See William James, *The Moral Equivalent of War*, 1910. Cp. H. Peterson, A. Johnson, L. K. Frank, 'The Moral Equivalent of War', in G. Murphy (ed.), *Human Nature and Enduring Peace*, Cambridge, Mass., 1945.
24. Cp. A. J. P. Taylor, 'If the present government pursue their retrograde policy much further, we shall have to have another war in order to start up social progress (joke)', *New Statesman*, 25 November 1966. The parenthesis was necessary because readers of the *New Statesman* are serious, peace-loving people.

Bibliography

Place of publication is London unless otherwise stated

A. MAIN PRIMARY MATERIALS

A number of manuscript collections are now available for parts of the period under review. It happens that I have consulted some of them while pursuing ancillary projects, but I have made no systematic use of them for this study, save in the case of the newly-released papers in the Public Record Office (P.R.O.) which, at time of writing, covered the years up to 1922 (and are now governed by the thirty-year rule). For the main social groups and themes of change discussed there is an abundance of published literature.

At the centre there are the *Acts of Parliament*, the *Parliamentary Debates* and, most important, the *Sessional (or 'Parliamentary') Papers* (cited, with Session and Volume numbers, as P.P.), the many publications of individual departments and offices, such as the *Labour Gazette*, the *Board of Trade Journal*, and those of the Central Statistical Office and the Central Office of Information (for the later period).

Otherwise I have used the *Reports* and *Miscellaneous Publications* of such organizations as the Federation of British Industries, the Conservative Party, the Liberal Party, the Fabian Society, the Labour Party, the Independent Labour Party, the Trades Union Congress, the Communist Party (and the various 'Reform Groups', etc., within or related to these organizations, e.g. the Bow Group or the Socialist League), and the British Association for the Advancement of Science. Other organizations of more temporary importance are listed separately below.

Newspapers and periodicals (which, as will be seen from the text, I have used intensively at certain points of crisis and selectively at other times) are invaluable both for the opinions and actions of specialized groups and for descriptive history. The *Annual Register*, though ultra-conservative, is still of great value. Working briefly with Tony Essex at the B.B.C. I was able to see a goodly amount of newsfilm: such programmes as *The Great War* and *1940* should have a place in any decently-equipped school or university history department. Only the novels, poems and plays specifically mentioned in the text have been noted in the second part of this bibliography.

For the whole of the second half of the book I have relied heavily on the publications of Political and Economic Planning, and also on the surveys of such bodies as Mass Observation, the Economic Research Council (later called the Christian Economic and Social Research Foundation), Research Services Ltd and the British Institute of Public Opinion. The London and Cambridge Economic Service, *The British Economy, Key Statistics 1900–1966*, 1967, is a useful compilation of official statistics culled from many quarters. Other individual surveys are itemized below.

B. OTHER CONTEMPORARY MATERIALS, MEMOIRS, AND SECONDARY SOURCES

(There are excellent annotated bibliographies on all aspects of the period by A. J. P. Taylor, *English History 1914–1945*, 1965, pp. 602–39, H. R. Winkler in E. Furber (ed.), *Changing Views on British History*, 1966, pp. 289–319, and A. F. Havighurst, *Twentieth Century Britain*, 1966 edn, pp. 536–47. I mention only books relevant to my major topics. For a fuller bibliography on the social history of the First World War than there is space for here, the reader may consult my *The Deluge: British Society and the First World War*, 1965, pp. 316–27.

(i) *General*

Abrams, M., *The Condition of the British People 1911–1945*, 1945.

Adams, T. W. R., *Modern Town and Country Planning*, 1952.

Andrzewski, S., *Military Organization and Society*, 1954.

Aron, R., *The Century of Total War*, 1945.

Ashworth, W., *The Genesis of Modern British Town Planning*, 1954.

Ashworth, W., *An Economic History of England 1870–1939*, 1960.

Avon, Earl of, *Memoirs of Anthony Eden, Earl of Avon*, 3 vols, 1960–65.

Bagehot, W., *The English Constitution*, 1868, 1872 and (ed. R. Crossman) 1965.

Banks, O., *Parity and Prestige in English Secondary Education*, 1955.

Barraclough, G., *History in a Changing World*, 1955.

Barton, A. H., *Social Organization under Stress*, Washington, D.C., 1963.

Bealey, F., 'Les Travaillistes et la Guerre des Boers', *Le Mouvement Social*, no. 45, 1963.

Beer, S. H., *Modern British Politics*, 1965.

Beloff, M., *New Dimensions in Foreign Policy*, 1961.

Bernal, J. D., *Science in History*, 1954 and 1965.

Beveridge, W., *Power and Influence*, 1953.

Booth, C., *Life and Labour of the People in London,* 17 vols, 1902–3.

Boulding, K., *The Meaning of the Twentieth Century,* 1964.

Bowley, M., *Housing and the State, 1945.*

Brand, C. F., *The British Labour Party: A Short History,* 1964.

Briggs, A., *Friends of the People,* 1956.

Briggs, A., *History of Birmingham,* vol II, 1955.

Briggs, A., *History of Broadcasting in Great Britain,* 2 vols, 1961–65.

Briggs, A., *Social Thought and Social Action: A Study of Seebohm Rowntree,* 1961.

Briggs, A., *They Saw It Happen,* 1960.

Briggs, A., 'The Welfare State in Historical Perspective', *Archives Européennes de Sociologie,* 1961.

Brookes, J., *The Great Leap: the Past Twenty-Five Years in America,* New York, 1966.

Bruce, M., *The Coming of the Welfare State,* 1961.

Bullock, A., *The Life and Times of Ernest Bevin,* 2 vols, 1960–7.

Bulmer-Thomas, I., *The Party System in Great Britain,* 1953.

Burnett, J., *Plenty and Want,* 1966.

Butler, D. E., *The Electoral System in Britain since 1918,* 2nd edn, 1963.

Calder, R., *Profile of Science,* 1951.

Citrine, Lord, *Men and Work,* 1964.

Clarke, I. F., *Voices Prophesying War 1763–1984,* 1966.

Clarkson, J. D. and Cochran, T. (eds.), *War as a Social Institution,* New York, 1941.

Cole, G. D. H., *History of the Labour Party since 1914,* 1948.

Cole, G. D. H., *Studies in Class Structure,* 1955.

Cole, M. I., *The Story of Fabian Socialism,* 1961.

Crowther, J. G., *British Scientists of the Twentieth Century,* 1952.

Daalder, H., *Cabinet Reform in Britain, 1914–1963,* 1964.

Dalton, H., *Memoirs,* 3 vols, 1953–62.

Davenport, N., *The Split Society,* 1964.

Deane, P. and Cole, W. A., *British Economic Growth 1688–1959,* 1962.

de Schweinitz, K., *Britain's Road to Social Security,* 1941.

Dicey, A. V., *Lectures on the Relationship between Law and Public Opinion in England in the Nineteenth Century,* 1905.

Dickinson, W., Donaldson, G., and Milne, I., *Source Book of Scottish History,* vol. I., 1955.

Ehrman, J., *Cabinet Government and War,* 1958.

Ensor, R. C. K., *England 1870–1914,* 1936.

Ervine, St J., *George Bernard Shaw: His Life, Work and Friends,* 1956.

Escott, T., *England: Her People, Polity and Pursuits*, 1879.

Feldman, G., *Army Industry and Labor in Germany 1914–1918*, Princeton, N.J., 1966.

Galbraith, J. K., *The Affluent Society*, 1958.

Galbraith, J. K., *The New Industrial State*, Boston, 1967.

Gibbs, N. H., *et al.* 'War and Society', *Listener*, 6 October–17 November, 1955.

Ginsberg, M. (ed.), *Law and Opinion in England in the Twentieth Century*, 1959.

Guttsman, W. L., *The British Political Élite*, 1963.

Halévy, E., *The Era of Tyrannies* (trs. R. K. Webb), New York, 1965.

Hallett, G., *The Economics of Agricultural Land Tenure*, 1960.

Harding, A., *Social History of English Law*, 1966.

Harrod, R. F., *The British Economy*, 1963.

Harrod, R. F., *The Life of John Maynard Keynes*, 1951.

Havighurst, A. F., *Twentieth Century Britain*, 1962 and 1966.

Heath, H. F. and Hetherington, A. L., *Industrial Research and Development in the United Kingdom*, 1946.

Hinsley, F. H., *Power and the Pursuit of Peace*, 1963.

Hollis, C., 'The Conservative Party in History', *Political Quarterly*, 1961.

Ilké, F. C., *The Social Impact of Bomb Destruction*, Norman, Okla., 1958.

Ince, G., *The Ministry of Labour and National Service*, 1960.

Iremonger, F. A., *William Temple, Archbishop of Canterbury*, 1948.

James, W., *The Moral Equivalent of War*, 1910.

Janis, I. L., *Air War and Emotional Stress: Psychological Studies of Bombing and Civilian Defense*, New York, 1951.

Jennings, I., *Cabinet Government*, 3rd edn, 1959.

Jennings, I., *Party Politics*, 3 vols, 1960–62.

Jewkes, J., *Public and Private Enterprise*, 1965.

Jewkes, J., *et al.*, *The Sources of Invention*, 1958.

Jones, T., *A Diary with Letters, 1931–1950*, 1954.

Kelsall, R. K., *Higher Civil Servants in Britain*, 1955.

Kornhauser, W., *The Politics of Mass Society*, Glencoe, 1959.

Krieger, L., 'The Idea of the Welfare State in Britain and the United States', *Journal of the History of Ideas*, 1963.

Lee, J. M., *Social Leaders and Public Persons*, 1964.

Lekachman, R., *The Age of Keynes*, 1966.

Lewis, R. and Maude, A., *The English Middle Classes*, 1949.

Lewis, R. and Maude, A., *Professional People*, 1952.

Low, D., *The Years of Wrath*, 1946.

Mackenzie, R. T., *British Political Parties,* 1955.

Mackenzie, W. J. M., and Grove, J. W., *Central Administration in Britain,* 1962.

Mackerness, E. D., *Social History of English Music,* 1964.

Mackintosh, J. P., *The British Cabinet,* 1960.

Mansergh, N. (ed.), *British Commonwealth Documents 1931–1952,* 2 vols, 1959.

Marsh, D. C., *The Changing Social Structure of England and Wales 1871–1951,* 1958.

Marshall, N., *The Other Theatre,* 1947.

Marshall, T., *Citizenship and Social Class,* 1950.

Marwick, A., 'The Labour Party and the Welfare State in Britain 1900–1948', *American Historical Review,* December 1967.

Marwick, A., 'The Impact of the First World War on Britian', *Journal of Contemporary History,* January 1968.

Marwick, W. H., *Modern Scotland,* 1965.

Marx, K., *The Eastern Question,* 1897.

Mendelsohn, R., *Social Security in the British Commonwealth,* 1954.

Miliband, R., *Parliamentary Socialism,* 1962.

Minney, R. J., *The Private Papers of Hore-Belisha,* 1960.

Mitchell, J. B. (ed.), *Great Britain: Geographical Essays,* 1962.

Morrison, Lord, *Autobiography of Herbert Morrison,* 1960.

Mowat, C. L., 'The Approach to the Welfare State in Great Britain', *American Historical Review,* 1953.

Nef, J. U., *War and Human Progress,* 1950.

Nicholson, M., *The System,* 1967.

Osborne, G. S., *Scottish and English Schools,* 1966.

Ostrogorski, M., *Political Parties,* 1902.

Pear, T. H., (ed.), *Psychological Factors of Peace and War,* 1950.

Pelling, H. M., *The British Communist Party: an Historical Profile,* 1958.

Pollard, S., *The Development of the British Economy 1914–1950,* 1960.

Prince, S. H., *Catastrophe and Social Change,* New York, 1920.

Roberts, B. C., *National Wages Policy in War and Peace,* 1958.

Robson, W. A. (ed.), *The Civil Service in Britain and France,* 1956.

Robson, W. A., *The Development of Local Government,* 1958.

Runciman, W. G., *Relative Deprivation and Social Justice,* 1966.

Russell, B., *The Impact of Science on Society,* 1953.

Ruth, G., *Occupation and Pay in Great Britain,* 1964.

Salter, Lord, *Memoirs of a Public Servant,* 1961.

Seaman, L. C. B., *Post-Victorian Britain,* 1965.

Sedgwick, R. (ed.), *Lord Hervey's Memoirs*, 1963.

Semmell, B., *Imperialism and Social Reform*, 1960.

Schumpeter, J. A., *Capitalism, Socialism and Democracy*, revised edn, 1950.

Scott, J. D., *Vickers: A History*, 1962.

Sjoberg, G., 'Disasters and Social Change' in G. W. Baker and D. W. Chapman (eds.), *Man and Society in Disaster*, New York, 1962.

Smith, T. B., *Scotland – The Development of its Laws and Constitution*, 1962.

Sorokin, P. A., *Man and Society in Calamity*, New York, 1942.

Spinks, G. (ed.), *Religion in Britain since 1900*, 1952.

Steinmetz, S. R., *Soziologie des Krieges*, Leipzig, 1929.

Tawney, R. H., *Equality*, 4th edn, 1952.

Taylor, A. J. P., *English History, 1914–1945*, 1966.

Thompson, E. P., *The Making of the English Working Class*, 1963.

Thompson, F. M. L., *English Landed Society in the Nineteenth Century*, 1963.

Toynbee, A. J., *A Study of History*, 10 vols, 1934–54.

Tropp, A., *The School Teachers*, 1957.

Waller, W. (ed.), *War in the Twentieth Century*, New York, 1940.

Waltz, K. N., *Man, the State and War*, 1959.

Watson, J. Wreford, *The British Isles: A Systematic Geography*, 1964.

Watt, D. C., *Personalities and Policies*, 1965.

Wheeler-Bennett, J. W., *Sir John Anderson*, 1962.

Wickwar, H. and M., *The Social Services*, 1949.

Williams, F., *Dangerous Estate*, 1957.

Williams, R., *Culture and Society 1780–1950*, 1958.

Williams, R., *The Long Revolution*, 1960.

Williams, R., *Mass Communications*, 1964.

Wood, N., *Communism and the British Intellectuals*, 1959.

Woolf, L., *Sowing*, 1960, *Growing*, 1961, *Beginning Again*, 1963, *Downhill all the Way*, 1967.

Wright, Q. B., *A Study of War*, 2 vols, Chicago, 1942.

Young, M., *The Rise of the Meritocracy*, 1959.

Youngson, A. J., *The British Economy 1920–1957*, 1960.

(2) *The First World War and After*

Abrams, P., 'The Failure of Social Reform: 1918–1920', *Past and Present*, 1963.

Aldington, R., *Death of a Hero*, 1929.

Aldington, R., *Roads to Glory*, 1930.

Addison, C., *Politics From Within 1911–1918*, 2 vols, 1924.

Addison, C., *Practical Socialism*, 1926.

Archer, W., *The Great Analysis*, 1911.

Arnot, R. Page, *The Miners: Years of Struggle*, 1953.

Attlee, C. R., *The Social Worker*, 1920.

Auden, W. H., *Collected Shorter Poems*, 1950.

Auden, W. H. and Isherwood, C., *The Dog Beneath the Skin*, 1935.

Baldwin, A. W., *My Father*, 1955.

Barnett, C., *The Sword Bearers*, 1964.

Bassett, R., *1931 Political Crisis*, 1958.

Beales, H. L. and Lambert, R. S. (eds.), *Memoirs of the Unemployed*, 1934.

Bealey, F. and Pelling, H., *Labour and Politics 1900–1906*, 1959.

Beaverbrook, Lord, *Politicians and the War 1914–1916*, 1928.

Beaverbrook, Lord, *Men and Power 1917–1918*, 1956.

Beaverbrook, Lord, *Decline and Fall of Lloyd George*, 1963.

Blumenfeld, R. D., *All in a Lifetime*, 1931.

Blunden, E., *War Poets 1914–1918*, 1958.

Boothby, R., *The New Economy*, 1943.

Bowley, A. L., *The Division of the Product of Industry*, 1919.

Bowley, A. L., *Some Economic Consequences of the Great War*, 1930.

Bowley, A. L., *Studies in the National Income*, 1942.

Bowley, A. L., *Wages and Income in the U.K. since 1860*, 1937.

Bowley, A. L. and Burnett-Hurst, A. R., *Livelihood and Poverty*, 1915.

Bowley, A. L. and Hogg, M., *Has Poverty Diminished?*, 1925.

Bowley, A. L. and Stamp, J., *The National Income, 1924*, 1927.

Boyd Orr, J., *Food, Health and Income*, 1936.

Brailsford, H. N., et al., *The Living Wage*, 1926.

Brend, W. A., *Health and the State*, 1917.

British Empire Exhibition at Wembley, 1923.

Brittain, V., *Testament of Youth*, 1933.

Brooke, R., *Collected Poems*, 1918.

Brophy, J. and Partridge, E., *Songs and Slang of the British Soldier, 1914–1918*, 1950.

Bryant, A., *The Spirit of Conservatism*, 1929.

Burn, D. L., *Economic History of Steelmaking*, 1940.

Cardiff, *Annual Report of Medical Officer of Health for 1936*, 1937.

Carnegie Endowment for International Peace, *Economic and Social History of the World War, British series*, 24 vols, Washington and Oxford, 1918–40.

Carrington, C., *Soldier from the Wars Returning*, 1965.

Carr-Saunders, A. M. and Jones, D. C., *Social Structure of England and Wales*, 1927 and 1937.

Cecil, Viscount, *All the Way*, 1949.

Chester, L., *et. al*, *The Zinoviev Letter*, 1967.

Churchill, R., *Winston Spencer Churchill*, vol. 1, 1966.

Clark, C., *National Income and Outlay*, 1937.

Clay, H., *Lord Norman*, 1957.

Clephane, I., *Towards Sex Freedom*, 1936.

Clifford, J., *Our Fight for Belgium and What it Means*, 1917.

Cline, C., *Recruits to Labour*, 1961.

Clynes, J. R., *Memoirs*, 2 vols, 1937.

Cole, G. D. H. and M., *The Condition of Britain*, 1937.

Cohen, G., *Disarmament and Peace in Labour Politics*, 1959.

Coxon, S. (ed.), *Dover during the Dark Days*, 1919.

Crawford, W., *The People's Food*, 1938.

Crook, W. H., *The General Strike*, 1931.

Cross, C., *The Fascists in Britain*, 1963.

Council of Action for Peace and Reconstruction, *Pamphlets*, 1935–36.

Cuckfield Rural District Council, *Annual Report of Medical Officer of Health for 1936*, 1937.

Daily Mail 7th Ideal Home Exhibition, 1923.

Dampier-Whetham, W. C., *The War and the Nation, a Study in Constructive Politics*, 1917.

Dawson, W. H. (ed.), *After War Problems*, 1917.

Dearle, N. B., *The Labour Cost of the World War to Great Britain*, 1940.

Denman, R. D., *Political Sketches*, Carlisle, 1948.

Dickinson, G. L., *The International Anarchy 1900–1914*, 1914.

Dilnot, F., *England After the War*, 1920.

Dowse, R. E., *Left in the Centre*, 1966.

'Economist', *The Economics of War, with some arguments for better pay and security for those serving their country*, 1914.

Edmonds, C. (i.e. C. Carrington), *A Subaltern's War*, 1929.

Edmonds, J. E., *Short History of World War I*, 1952.

The Elements of Reconstruction, 1916.

Elton, Lord, *Among Others*, 1938.

Engall, J. S., *A Subaltern's Letters*, 1918.

Ensor, R. C. K., *England 1870–1914*, 1936.

Falls, C., *The First World War*, 1960.

Fawcett, M. G., *The Women's Victory and After*, 1920.

BIBLIOGRAPHY

Fisher, H. A. L., *An Unfinished Autobiography*, 1940.

Ford, F. M., *Parade's End*, 1924–28.

Fulford, R., *Votes for Women*, 1957.

Fyfe, H. H., *Behind the Scenes of the Great Strike*, 1926.

Gallacher, W., *Revolt on the Clyde*, 1936.

Galsworthy, J., *A Modern Comedy*, 1929.

Gilbert, B. B., *The Evolution of National Insurance in Great Britain: The Origins of the Welfare State*, 1966.

Gilbert, M., *The Roots of Appeasement*, 1966.

Gollin, A. M., *Proconsul in Politics: A Study of Lord Milner*, 1964.

Graubard, S. R., *British Labour and the Russian Revolution*, 1956.

Graubard, S. R., 'Military Demobilization in Britain following the First World War', *Journal of Modern History*, 1947.

Graves, R., *Goodbye to All That*, 1929.

Graves, R. and Hodge, A., *The Long Week-End*, 1940.

Gray, J. L., *Wartime Control of Industry*, New York, 1918.

Greene, G., *It's a Battlefield*, 1934.

Greenwood, W., *Love on the Dole*, 1933.

Greenwood, W., *There was a Time*, 1967.

Guinn, P., *British Strategy ond Politics 1914–1918*, 1965.

Gwynn, S. (ed.), *The Anvil of War: Letters from F. S. Oliver to his Brother*, 1936.

Hanak, H. H., 'The Union of Democratic Control during the First World War', *Bulletin of Institute of Historical Research*, 1963.

Hancock, W. K., *Survey of British Commonwealth Affairs*, 2 vols, 1937 and 1942.

Hankey, Lord, *The Supreme Command 1914–1918*, 2 vols, 1961.

Hannington, W., *Unemployed Struggles 1919–1936*, 1936.

Harper, R., *Romance of a Modern Airway*, 1931.

Hart, B. Liddell, *The Real War*, 1930.

Haxey, S., *Tory M.P.*, 1939.

Hearnshaw, L. S., *A Short History of British Psychology 1840–1940*, 1964.

Heindel, R. H., *The American Impact on Great Britain 1898–1914*, 1940.

Henderson, H. D., *"The Inter-war Years" and Other Papers*, 1965.

Hendrie, J., *Letters of a Durisdeer Soldier*, n.d. (1918?)

Higham, R., *The Military Intellectuals in Britain 1918–1939*, 1966.

Hilton, J., *et al*, *The Other War*, n.d. (1917?)

Hilton, J., *Rich Man, Poor Man*, 1944.

Hirst, F. W., *The Consequences of the War to Great Britain*, 1934.

Hobson, J. A., *Imperialism*, 1902.

Hobson, J. A., *Confessions of an Economic Heretic*, 1938.

Hobson, J. A., *Democracy after the War*, 1917.

Horsfall, T. C., *National Service and the Welfare of the Community*, 1906.

Houseman, L. (ed.), *Letters of Fallen Englishmen*, 1931.

Hurwitz, S. J., *State Intervention in Great Britain*, New York, 1949.

Huxley, A., *Brave New World*, 1931.

Jenkins, R., *Asquith*, 1964.

Jones, D. C. (ed.), *Social Survey of Merseyside*, 3 vols, 1934.

Jones, T., *Lloyd George*, 1951.

Kahn, A. E., *Great Britain in the World Economy*, 1946.

Keeling, F. H., *Keeling Letters and Reminiscences*, 1918.

Kendall, W., *Revolutionary Movements in Britain 1900–1921*, 1967.

Kenney, A., *Memories of a Militant*, 1924.

Keynes, J. M., *The Economic Consequences of the Peace*, 1920.

Keynes, J. M., *The End of Laissez-Faire*, 1920.

Keynes, J. M., *The General Theory of Employment, Interest and Money*, 1936.

Kirkwood, D., *My Life of Revolt*, 1935.

Laski, H. J., *The Crisis and the Constitution: 1931 and After*, 1932.

Le Corbusier, *The City of Tomorrow and its Planning* (trs. C. E. Jeanneret-Gris, intro. by F. Etchells), 1929.

Leeson, C., *The Child and the War*, 1917.

Leicester Galleries, *Catalogue of Exhibitions 1917–1918*.

Lewis, C. Day, *The Magnetic Mountain and Other Poems*, 1933.

Liberal Industrial Inquiry, *Britain's Industrial Future*, 1928.

Liberty and Democratic Leadership, 1934.

Lloyd, E. M. H., *Stabilization*, 1923.

Lloyd George, D., *The Great War*, 1914.

Lloyd George, D., *The Allied War Aims*, 1918.

Lloyd George, D., *War Memoirs*, 6 vols, 1933–36.

Lovat Fraser, J. A., *Why a Tory joined the Labour Party*, 1921.

Lucy, H., *Diary of a Journalist*, 1922.

Lyman, R., *The First Labour Government 1924*, 1957.

McBriar, A. M., *Fabian Socialism and English Politics 1884–1918*, 1963.

MacDonagh, M., *In London during the Great War*, 1935.

McEwan, J. M., 'The Coupon Election of 1918 and the Unionist Members of Parliament', *Journal of Modern History*, 1962.

Macfarlane, L., *The British Communist Party, Origins and Development to 1930*, 1966.

McGonigle, G. E. W. and Kirby, J., *Poverty and Public Health*, 1936.

Macleod, I., *Neville Chamberlain*, 1961.

Macmillan, H., *Reconstruction*, 1933.

Macmillan, H., *The Middle Way*, 1938.

Macmillan, H., *Winds of Change*, 1966.

Mansergh, N., *Survey of British Commonwealth Affairs: Problems of External Policy 1931–1939*, 1952.

Marder, A., *From Dreadnought to Scapa Flow*, 3 vols, 1961–66.

Marwick, A., *Clifford Allen: The Open Conspirator*, 1964.

Marwick, A., *The Deluge: British Society and the First World War*, 1965.

Masterman, C. F. G., *The Condition of England*, 1909.

Masterman, C. F. G., *England After the War*, 1922.

Meech, T. C., *This Generation 1900–1926*, 2 vols, 1928.

Middlemass, R. K., *The Clydesiders*, 1965.

Money, L. C., *Riches and Poverty*, 1905 and 1913.

Montague, C. E., *Disenchantment*, 1922.

Montgomery, J., *The Twenties*, 1957.

Moore, H. K. and Sayers, B., *Croydon and the Great War*, 1920.

Morgan, E. V., *Studies in British Financial Policy 1914–1925*, 1952.

Mosley, O., *A National Policy*, 1931.

Mosley, O., *Ten Points of Fascist Policy*, n.d.

Mowat, C. L., *Britain between the Wars*, 1955.

Mowat, C. L. *The Charity Organization Society 1869–1913*, 1961.

Nash, P., *Outline, An Autobiography and Other Writings*, 1949.

National Council on Public Morals, *The Declining Birth Rate*, 1916.

National Council on Public Morals, *The Ethics of Birth Control*, 1925.

National Labour Committee, *Pamphlets 1931–35*.

Nevinson, C. R. W., *Modern War*, 1917.

Newcastle-on-Tyne, *Annual Report of Medical Officer of Health for 1936*, 1937.

Newton, A. P. (ed.), *The Empire and the Future*, 1916.

The Next Five Years: An Essay in Political Agreement, 1935.

Nicolson, H., *The Diaries of Harold Nicolson*, vol. I, 1966.

Northedge, F. S., *The Troubled Giant: Britain Among the Great Powers 1916–1939*, 1966.

Nowell-Smith, S. (ed.) *Edwardian England*, 1964.

Official History of the Ministry of Munitions, 8 vols, 1918–22.

Orton, W. A., *Labour in Transition*, 1921.

Orwell, G., *The Road to Wigan Pier*, 1937.

Orwell, G., *Coming Up For Air*, 1939.

Owen, W., *Collected Poems,* (ed. C. Day Lewis), 1963.

The Oxford Pamphlets, 1914–15.

Peel, C. S., *How We Lived Then 1914–1918,* 1929.

Peel, J., 'The Manufacture and Retailing of Contraceptives in England', *Population Studies,* vol. XVII.

Pilgrim Trust, *Men Without Work,* 1938.

Playne, C. E., *The Pre-War Mind in Britain,* 1928.

Playne, C. E., *Society at War 1914–1918,* 1931.

Playne, C. E., *Britain Holds On 1917–1918,* 1933.

Plummer, A., *New British Industries,* 1937.

Pribicevik, B., *The Shop Stewards' Movement and Workers' Control 1910–1922,* 1959.

Priestley, J. B., *Angel Pavement,* 1930.

Priestley, J. B., *English Journey,* 1934.

Priestley, J. B., *Margin Released,* 1962.

Purdom, C. B., (ed.), *Everyman at War,* 1930.

Repington, C. à C., *The First World War,* 2 vols, 1920.

Rhodes James, R., *Gallipoli,* 1965.

Richards, F., *Old Soldiers Never Die,* 1933.

Richards, J. M., *Castles on the Ground,* 1946.

Richardson, H. W., *Economic Recovery in Britain, 1932–39,* 1967.

Rowntree, B. S., *Poverty: A Study of Town Life,* 1901.

Rowntree, B. S., *The Human Needs of Labour,* 1918.

Rowntree, B. S., *Poverty and Progress,* 1940.

Rowntree, B. and Pierce, J., 'Birth Control in Britain', *Population Studies,* vol. XV.

Russell, B., *The Autobiography of Bertrand Russell,* vol. I, 1967.

Sassoon, S., *Collected Poems,* 1961.

Shaw, G. Bernard, *Man and Superman,* 1901–3.

Sinclair, R., *Metropolitan Man,* 1937.

Skidelski, R., *Politicians and the Slump,* 1967.

Smith, H. L. (ed.), *New Survey of London Life and Labour,* 9 vols, 1930–35.

Spender, S., *Forward from Liberalism,* 1937.

Strachey, L., *Eminent Victorians,* 1918.

Strachey, R. (ed.), *Our Freedom and Its Results,* 1936.

Symons, J., *The General Strike,* 1957.

Symons, J., *The Thirties,* 1960.

Tawney, R. H., 'The Abolition of Economic Controls, 1918–1921', *Economic History Review,* 1943.

Taylor, A. J. P., *The Origins of the Second World War*, 1961.

Taylor, A. J. P., *Politics in Wartime*, 1964.

Taylor, H. A., *Robert Donald*, 1934.

Terraine, J., *Douglas Haig, the Educated Soldier*, 196?

Thomas, H., *The Spanish War*, 1961.

Thorne, C., *The Origins of the Second World War*, 1967.

Titmuss, R. M., *Poverty and Population*, 1938.

Tout, H., *The Standard of Living in Bristol*, 1938.

Trevelyan, C. P., *From Liberalism to Labour*, 1921.

Trotter, W. B., *The Instinct of the Herd in Peace and War*, 1919.

Watt, D. C., 'German Plans for the Reoccupation of the Rhineland', *Journal of Contemporary History*, 1966.

Webb, B., *Diaries*, 1952–56.

Williams, D., 'London and the 1931 Financial Crisis', *Economic History Review*, 1963.

Willis, I. C., *England's Holy War*, New York, 1929

Wilson, J. Dover (ed.), *The Schools of England*, 1928.

Wilson, T., *The Downfall of the Liberal Party*, 1966.

Winkler, H. R., *The League of Nations Movement in Great Britain 1914–1919*, New Brunswick, 1952.

Winkler, H. R., 'The Emergence of a Labor Foreign Policy in Great Britain 1918–1929, *Journal of Modern History*, 1956.

Woodward, E. L., *Short Journey*, 1941.

Worsfold, W. B., *The War and Social Reform*, 1919.

Workers' and Soldiers' Councils, 1917.

Wrench, E., *Struggle 1914–1920*, 1935.

Young, K., *Arthur James Balfour*, 1964.

(3) *Second World War and After*

Abercromby, P., *Greater London Plan*, 1944.

Abrams, M. and Rose, R., *Must Labour Lose?*, 1960.

Acland, R., *Unser Kampf*, 1940.

Acland, R., *What it will be like in the New Britain*, 1942.

Acton Society Trust, *Management Succession*, 1956.

Allen, V. L., *Trade Unions and the Government*, 1960.

Allsop, K., *The Angry Decade*, 1958.

Amis, K., *Lucky Jim*, 1953.

Amis, K., *Take a Girl Like You*, 1960.

Armytage, W. H. G., *Civic Universities*, 1955.

Arnot, R. Page, *The Miners in Crisis and War*, 1961.

Arts Council, *The Arts in Wartime*, 1946.

Arts Council, *Annual Reports*, 1945–67.

Astbury, B. E., *Letters from an English Social Worker in Wartime*, New York, 1942.

Attlee, C. R. and Williams, F., *A Prime Minister Remembers*, 1961.

Barker, A. J., *Suez: The Seven Days' War*, 1965.

Bartlett, B., *My First War: An Army Officer's Journal for May 1940*, 1940.

Beveridge, J., *Beveridge and his Plan*, 1943.

Beveridge, W., *The Pillars of Security*, 1943.

Beveridge, W., *Full Employment in a Free Society*, 1944.

Bevin, E., *The War and the Workers*, 1940.

Birkenhead, Lord, *The Prof in Two Worlds*, 1961.

Blackburn, R., *I am an Alcoholic*, 1959.

Bonham, J., *The Middle-Class Vote*, 1954.

Boyd, F., *British Politics in Transition 1945–63*, 1964.

Boyd, F., *Richard Austen Butler*, 1956.

Boyd, W. (ed.), *Evacuation in Scotland*, 1942.

Boyd Orr, J., *Feeding the People in Wartime*, 1940.

Brady, R., *Crisis in Britain*, 1950.

Braine, J., *Room at the Top*, 1957.

British Institute of Public Opinion, *The Beveridge Report and the Public*, 1943.

Brittain, V., *England's Hour*, 1941.

Brockway, A. F., *Outside the Right*, 1963.

Brown, W. J., *So Far*, 1943.

Burn, D., *The Steel Industry, 1939–1959*, 1961.

Calder, R., *The Lesson of London*, 1941.

Calder, R., *Start Planning Britain Now*, 1941.

Camps, M., *Britain and the European Community 1955–1963*, 1964.

Carr-Saunders, A. M., Jones, D. C. and Moser, C. A., *Social Conditions in England and Wales*, 1957.

Carter, A. M., *The Redistribution of Income in Post-War Britain*, 1950.

Central Office of Information, *Post-War Britain 1948–49*, 1949.

Chandos, Viscount, *Memoirs*, 1962.

Chapman, D., *Social Survey of Middlesbrough*, 1944.

Chester, D. N., (ed.) *Lessons of the British War Economy*, 1951.

Christiansen, A., *Headlines All My Life*, 1961.

Churchill, W. S., *Sinews of Peace*, 1948.

Churchill, W. S., *The Second World War*, 6 vols, 1948–53.

Churchill, W. S., *War Speeches* (ed. C. Eade), 4 vols, 1950.

Churchill, W. S., *Europe Unite*, 1950.

Clark, C., *Welfare v. Taxation*, 1952.

Clarke, R., *Sir Henry Tizard*, 1965.

Clements, R. V., *Managers, A Study of their Careers in Industry*, 1958.

Cole, G. D. H., *Post-War Condition of Britain*, 1956.

Collier, B., *The Battle of Britain*, 1962.

Cooke, C., *Sir Stafford Cripps*, 1957.

Cooper, W., *Scenes from Provincial Life*, 1950.

Cosens, M., *Evacuation: a Social Revolution*, 1940.

Crosland, C. A. R., *The Future of Socialism*, 1956.

Crossman, R. H. S. (ed.), *New Fabian Essays*, 1952.

Croydon and the Second World War, 1946.

Cudlipp, H., *Publish and Be Damned*, 1953.

Dean, B., *The Theatre at War*, 1956.

Dent, H. C., *The Education Act 1944*, 1944.

Dent, H. C., *Growth in English Education 1946–52*, 1954.

Dent, H. C., *Universities in Transition*, 1961.

Divine, D., *The Nine Days of Dunkirk*, 1959.

Dow, J. C. R., *The Management of the British Economy 1945–1960*, 1962.

D.S.I.R., *Science at War*, 1946.

Duff, A. C., *Britain's New Towns*, 1952.

Dunning, J. H., *American Investment in British Manufacturing Industry*, 1958.

Eckstein, H., *The English Health Service*, 1958.

Eckstein, H., *Pressure Group Politics: The Case of the British Medical Association*, 1960.

Epstein, L. D., *Britain, Uneasy Ally*, 1954.

Epstein, L. D., *British Politics in the Suez Crisis*, 1964.

Falls, C., *The Second World War*, 1960.

Faviell, F., *The Chelsea Concerto*, 1959.

Ferris, P., *The City*, 1960.

Fitzgerald, H., *A Guide to the National Health Service Act*, 1946.

Fitzgibbon, C., *The Blitz*, 1957.

Floud, J., *et al.*, *Social Class and Educational Opportunity*, 1956.

Flower, D. and Reeves, J. (eds.), *The War 1939–45*, 1960.

Foot, M., *Aneurin Bevan*, vol. I, 1962.

Fyfe, H. H., *Britain's Wartime Revolution*, 1944.

Gallacher, W., *The Last Memoirs of Willie Gallacher*, 1966.

Gillespie, R. D., *Psychological Effects of War on Citizens and Soldiers*, New York, 1942.

Glass, D. V. (ed.), *Social Mobility in Britain*, 1956.

Gordon, A., *A Guide to the National Insurance Act of 1946*, 1946.

Gordon Walker, P., 'On being a Cabinet Minister', *Encounter*, April 1956.

Graves, C., *The Home Guard of Britain*, 1943.

Graves, C., *Women in Green: the Story of the WVS*, 1948.

Greenwood, A., *Why We Fight: Labour's Case*, 1940.

Gregg, P., *The Welfare State: A Social and Economic History of Britain from 1945 to the Present*, 1967.

Grundy, F., *The New Public Health*, 1946.

Hall, M. P., *The Social Services of Modern England*, 1952.

Harrison, M., *Trade Unions and the Labour Party since 1945*, 1960.

Harrisson, T., *Britain Revisited*, 1961.

Hayes, D., *Challenge of Conscience*, 1949.

Hinchingbrooke, Viscount, *Full Speed Ahead: Essays in Tory Reform*, 1944.

H.M.S.O., *History of the Second World War: Civil Series*, 27 vols, 1949–64.

Hodson, J. L., *The Way Things Are*, 1949.

Hoffman, J. D., *The Conservative Party in Opposition 1945–1951*, 1964.

Hoggart, R., *The Uses of Literacy*, 1952.

Hopkins, H., *The New Look*, 1963.

Houghton, D., *The Family Circle*, 1946.

Hoyle, F., *A Decade of Decision*, 1953.

Hulton Press, *Patterns of British Life*, 1950.

Huxley, A., *Brave New World Revisited*, 1959.

Hyams, E., *Gentian Violet*, 1953.

Idle, E. D., *War over West Ham*, 1943.

International Labour Review, vol. XL, 1939: 'Social Legislation in Wartime'.

Isaacs, S. (ed.), *Cambridge Evacuation Survey*, 1941.

Jacob, N., *Me – in Wartime*, 1940.

Jesse, F. T. and Harwood, H. M., *London Front: Letters Written to America*, 1940.

Jewkes, J., *Ordeal by Planning*, 1948.

Keynes, J. M., *How to Pay for the War*, 1940.

Kilmuir, Viscount, *Political Adventure*, 1964.

King, G. S., *The Ministry of Pensions and National Insurance*, 1958.

King George's Jubilee Trust, *Citizens of Tomorrow*, 1955.

Kipping, N., *The Federation of British Industries*, 1954.

Laski, H., *Reflections on the Revolution of Our Time*, 1943.

Lee, J., *This Great Journey*, 1963.

Lindsey, A., *Socialized Medicine in England and Wales*, 1962.

Lockwood, D., *The Black-coated Workers*, 1958.

Lowndes, G. A. N., *The British Educational System*, 1955.

McCallum, R. B. and Readman, A., *The British General Election of 1945*, 1947.

Mackay, R. W. G., *Britain in Wonderland*, 1948.

Mackenzie, N. (ed.), *Conviction*, 1958.

Macmillan, H., *Blast of War, 1939–1945*, 1967.

Madge, C., *Industry After the War*, 1943.

Mansergh, N., *Survey of Commonwealth Affairs: Problems of Wartime Cooperation and Post-war Change 1939–1952*, 1958.

Manvell, R., *The Film and the Public*, 1956.

Marsh, D. C., *National Insurance and Assistance in Great Britain*, 1951.

Mass Observation, *People in Production*, 1941.

Mass Observation, *War Begins at Home*, 1941.

Mayer, J. P., *British Cinemas and their Audiences* 1948.

Ministry of Information, *Modern Publicity and War*, 1941.

Ministry of Information, *Front Line 1940–41*, 1942.

Mitchell, J., *Crisis in Britain*, 1963.

Montgomery, J., *The Fifties*, 1965.

Murrow, E., *This is London*, New York, 1941.

Nicholas, H. G., *The British General Election of 1950*, 1951.

Nicolson, H., *The Diaries of Harold Nicolson*, vol. II, 1967.

Nisbet, J. W., *et al.*, *Beveridge and his Plan*, 1943.

Northedge, F. S., *British Foreign Policy: The Process of Readjustment 1945–61*, 1962.

Nutting, A., *No End of a Lesson: The Story of Suez*, 1967.

Orwell, G., *The Lion and the Unicorn*, 1941.

Orwell, G., *1984*, 1949.

Osborn, F. J., *New Towns After the War*, 1944.

Osborn, F. J. and Whittick, A., *The New Towns*, 1963.

Osborne, J., *Look Back in Anger*, 1956.

Owen, J., *War in the Workshops*, n.d.

Padley, R. and Cole, M., *Evacuation Survey*, 1943.

Peacock, A. T. (ed.), *Income Redistribution and Social Policy*, 1954.

Pear, T. H., *English Social Differences*, 1955.

Pick, F., *Britain Must Rebuild*, 1941.

Potter, A., *Organized Pressure Groups in British National Politics*, 1961.

Priestley, J. B., *Blackout in Gretley*, 1942.

Priestley, J. B., *Daylight on Saturday*, 1943.

Priestley, J. B., *Postscripts*, 1940.

Priestley, J. B., *Three Men in New Suits*, 1945.

Robertson, T., *Crisis, The Inside Story of the Suez Conspiracy*, 1961.

Robson, W. A. (ed.), *Social Security*, 1943.

Robson, W. A., *Nationalized Industry and Public Ownership*, 1960.

Rogow, A. A., *The Labour Government and British Industry*, 1955.

Ross, A., *The Forties*, 1950.

Rowntree, B. S. and Lavers, J., *Poverty and the Welfare State*, 1951.

Rowntree, B. S. and Lavers, J., *English Life and Leisure*, 1951.

Sansom, W., *Westminister in War*, 1947.

Sargant, W., *The Unquiet Mind*, 1967.

Seers, D., *Changes in the Cost of Living and Distribution of Income since 1938*, 1948.

Self, P. and Storing, H. J., *The State and the Farmer*, 1962.

Sillitoe, A., *Saturday Night and Sunday Morning*, 1958.

Sissons, M. and French, P. (eds.), *The Age of Austerity*, 1963.

Snow, C. P., *The New Men*, 1954.

Snow, C. P., *Homecomings*, 1956.

Snow, C. P., *Science and Government*, 1959.

Socialist Medical Association, *Aneurin Bevan, an Assessment of his Service to the Health of the People*, 1961.

Spraos, J., *The Decline of the Cinema*, 1962.

Stacey, M., *Tradition and Change: A Study of Banbury*, 1960.

Strachey, J., *Post D*, 1941.

Strachey, J., *A Programme for Progress*, 1940.

Thomas, H. (ed.), *The Establishment*, 1959.

Thomas, H., *The Suez Affair*, 1967.

Thompson, L., *1940*, 1966.

Titmuss, R. M., *Essays on the 'Welfare State'*, 1958.

Titmuss, R. M., *Income Distribution and Social Change*, 1962.

Titmuss, R. M. and Abel-Smith, B., *The Cost of the National Health Service*, 1956.

Towndrow, F. E. (ed.), *Replanning Britain*, 1941.

Turner, E. S., *The Phoney War on the Home Front*, 1961.

Vaizey, J., *The Cost of Education*, 1958.

Watkins, E., *The Cautious Revolution*, 1950.

Watson, J. P. and Abercromby, P., *Plan for Plymouth*, 1943.

Watt, D. C. (ed.), *Documents on the Suez Crisis*, 1957.

Waugh, E., *Sword of Honour*, 1952–61.

Wedderburn, D. C., 'Facts and Theories of the Welfare State', *Socialist Register*, 1965.

Weymouth, A., (Ivo Geikie-Cobb). ed., *The English Spirit*, 1942.

Weymouth, A., *Journal of the War Years*, 2 vols, Worcester, 1948.

Whittle, F., *Jet, The Story of a Pioneer*, 1953.

Wilson, H. H., *Pressure Group: The Campaign for Commercial Television*, 1961.

Wilson, T., *Modern Capitalism and Economic Progress*, 1950.

Winant, J. G., *A Letter from Grosvenor Square*, 1947.

Wintringham, T., *People's War*, 1942.

Women's Group on Public Welfare, *Our Towns*, 1943.

Wood, A., *Mr Rank*, 1952.

Woolton, Lord, *Memoirs*, 1959.

Worswick, G. D. N. and Ady, P., *The British Economy 1945–1950*, 1953.

Worswick, G. D. N. and Ady, P., *The British Economy in the Nineteen-Fifties*, 1962.

Wyatt, W., *Into the Dangerous World*, 1952.

Young, K., *Churchill and Beaverbrook*, 1966.

Young, M. and Wilmot, P., *Family and Kinship in East London*, 1957.

Zweig, F., *The British Worker*, 1952.

(4) *Contemporary Britain*

Abel-Smith, B. and Stevens, R., *Lawyers and the Courts*, 1966.

Abel-Smith, B. and Townsend, P., *The Poor and the Poorest*, 1966.

Archer, P., *The Queen's Courts*, 1963.

Bagrit, L., *The Age of Automation*, 1965.

Beckerman, W. and associates, *The British Economy in 1975*, 1965.

Bennet, A., *et al.*, *Beyond the Fringe*, 1962.

Bernal, J. D., *Britain's Part in the New Scientific Industrial Revolution*, 1964.

Brandon, H., *In the Red: The Struggle for Sterling 1964–1966*, 1966.

Buchanan, C., *Mixed Blessing: The Motor in Britain*, 1958.

Butler, D. E. and King, A., *The British General Election of 1964*, 1965.

Butler, D. E. and King, A., *The British General Election of 1966*, 1966.

Butler, D. E. and Rose, R., *The British General Election of 1959*, 1960.

Camps, M., *European Unification in the Sixties*, 1967.

Carstairs, G. M., *This Island Now*, 1962.

Catherwood, H. F. R., *Britain with the Brakes Off*, 1966.

Central Office of Information, *Britain: An Official Handbook*, 1967.

Central Office of Information, *Social Changes in Britain*, 1962.

Chaplin, S., *The Day of the Sardine*, 1961.

Chapman, B., *British Government Observed*, 1963.

Churchill, R. S., *The Fight for the Tory Leadership*, 1964.

Cole, D. and Utting, J., *The Economic Circumstances of Old People*, 1962.

Cole, R., *Comprehensive Schools in Action*, 1964.

Cooper, B. and Gaskell, T. F., *North Sea Oil – The Great Gamble*, 1966.

Crick, B., *The Reform of Parliament*, 1964.

Crosland, C. A. R., *The Conservative Enemy*, 1963.

Cullingworth, J. B., *Housing and Local Government in England and Wales*, 1966.

Dickie, J., *The Uncommon Commoner: A Study of Sir Alec Douglas-Home*, 1964.

Driver, C., *The Disarmers: A Study in Protest*, 1964.

Fogarty, M. P., *Under-Governed and Over-Governed*, 1962.

Foot, P., *Immigration and Race in British Politics*, 1965.

Freeman, T. W., *The Conurbations of Great Britain*, 2nd edn, Manchester, 1966.

Gardiner, Lord, *Law Reform Now*, 1963.

Goldman, P., *The Welfare State*, 1964.

Goldthorpe, J. H. and Lockwood, D., 'Affluence and the British Class Structure', *Sociological Review*, 1963.

Gosling, J. and Craig, D., *The Great Train Robbery*, New York, 1964.

Gross, R. E., *British Secondary Education, Overview and Appraisal*, 1965.

Hamilton, W. B., Robinson, K. and Goodwin, C. D. W., *A Decade of Commonwealth 1955–1964*, Durham, N.C., 1966.

Hartley, A., *A State of Britain*, 1963.

Hignett, S., *A Picture to Hang on the Wall*, 1966.

Hill, A. and Whichelow, A., *What's Wrong with Parliament?*, 1964.

Howard, A. and West, R., *The Making of the Prime Minister*, 1965.

Hunter, L., *The Road to Brighton Pier*, 1959.

Institute of Economic Affairs, *Occasional Papers*, 1957–1967.

Irving, C., *et al.*, *Scandal '63: A Study of the Profumo Affair*, 1963.

Jackson, B., *Streaming, An Education System in Miniature*, 1964.

Jackson, B., and Marsden, D., *Education and the Working Class*, 1962.

Jackson, R. M., *The Machinery of Justice in England*, 4th edn, 1964.

Johns, E. A., *The Social Structure of Modern Britain*, 1965.

Kaufman, G. (ed.), *The Left*, 1966.

Kelly, T., *et al.*, *A Competitive Cinema*, 1966.

King, A. (ed.), *British Politics*, 1966.

Koestler, A. (ed.), *Suicide of a Nation?*, 1964.

Mabey, R. (ed.), *Class: A Symposium*, 1967.

MacInnes, C., *England, Half-English*, 1961.

Magee, B., *The New Radicalism*, 1962.

Malik, R., *What's Wrong with British Industry?*, 1964.

Mander, J., *Great Britain or Little England?*, 1963.

Marriott, O., *The Property Boom*, 1967.

Marsh, D. C., *The Future of the Welfare State*, 1964.

Millar, R., *The New Classes*, 1966.

Morris, J., *The Outriders: A Liberal View of Britain*, 1963.

Peacock, A., *The Welfare Society*, 1960.

Peacock, A. and Wiseman, J., *Education for Democrats; A Study of the Financing of Education in a Free Society*, 1964.

Pressure for Economic and Social Toryism, *Will the Tories Lose?*, 1965.

Raison, T., *Why Conservative?*, 1964.

Rasmussen, J. S., *The Liberal Party: A Study in Retrenchment and Revival*, 1965.

Rex, J. and Moore, R., *Race, Community and Conflict – A Study of Sparkbrook*, 1966.

Robinson, J., *Economics: An Awkward Corner*, 1966.

Robson, W. A., *Local Government in Crisis*, 1966.

Rose, R. (ed.), *Studies in British Politics*, 1966.

Sampson, A., *Anatomy of Britain*, 1962.

Sampson, A., *Anatomy of Britain Today*, 1965.

Seldon, A. (ed.), *Rebirth of Britain*, 1964.

Shanks, M., *The Stagnant Society*, 1961.

Shrimsley, A., *The First Hundred Days of Harold Wilson*, 1965.

Smith, L., *Harold Wilson: the Authentic Portrait*, 1964.

Snyder, W. P., *Politics of British Defence Policy*, 1966.

Stevens, R., *Medical Practice in Modern England*, 1966.

Sutherland, D., *The Landowners*, 1967.

Theobald, R. (ed.), *Britain in the Sixties*, 1961.

Third Statistical Account of Scotland, *The City of Edinburgh*, 1966.

Titmuss, R., *Commitment to Welfare*, 1968.

Titmuss, R. M., *The Irresponsible Society*, 1960.

Townsend, P., 'The Meaning of Poverty', *British Journal of Sociology*, 1962.

Walker, N. D., *Crime and Punishment in Britain*, 1965.

Wickenden, J., *Colour in Britain*, 1958.

Wigham, E., *What's Wrong with the Unions?*, 1961.

Willey, F. T., *Education Today and Tomorrow,* 1964.

Williams, F., *The American Invasion,* 1962.

Willmott, P., *Consumers Guide to the Social Services,* 1967.

Wootton, B., 'Is there a Welfare State?', *Political Science Quarterly,* 1963.

Wootton, G., *Workers, Unions and the State,* 1966.

Younger, K., *Changing Perspectives in British Foreign Policy,* 1964.

Zweig, F., *The Worker in an Affluent Society,* 1961.

INDEX